Frommer's™

Best Hiking Trips in British Colombia

D0757153

My British Columbia

by Christie Pashby

BRITISH COLUMBIA IS UNQUESTIONABLY one of the world's most beautiful places. From the rugged beauty of the Pacific Coast to the towering Rocky Mountains, it's a wildly diverse and scenic province—boasting more than 50 mountain ranges, the only desert in Canada, towering waterfalls, sandy coastal beaches, ancient forests, giant granite monoliths, and majestic glaciers. From lush old-growth forests to high alpine tundra, it's all here.

Hiking may be the best way of all to explore BC. With hundreds of trails and more than 850 parks and protected areas, what is constant is the adventure: whatever your taste, you can enjoy a gentle walk through wine country, a bird-watching outing along a coastal beach, or a challenging high-mountain trek. Exploring is a passion for the locals, who hit the trails near and far, urban and wild, throughout the long hiking season. They'll happily introduce you to their favorite trails.

And as you roam and make your own discoveries, there's a good chance you'll also discover something about yourself. Or at least you can close your eyes and imagine what it would be like to have the time to hike every trail. Enjoy!

First page: top, ©Randy Lincks/All Canada Photos; bottom, ©Chloë Ernst

©All Canada Photos

©Chloë Ernst

STANLEY PARK (opposite page) This 1,000-acre park on the edge of downtown is an oasis for Vancouverites and one of the jewels of the city. Larger than New York's Central Park, it retains a wildness like few other urban green spaces—with more than half a million trees, many of them hundreds of years old, it's the easiest way to appreciate British Columbia's renowned forests. Along the perimeter is the spectacular 8.8km (5.5 mile) seawall, where walkers, cyclists and in-line skaters take in the majesty of the Pacific and the Vancouver skyline.

From **LIGHTHOUSE PARK (above)** in West Vancouver, hikers can admire views of the Coast Mountains, picnic on the rocks, and take part in some "ferry spotting." When you tire of the scenery, hike a variety of trails through old-growth forests, and then be back downtown in under an hour.

The **WEST COAST TRAIL (right)** is not for the faint-hearted. The week-long route travels 75km (46.6 miles) and traverses elaborate bridges, changing tides and sets of ladders that can stretch 50 storeys. But the rewards—ancient cedars and temperate rainforest, isolated sandy beaches, and beautiful wildlife—make it arguably Canada's top hike. A true once-in-a-lifetime experience.

©All Canada Photos

©Chloë Ernst

Sometimes a little extra effort is worth it. **STRATHCONA PROVINCIAL PARK (above)** lies in the remote northern corner of Vancouver Island, but the reward is a startling landscape often compared to the Alps or Norwegian fjords. With few people making the trek this far, you'll have extra time to stop and drink in the astounding beauty.

One of the most difficult things to adjust to in British Columbia is the astonishing scale—sometimes it feels as if you've stepped inside the pages of *Gulliver's Travels.* This is particularly true in and around **WHISTLER (right)**, where the towering peaks are equaled by the incredible size of the centuries-old red cedars.

©Randy Lincks/All Canada Photos

UPPER JOFFRE LAKE sits in a cirque of towering mountains topped with glaciers, less than an hour from Whistler. The turquoise-colored lakes here reflect glacial sediment that's fallen into the water, and are further cooled by being nearly a mile above sea level.

©Chloë Ernst

Inland waterways run more than 50km (31.3 miles) from the Pacific Ocean to the **BELLA COOLA VALLEY (above)**, making it an excellent spot to watch the autumn salmon run.

©Chloë Ernst

The gentle **OKANAGAN VALLEY (right)** lies wedged between two mountain ranges in British Columbia's interior, giving it a unique ecology that includes Canada's only true desert. More prominent are its award-winning vineyards and wineries, and the fruit orchards that supply much of the province.

The path around **LAKE O'HARA (below)** is a true Rocky Mountain classic—and the fact that advance permits are required for the 42 hikers allowed on the trail each day means it is one of the most rarely seen. The reward for those who plan ahead is a variety and grandeur matched in very few places: spectacular glaciers, thundering waterfalls, famous backcountry lodges and landscapes that have been captured by artists from around the globe.

©Chris Cheadle/All Canada Photos

©Ron Watts/All Canada Photos

©Josh McCulloch/All Canada Photos

Yoho National Park lies in the shadow of its more famous cousin—Banff National Park, just on the other side of the British Columbia/Alberta border—but its beauty is no less spectacular. The easygoing route around **EMERALD LAKE (above)** was only discovered in 1882 while planning a route for the Canadian Pacific Railroad, but the area does not lack for history—the 515-million-year-old Burgess Shale lies just above the lake. Its diverse range of fossils transformed archaeologists' understanding of how life on Earth evolved, with half the animal species preserved in the shale having gone extinct millions of years ago.

©Bruce Whittington

BC is home to six subspecies of black bear, ranging in color from black through blue-grey, brown, and cinnamon to the white form known as the Spirit Bear. Their diet includes vegetation, animal prey when available, and on the coast, spawning salmon in the fall.

Grizzly bears (known as brown bears in Alaska) have distinct humps on their shoulders and flatter faces. They occupy more open habitat and are more likely to be seen at higher elevations than black bears.

Bears avoid humans unless they smell food or sense a threat to their young, food, or territory.

BLACK BEAR

Length: 1.5–1.8m (5–6 ft.)

Weight: 90–275kg (198–606 lb.)

Identifying features: "Roman" nose, tan muzzle

Best sighting time: April–October, later on the coast

Where to see them: All regions; most often in open subalpine areas, and along coastal salmon streams in fall

GRIZZLY BEAR

Length: 1.8–2.5m (6–8 ft.)

Weight: 145–675kg (320–1,488 lb.)

Identifying features: Flatter face, shoulder hump

Where to see them: Most likely seen in the Rockies, Kootenays, and Whistler and surrounding areas

©Bruce Whittington

The hoary marmot, or whistler, is a rotund cat-sized resident of alpine and subalpine meadows and talus slopes. These rodents have a short, active summer season during which they mate and feed on lush vegetation. They are true hibernators, whose body temperature may drop to less than 5°C (41°F) during their long winter sleep from September to April.

Marmots are often heard before they are seen, their piercing alarm calls echoing off the rocky slopes.

This species has cousins in other habitats. The yellow-bellied marmot is found in the southern interior of BC, and the groundhog or woodchuck is widespread in open parkland.

HOARY MARMOT

Length: 66–76cm (26–30 in.)

Weight: 3.6–9kg (8–20 lb.)

Identifying features: Frosty color, white snout, whistling call

Best Sighting Time: May through August, daytime

Where to see them: Alpine areas of the Canadian Rockies and Kootenays, Whistler and surroundings, Cariboo coast and the north. The Yellow-bellied Marmot is more common in open, rocky, lower-elevation sites in the Okanagan Valley.

DEER

Length: 132–168cm (52–66 in.) Columbian blacktail; 127–188cm (50–74 in.) mule deer

Weight: 32–113kg (70–250 lb.) Columbian blacktail; 54–181kg (120–400 lb.) mule deer

Identifying features: Bucks (males) have forked antlers; tails all black (except underside). Tails of whitetail deer are white, tipped with black.

Best sighting time: Active year-round, but most active at dawn and dusk

Where to see them: Suburban areas on Vancouver Island and in the Vancouver area; widespread elsewhere

©Bruce Whittington

Blacktail deer seek cover in forested habitat but often come to meadows to feed, sometimes above the tree line. There are three subspecies, with mule deer the largest. They occupy most of the interior of the province. On the coast, Columbian blacktails are found north to about Calvert Island, where they are replaced by Sitka blacktail deer. Both are much smaller than mule deer, with some females the size of a large dog.

Whitetail deer may be found in southeastern British Columbia. The antlers of the bucks differ from the forked antlers of blacktail deer in having all tines rise individually from the main stem.

RED SQUIRRELS

Length: 28–35cm (11–14 in.)

Weight: 198–255g (7–9 oz.)

Identifying features: Reddish-brown upperparts, noisy chattering

Best sighting time: Active year-round, mostly during the daytime

Where to see them: Found in forested areas of all regions in this guide

©Bruce Whittington

Red squirrels are found almost everywhere there is forest to support them in BC. Their bold chattering warns hikers that this territory is taken long before the diminutive owner is seen. They remain active through all but the most bitter winter weather, when they retreat to warm dens in tree cavities or leaf-nests called dreys.

They spend much of their time gathering and caching nuts and cones that will be retrieved during the winter. Squirrels also eat flowers, mushrooms, insects, and the eggs or nestlings of birds.

©iStockphoto.com

This species has expanded its range in recent years, including a move into suburban areas. Coyotes may be encountered from the Fraser River delta to alpine areas in the south, and to the grasslands and aspen parklands of the north. They are absent from the coast and islands. They are medium-sized members of the dog family.

Coyotes eat primarily small mammals and carrion but may attack larger animals, and farm animals and household pets. They are social animals, and a chorus of coyotes yelping at the moon is unforgettable.

COYOTES

Length: Averages 119cm (47 inches)

Weight: Averages 14kg (30 lb.)

Identifying features: Cinnamon-buff in summer, grey in winter, with a long bushy tail

Best sighting time: Active year-round; seen by day, often heard at night

Where to see them: Look for coyotes in open grassland, parkland, and alpine areas. Increasing in suburban areas of Vancouver and the Fraser Valley.

©Bruce Whittington

BC's provincial bird is the Steller's jay, its brilliant blue plumage a product not of feather pigment, but of feather structure that reflects the blue wavelength of light. These birds are opportunistic feeders and often prey on the eggs and young of other forest-nesting species.

In the fall, Steller's jays sometimes move out of the woods to forage. They fill an expandable pouch in the throat, called a crop, with seeds to be buried for winter use.

These jays are cheeky and raucous, and they readily mimic the calls of other birds. Many have learned to use the descending scream of the red-tailed hawk to warn off potential interlopers.

STELLER'S JAY

Length: 29cm (11 in.)

Identifying features: Look for iridescent blue plumage, prominent crest, and raucous calls.

Best sighting time: Coniferous forest in spring and summer, valley bottoms in most winters

Where to see them: In summer months, look for them in coniferous forests throughout the province. In winter, they often move into suburban areas of Vancouver Island, the Vancouver area, and the Okanagan Valley.

BALD EAGLE

Length: 79–94cm (31–37 in.)

Wingspan: 178–229cm (70–90 in.)

Identifying features: Adults have white heads and tails; immatures are brown, variably mottled with white.

Best sighting time: Year-round in most areas; many move to coast late summer and fall; some northern populations move south or to the coast in winter

Where to see them: Abundant on Vancouver Island, the central coast, and in the Vancouver area; look also along major rivers and lakes in the Okanagan Valley, Kootenays, and Cariboo.

©Bruce Whittington

Bald eagles are members of the sea eagle family and almost always nest near large bodies of water, typically in large trees, but rocky ledges are used where suitable trees are scarce.

Females are larger than males, sometimes noticeably so when a pair is seen together. Young birds are dark brown, changing gradually to the familiar adult plumage over 5 years. Eagles eat a lot of fish and seabirds, but they happily eat carrion, as well, and rob other raptors of their prey.

RAVENS

Length: 61cm (24 in.)

Wingspan: 135cm (53 in.)

Identifying features: All glossy black, heavy bill with flat forehead, tail diamond-shaped in flight

Best sighting time: Active year-round during daytime

Where to see them: Common in forested areas in all regions in this guide; often numerous where food is available at salmon streams, landfills, and so on

©Bruce Whittington

Common ravens figure prominently in First Nations creation stories and family clan histories.

They have been observed cooperating in food-gathering and engaging in forms of play. They have a remarkable array of calls, but their signature hollow croaking is one of the icons of the woods. Carrion is an important part of the diet, but ravens also prey on small mammals, and birds' eggs and nestlings. They mate for life and often return to the same nest site.

Ravens are master aviators, regularly practicing spectacular rolls and dives, often in pairs. In flight, they exhibit diamond-shaped tails which help to distinguish them from the common crow.

©Bruce Whittington

COMMON PAINTBRUSH

Height: 20–79cm (8–31 in.)

Identifying features: This species has bright orange-red "flowers" with slightly hairy leaves.

Best sighting time: Blooms mid-to-late summer

Where to see them: Look for it in roadsides, alpine meadows, open parkland, and coastal estuaries in all regions covered by this guide.

On almost any summer walk in BC, you are likely to encounter paintbrush. The family includes about 40 species, which range in color from magenta through red and yellow to white, in some cases.

Common red paintbrush is one of the most widespread of all. The brightly colored "petals" are in fact modified leaf bracts that surround the inconspicuous flowers. All paintbrushes are perennial and derive some of their nutrients through parasitism on the roots of other plants.

The many species of paintbrush create scarlet drifts in alpine meadows and flashes of color in open pine forests and coastal estuaries.

©Bruce Whittington

BUNCHBERRY

Height: 5–25cm (2–10 in.)

Identifying features: Four white "petals" in spring and summer; bright shiny red berries in fall

Best sighting time: Blooms as early as May, occasionally again in summer. Berries in August.

Where to find them: Look for Bunchberry in moist forests and edges throughout the province.

Bunchberry is a ground-hugging member of the dogwood family found in a variety of habitats from seashore to alpine slopes. The white "flowers" are modified leaves that draw pollinators to the small clusters of true flowers.

Bunchberry carpets open areas where it is established and clambers over decaying stumps and logs.

In late summer, the flowers produce tight clusters of shiny red berries. These are edible but somewhat bland and pulpy, although they are popular with deer. As autumn approaches, the leaves turn a rich red, burnishing the alpine slopes with color.

ARCTIC LUPINE

Height: to 60cm (24 in.)

Identifying features: Purplish-blue pea-like flowers in spring and summer; hairy pea-like seed pods in late summer and fall

Best sighting time: Blooms in April in the south, through late summer further north and at higher elevations

Where to see them: Widespread in open parkland and meadows; more common at middle to subalpine elevations

©iStockphoto.com

In gardens and clear-cuts, along roadsides and on glacial outwash plains, lupines lend their colorful spires to the landscape. Arctic lupine is the most widespread of some two dozen species in the province, and many hybrids occur. Most are blue or violet, but there are white and yellow species, and many color forms. Alpine species may be quite low-growing, but some lupine species growing in good conditions may be 1.2m (4 ft.) tall.

Like other members of the pea family, they fix atmospheric nitrogen in the soil with the help of bacteria. Their seeds are produced and dispersed in pea-like pods. Some Arctic lupine seeds retrieved from an ancient ground squirrel cache were carbon-dated at over 10,000 years old, yet germinated in 48 hours and bloomed.

FIREWEED

Height: Average 120cm (47 in.) tall fireweed

Identifying features: Tall spikes of pink flowers, downy seeds in fall

Best sighting time: Blooms mid-June to late summer

Where to see them: Widespread across British Columbia, especially in disturbed open areas, but not common in the drier parts of the Okanagan Valley

©Bruce Whittington

Fireweed in BC is often the first new growth to appear after the devastation of a forest fire. Its seeds are equipped with downy parachutes and are dispersed widely on the wind. It is a pioneer species in glaciated and human-disturbed landscapes, as well.

The species most familiar and visible is tall fireweed, with its spikes of flowers waving in the breeze. River Beauty is a much lower-growing and more compact species that likes gravel bars in rivers and glacial meltwater streams, and also grows at higher elevations.

Fireweed produces an abundance of nectar, and large patches are sought after by beekeepers who leave hives there. Fireweed honey is a favorite in the West.

©Bruce Whittington

COW-PARSNIP

Height: 1–3m (3–10 ft.)

Identifying features: Large size, broad umbrella-like white flower heads

Best sighting time: Blooms in May at low altitudes and latitudes, progressively later elsewhere

Where to see them: Look for it in moist environments in all regions covered by this guide.

Cow-parsnip is possibly BC's largest perennial wildflower, a lush plant with plate-sized white flower heads atop its large, branching stems. It grows in moist environments, from sea level stream banks to alpine avalanche tracks.

This plant is a member of the carrot family, and there is a strong resemblance to other plants in the family, such as Kneeling Angelica, sea-coast Angelica, and Queen Anne's lace.

Native people have long used the peeled young stems of these plants for food, but care must be taken not to confuse them with the deadly poisonous Douglas's water-hemlock.

©iStockphoto.com

BLUEBERRIES

Height: 10cm–3m (4 in.–10 ft.)

Identifying features: Look for shrubs with many berries, not small plants with very few berries; look for residual flower on the end.

Best sighting time: Blooms May-June; berries ripen July and later

Where to see them: Different species are found in most forest habitats and some open areas, flowering in spring with berries ripening by July.

There are many plants with blue berries, but nothing tastes quite so good as blueberries. They belong to the genus vaccinium, which includes blueberries, huckleberries, bilberries, some cranberries, and more. There are several species of blueberries, and one or more may be found from sea level to alpine meadows.

The plants range from ground-carpeting mats to shrubs 3m (10 ft.) in height. The flowers are like tiny suspended lanterns, most often white with pink accents. The berries are blue and retain remnants of the flower on the end.

Most have a whitish "bloom." There are a few plants with blue berries that are poisonous, so don't eat anything if you aren't sure.

REDCEDAR

Height: To 60m (197 ft.)

Identifying features: Yellow-green scaly foliage; mature trees often have dead tops.

Best sighting time: Flowers in April-May; cones evident by August

Where to see them: Vancouver Island and coastal BC, Vancouver area, major valleys in the Kootenays and Rockies

©Bruce Whittington

Western redcedar is not a true cedar, but belongs to the *arborvitae* family—a name that means literally "tree of life." For thousands of years, West Coast First Nations people have used its bark for the weaving of garments and baskets, and the manufacture of rope. Its wood, light and pest-resistant, is used for carved implements and unique bentwood boxes. Seagoing dugout canoes were carved from single trees, and totems and houses were constructed from the wonderful wood.

Redcedar is a conifer, but its leaves are scale-like instead of needle-like. It produces small cones with only a few scales, but each tree produces millions of tiny seeds.

This species is most common in moist forests in the southern half of the province, to about 853m (2,800 ft.).

SUBALPINE FIR

Height: To 46m (150 ft.)

Identifying features: Distinctive narrow, tapering shape; cones erect on branches

Best sighting time: Blue pollen cones visible in spring; seed cones ripen in autumn.

Where to see them: Higher elevations of central Vancouver Island, the Vancouver and Whistler areas, and the Kootenays and Rockies

©Bruce Whittington

Of all the coniferous tree species in BC, subalpine fir is the most widely distributed. As its name suggests, it is the species found at the edges of subalpine meadows, but it also grows as low as 610m (2,000 ft.) in some places.

Amabilis fir grows at lower elevations along the coast north to the Alaska panhandle. Grand fir is found on the south coast and in low- to mid-elevation valleys in southeastern British Columbia. These "true firs" produce cones that stand erect on the tops of the branches, rather than hanging like those of the spruces and Douglas fir.

Douglas fir is a large tree famous for its great height of over 91m (300 ft.) on the south coast. The interior subspecies is widespread at low to mid-elevations, but is not hardy enough to survive where subalpine fir do.

Frommer's®

Best Hiking Trips in British Columbia

1st Edition

by Christie Pashby, Darlene West, Chloë Ernst, Anne Tempelman-Kluit, Judi Lees, Amanda Castleman, Andrew Hempstead, and Judy McKinley

Wildlife Guide by Bruce Whittington

Here's what the critics say about Frommer's:

"Amazingly easy to use. Very portable, very complete."

—BOOKLIST

"Detailed, accurate, and easy-to-read information for all price ranges."

—GLAMOUR MAGAZINE

"Hotel information is close to encyclopedic."

—DES MOINES SUNDAY REGISTER

"Frommer's Guides have a way of giving you a real feel for a place."

—KNIGHT RIDDER NEWSPAPERS

John Wiley & Sons Canada, Ltd.

Published by:

JOHN WILEY & SONS CANADA, LTD.

6045 Freemont Blvd.
Mississauga, ON L5R 4J3

Copyright © 2009 John Wiley & Sons Canada, Ltd. All rights reserved. No part of this work covered by the copyright herein may be reproduced or used in any form or by any means—graphic, electronic or mechanical—without prior written permission of the publisher. Any request for photocopying or other reprographic copying of any part of this book shall be directed in writing to The Canadian Copyright Licensing Agency (Access Copyright). For an Access Copyright license, visit www.accesscopyright.ca or call toll free, 1-800-893-5777.

Frommer's is a trademark or registered trademark of Arthur Frommer. Used under license.

Wiley and the Wiley Publishing logo are trademarks or registered trademarks of John Wiley & Sons, Inc. and/or its affiliates. Frommer's is a trademark or registered trademark of Arthur Frommer. Used under license. All other trademarks are the property of their respective owners. Wiley Publishing, Inc. is not associated with any product or vendor mentioned in this book.

ISBN 978-0-470-15990-3

Editor: Gene Shannon
Project Manager: Elizabeth McCurdy
Project Editor: Pauline Ricablanca
Editorial Assistant: Katie Wolsley
Project Coordinator: Lynsey Stanford
Cartographer: Lohnes+Wright
Vice President, Publishing Services: Karen Bryan
Production by Wiley Indianapolis Composition Services

Front cover photo: A hiker basks in rays of sunlight piercing the mist along a forest trail in British Columbia.

SPECIAL SALES

For reseller information, including discounts and premium sales, please call our sales department: Tel. 416-646-7992. For press review copies, author interviews, or other publicity information, please contact our marketing department: Tel. 416-646-4584; Fax: 416-236-4448.

Wiley also publishes its books in a variety of electronic formats. Some content that appears in print may not be available in electronic formats.

Manufactured in the United States of America

1 2 3 4 5 RRD 13 12 11 10 09

CONTENTS

5 VANCOUVER ISLAND HIKES 78

6 WHISTLER & SEA-TO-SKY COUNTRY HIKES 124

7 CARIBOO COUNTRY, CHILCOTIN, COAST & NORTHERN BC HIKES 152

8 THE OKANAGAN VALLEY HIKES 191

9 THE CANADIAN ROCKIES & THE KOOTENAYS HIKES 219

APPENDIX: FAST FACTS, TOLL-FREE NUMBERS & WEBSITES 254

INDEX 263

Table of Hikes

Hike	Distance
Vancouver & The Sunshine Coast	
1 Stanley Park	9 km (5.6 miles) round trip
2 Capilano River Regional Park	7 km (4.3 miles) round trip
3 St. Mark's Summit, Howe Sound Crest Trail	11 km (6.8 miles) round trip
4 Lighthouse Park	2 km–6 km (1.2 miles–3.7 miles) on a variety of loop trails
5 The Grouse Grind	2.9 km (1.8 miles) one way
6 Lynn Canyon Park	2 km (1.2 miles)
7 Mount Seymour Trail	9.5 km (5.9 miles) round trip
8 Pacific Spirit Park	5 km (3 miles) one way
9 Point Grey Foreshore, From Spanish Banks to Wreck Beach	10 km (6.2 miles) round trip
10 Iona Beach Regional Park	9 km (5.6 miles) round trip
11 Skookumchuck Narrows Provincial Park	8 km (5 miles) round trip
12 Smuggler Cove Provincial Park	2.5 km (1.6 miles) round trip
13 Killarney Lake, Bowen Island	9 km (5.6 miles) round trip
14 Mount Daniel	2.5 km (1.6 miles) round trip
Vancouver Island	
1 Mount Finlayson Goldstream Provincial Park	7.4 km (4.6 miles) round trip
2 West Coast Trail	75 km (46.6 miles) round trip
3 Ruckle Provincial Park, Saltspring Island	6.7 km (4.2 miles) round trip
4 American Camp, San Juan Island National Historic Park	14 km (8.7 miles) round trip; shorter options available
5 The Galloping Goose Todd Trestle—Hutchinson Cove	20.5 km (12.7 miles) round trip
6 Juan de Fuca Marine Trail	10 km (6.2 miles) round trip
7 Newcastle Island Provincial Marine Park	7.5 km (4.7 miles) round trip; shorter options available
8 Wild Pacific Trail	7.8 km (4.8 miles) round trip
9 Big Cedar Trail, Meares Island	1.2 km (.7 miles) or 2.6km (1.6 miles) round trip
10 Bedwell Trail, Strathcona Provincial Park	12 km (7.5 miles) round trip
Whistler & Sea-to-Sky Country	
1 Cal-Cheak to Brandywine Falls	8 km (5 miles) round trip
2 Stawamus Chief (Centre And North Peaks)	5.5 km (3.4 miles) round trip
3 Joffre Lakes	11 km (6.8 miles) round trip
4 Lost Lake Nature Trail	4 km (2.5 miles) round trip
5 Panorama Ridge	31 km (19 miles) round trip
6 High Note via Half Note Trail	5.5 km (3.4 miles) (one way?)
7 Stein Valley Nlaka'pamux Heritage Park	9 km (5.6 miles) round trip

Difficulty	Best Time to Go	Star rating	page number
Easy	Summer to enjoy water activities	★★	30
Easy	Spring when the river is high or late summer and fall for the salmon run	★	34
Moderate	Sept.–Oct.	★★	40
Easy to moderate	The park is particularly lovely in the fall.	★	36
Strenuous	Open mid-May to mid-Sept.		43
Easy to moderate	Fall for the misty atmosphere.	★	46
Strenuous	Sept.	★★	49
Easy to moderate	Spring and summer for the new growth and bird-song.		52
Easy	July and Aug. for swimming and sunbathing	★	55
Easy	Early morning to see eagles perched along the jetty or at sunset for spectacular ocean views.	★	58
Easy	In winter, for the highest tides.	★★	61
Easy	Summer is best to enjoy the waterfront.	★	64
Easy	Spring and fall		67
Moderate	Spring or fall	★★	70
Moderate to strenuous	Spring and autumn.		81
Very strenuous	The best weather usually falls in Aug. or Sept.	★★★	85
Easy to moderate	Mid-Sept. for the fall fair.		94
Moderate	This park dazzles most in early autumn sunshine.	★★★	98
Moderate	Especially pleasant when autumn ignites the foli-age.		102
Moderate	Pods of gray whales often draw close to shore May–Aug.		105
Easy	Newcastle Island's ferries run most frequently from mid-May to early Sept.	★★	108
Easy	Superb storm-watching opportunities in winter.		111
Easy	In summer, when more light pierces the thick rainforest canopy.		114
Strenuous	Late summer provides the warmest treks in this alpine environment.		117
Moderate	July–Sept.	★	129
Strenuous	June–Oct.	★★	132
Moderate	July–Sept.	★★★	135
Easy	Apr.–Nov.		138
Strenuous	July–Aug.	★★★	140
Moderate	Late July–Sept.	★★	143
Easy	Year-round	★★	149

continues

Table of Hikes

Hike	Distance
Cariboo Country, Chilcotin, Coast & Northern BC	
1 Mount Bowman	15 km (9.3 miles) round trip
2 Williams Lake River Valley Trail	9.8 km (6.1 miles) round trip
3 Junction Sheep Range	7 km (4.3 miles) round trip
4 Perkins Peak	9.6 km (6 miles) round trip
5 Burnt Bridge Creek Loop	4.8 km (3 miles) round trip
6 Rainbow Range	17 km (11 miles) round trip
7 Barkerville to Summit Rock and Groundhog Lake	17 km (11 miles) round trip
8 Bergeron Cliffs and Falls	12.2 km (7.6 miles) round trip
9 Heritage River Trail	9 km (5.6 miles) one way
10 Cape Fife Trail	35 km (21.9 miles) round trip
The Okanagan Valley	
1 Enderby Cliffs	10 km (6.2 miles) round trip
2 Myra Canyon on the Kettle Valley Railway	12 km (7.5 miles) round trip
3 Knox Mountain Park Apex Trail	5.5 km (3.4 miles) round trip
4 Stave Pipe Trail to Pincushion Mountain	8.4 km (5.2 miles) round trip
5 Kettle Valley Railway: Penticton To Naramata	10 km (6.2 miles) round trip
6 Golden Mile Trail	8.5 km (5.3 miles) round trip
7 International Hike & Bike Trail	11 km (6.8 miles) round trip
8 Giant Cleft & the Rim Trail Via Ladyslipper Lake, Cathedral Provincial Park	12 km (7.5 miles) round trip
The Canadian Rockies & the Kootenays	
1 Abbott Ridge Trail, Glacier National Park	10 km (6.2 miles) round trip
2 Bugaboo Spires	10 km (6.2 miles) round trip
3 Emerald Lake	5.2 km (3.2 miles) round trip
4 Iceline, Celeste Lake & Twin Falls	24 km (15 miles) round trip
5 Kindersley Pass	13 km (8 miles) round trip
6 Mount Robson Provincial Park & Kinney Lake	6.5 km (4.1 miles) one way
7 Kokanee Lakes	17 km (11 miles) round trip
8 Lake of The Hanging Glacier	16 km (10 miles) round trip
9 Lake O'Hara Circuit	10.1 km (6.3 miles) round trip
10 Stanley Glacier	9 km (5.6 miles) round trip

Difficulty	Best Time to Go	Star rating	page number
Strenuous	July–Sept.	★★	156
Easy	July–Sept.	★	158
Moderate	June, Sept.–Oct.	★★★	161
Moderate	Aug.–Sept.	★★	164
Easy to moderate	June–Sept.	★★	167
Strenuous	July–Sept.	★★★	170
Moderate	Aug.–Sept.	★★★	172
Moderate	May–Sept.		176
Easy	May–Sept.		178
Moderate	May–Sept.	★★	182
Strenuous	Spectacular wild flowers come into bloom from late June to early July.		194
Easy	Dodge the crowds with an early start.	★	196
Moderate	Wildflowers are spectacular in May and June.		199
Moderate	June or Sept. to avoid mid-summer heat.		202
Easy	Enjoy a patio lunch in June or Sept.		205
Easy	In early Oct., catch local and regional grape harvest and wine festival events.		208
Easy	In may, The Meadowlark Festival hosts dozens of birding and naturalist events in the South Okanagan.		210
Strenuous	Weather is nicest and wildflowers at their showiest in July and Aug.	★★★	213
Strenuous	July–Sept.	★	222
Moderate	July–Sept.	★	225
Easy	June–Sept., late afternoon to avoid crowds	★	228
Strenuous	Late June–Sept.	★★	230
Strenuous	June–Sept.	★	234
Easy	May–Oct.		237
Moderate	Larches are stunning in Sept.	★★	239
Strenuous	Mid-July to Sept only. Bridges are removed and make hiking here impossible during the rest of the year.	★★	242
Strenuous	Mid-June to early Oct. Fall is particularly lovely.	★★★	245
Moderate	Late June to Oct. Before 9am or after 3pm to avoid crowds.	★	248

LIST OF MAPS

Map Legend

Trail	*Mountain Peak*
Alternate Trail	Point of Interest
Freeway	Overview
Major Road	Trailhead
Minor Road	Picnic Spot
Lake & River	Campground
Park	Washroom
Land	Parking
	Information/Ranger Station
	Drinking Water
	Waterfall

ABOUT THE AUTHORS

Christie Pashby is the author of *Frommer's Banff & Jasper National Parks* and co-author of *Frommer's Argentina* and *Frommer's Chile*. A freelance editor, journalist, and translator, her writing has appeared in many of Canada's major daily newspapers and has been featured on BBC Radio and NBC television. She divides her time between the Canadian Rockies and Patagonia, Argentina. Her website is www.patagonialiving.com.

Anne Tempelman-Kluit is an award-winning writer living in Vancouver close to Spanish Banks Beach and Pacific Spirit Park, where she walks almost every day. She has lived in the Yukon where she did many long hikes – one of three weeks – and has written a number of books about Vancouver Parks, the Yukon, and Christmas.

Judi Lees lives on the Sunshine Coast and she and her dog hike in the woods near her home most days, except when she is traveling to exotic places in her guise as a well-known travel writer. She is the author of a book about soft-adventure in British Columbia and one of exploring Vancouver.

Amanda Castleman is a Seattle-based author and former wilderness guide. She won a 2007 Lowell Thomas award (travel writing's Pulitzer) for adventure coverage. Amanda now plans to dive some of the tremendous landscapes she explored on Vancouver Island for this book. Her website is www.amandacastleman.com and she ego-casts further at http://roadremedies.blogspot.com.

From Welsh mountains to Bolivian cloud forests, **Chloë Ernst** has always enjoyed exploring the backcountry. Over the past six years of ranging through British Columbia she has skied on the slopes overlooking her Vancouver home, retraced the Gold Rush in the central interior, and caught waves on the Pacific coast. Chloë holds a Bachelor of Journalism and Spanish from the University of King's College and writes for various print and online publications. Read more about the travel and lifestyle writer's journeys at www.chloeernst.com.

Darlene West has written about travel, lifestyle, and outdoor adventure for regional and national magazines in both Canada and the U.S. She is also the author of *Frommer's Calgary* and *Canadian Rockies For Dummies*. She lives in Oliver, British Columbia.

Andrew Hempstead, a resident of Banff, Alberta, is a keen hiker who has been writing about and photographing western Canada since the early 1990s. He is the author of over 20 guidebooks and his images have been published in hundreds of books, magazines, and graphic products

Judy McKinley is a writer, playwright, and artist living in the north end of beautiful Haida Gwaii. Haida Gwaii is one of the rare places you can still live off the land and sustainably, and where the original peoples have never signed a treaty: She hopes she can be a part of sustaining this Haida Gwaii.

AN INVITATION TO THE READER

In researching this book, we discovered many wonderful places—hotels, restaurants, shops, and more. We're sure you'll find others. Please tell us about them, so we can share the information with your fellow travelers in upcoming editions. If you were disappointed with a recommendation, we'd love to know that, too. Please write to:

Frommer's Best Hiking Trips in British Columbia, 1st Edition

John Wiley & Sons Canada, Ltd. • 6045 Freemont Blvd. • Mississauga, ON L5R 4J3

AN ADDITIONAL NOTE

Please be advised that travel information is subject to change at any time—and this is especially true of prices. We therefore suggest that you write or call ahead for confirmation when making your travel plans. The authors, editors, and publisher cannot be held responsible for the experiences of readers while traveling. Your safety is important to us, however, so we encourage you to stay alert and be aware of your surroundings. Keep a close eye on cameras, purses, and wallets, all favorite targets of thieves and pickpockets.

Other Great Guides for Your Trip:

Frommer's British Columbia & the Canadian Rockies

Frommer's Vancouver & Victoria

Frommer's Vancouver & Whistler Day by Day

Frommer's Vancouver Island, the Gulf Islands & the San Juan Islands

FROMMER'S STAR RATINGS, ICONS & ABBREVIATIONS

Every hotel, restaurant, and attraction listing in this guide has been ranked for quality, value, service, amenities, and special features using a **star-rating system.** In country, state, and regional guides, we also rate towns and regions to help you narrow down your choices and budget your time accordingly. Hotels and restaurants are rated on a scale of zero (recommended) to three stars (exceptional). Attractions, shopping, nightlife, towns, and regions are rated according to the following scale: zero stars (recommended), one star (highly recommended), two stars (very highly recommended), and three stars (must-see).

In addition to the star-rating system, we also use **seven feature icons** that point you to the great deals, in-the-know advice, and unique experiences that separate travelers from tourists. Throughout the book, look for:

Finds	Special finds—those places only insiders know about
Fun Facts	Fun facts—details that make travelers more informed and their trips more fun
Kids	Best bets for kids and advice for the whole family
Moments	Special moments—those experiences that memories are made of
Overrated	Places or experiences not worth your time or money
Tips	Insider tips—great ways to save time and money
Value	Great values—where to get the best deals

The following **abbreviations** are used for credit cards:

AE American Express	DISC Discover	V Visa
DC Diners Club	MC MasterCard	

FROMMERS.COM

Now that you have this guidebook to help you plan a great trip, visit our website at **www.frommers.com** for additional travel information on more than 4,000 destinations. We update features regularly to give you instant access to the most current trip-planning information available. At Frommers.com, you'll find scoops on the best airfares, lodging rates, and car rental bargains. You can even book your travel online through our reliable travel booking partners. Other popular features include:

- Online updates of our most popular guidebooks
- Vacation sweepstakes and contest giveaways
- Newsletters highlighting the hottest travel trends
- Podcasts, interactive maps, and up-to-the-minute events listings
- Opinionated blog entries by Arthur Frommer himself
- Online travel message boards with featured travel discussions

1

The Best Hiking in British Columbia

British Columbia is a very large province, larger than California, Oregon, and Washington State all put together. Most of it is wild and remote. Hiking opportunities abound. From urban-backyard hikes in Vancouver to ferry-accessed trail heads on the far Northwest, there is a lot of territory to explore on the coast. Further inland, there are hundreds and hundreds of kilometers of high mountains calling trekkers and nature-lovers. Whether you want a leisurely stroll in a lush forest or a challenging full-day high-mountain hike, you'll find lots of options in "Beautiful BC." In this chapter, we highlight the best of all that BC has to offer—the best trails for kids, the best challenging hikes, best hikes for scenery, and even the best mountain lodges. So, read on and start planning!

1 THE BEST HIKES FOR FAMILIES

- **Kinney Lake** (Mt. Robson Provincial Park): This gentle mountain ramble is many families' introduction to the joys of hiking in the Rockies. Kinney Lake, in the shadow of the Canadian Rockies' highest peak, makes a great picnic spot. See p. 237.
- **Lost Lake Nature Trail** (Whistler): Even with Whistler's notoriously radical mountain bikers whizzing by, this is a calm, easy hike that leads out from the heart of Whistler Village. See p. 138.
- **Williams Lake River Valley Trail** (Williams Lake): Kids will love all the bridges here. There's also a beaver dam and lots of fish! Watching the Williams Lake River merge with the Fraser River is a lesson in the geography and history of British Columbia. See p. 158.
- **Lighthouse Park** (North Vancouver): Who doesn't find lighthouses magical? At Vancouver's doorstep, this large park has a lush forest and a truly picture-perfect well-preserved lighthouse. Great picnic spot! See p. 36.
- **Stawamus Chief** (Squamish): Most people hike the monolithic "Chief" via the South Peak. Our version also goes past Shannon Falls, but then it goes north to a quieter, higher, and more technical trail. This is an appropriate hike for experienced teens. See p. 132.

2 THE BEST EASY HIKES

- **Kettle Valley Railway** (Penticton to Naramata): A 10km (6¼-mile) leisurely hike that heads out of suburbia along a historic trestle bridge and ends at a gorgeous winery. Cheers! See p. 196.
- **Smuggler Cove Provincial Park** (Sunshine Coast): A classic West Coast half-hour ramble, this is the Sunshine Coast at its best. If you like birding, swimming, forests, pirates, and cool breezes, you'll like it here. See p. 64.

- **Pacific Spirit Park** (Vancouver): If you've got 2 hours to spare in downtown Vancouver, take a bus out to the coastal forests behind UBC and see how simply the city turns wild here. See p. 52.
- **High Note via Half Note Trail** (Whistler): Don't like hiking up but want to take in the mountain air? Take the Whistler Village Gondola and the Peak Chair to the top of the ski resort. See p. 143.
- **Emerald Lake** (Yoho National Park): This is not your average walk in a park. Flat, scenic, and circling around a jewel-like lake, there are interpretive signs in front, avalanches above, wildflowers below, and a great bistro at the end. See p. 228.
- **Big Cedar Trail, Meares Island** (Tofino): Paddle a kayak from Tofino to this amazing corner of Clayoquot Sound to see 2,000-year-old giant cedar trees. A true treasure for humankind. See p. 113.

3 THE BEST MODERATE HIKES

- **St. Mark's Summit** (Cypress Provincial Park): Just a bit longer than a half-day hike, this is a shorter version of the renowned Howe Crest Sound Trail, and it's in Vancouver's backyard. See p. 40.
- **Juan de Fuca Marine Trail** (Vancouver Island): A quick way to sample one of BC's most important backpacking trips, this hike has little elevation gain. Watch for orca whale out at sea, bald eagles in ancient trees, and starfish in the numerous tide pools. See p. 104.
- **Kokanee Lakes** (Kokanee Glacier Provincial Park): The best hike in the beautiful Kootenay Mountains of interior British Columbia takes you high into an alpine region dotted with turquoise lakes. See p. 239.
- **Mount Daniel** (Sechelt): There aren't many hikes in this book that take you to such great summit lookouts so quickly. Yes, it's steep. But the view takes in the gently-dotted harbors, islands, and rambling coastline of the Sunshine Coast. See p. 70.
- **Cal-Cheak to Brandywine Falls** (Whistler): This is a little-visited area south of Whistler. The legendary falls in question are hidden in the wilderness. The trail heads past a handful of little lakes, a suspension bridge, and a lush mountain meadow. See p. 129.

4 THE BEST DIFFICULT HIKES

- **Rainbow Range** (Cariboo Chilcotin Coast): Leading into the little-known but magic Rainbow Range, deep in the heart of the remote Tweedsmuir Provincial Park, this hike will challenge those looking for remoteness and route-finding challenges, and to see the rarely seen. See p. 170.
- **The Grouse Grind** (North Vancouver): One of the iconic hikes of BC, this is where Vancouver's athletic folk challenge themselves weekend after weekend. It's short but steep, a classic endurance test called God's Stairmaster—no active visit to Vancouver is complete without it. See p. 43.
- **Bedwell Trail** (Strathcona Provincial Park): There are some surprisingly high mountains on Vancouver Island. In the middle of the island, this takes you to alpine waterfalls, meadows, and midsummer snowfields. See p. 116.

- **Iceline Trail** (Yoho National Park): This trip can be done many ways, but our 18km (11-mile) version has it all: glaciers, waterfalls, high alpine peaks, and raging milky rivers. It's a classic Rocky Mountain trail rich in history and that elusive "Rocky Mountain high." See p. 230.
- **Panorama Ridge** (Garibaldi Provincial Park): A whopping 1,500m (4,921 ft.) elevation gain pays off on the shores of Garibaldi Lake. You can knock the Helm Glacier, the Barrier cliff, Black Tusk, the Table, and Taylor Meadows off your must-see list. See p. 140.
- **Mount Bowman** (Cache Creek): A dry summit next to the Mad Dog Mountain in the center of British Columbia, this is a remote trail leading to the summit of the highest peak in the Marble Ridge. The trip involves some challenging route-finding. See p. 156.
- **Mount Seymour Trail** (North Vancouver): There are three high summits to the north of Vancouver, and many trails taking you to them within Mt Seymour Provincial Park. The best trail takes in Mystery Lake first, and then takes in all three peaks. See p. 49.

5 THE BEST HISTORIC HIKES

- **Barkerville to Summit Rock** (Cariboo Chilcotin Coast): A moderate hike along the old wagon tracks of a historic highway that teemed with life during the gold rush that began in 1862. See p. 172.
- **Myra Canyon, Kettle Valley Railway** (Okanagan): You can take in a variety of sections of this historic railway, originally built between 1910 and 1915, and lovingly restored between 2006 and 2008. The trestle bridges in the parched land south of Kelowna make up the most thrilling parts of the trail. See p. 196.
- **Newcastle Island Provincial Park** (Vancouver Island): An easy 7.5km (4³/₄-mile) trail follows the coast of this island that once was the home to Salish villagers, herring salteries, and a sandstone quarry. Access is by a short ferry from Nanaimo. See p. 107.
- **Stein Valley Nlaka'Pamux Heritage Park** (Hope): A gorgeous trail through a sacred site of the Lytton First Nation, in a stunningly wild valley. Visit an "asking rock," pictographs, and a culturally-modified tree. See p. 147.
- **Burnt Bridge Creek Loop** (Bella Coola): The final section of the historic 420km (261-mile) Alexander Mackenzie Heritage Trail takes you over the same final steps the legendary explorer and mapmaker might have taken when he first reached the Pacific Ocean in 1793. The trail also has an even older Native history. See p. 167.

6 THE BEST HIKES FOR SEEING WILDLIFE

- **Wild Pacific Trail** (Vancouver Island): This is classic, dramatic West Coast terrain just outside the town of Ucluelet. Watch for gray whales in spring, and seals, sea lions, and surfers the rest of the year. On land, there are bears, cougars, and wolves. It's the kind of place where you want to sit still and soak it all in. See p. 110.
- **Mount Finlayson** (Vancouver Island): Where Victoria's weekend warriors challenge themselves, Goldstream is a

hive of activity when salmon spawn in autumn, drawing crowds of bald eagles. See p. 80.

- **American Camp** (San Juan Island): If you want to see orca whales, come here in summertime. Three pods regularly make their home in the waters off Lime Kiln Point and can often be seen from American Camp. See p. 97.
- **International Hike and Bike** (Oliver): A great spot for bird-watching, this leisurely trail in the South Okanagan may also offer up deer, painted turtles, coyotes, and beavers. Birders from around the world come here to see more than 200 species, including herons, orioles, goldfinch, and Canada's smallest woodpeckers. See p. 210.
- **Kindersley Pass** (Kootenay National Park): If you don't spot deer, bear, or mountain goats while hiking this full-day trail, just head down the road from the trail head towards Radium Hot Spring, where bighorn sheep hang out. Remember, dawn and dusk are the best times to see wildlife. See p. 234.

7 THE BEST SCENIC HIKES

- **Bugaboo Spires** (Bugaboo Spires Provincial Park): For those craving stunning and unique mountain sceneries, this is alpine paradise. It's a tough 5km (3-mile) climb, but no horizon in BC matches the Bugaboos' granite spires as seen from the Conrad Kain Hut. See p. 225.
- **Lake O'Hara Circuit** (Yoho National Park): This is the kind of alpine landscape dreams are made of. Lake O'Hara is a beautiful, magical area just west of the Continental Divide. Access is complicated, so plan ahead. See p. 245.
- **Joffre Lakes** (Joffre Provincial Park): A moderate 5-hour hike in the Coast Mountains north of Whistler takes you to three gorgeous turquoise lakes set amidst the cool and clear air coming off the Matier Glacier. See p. 135.
- **Junction Sheep Range** (Williams Lake): With rolling grasslands, deep eroded gullies, cliffs, and hoodoos, the landscapes here, where the Chilcotin and Fraser rivers meet, are unique and beautiful. A moderate 2-hour hike takes you to the Farwell and Fraser canyons. See p. 161.
- **Skookumchuck Narrows Provincial Park** (Sunshine Coast): It's worth the trip just to catch this natural phenomenon, one of the world's largest saltwater rapids. Be sure to time your hike with the twice-daily tide changes, otherwise there'll be nothing but still water! See p. 61.

8 THE BEST MOUNTAIN LODGES

- **West Coast Wilderness Lodge** (Egmont; ✆ **877/988-3838** or 604/883-3667; www.wcwl.com): Oceanfront property this divine on the Sunshine Coast is hard to come by. With a rustic vibe, friendly staff, a spa, and the cute village of Egmont nearby. See p. 75.
- **Nita Lake Lodge** (Whistler; ✆ **888/755-6482** or 604/966-5700; www.nitalakelodge.com): A luxury boutique lakeside lodge just steps from the Whistler Creekside is a great place to unwind and rest up for a day exploring the mountains. Rooms are mainly "deluxe studios" with modern amenities and a hip décor. See p. 150.

- **Cathedral Mountain Lodge** (Yoho National Park; ✆ **866/619-6442** or 250/343-6442; www.cathedralmountain.com): Located close to so many of the great hikes in the amazing Yoho National Park, this is a collection of cozy cabins tucked along the shores of the Kicking Horse River. See p. 251.
- **Spirit Ridge Vineyard Resort & Spa** (Osoyoos; ✆ **877/313-9463** or 250/495-5445; www.spiritridge.ca): Overlooking Okanagan Lake, with the valley in front of you and miles of vineyards all around, this new Santa Fe–inspired resort brings life to the desert. See p. 217.
- **Strathcona Park Lodge & Outdoor Education Centre** (Campbell River; ✆ **250/286-3122**): With cabins, chalets, and lodge rooms, this is one of Canada's most ethical and eco-friendly resorts. Great for families. See p. 120.

9 THE BEST RESTAURANTS

- **Araxi Restaurant & Bar** (Whistler; ✆ **604/932-4540**): Award-winning upscale dining in the chic heart of Whistler Village. Summer evening meals on the terrace are unforgettable. See p. 150.
- **Breakers Deli** (Tofino; ✆ **250/725-2559**): A popular informal eatery, this is a great place to pick up a picnic. Falafel wraps or smoked salmon burritos make great trail lunches! It's open early. See p. 121.
- **Cilantros on the Lake, Emerald Lake Lodge** (Yoho National Park; ✆ **250/343-6321**): Reward yourself post-hike with a grilled flatbread pizza, a pint of micro-brewed beer, and a truly stunning scene on the shores of the marvelous Emerald Lake. See p. 253.
- **Fresco** (Kelowna; ✆ **250/868-8805**): The Okanagan's most exciting and inspired eatery focuses on local and regional products, and of course, Okanagan wines. See p. 218.
- **Homer's Most Excellent Take Out** (Sooke; ✆ **250/642-7456**): A classic shake shack, fill up on fish and chips, wraps, burgers, *poutine,* or burritos. Fresh, cheap, and decadent, if not calorie-wise. See p. 122.
- **Salmon House on the Hill** (West Vancouver; ✆ **604/926-3212**): A Vancouver-area classic, this may be the best place to sample alder-grilled salmon in the world. Great views add to the appeal. Great wine list. See p. 76.

10 THE BEST CAMPGROUNDS

- **Riverside RV Resort & Campground** (Whistler; ✆ **604/905-5533;** www.whistlercamping.com): A fancy campground for a stylish town. Heated showers, a café, a putting green, and free shuttles into the Village make this the most happening campground on the Sea to Sky Highway. See p. 150.
- **Illecillewaet Campground** (Glacier National Park; ✆ **250/837-7500;** www.pc.gc.ca/glacier): Few campgrounds have so much at their doorstep. Awesome hikes, a historic site, a gushing alpine river, and a glacier in the background. This is a great base camp. No reservations are taken. See p. 251.

- **Bear Creek Provincial Park** (Kelowna; (✆ **800/689-9025** or 604/689-9025): Shady sites on the shores of Okanagan Lake, there are 5km (3 miles) of hiking trails right next door. Reservations are highly recommended. See p. 216.
- **Redstreak Campground** (Kootenay National Park; ✆ **877/737-3783;** www.pccamping.ca): With plenty of nearby trails, an outdoor theater, playground, and kitchen shelters, this large and full-service campground has more activities and amenities than most resorts. It's just 2.5km (1½ miles) from the village of Radium Hot Springs. Remember, you must reserve in advance! See p. 252.

2

Planning Your Hiking Trip to British Columbia

British Columbia is a mountain- and nature-lover's paradise. Vast and varied, there are hiking trails in just about every nook and cranny of this large province. The distances, like the options, are great. The main international airport, at Vancouver, is nearly 12 hours from the eastern side of the province by car and equally as far from the central and northern reaches of the province.

Getting here is easy, but getting around can be complicated. Don't bite off more than you can chew, as they say, when organizing your hiking trip. Trying to hike in both Tofino and Revelstoke on the same trip is really out of the question unless you have a few weeks. It's wise to narrow your goals into one or two geographical areas of the province outlined in this book.

Another important factor in your planning is the weather, which depends highly on the season. Seasons vary throughout the province; summer comes much earlier to the Lower Mainland area near Vancouver than it does to the central, eastern, and northern parts of the province. Hiking is an almost year-round activity on Vancouver Island, but in most of the province, the season usually runs from June through late September.

For additional help in planning your trip and for more on-the-ground resources in British Columbia, please turn to the "Fast Facts, Toll-Free Numbers & Websites" appendix on p. 254.

1 BEFORE YOU GO

VISITOR INFORMATION

For advance information, contact the official provincial tourism agency **Tourism British Columbia,** P.O. Box 9830, Stn. Prov. Govt., 1803 Douglas St., 3rd Floor, Victoria, BC V8W 9W5 (✆ **800/HELLO-BC** or 250/387-1642; www.hellobc.com).

PASSPORTS

All non-Canadians require a valid passport to visit Canada. The only alternative (and only for U.S. citizens) is a passport card (a new high-tech identity card which can speed up entry at U.S. land and sea ports-of-entry), a valid Merchant Mariner Document (MMD) when traveling in conjunction with official maritime business, or a valid U.S. military identification card while traveling on official orders. While photo ID and a declaration of citizenship are no longer accepted at the border, some combinations of government-issued photo identification, along with a second document showing proof of citizenship, can be acceptable for U.S. travelers crossing the border by land or sea—visit http://travel.state.gov/travel/cbpmc/cbpmc_2223.html for a list of acceptable documents. A valid passport is the only way to gain entry to Canada by air.

Any person under 18 traveling alone requires a letter from a parent or guardian granting him or her permission to travel

Plan Before You Hike at Frommers.com

Want to make your hiking vacation as smooth and enjoyable as possible? We've added lots of valuable information about how to plan the perfect hiking trip on our website at www.frommers.com/go/hiking. You'll find tips on how to get fit before your trip, suggestions on how best to plan your route, and useful packing tips. There are even bonus hike reviews for British Columbia not found in this book!

into Canada. The letter must state the traveler's name and the duration of the trip. It's essential that teenagers carry proof of identity, usually a passport; otherwise, their letter is useless at the border, and entry can be refused.

For additional information on passports and visas, please turn to the "Fast Facts, Toll-Free Numbers & Websites" appendix on p. 254.

CUSTOMS

What You Can Bring into Canada

Canada Customs is fairly liberal, except when it comes to firearms, plants, and meats. These are subject to rigorous inspection; without *precisely* the right paperwork, they won't make it across the border. Pepper sprays are also a big no. For a clear summary of Canadian rules, request the booklet *I Declare,* issued by the Canada Border Services Agency (© **800/461-9999** in Canada, or 204/983-3500; www.cbsa.gc.ca). Canada allows its citizens a C$750 exemption per 7-day absence, and you're allowed to bring back duty-free 1 carton of cigarettes, 1 can of tobacco, 1.5L (40 imperial oz.) of liquor, and 50 cigars. There is also a smaller 48-hour exemption (you can claim C$400 total), as well as a 24-hour exemption of C$50. You must be over 19 to purchase tobacco products and alcoholic beverages, and purchases have to accompany you in your checked or hand luggage.

What You Can Take Home from British Columbia

U.S. Citizens: For specifics on what you can bring back and the corresponding fees, download the invaluable free pamphlet *Know Before You Go* available online at **www.cbp.gov**. (Click "Travel," and then click "Know Before You Go! Online Brochure".) Or contact the **U.S. Customs & Border Protection (CBP),** 1300 Pennsylvania Ave., NW, Washington, DC 20229 (© **877/287-8667**) and request the pamphlet.

U.K. Citizens: For information, contact **HM Customs & Excise** at © **0845/010-9000,** or 020/8929-0152 from outside the U.K.; or consult their website at **www.hmce.gov.uk**.

Australian Citizens: A helpful brochure available from Australian consulates or Customs offices is *Know Before You Go.* For more information, call the **Australian Customs Service** at © **1300/363-263** or log on to **www.customs.gov.au**.

New Zealand Citizens: Most questions are answered in a free pamphlet available at New Zealand consulates and Customs offices: *New Zealand Customs Guide for Travellers, Notice no. 4.* For more information, contact **New Zealand Customs,** The Customhouse, 17–21 Whitmore St., Box 2218, Wellington, 6140 (© **04/473-6099** or 0800/428-786; **www.customs.govt.nz**).

2 WHEN TO GO

The height of the hiking season all across British Columbia is July and August. Warm summer days, coupled with later sunsets, make this prime trekking time. Hiking trails open up earlier, and stay snow-free later, on the Pacific Coast than in the interior mountains. Throughout the province, September makes a great month for a hiking trip. Crowds are thinner and most lodgings drop their rates.

Average Daytime Temperature & Total Precipitation for Vancouver, BC

	Jan	Feb	Mar	Apr	May	June	July	Aug	Sept	Oct	Nov	Dec
Temp (°F)	38	41	45	40	46	62	66	67	61	42	48	39
Temp (°C)	3	5	7	9	12	15	17	18	15	10	6	4
Precipitation (in.)	5.9	4.9	4.3	3	2.4	1.8	1.4	1.5	2.5	4.5	6.7	7
Number of days with precipitation	18	16.5	17	14	13	11	7	7	8.5	14.5	20	20

Weather is the hiker's constant companion, one with many moods and subject to change at anytime. Always get a weather forecast before your hike and adjust your schedule accordingly. For example, on a hot day, schedule your hiking for the cool of the morning and the late afternoon. Avoid hiking in exposed places when thunder and lightning storms are predicted.

Get local forecasts by going online to The Weather Network (www.weathernetwork.com), Environment Canada's Weather Office (www.weatheroffice.ec.gc.ca), or AccuWeather.com (www.accuweather.com). Note that most forecasts are oriented to populated areas and may not apply to where you're hiking. Call or drop-in at the local park office or ranger station for the latest in local weather conditions and advice about trail conditions in inclement weather.

British Columbia has a very full calendar of events going on throughout the year in every region. A good place to find out what's happening during your visit is www.whatsonwhen.com, where you can search by dates, categories, locations, and keywords. If you're visiting before, during, or shortly after the Vancouver 2010 Olympic and Paralympic Games, it's worth visiting www.vancouver2010.com to see what particular events are happening during your stay.

3 GETTING THERE & GETTING AROUND

BY PLANE

British Columbia is linked with the United States, Europe, Asia, and the rest of Canada by frequent non-stop flights. The Vancouver International Airport (airport code YVR) is the main hub, although destinations in the eastern part of the province (including the Canadian Rockies) are closer to the Calgary International Airport (airport code YYC) than to Vancouver, making this an alternative entry airport. Regional airlines connect to smaller centers like Cranbrook, Smithers, Prince George, Kamloops, Kelowna, Victoria, and Nanaimo.

See the "Fast Facts, Toll-Free Numbers & Websites" appendix on p. 254 for a list of Canadian and international airlines that serve the province.

What to Bring: The Hiker's Checklist

Day pack	First aid kit
Boots	Map and compass
Socks	Sunglasses
Underwear	Sun block
Pants and shorts	Insect repellant
Long-sleeved shirt or sweater	Pocket knife
Outerwear: parka or windbreaker	Flashlight/headlamp
Hat	Matches and fire starter
Water bottle	Plastic bags
Food	

Also consider these items:

Camera, battery charger, extra memory card

Trekking pole(s) (the collapsible, telescoping variety)

A bandana has many uses. Soak one in water and tie around your neck for an instant pick-me-up in hot weather; tie around your head for a sweatband; or use as a mask tied below your eyes to protect from wind and dust.

Heart-rate monitor on your wrist to track target heart rate, particularly if you have any physical infirmities that would require paying particular attention to over-exertion, especially on strenuous hikes at altitude or in extreme weather.

A good book for after the hike or to enjoy during a break on the trail. A paperback is lighter to carry around.

Complete information on what to bring on your hiking vacation can be found at www.frommers.com/go/hiking, including tips on day packs, clothing and equipment to pack, and recommendations for other things to bring with you.

There are 19 airports in British Columbia that have regular commercial service. They range from Victoria and Cranbrook in the south to Dawson Creek, Smithers, and Prince Rupert to the north. Besides Air Canada and WestJet (see Appendix), the following airlines offer commercial service within British Columbia: **Central Mountain Air** (✆ **888/865-8585;** www.flycma.com), **Pacific Coastal Airlines** (✆ **604/273-8666;** www.pacificcoastal.com), and **Hawkair** (✆ **800/487-1216;** www.hawkair.com). **Harbour Air Seaplanes** (✆ **800/665-0212;** www.harbourair.com) has floatplanes servicing Vancouver, Victoria, and Nanaimo.

BY CAR

Having a vehicle will greatly ease your hiking trip, allowing you to access trail heads on your own schedule and keeping you from having to rule out so many choices due to complex access points.

Many U.S.-based travelers should consider taking their own car to Canada. There are scores of border crossings; however, not all border crossing keep the same hours, and many are closed at night, so before departing, ascertain if it will be open when you arrive there.

In addition to having the proper ID to cross into Canada, drivers may also be asked to provide proof of car insurance and show the car's registration. If you're driving a rental car, you may be asked to show the rental agreement. Firearms are allowed across the border only in special circumstances; handguns are almost completely outlawed.

Once in Canada, you'll find that roads are generally in good condition. Speed limits on highways are either 80kmph (50 mph) or 100kmph (62 mph).

Canadians from other provinces will also find it very appealing to visit these hiking areas with their own cars. They will enter BC from Alberta, the province's eastern neighbor.

Hwy. 1, the Trans-Canada Highway, connects the province from east to west; Hwy. 99 (an extension of the US I-5) begins at the Canada/U.S. border and then travels into Vancouver and on to Whistler; Hwy. 97 runs south to north from Osoyoos all the way to the Yukon Territory. Hwy. 16, the Yellowhead Highway, traverses central British Columbia from Mount Robson Provincial Park to Prince Rupert. Hwy. 5 travels through the Thompson and Okanagan regions through to Hope. On Vancouver Island, Hwy. 1 runs from Nanaimo to Mile Zero in Victoria. Hwy. 4 takes you west from Nanaimo to Tofino and Ucluelet. Finally, Hwy. 19 heads north from Nanaimo to the far north of the island.

The distance within British Columbia can be very long. From Vancouver to Calgary, the drive is 1,057km (657 miles) and can take more than 13 hours.

Note: Logging roads are open to the public unless otherwise posted. Built for industrial traffic and frequently unpaved, special care should be taken. Be aware that logging trucks have right-of-way.

BY TRAIN

VIA Rail (**✆888/842-7245**; www.viarail.ca), Canada's national passenger rail service, has three routes in BC, connecting Vancouver with Jasper, Alberta, Prince George, Prince Rupert, and Smithers. You can get off at any point along the route as long as you request a "special stop" in advance. The **Whistler Mountaineer** (**✆ 888/687-RAIL;** www.whistlermountaineer.com) is another rail service connecting Vancouver with Whistler. In general, rail travel is slower than air but gives you a chance to enjoy the scenery. Still, from train stations, you'll have to solve the problem of getting to trail heads. Again, a rental car will ease this greatly.

BY BUS

Bus lines service almost every city and town in BC and will help you connect short distances. Most of the time, though, you'll have to find your own way from a main highway to a trail head. **Greyhound Canada** (**✆ 800/661-8748;** www.greyhound.ca) serves nearly 300 destinations across the entire province. **Pacific Coach** (**✆ 800/661-1725;** www.pacificcoach.com) links Vancouver with Vancouver Island and has an express bus from the Vancouver International Airport to Whistler. **Perimeter** (**✆ 877/317-7788;** www.perimeterbus.com) also links to Whistler. **Tofino Bus** (**✆ 866/986-3466;** www.tofinobus.com) has daily service from Vancouver, Victoria, and Nanaimo to Tofino and Ucluelet.

4 CHOOSING A HIKE

For such a rich and diverse hiking destination as British Columbia, there are obviously thousands of different trails you could take—so what makes these hikes the best? While any choice is going to be subjective, we've used our years of experience hiking in the area to choose the best hikes for all kinds of interests: the best hikes for spectacular views, the best to see wildlife, the best forest walks, the best coastal routes, the best challenges, and the best to explore the culture while you walk. Above all, we've strived to provide hikes that show you something unique about British Columbia that you won't likely find where you've come from.

ELEMENTS OF A FROMMER'S "BEST HIKING TRIP"

At the beginning of each hike review, there is lots of information to help you decide if a particular hike is right for you. Keeping in mind what kind of vacation experience you want, use these tools to help you plan your hike and get the most out of your vacation.

Star Ratings and Icons

Located in the title bar at the beginning of the hike review, these ratings are the quickest way to see what we believe are "the best of the best."

All hikes in this book have been carefully recommended and make for an excellent hiking experience; however, a few routes are so exceptional that they deserve special attention. For these hikes, we've awarded a star (or two or three stars) for easy identification.

Likewise, some hikes have special qualities that deserve recognition:

- **Finds** Are lesser-known hikes that don't have the crowds of some of the more popular routes—the hidden treasures.
- **Kids** These hikes are ones best-suited for doing with young families, with easier terrain and lots to see and do to keep children engaged.
- **Moments** These routes contain experiences that are so special they will leave lasting memories—something you may never have seen before, but will never forget.

Difficulty Rating

A trail's **degree of difficulty** greatly affects hiking time. Park agencies and guidebook writers rate the degree of challenge a trail presents to the average hiker. Of course the "average" hiker varies widely, as does the average hiker's skills, experience, and conditioning; assessing "degree of difficulty" is inevitably subjective.

A path's elevation gain and loss, exposure to elements, steepness, climactic conditions, and the natural obstacles a hiker encounters along the way (for example, a boulder field or several creek crossings would increase the difficulty rating) figure prominently in determining the hike's difficulty rating.

In this book, hikes are rated with an Easy-Moderate-Strenuous system. The hike rating in brief is:

- **Easy:** Less than 2 hours, with relatively flat, even terrain. An easy day hike is suitable for beginners and children. No hiking boots or special equipment necessary.
- **Moderate:** A hike that can take up to 5 hours to complete. Suitable for hikers with moderate fitness levels and for older children. May include sections with significant elevation or difficult terrain. No excessive difficulty or navigational skills requires. You should be reasonably fit for these.
- **Strenuous:** Day hikes in excess of 6 hours, or shorter hikes that feature particularly challenging terrain or require skilled navigation. The trail may include difficult terrain like scree, dense vegetation, swampy sections, boulders to traverse, or ladders. Not suitable for children or people of questionable fitness.

Distance

Distance is expressed in kilometers and miles for the complete distance to walk beginning at the trail head. The hikes in this guide range from 2km to 31km (1.2 miles–19 miles) round trip. We also indicate whether the hike brings you back to your starting point (round-trip) or is a one-way path (where another means of transport returns you to the trail head).

Estimated Time

Estimated time needed to complete the hikes in this guidebook is based on the expected performance of a person in average physical and aerobic condition, traveling at a moderate pace. Age, fitness, and trail experience vary widely among hikers, and the estimated time may be far too long for some hikers, far too short for others. The estimate also includes recommended amounts of time for taking breaks along the route.

Elevation Gain

Elevation gain measures the *net* gain from the trail head to the hike's highest point. Overall gain (or gross gain), on a trail with rolling terrain that climbs and loses elevation, could be substantially more. The elevation chart that appears with the trail map for each hike will show the route's topography.

Costs & Permits

Every national park in Canada has an entry fee. Provincial parks often do, as well. A day fee costs C$9.80 for adults, C$8.30 for seniors, C$4.90 for youth 6 to 16 years of age. A family permit costs C$19.60 per day. If you plan to be in a national park for more than a day, your best bet is to buy a Annual Discovery Package, which costs C$84.40 for a family of up to seven people arriving together, and includes entrance into all the national parks in Western Canada. You must have a permit on your vehicle's dashboard when you leave it in a National Park parking lot.

Day hiking and parking are generally free at British Columbia's provincial parks. For the rest of the trails in this book, unless otherwise indicated, there are either no permits required or simply forms to fill out at a self-service kiosk at the trail head.

Pet-Friendly

In Canada's national and provincial parks, pets are allowed on most trails, but they must be on a leash. Remember that they pose a danger to other wildlife. Dogs are not permitted on most beaches in British Columbia. If the hike introduction does not specifically state if a particular hike is pet-friendly, then no hazards for pets are present.

Best Time to Go

We have suggested time periods that are best to enjoy the particular hike. There are a few areas of British Columbia that offer four-season hiking, but some climatic restrictions must be heeded. Elsewhere, hiking is a summer activity only. Heavy rains can lead authorities to close trails to public use any time of the year.

The suggested times are intended to show the best time for maximum enjoyment of the trail, but the trail may also be accessible outside of the suggested time period. Visit the suggested website for details on times when the trail is closed.

Website

The suggested website is the best place to go to get further information on the trail and surrounding area.

Recommended Map

We've listed our favorite trails maps, those that are reasonably easy for the traveler to obtain. These will likely provide additional detail to the map provided in this guide.

Trail Head GPS

We've listed the GPS coordinates for where the recommended trail begins. The intent is to get you to the start of the trail easily by entering the coordinates into a handheld or automotive GPS device, GPS-enabled cellphone, or online mapping program.

Trail Head Directions

Directions to the hike starting point are given from the nearest highway or major road to the parking area for the trail head. For trails having two desirable trail heads, directions to both are given. A few trails can be hiked one way with the possibility of a car shuttle. Suggested car shuttle points are noted.

NAVIGATION ASSISTANCE

Maps

Each trail in this guide has a map. Familiarize yourself with the map legend. To follow the map easily, first look for the north. Then, find the trail head and follow the directions given to each waypoint.

The best road maps for British Columbia are designed by the Canadian Automobile Association (CAA) (www.caa.ca). Maps are free to CAA and American Automobile Association (AAA) members, and available for purchase by nonmembers.

Google Maps are particularly useful for finding your way to parks, most of which have well-signed trail heads for particular trails. Google Maps provide highly specific driving directions from Point A to Point B—that is to say, from the city to the country and from one park to another.

Google Maps provide road maps and, in many cases, also show Canadian national and provincial park trails. A more specific Terrain Maps view displays a topographic view. In addition, the satellite view shows terrain in a more three-dimensional way. You can create and edit Google Maps on your home computer before your trip or download them to a wireless device.

MapQuest (www.mapquest.com) has excellent mapmaking capabilities and will enable you to get maps and directions to parks and trail heads. The company also offers a product called MapQuest Navigator 5.0 that provides a GPS car navigation experience right on your phone without the need to buy another navigation device.

Detailed Local Maps

Detailed topographical maps are produced by **Natural Resources Canada** (615 Booth St., Rm. 180, Ottawa, Ontario K1A 0E9; ✆ **800/465-6277**; www.maps.nrcan.gc.ca) and sold at shops across the country. The NRC website has a good list of where to buy the maps.

Another good resource is **Maptown** (✆ **877/776-2365;** www.maptown.com), which has a wide selection of topo maps, forest district maps, road maps, and hiking maps. Based in Richmond, BC, **International Travel Maps and Books** (✆ **604/237-1400;** www.itmb.com) also has a great selection. Make sure any map you purchase is up to date!

Most of the hikes in this guide are in Canadian national parks (www.pc.gc.ca) or in British Columbia provincial parks (www.env.gov.bc.ca/bcparks), two park agencies with large, user-friendly websites that have downloadable PDF maps of

Google That Trail Head

Besides accepting addresses for providing directions, Google Maps (http://maps.google.com) can also understand GPS coordinates. So, for a sure-fire way to reach any trail in this guide, simply click on Get Directions, enter the address where you'll be starting from on the From line, and then enter the GPS coordinates for the trail head (given at the beginning of each hike in this book) in the To line. Click the Get Directions button, and you can then print off step-by-step directions to get you directly to the trail.

It's Easy Being Green

Here are a few simple ways you can help conserve fuel and energy when you travel:

- Each time you take a flight or drive a car, greenhouse gases release into the atmosphere. You can help neutralize this danger to the planet through "carbon offsetting"—paying someone to invest your money in programs that reduce your greenhouse gas emissions by the same amount you've added. Before buying carbon offset credits, just make sure that you're using a reputable company, one with a proven program that invests in renewable energy. Reliable carbon offset companies include **Carbonfund** (www.carbonfund.org) and **TerraPass** (www.terrapass.org).
- Whenever possible, choose nonstop flights; they generally require less fuel than indirect flights that stop and take off again. Try to fly during the day—some scientists estimate that nighttime flights are twice as harmful to the environment. And pack light—each 6.8kg (15 lb.) of luggage on a 8,047km (5,000-mile) flight adds up to 23kg (50 lb.) of carbon dioxide emissions.
- Where you stay during your travels can have a major environmental impact. To determine the green credentials of a property, ask about trash disposal and recycling, water conservation, and energy use; also, question if sustainable materials were used in the construction of the property. The website **www.greenhotels.com** recommends green-rated member hotels around the world that fulfill the company's stringent environmental requirements. Also consult **www.environmentallyfriendlyhotels.com** for more green accommodation ratings.
- At hotels, request that your sheets and towels not be changed daily. (Many hotels already have programs like this in place.) Turn off the lights and air-conditioner (or heater) when you leave your room.
- Use public transport where possible—trains, buses, and even taxis are more energy-efficient forms of transport than driving. Even better is to walk or cycle; you'll produce zero emissions and stay fit and healthy on your travels.
- If renting a car is necessary, ask the rental agent for a hybrid, or rent the most fuel-efficient car available. You'll use less gas and save money at the pump.
- Eat at locally owned and operated restaurants that use produce grown in the area. This contributes to the local economy and cuts down on greenhouse gas emissions by supporting restaurants where the food is not flown or trucked in across long distances. Visit **www.eatwellguide.org** for tips on eating sustainably in the U.S. and Canada.

almost all the parks in their respective jurisdictions. These park maps show all areas of the parks, including roads, picnic areas, scenic features, trail heads, and most hiking trails.

National park maps are available for free with paid admission to a national park, usually available from the park visitor center. Many provincial parks, especially the remote ones, have no visitor center or registration office, and thus it can be more difficult to get park maps.

Reading GPS Coordinates

Every spot on the Earth can be numbered by the coordinates on a GPS unit. Latitude is noted in North or South; in the case of British Columbia destinations, it's North. Longitude is shown as East or West; in British Columbia, the location is West. For example, the trail head for the Juan De Fuca Marine Trail on Vancouver Island is located at N 48 31.976, W 124 26.637. Latitude and longitude are measured in degrees, which translate into distance from the 0 line (longitude) in England or the Equator (latitude).

Hikes can be broken up with waypoints, or stops along the way. These waypoints can guide you back to the trail if you are lost, by checking the coordinates for where you are and aiming yourself towards the coordinates of the nearest waypoint.

Having a GPS reading of the trail head and of certain trail waypoints can be both helpful and confusing. Such readings can be particularly helpful as a supplement to a map for finding obscure trail heads, unsigned junctions, or going off-trail—situations you will rarely encounter while hiking any of the high-quality trails in this guide.

A GPS reading can be confusing to the less experienced hiker and GPS user at times because a GPS device shows direction or gives distance only "as the crow flies," or in a straight line. But hikers are not crows! Most trails don't take a straight line from Point A to Point B, so be sure to consult the map included with the hike description, along with your GPS readings.

5 HIKING SAFETY

The overall condition of the trails in British Columbia's provincial parks, national parks, and regional and forest service areas ranges from good to excellent. Trail head parking, interpretive panels and displays, as well as signage, are generally excellent. Backcountry junctions are usually signed, and trail conditions generally range from good to excellent. That said, it never hurts to take precautions—no one wants to come home with stories about how good the medical service is in British Columbia.

COMMON AILMENTS

Drinking Water

Do not drink water from any lakes, rivers, or streams in British Columbia! Though it may be some of the cleanest water on the planet, and free from industrial chemicals, water may contain harmful bacteria and parasites. Boil or filter untreated water, or carry water from a treated water source. Tap water is generally potable.

Mosquitoes & Ticks

Ticks are present in many locales in British Columbia, particularly in wooded areas with lots of leaf litter and in dense underbrush characteristic of the coastal environment. They attach to human hosts in warm areas where they will go undisturbed—behind the ears or knees, armpits, and in the scalp.

At the conclusion of a hike in an area where ticks are present, check your fellow hikers (and have them check you!) for ticks. Brush off your clothes. In a post-hike shower, scan your body one more time. Make sure to wash your hiking clothes.

To remove a tick, dab rubbing alcohol on the skin around the tick and on the tick itself. It sterilizes the area and some experts argue that it causes the tick to loosen its grip, making it easier to pull out. Firmly grab the tick with a pair of sharp-pointed tweezers right where the head meets the skin. Slowly pull the tick straight out.

Like ticks, mosquitoes feed on the blood of animal hosts. But unlike ticks, only the females bite. They lay eggs in standing water, in anything from marshy meadows to tiny puddles, which makes it nearly impossible to avoid them on many summertime hikes.

The strongest and most effective insect repellants contain DEET, which overpowers the scent that mosquitoes and other biting insects normally pick up from humans.

Poison Ivy

This infamous plant, also known as poison oak, grows abundantly throughout British Columbia. It's most commonly a bush but may also take the form of a vine and climb up trees. "Leaflets three, let it be" is the warning for poison oak leaves that have three lobed leaves, one to four inches long and glossy, as if waxed.

All parts of the plant at all times of the year contain poisonous sap that can severely blister skin and mucous membranes. Its sap is most toxic during spring and summer. In fall, poison oak is particularly conspicuous; its leaves turn to flaming crimson or orange. However, its color change is more a response to heat and dryness than season; its "fall color" can occur anytime in British Columbia.

A long-sleeved shirt and long pants comprise a helpful barrier, but not an impenetrable one. Rash outbreaks can occur as quickly as 6 to 12 hours after exposure, but usually in the 24- to 48-hour range. Most common of a multitude of remedies is the regular application of calamine lotion or cortisone cream.

WILDLIFE & WILDLIFE ENCOUNTERS

The rugged wilderness of British Columbia is also home to a varied and active population of wildlife. Hiking here is hiking in wildlife territory; that's part of the appeal, of course. But it's extremely important that you are prepared for any wildlife encounter you may have on the trail, at the trail head, or on the road to the parking lot.

Wildlife in British Columbia includes black and grizzly bears, cougars (mountain lions), bighorn sheep, elk, moose, deer, skunks, lynx, fox, coyotes, and many other mammals. See the front of this guide for more information on some of the noteworthy wildlife you may encounter.

General wildlife rules include

- Never feed, entice, or disturb wildlife.
- Photograph wildlife from a distance.
- Don't make sounds to startle an animal.
- Keep pets on a leash at all times.
- Keep children within close reach at all times and never encourage them to pet or feed wild animals.

Bears

Bears are very intelligent and complex animals. They can frequently be seen in the mountains of BC, but bear attacks are extremely rare. Each bear and each bear encounter is unique; there is no single strategy that will work in all situations. Bears do not like surprises. When hiking in bear country, sing, chat loudly, yodel, and make as much noise as possible. Bear bells will help with this no-surprise factor. And bear spray, when used properly, should effectively turn back a bear that is at close range (make sure you thoroughly read instructions before hitting the trail!). But it's best to never get close enough to actually need bear spray.

Here are some important tips on how to deal with a bear encounter (review them *before* hitting the trail):

- Stay calm: Bears usually don't want to attack; they are more curious first to determine if you are a threat. They often bluff an attack to gauge a reaction.
- Immediately pick up small children.
- Stay in a group.

What Really Lost Hikers Should Do

- S.T.O.P. (Stop, Think, Observe, Plan).
- Blow a whistle to signal you need assistance.
- Stay put. Most likely, if you've informed friends and authorities of your itinerary, a rescue effort will be launched quickly on your behalf after you fail to show up at the appointed time.
- Drink enough water.
- Put on your extra clothing. Avoid getting cold or hypothermic.
- If appropriate, build a fire for warmth and as a locator. Make sure to build a simple fire pit so that you don't set the woods on fire with your blaze.

- Don't drop your backpack.
- Back away slowly—never run!
- Talk firmly, calmly, and loudly to the bear. If a bear rears on its hind legs, it is trying to identify you. Remain calm and continue talking so it knows you are not a prey animal. Screaming or quick movements may startle the bear.
- Leave the area: As soon as possible, back away, always leaving the bear an escape route.
- If a bear attacks, do not play dead. First, try to escape, preferably in a building, in a car, or up a tree. Use bear spray, if possible. Shout and do anything you can to intimidate the bear.

Elk

Elk are dangerous animals, particularly in calving season (mid-May to the end of June). Give them the right of way and stay at least three bus lengths away.

Cougars

The cougar, or mountain lion, is solitary, elusive, and active mainly at night. Avoid meeting a cougar on a trail by hiking in groups and making lots of noise. If you encounter a cougar

- Immediately pick up small children.
- Face the animal and retreat slowly. Do not run or play dead.
- Try to appear bigger by waving your arms.

TRAIL HEAD SAFETY & PARKING PRECAUTIONS

Returning to the trail head after a joyful day on the trail to find a car window smashed and valuables missing can ruin your hiking vacation. Many of the featured hikes in this guide begin at what land managers characterize as "developed trail heads"—which is to say, they're usually safer and better patrolled than undeveloped trail heads, such as pullouts and dirt lots hidden far from the highway. Others are very remote; yours may be the only car parked there all day.

Statistics suggest that after 3 decades of "Lock your Car and Take your Valuables With You" signs and campaigns in North America, hikers are finally heeding this safety advice, resulting in fewer reported car break-ins.

A few simple steps can minimize the likelihood of your car being broken into: Don't leave valuables in the car (best idea); lock valuables in the trunk (second best idea); bring at least your wallet and keys with you, rather than hiding them in your vehicle.

Another important issue at many trail heads in British Columbia are the critters who live nearby. Porcupines, in particular, have gotten used to the salty tidbits they find on many vehicles and have wreaked havoc on brake lines. In such trail head parking lots, hikers have taken matters into their own hands. With the help of parks staff, chicken wire is available for you to wrap tightly around the base of your car. Use nearby stones to secure the wire in place and make sure you cover all four wheels.

6 GUIDED HIKING TOURS

A number of companies offer outstanding hiking trips in British Columbia.

Coastal Revelations Nature and Heritage Tours (✆ **866/954-0110;** www.coastalrevelations.com) has trekking and nature tours up and down the Pacific Coast.

Sea to Sky Expeditions (✆ **800/990-8735;** www.seatoskyexpeditions.com) has unique hiking trips in BC's Chilcotin Mountains and on the Chilkootin Trail, as well as hiking trips in the Canadian Rockies and along the Pacific Coast.

Yamnuska Mountain Adventures (✆ **866/678-4164;** www.canadianrockieshiking.com) has guided backpacking and hiking trips in the Canadian Rockies.

WildEarth Adventures (✆ **800/378-9810;** www.wildearth-adventures.com) has a 12-day hiking trip along the Mackenzie River in a stunning area of northern British Columbia.

To find a qualified mountain guide to lead you on the trail, contact the **Association of Canadian Mountain Guides** (✆ **403/678-2885;** www.acmg.ca).

For more information on package tours and for tips on booking your trip, see www.frommers.com/planning.

Frommers.com: The Complete Travel Resource

Planning a trip or just returned? Head to **Frommers.com** (www.frommers.com), voted Best Travel Site by *PC Magazine.* We think you'll find our site indispensable before, during, and after your travels—with expert advice and tips; independent reviews of hotels, restaurants, attractions, and preferred shopping and nightlife venues; vacation giveaways; and an online booking tool. We publish the complete contents of over 135 travel guides in our **Destinations** section, covering over 4,000 places worldwide. Each weekday, we publish original articles that report on **Deals and News** via our free **Frommers.com Newsletters.** What's more, **Arthur Frommer** himself blogs 5 days a week, with cutting opinions about the state of travel in the modern world. We're betting you'll find our **Events** listings an invaluable resource; it's an up-to-the-minute roster of what's happening in cities everywhere—including concerts, festivals, lectures, and more. We've also added weekly **podcasts, interactive maps,** and hundreds of new images across the site. Finally, don't forget to visit our **Message Boards,** where you can join in conversations with thousands of fellow Frommer's travelers and post your trip report once you return.

3 Suggested Itineraries

From the coast to the mountains, a lifetime may not be long enough to explore all the hiking trails of British Columbia. Each pocket of the province offers enough for a hiking trip of its own. You could spend 10 days in the Canadian Rockies alone; ditto for Vancouver Island or the Whistler area, for example. Still, vacations are treasured breaks, and it's important to make the most of every single day. Remember that distances here can be large; don't bite off more than you can chew or try to take in too much. Otherwise, you'll end up spending more time behind the wheel than on the trail. These itineraries are blueprints that can be adapted and modified to suit your needs. They will help you narrow things down, plan ahead, and spend as much time as possible on the trail.

1 A LONG WEEKEND IN WHISTLER

Whistler is synonymous with adventures, and its location, just 2 hours north of Vancouver, makes it an ideal getaway for weekend warriors. By adding an extra day to your weekend, you can fill your spirit up with challenging hikes and high alpine glory.

Head north from Vancouver on the Sea-to-Sky Highway and enter a fantastic world of high alpine lakes, giant rock-walls, remote glaciers, and (of course) one of the world's finest mountain resort towns, Whistler, at the center of it all.

Day ❶:

Get a head start on the weekend, heading out late on a Friday afternoon from Vancouver towards Squamish. Spend the night in a cozy cabin at the **Sunwolf Outdoor Centre** (p. 150).

Day ❷:

You can't miss the gigantic **Stawamus Chief** (p. 132) rock-wall, which is the dramatic backdrop of Squamish. The 4-hour hike to the Centre and North Peaks at the top of the Chief is steep but will give you your first glimpse of the mountains to the north. Back down at your car, continue to Whistler for lunch. For something fast and healthy, try **Ingrid's Village Café** (p. 151). Then, hop on the Whistler Village Gondola and on to the Peak Chair. Suddenly, you're above 2000m (6,562 ft.), with high alpine glory all around you. Stroll the gentle **High Note to Half Note Trail** (p. 143) for views of the Black Tusk. Check into your luxury room at the **Nita Lake Lodge** (p. 150).

Day ❸:

Panorama Ridge (p. 140) is a full-day, challenging hike. The trail head is 25km (16 miles) south of Whistler. With 1,505m (4,938 ft.) of elevation gain, you're going to work hard here. But the reward is a stunning panorama view of Garibaldi Lake, The Barrier peak, and glaciers galore. There are more rewards to be had later with dinner at the outstanding **Araxi Restaurant** (p. 150).

Day ❹:

Grab breakfast at **Crepe Montagne** (p. 151). If you've still got some energy left (and aren't tempted by Whistler's many

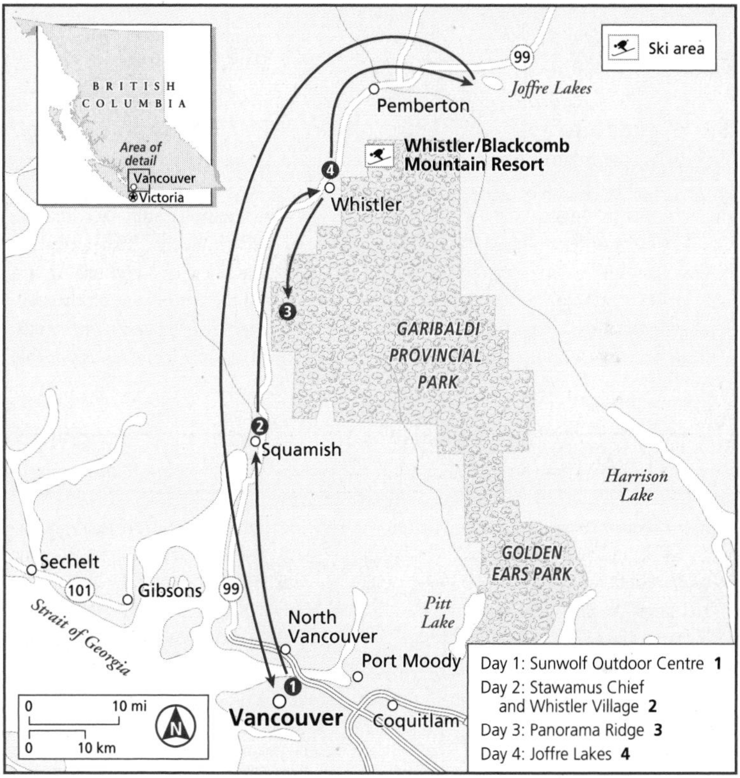

Ski area

Day 1: Sunwolf Outdoor Centre **1**
Day 2: Stawamus Chief and Whistler Village **2**
Day 3: Panorama Ridge **3**
Day 4: Joffre Lakes **4**

spas), then drive north to Joffre Provincial Park. The 5-hour hike to **Joffre Lakes** (p. 135) leads to the cool, crisp air beneath the Matier Glacier and the three jewel-green Joffre Lakes. Then, head back to Vancouver.

2 HIKING IN WINE COUNTRY: A FALL LONG WEEKEND IN THE OKANAGAN

Where better to frolic in the fall than BC's Okanagan Valley? It's very hot here in the summer, so make this the destination for an autumn getaway, coinciding with the wine harvest. A half-day drive from Vancouver, this wide valley offers great outdoor adventures. Base yourself in Naramata or Kelowna.

Day 1:

Saturday morning begins with a 3-hour hike on the **Golden Mile Trail** (p. 208) from the west bench of Okanagan River Valley. Sage meadows above and vineyards below finish the trail with a visit to Tinhorn Creek, a nearby winery that happens to be the trail head. Head into Osoyoos for dinner with lake views at **Passatempo** (p. 218).

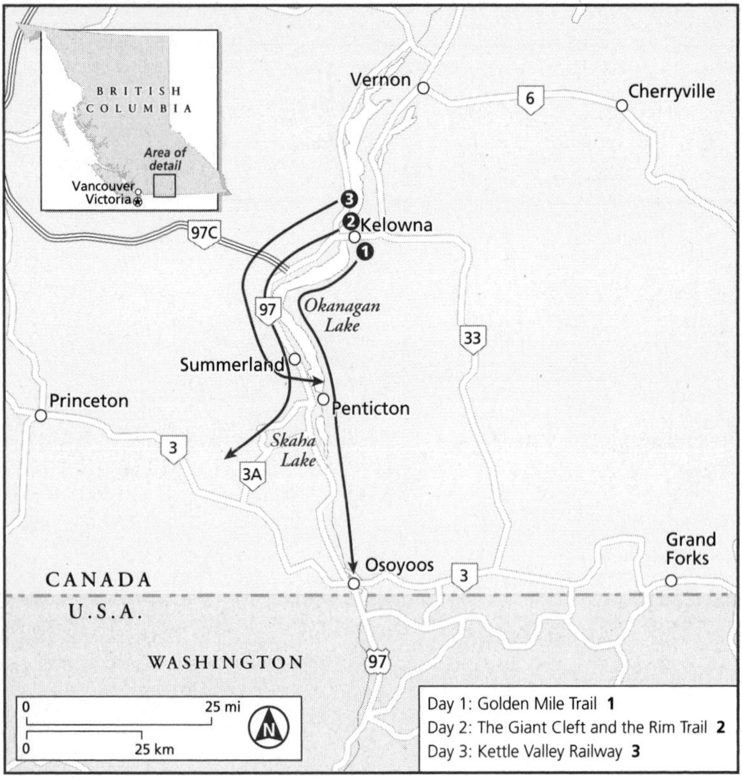

Day ❷:

If yesterday was about hedonism and good wine, then today is about exertion and natural bliss. **The Giant Cleft and the Rim Trail** (p. 213) in Cathedral Provincial Park visits three of seven exquisite alpine lakes between the Cascade Mountains and Okanagan. In the fall, larch trees are golden. It's an 8-hour trip, so bring a good lunch. For dinner, head to the **Bouchons Bistro** (p. 217) on Sunset Drive in Kelowna.

Day ❸:

Your final hike on Monday morning blends exercise with history. This section of the historic **Kettle Valley Railway** (p. 205) leads right out of suburban Penticton into one of the hottest, driest parts of Canada. It crosses an amazing trestle bridge and leaves you at a great lunch spot: the beautiful **Hillside Estates Winery.**

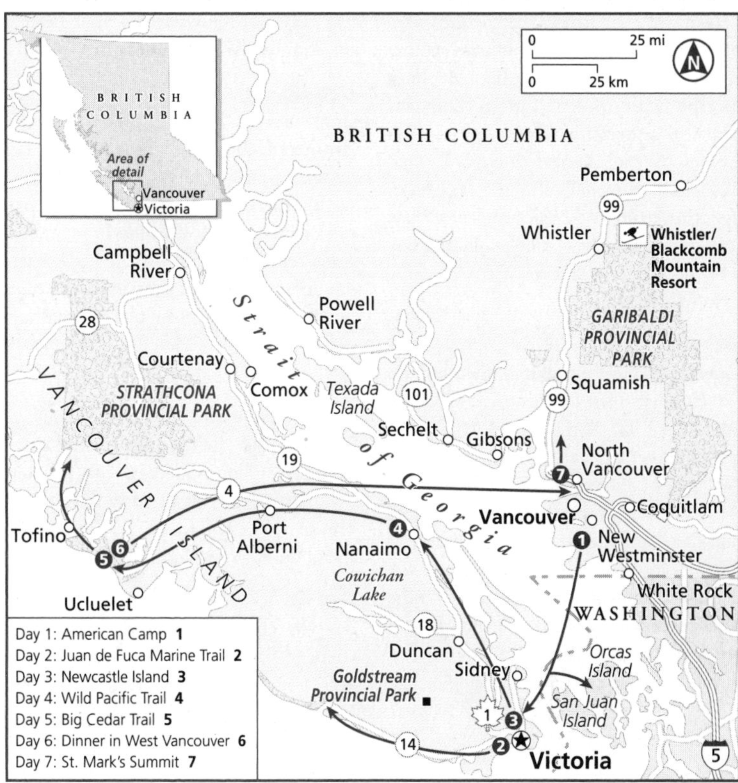

3 A WEEK HIKING ON THE COAST

There is so much nature to discover on the West Coast of British Columbia. A rich marine life, coupled with temperate rainforests, means there is plenty to keep you interested. Since the hiking season starts earlier and finishes later here than other parts of the province, why not come here in spring?

Distances and dependence on ferry travel, however, will be the fundamental nuts and bolts determining your itinerary. Plan ahead, with help from ferry schedules.

Day 1:

Catch the morning ferry from Tsawassen to Schwartz Bay on Vancouver Island. Drive to Sydney and board the ferry to Washington State's San Juan Island. From Friday Harbor, head to the historic **American Camp** (p. 98) interpretive hike, a great beachcombing warm-up. Watch for pods of orca whales off Lime Kiln Point. Spend the night in Victoria, first strolling the harbor and dining at **rebar** (p. 122).

Day 2:
Pick up lunch supplies at **Lifestyle Markets** on Douglas Street. Then, from Victoria, drive west to the far southwest corner of Vancouver Island. The **Juan de Fuca Marine Trail** (p. 105), from Botanical Beach, is a shortened version of the West Coast Trail and journeys through a splendid seaside temperate rainforest. The highlights are many: waterfalls, eagles, surfers, seals, sandstone bluffs, tide pools, and history. Back to Victoria for dinner at **Café Brio** (p. 122).

Day 3:
Drive up-island to Nanaimo, then hop on the 10-minute ferry to historic **Newcastle Island** (p. 108). A tiny island with a rich heritage, the highlight here is the 7.5km (4¾-mile) perimeter loop. Grab lunch at the **Pavillion Restaurant** and then set out; there's more than enough to keep you moving for half a day here. Keep the mariner theme alive by checking into the **Buccaneer Inn** (p. 120) and then head a few blocks up the hill for dinner at the **Fox & Hounds** pub (p. 122).

Day 4:
Continuing past Nanaimo, turn west at Hwy. 4 and drive west to spectacular Ucluelet. The **Wild Pacific Trail** (p. 111) covers classic West Coast landscapes and is the home to interesting marine wildlife, including seals, sea lions, and surfers. The ocean here is wild and dramatic. Give yourself time to sit still on a bench and soak in the views. Dinner could be at **SoBo** or **Shelter** (p. 122) in Tofino, and lay your head at the stunning **Wickaninnish Inn** (p. 121).

Day 5:
After picking up a takeaway lunch at **Breakers Deli** (p. 122), head by water taxi or sea kayak to the **Big Cedar Trail** on Meares Island (p. 114). In the 1980s, environmentalists saved this amazing stretch of giant cedar trees, part of the giant Clayoquot Sound. It's not a tough trail to hike, but it's one with incredible spiritual and political value.

Day 6:
Today is a **travel day.** Head back to Nanaimo and catch the ferry from Departure Bay to Horseshoe Bay. This will take you most of the day. Head to the **Salmon House on the Hill** (p. 76) for dinner, then spend the night in West Vancouver.

Day 7:
For your final day hiking on the West Coast of British Columbia, West Vancouver's Cypress Provincial Park calls. After loading up with fuel over brunch at **Crave Beachside** (p. 75), follow the signs, and the road, uphill. Hiking **St. Mark's Summit** (p. 40), a spectacular section of the renowned Howe Sound Crest Trail, gives you fantastic views and a chance to bid farewell to the lush, varied, and fascinating landscape of the Pacific Coast.

4 A WEEK HIKING IN THE ROCKY MOUNTAINS & CENTRAL BC

A hiking trip to the majestic British Columbia Rocky Mountains and Cariboo Mountains is a trekker's dream. It's easier and faster to access the BC Rockies from Calgary, Alberta than it is from Vancouver (Calgary is only 2½ hr. from Yoho National Park; Vancouver is a 9- to 10-hr. drive). If your goal is to hike in the Canadian Rockies alone, it's worth considering flying into and out of Calgary. If you are driving from elsewhere in BC to the Rockies, or want to combine the area with another region as you tour the province, give

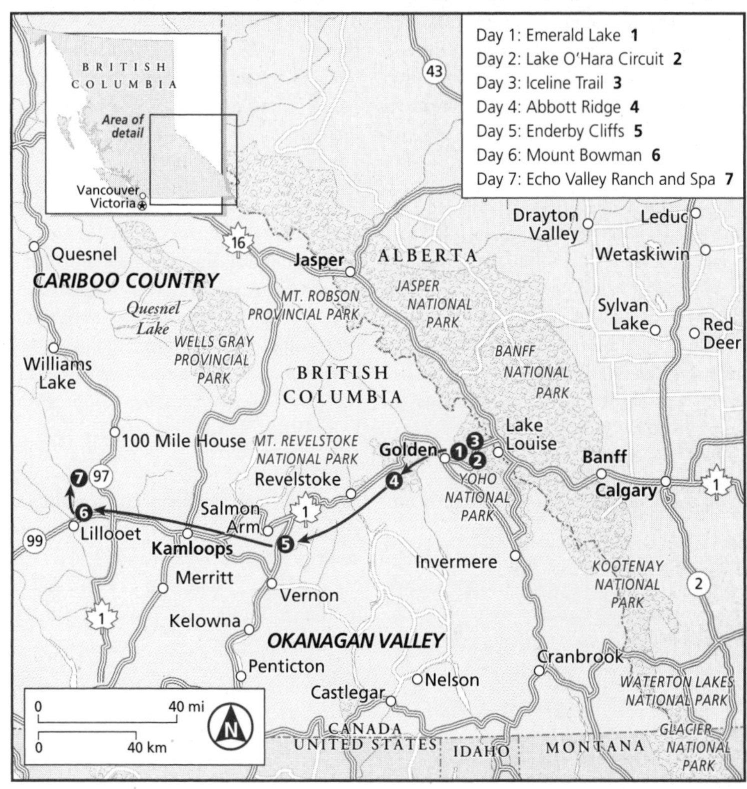

yourself most of a day to get to the starting point for this trip. Or simply do it in reverse, starting in the Cariboo. From the trip's end, north of Kamloops, you are 4 or 5 hours from Vancouver. This trip includes 4 nights in a lodge and 2 nights camping.

Day ❶:

The day begins in Yoho National Park. Check into the superbly located cabins at **Cathedral Mountain Lodge** (p. 251). Stop by the Field Visitor Center first thing in the morning and schedule your trip for the following day to Lake O'Hara. Remember, you must make a reservation ahead of time to get a spot on the bus to the lake, and space is very limited. After the visitor's center, head out to **Emerald Lake** (p. 228) to stretch your legs with a gentle 2-hour stroll around the lake. Treat yourself with a beer and a gourmet pizza on the patio at **Cilantro's** (p. 253). Pick up supplies for tomorrow's lunch in Field at the **Chercher La Vache Café** (p. 252).

Day ❷:

The **Lake O'Hara Circuit** (p. 245) isn't easy to get to, but it is very easy to fall in love with. The sublime landscapes, coupled with lovingly laid hiking trails, keep hikers coming back here year after year. When you factor in the bus trip up and down from the lake, and the challenging nature of the trail, it's a long day. But this will surely be the highlight of your trip. Return to your cabin at Cathedral Mountain Lodge.

Day 3:

The **Iceline Trail** (p. 230) is one of the finest trails in the Rockies, taking in all the wonders of the Little Yoho Valley, including a handful of stellar waterfalls, massive glacial ice fields, and views that stretch on and on. Don't forget to get lunch for the following day at the **Chercher Le Vache** (p. 252) in Field!

Day 4:

Say goodbye to Yoho and head down into the Columbia Valley. Stop in Golden for supplies, then continue west on the Trans-Canada Highway to Rogers Pass. Set up camp at the **Illecillewaet Campground** (p. 251) and then make your way up **Abbott Ridge** (p. 222) to take in the full majesty of Glacier National Park.

Day 5:

Continue west on the Trans-Canada Highway past Revelstoke and south to Enderby, heading for the Enderby Cliffs. This four-hour hike takes you above the Shushwap Valley. Continue on to Kamloops and then north to Clinton, arriving at the **Cariboo Lodge Resort** for the night. (p. 188).

Day 6:

In the morning, head out for a half-day hike at the wild and rugged **Mount Bowman** (p. 156) north of Cache Creek in the little-visited Marble Range. Tonight, you'll reward yourself with a final night in one of the gems of the Cariboo Country, the **Echo Valley Ranch and Spa** (p. 188).

Day 7:

Indulge in some well-deserved pampering at the spa in the morning, a great way to wrap up a busy and exhilarating week hiking in the high mountains of BC. Then, it's time to hit the road and head home.

4

Vancouver & the Sunshine Coast Hikes

by Anne Tempelman-Kluit & Judi Lees

Cradled between the Rocky Mountains and the Pacific Ocean, southwestern British Columbia's topography is unique. From lofty mountain peaks with breathtaking, wrap-around views to the tranquility of deep, lush river valleys; sweeping sandy beaches; or aromatic, thickly wooded trails, it's no wonder the city is frequently called Lotus Land.

It also has rain. Clouds unimpeded across the Pacific Ocean meet the Coast Mountains and drop their moisture, nourishing the lakes, rivers, and vegetation. Trekking a wilderness trail under a leafy canopy, rain pattering overhead, is a soul-soothing experience. Equally, as you challenge yourself to conquer a mountain peak, there's the euphoric feeling that you are on top of the world as the panoramic views unfold before you.

Consistently considered one of the world's most livable cities, the City of Vancouver is now home to more than 600,000 people, with more than one million in the surrounding Lower Mainland. It is one of the few cities in Canada not to have a freeway through town, so be prepared for traffic congestion downtown. It also has an excellent transportation system that includes an ocean-going SeaBus to North Vancouver and an elevated SkyTrain to the suburbs.

The real bonus of being here, however, is how close your urban base is to the great outdoors. Vancouver is a city with wilderness at its doorstep. Stanley Park has old-growth forests, kilometers of beautiful beaches, and a matchless seawall walk, all in the heart of downtown. From the elegant urbanity of the downtown core, cross a bridge and you are less than 30 minutes from high-mountain hikes, roaring riverside scrambles, and oceanside strolls.

The choices are mindboggling. Wilderness parks boast remote, challenging trails or short, easy walks through forest and bush, sometimes with civilization mere meters away. Hike up a mountain, but at the top, relax over a coffee, and if you wish, take the easy way down. You can drive almost to a river's edge as the roiling waters rush to meet the sea or hike along its banks through dense bush and towering trees. The ocean may seem tame as it laps against sandy beaches or rocky outcrops, but in a storm, it is exhilarating to watch waves crashing over seaside paths, spray drenching those who venture out.

The Sunshine Coast is a 40-minute ferry ride from West Vancouver but eons away from the city lifestyle. The 180km (112-mile) greenbelt, divided into the Lower and Upper Sunshine Coast, is accessed at each end by ferries. Explore small villages and oceanfront communities, visit artist's studios, and delve into the great outdoors—everything from water sports to hiking is nearby.

Trails, many maintained by local enthusiasts, weave up forested hillsides and along the ocean, revealing astounding scenery and possible wildlife sightings, including deer, bear, elk, eagles, and more. Tame or tempestuous, wild or urbane, the combination of easy access to a varied wilderness and the mild, temperate climate makes this a Mecca for outdoor lovers.

ESSENTIALS

GETTING THERE

By Plane

You arrive at **Vancouver International Airport** (✆ **604/207-7077;** www.yvr.ca); Canada's second largest airport services more than 17 million passengers annually, arriving and departing on some 31 airlines, including **Air Canada** (✆ **888/247-2262;** www.aircanada.ca), **Horizon Air** (✆ **800/547-9308;** www.alaskaair.com), and **WestJet** (✆ **888/937-8538;** www.westjet.com). The airport is located in Richmond about 13km (8 miles) south of Vancouver.

The Airporter bus (✆ **800/668-3141** or 604/946-8866; www.yvrairporter.com) provides transportation to major hotels in downtown Vancouver and to the Canada Place Cruise Ship Terminal. It takes about 30 minutes to reach the city. Buses leave daily every 30 minutes from the International Terminal from 8:20am to 9:45pm and from the Domestic Terminal from 8:25am to 9:50pm. The adult fare is C$13.50 one way.

For taxi service, three companies that service the airport are **Yellow Cab** (✆ **604/681-1111**), **Black Top & Checker Cabs** (✆ **604/731-1111**), and **Vancouver Taxi** (✆ **604/255-5111**). One-way fare is approximately C$30.

Twenty-four-hour limousine service is available with **Limojet Gold** (✆ **800/178-8742** or 604/273-1331; www.limojetgold.com), Limousines are located outside the Domestic and International terminals. The fare to downtown is C$39 to C$45, plus the Goods and Services Tax (GST); the fare to Whistler is C$295.

By Car

Highway 1 (Trans-Canada Hwy) runs through Vancouver. It comes into the city from the east via the Fraser Valley and goes west via Highway 99 to Horseshoe Bay (BC Ferry terminal with ferries to Bowen Island, Sunshine Coast, and Nanaimo on Vancouver Island) as well as on to Whistler. (Hwy 99 to Whistler is well known as the Sea-to-Sky Highway.) Highway 99 goes south to the U.S. border at Blaine, Washington.

By Public Transit

Vancouver's transit system consists of buses, several ferries, a commuter train, and SkyTrain (✆ **604/953-3333;** www.translink.bc.ca). The latter is a mostly above-ground, electrical rapid transit system. In 2009, SkyTrain's Canada Line will link the airport with downtown. Trains travel every 2 to 8 minutes, and tickets can be purchased from vending machines (which accept C$5, C$10, C$20, coins, and credit and debit cards) at each station. Routes are divided by zones: fares are C$2.50 for one zone, C$3.75 for two, and C$5 for three zones. Tickets can be used on the SkyTrain, as well as buses and the SeaBus that connects Vancouver to North Vancouver.

By Train

VIA Rail Canada (✆ **888/842-7245;** www.viarail.ca) trains arrive at Pacific Central Station, 1150 Station St., near the corner of Terminal and Main streets. This is the western terminus of the national railway's cross-Canada route.

By Bus

The Pacific Central Station is also the terminal for **Greyhound** (✆ **800/661-8747;** www.greyhound.ca), which services all of North America, and **Pacific Coach Lines**

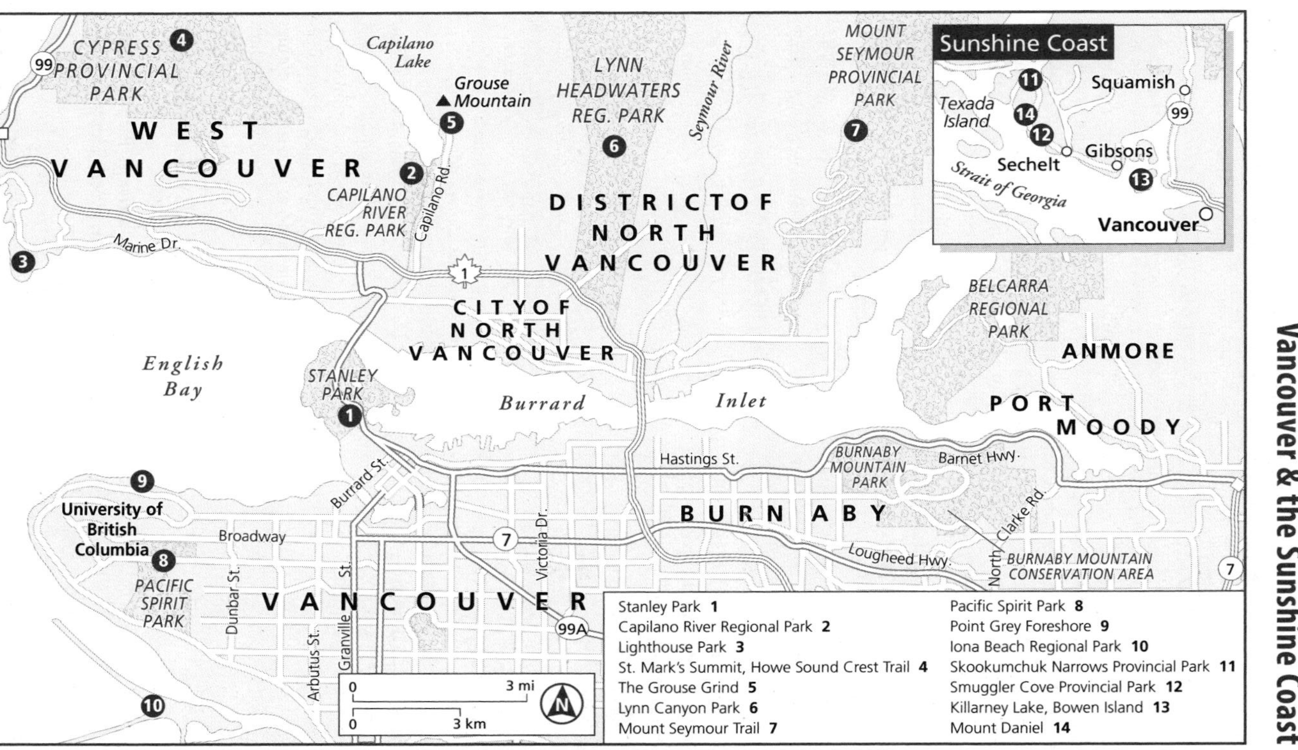
Sunshine Coast
Squamish
Texada Island
Gibsons
Sechelt
Strait of Georgia
Vancouver
CYPRESS PROVINCIAL PARK
WEST VANCOUVER
Capilano Lake
Grouse Mountain
CAPILANO RIVER REG. PARK
Capilano Rd.
Marine Dr.
LYNN HEADWATERS REG. PARK
Seymour River
DISTRICT OF NORTH VANCOUVER
MOUNT SEYMOUR PROVINCIAL PARK
CITY OF NORTH VANCOUVER
BELCARRA REGIONAL PARK
ANMORE
PORT MOODY
English Bay
STANLEY PARK
Burrard Inlet
Hastings St.
BURNABY MOUNTAIN PARK
Barnet Hwy.
Burrard St.
University of British Columbia
Broadway
BURNABY
North Clarke Rd.
Victoria Dr.
Lougheed Hwy.
BURNABY MOUNTAIN CONSERVATION AREA
PACIFIC SPIRIT PARK
Dunbar St.
Arbutus St.
Granville St.
VANCOUVER
0 3 mi
0 3 km
Stanley Park 1
Capilano River Regional Park 2
Lighthouse Park 3
St. Mark's Summit, Howe Sound Crest Trail 4
The Grouse Grind 5
Lynn Canyon Park 6
Mount Seymour Trail 7
Pacific Spirit Park 8
Point Grey Foreshore 9
Iona Beach Regional Park 10
Skookumchuk Narrows Provincial Park 11
Smuggler Cove Provincial Park 12
Killarney Lake, Bowen Island 13
Mount Daniel 14

(✆ **800/661-1725** or 604/662-7575; www.pacificcoach.com) that provides service in the Lower Mainland, including Whistler and Southern Vancouver Island.

By Ferry

BC Ferries (✆ **888/BCFERRY** [888/223-3779]; www.bcferries.com) offers crossings from the mainland to various points on Vancouver Island, the Gulf Islands, the Sunshine Coast, and locations along the coast of BC.

VISITOR INFORMATION

The **Tourism Vancouver Info Centre** (Plaza Level, 200 Burrard St.; ✆ **604/683-2000;** www.tourismvancouver.com) provides everything from where to dine and sleep to everything else you need to know about the Lower Mainland. Open daily 8:30am to 6pm. Also, check out Tourism British Columbia's website: www.hellobc.com.

1 STANLEY PARK ★★

Difficulty rating: Easy

Distance: 9km (5.6 miles)

Estimated time: 2 hr.

Elevation gain: Minimal

Costs/permits: None

Best time to go: Summer months to enjoy the many water activities

Website: www.vancouverparks.ca

Recommended map: Pick up map at any concession or information booth on route.

Trail head GPS: N 49 17.820, W 123 08.121

Trail head directions: From downtown Vancouver, drive 1.9km (1¼ miles) north along Georgia St., following the signs to Stanley Park (stay in the right lane), and turn right just opposite Lost Lagoon. Park nearby and begin.

Whatever else you don't do in Vancouver, make time to walk the Stanley Park Seawall. Two hours of brisk moving will allow you to complete the walk; however, it is better not to rush. Instead, stroll this peaceful peninsula, enjoying the unsurpassed scenery, the forest, the history, the birds, the seals, the beaches, the swimming pool, the boats, the restaurants, the miniature railway, the children's farmyard, and more.

Before starting your seawall walk, visit Lost Lagoon. The famed body of water near the park entrance is home to swans, ducks, herons, and geese year round, and in winter, it teems with birds. The fountain is spectacular at night when illuminated. Sky-reaching Douglas firs and western hemlock, maple, and red alder, found throughout the park, surround the lagoon, along with dense shrubbery providing homes to well-fed raccoons, skunks, and coyotes, whom you are unlikely to see, along with more visible rabbits, squirrels, and many birds.

Stanley Park sustained millions of dollars worth of damage during a major storm in December 2006, in which more than 3,000 trees were blown down or broken off. Work continues to clean up the debris. The seawall was also badly damaged but has since been repaired.

❶ Kilometer 0 Walking counterclockwise, each half-kilometer and half-mile along the seawall is marked by a plaque. The Vancouver Rowing Club (single sculls and eights are out early in the morning) marks kilometer 0.

Look on the lawn across from the Rowing Club to the statue of Lord Stanley. His foresight set aside this 405-hectare (1,000-acre) park in 1889, when the then

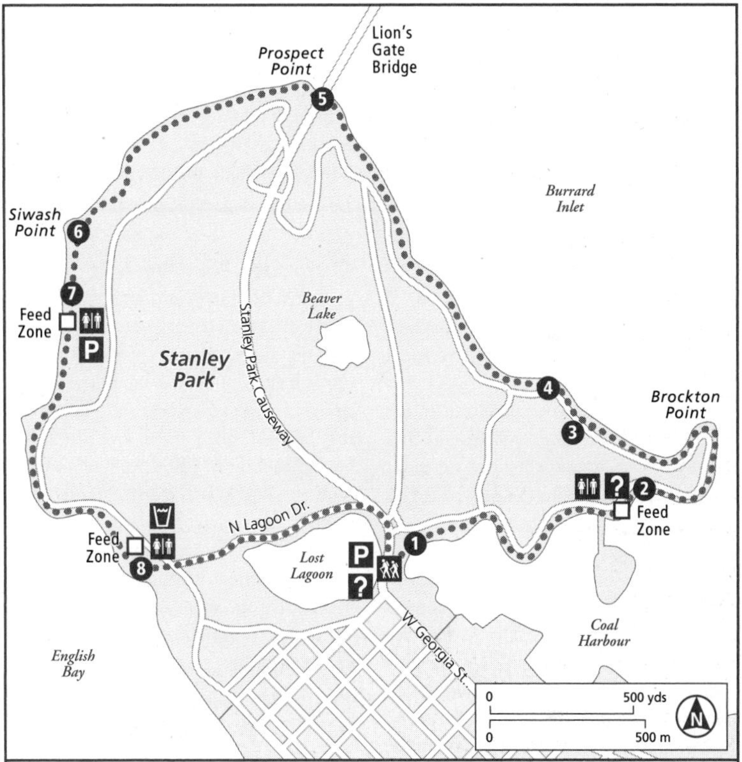

Lion's Gate Bridge
Prospect Point
Burrard Inlet
Siwash Point
Feed Zone
Beaver Lake
Stanley Park
Stanley Park Causeway
Brockton Point
N Lagoon Dr.
Feed Zone
Lost Lagoon
Feed Zone
W Georgia St.
Coal Harbour
English Bay
0 500 yds
0 500 m
N

1 km
2
3
4
5
6
7
8
9
225
150
75
0 m

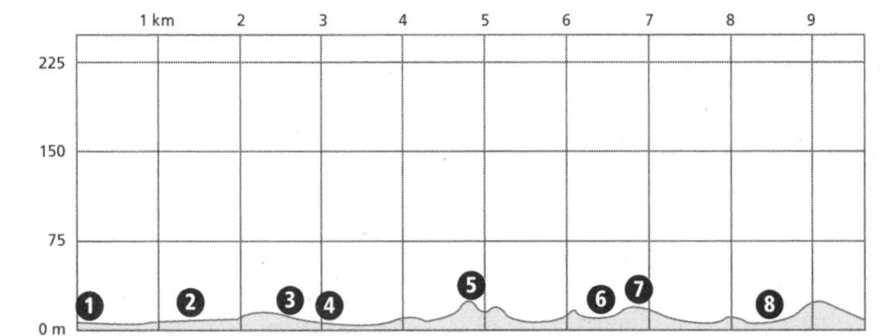

N 49 17.820, W 123 08.121 (0 km): Trail head
❶ N 49 17.814, W 123 08.050 (0.1 km): Vancouver Rowing Club and Kilometre 0 of Seawall
❷ N 49 17.922, W 123 07.247 (1.4 km): Stop for totem poles, gift shop, and interpretive center
❸ N 49 17.977, W 123 07.512 (2.6 km): Watch some cricket or rugby at Brockton Point Oval
❹ N 49 18.148, W 123 07.568 (3.1 km): Girl in a Wetsuit statue
❺ N 49 18.774, W 123 08.454 (4.8 km): Pass underneath the Lion's Gate Bridge
❻ N 49 18.515, W 123 09.355 (6.4 km): Siwash Rock
❼ N 49 18.244, W 123 09.376 (6.9 km): Third Beach
❽ N 49 17.677, W 123 08.998 (8.5 km): Take in the many activities at Second Beach

Tips Get on the Bus

From mid-June to mid-September, a free shuttle bus operates throughout the park, with stops approximately every half-kilometer. Hop on and off as the mood takes you. Another novel way to explore the park while resting your feet is to take a leisurely horse-and-carriage ride. The tours run from mid-March to late October, and you can get tickets from the Horse-Drawn kiosk at the parking area near the park entrance. The cost is C$24.99 adults, C$14.99 for children (2008 prices).

Governor General of Canada dedicated Stanley Park "to the use and enjoyment of people of all colors, creeds, and customs for all time." Lord Stanley also instigated hockey's famous Stanley Cup.

In a few minutes, you come to Painter's Circle, where on summer weekends and evenings, artists display their canvasses. It's a 2-minute detour from the seawall.

A short distance on, notice the Royal Vancouver Yacht Club, backed by a forest of masts. Just past the 1km marker, you pass a causeway leading to Deadman's Island, which is not officially part of the Park. The Royal Canadian Navy uses this island as a naval training center, called (somewhat confusingly) HMCS Discovery.

Take a moment to absorb the great views here of Canada Place, its soaring sails, and the cruise ship terminals.

2 Totem Poles When you reach the totem poles, you may have to wait for your turn to take a photo of these beautifully carved poles, unique to the Northwest Coast people. Backed by towering trees and the North Shore Mountains, these poles, carved with real and mythical creatures, are a Mecca for photographers and artists. The Interpretive Centre here is home to the Legends of the Moon gift shop.

Soon, you come to the Nine O'clock Gun in its glass cage beside the water. It has been fired at precisely 9pm each evening since 1894—except during World War II—to help ships, and now locals, set their clocks.

3 Brockton Point Oval If you love a good match, stop at Brockton Point Oval, where cricket and rugby are often played and the running track is always in use. From here, you are facing Burrard Inlet, speckled with freighters, sailboats, and the SeaBus, all framed by the North Shore Mountains. Wander on for about 15 minutes until you reach an elaborate, fire-breathing dragon's head, the figurehead of the Empress of Japan, one of the Pacific Empress fleet that plied these waters between Japan and Vancouver from 1891 to 1922, bringing silks to the city.

4 Statue Scan the boulders near the ocean's edge for the statue The Girl in a Wet Suit, unveiled in 1972; it's most commonly compared to Denmark's Little Mermaid, but this statue's scuba suit and mask make her uniquely West Coast. The bronze, sculpted by Elek Imredy, perches on a rock, usually crowned with a seagull for company.

TAKE A BREAK

You've now covered 3km (1¾ miles) of the seawall, but at Lumberman's Arch, it is difficult not to slow down, have a snack, and join in the activity around this pleasant, grassy meadow. Lumberman's Arch, formed by two huge tree trunks, is a tribute to the province's logging industry. Kids love the sandy beach and the waterpark. Kids will also be enamored by the Vancouver Mounted Police, who patrol the park on horseback. Picnic tables and lots of benches invite you to relax and enjoy the cheerful activity.

Many excellent attractions for children are nearby. Walk across the meadow to the Children's Farmyard and miniature railway, or follow the signs to the Vancouver Aquarium, one of the largest in North America.

Continuing along the seawall—watch for seals in the water—you soon hear traffic crossing the Lion's Gate Bridge as it comes into view. Just before the bridge, after covering 5km (3 miles) on the trail, you reach Prospect Point, accessible from the seawall by a short, steep switchback dirt trail. Prospect Point, the highest point in the park, received the most storm damage in 2006. The popular Prospect Point Café is here, as well as a wonderful flower garden.

5 Lion's Gate Bridge Under the Lion's Gate Bridge, fisher folk cast their lines into the rough water around the bridge supports, watched by a line-up of interested seagulls and pigeons.

6 Siwash Rock After you emerge from the shadow of the bridge, wander on to Siwash Rock at 6km (3¾ miles) along the seawall.

While your attention will be focused on the ocean, take time to look at the sandstone cliffs, firs, cedars, and hemlocks beside you. Smell the sweet air, underlain by the crisp tang of seaweed and ocean. Benches, and access to the beaches with their logs and boulders, invite you to pause a while and savor the unique beauty of your surroundings.

Native American legends have been woven around this seemingly indestructible rocky pinnacle, crowned by a small tree, that endures through the centuries. Possibly the most photographed spot in the park, legend has it that a warrior and his wife were swimming in Burrard Inlet, cleansing themselves before the birth of their child. When his wife went into the forest for the birth, the father continued swimming, defying the orders of the gods, who came by in their canoe. Because he put his child's future before the demands of the gods, he was made immortal as an example of pure fatherhood.

The rock is actually a volcanic remnant, carved by wave-action, that remained after softer rock around it eroded away.

7 Third Beach Next on your promenade, after traveling 6.5km (4 miles), you reach Third Beach, another popular family bathing beach. A few minutes past here, The Sequoia Grill crowns Ferguson point at the 7km (4¼-mile) mark; this is also the perfect place to watch the marine activity on the Pacific Ocean.

8 Second Beach This beach is jumping in summer. Locals gather to watch a sunset from the long, sandy beach, and the (slightly) heated salt-water swimming pool is open from mid-May to early September. Nearby is the Ceperley children's playground, a popular spot with a fire engine, picnic area, and washrooms. You can indulge in pitch and putt, shuffleboard, lawn bowling, and tennis beside the Fish House restaurant. Hundreds of rhododendrons and azaleas are a spectacular blaze of color in July and August.

The seawall ends here, and you turn left on North Lagoon Drive at the edge of the park to pass the lagoon and arrive back at your starting point. If you are still keen, stop at the Nature House (www.stanleyparkecology.ca) beside Lost Lagoon.

Or you might prefer to walk along Denman Street to have lunch or dinner at one of the diverse eateries along this busy street.

Fun Facts **A Lifetime of Construction**

Completed in 1980, the Stanley Park Seawall is the longest in Canada. It was constructed in financial fits and starts over 60 years. Master stonemason James Cunningham spent more than 30 years supervising the work, although he died before it was completed. A plaque near Siwash Rock commemorates his achievement.

2 CAPILANO RIVER REGIONAL PARK ★

Difficulty rating: Easy
Distance: 7km (4.3 miles) roundtrip
Estimated time: 4 hr.
Elevation gain: 90m (295 ft.)
Costs/permits: None
Pet friendly: Yes (dogs must be leashed)
Best time to go: Spring, when the river is high or late summer and fall for the salmon run
Website: www.metrovancouver.org
Recommended map: Pick up a map from the information kiosk in Cleveland Dam parking area.
Trail head GPS: N 49 21.545, W 123 06.418
Trail head directions: From Vancouver, cross Lion's Gate Bridge onto Marine Dr. E. Get into the left lane to turn north on Capilano Rd., following signs to the Cleveland Dam parking lot (not to be confused with the Capilano Suspension Bridge, shortly before the Dam).

This is a walk in the forest, but it's so much more. Spanning the boundary of North and West Vancouver, the park encompasses the immense Cleveland Dam, which provides the water supply for Greater Vancouver, and the frothing white water pounding down the dam's spillway is mesmerizing. Nearby, through a glass-fronted fish ladder at the fish hatchery, watch salmon as they fight to reach their spawning grounds upstream. Then, wander a forested walk beside the impressive Capilano River. Grassy meadows, picnic tables, riotous flower gardens, washrooms, and drinking water make this a popular picnic spot.

Anglers should bring a rod, as you can fish in these rushing waters with a BC Non-Tidal Angling License. The river is deep, fast, and cold, so wading is not recommended. The water level also fluctuates with the amount of water spilling down the dam, so it must be watched carefully.

The park is well-named, since everywhere you go, the sound—and often the sight—of the Capilano River keeps you company. Nowhere is the river more spectacular than where it cascades down the dam spillway. Walk over the dam on the concrete roadway beside the parking area and watch the water plunge 90m (295 ft.) into the river, where rainbows dance on the surface. The dam is in stark contrast to the calm waters of Capilano Lake Reservoir behind you, beautifully framed by the Coast Mountains.

The dam, completed in 1954, is named for the Vancouver Water Board's first Commissioner, Ernest Cleveland. Follow the short trail on the east edge of the dam for a close-up of the spillway and the vegetation clinging to the weather-beaten granite canyon walls. Wait in line to take photographs here.

To reach the fish hatchery, stay on the east side of the dam on the Palisades Trail; a steep section at the north end of the trail is navigated by several flights of stairs cut into the earth. This winding trail is less than 1km (1/2-mile) long but leads you past some of the most massive trees in the park, many clothed so heavily in moss that they appear to be dressed in green velvet.

❶ Fish Hatchery The low, sprawling hatchery building is surrounded by an attractive picnic area, with tables set back into the trees, ample parking, and washrooms, drinking water, and phones.

Plan to spend time here. Displays and fish tanks chronicle the Pacific salmon's life cycle. Breeding tanks hold minute salmon

Capilano Lake
Nancy Greene Way
Palisades Trail
Capilano River Regional Park
Giant Fir
Coho Loop
Capilano Rd.
Capilano Park Rd.
Stevens Dr.
Capilano Pacific Trail
Capilano River
0 300 yds
0 300 m
N

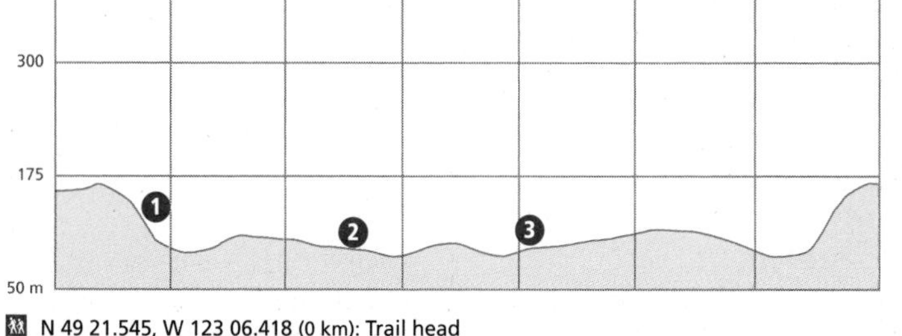

N 49 21.545, W 123 06.418 (0 km): Trail head

❶ N 49 21.393, W 123 06.618 (0.9 km): Fish hatchery

❷ N 49 21.121, W 123 06.726 (2.6 km): Pick up the Capilano Pacific Trail past Camp Capilano

❸ N 49 20.943, W 123 06.990 (4.1 km): Double back when you hit Rabbit Lane junction

and trout fry, with netting strung over the open tanks, frustrating aerial poachers. Through the glass-fronted observation area of the fishways, it's mesmerizing to watch salmon hanging motionless in relatively calm waters between the steps, resting before taking the next leap. September and October are the best months to see the salmon. There is information here on good fishing spots, too.

Expert whitewater paddlers can also put in here, but should check water levels and conditions first. At high water, the river can be dangerous.

For a short, easy hike through lush forest and views of the best fishing pools (Cable, Dog Leg, and House Rock), cross the wooden Cable Pool Bridge and take in the spectacular canyon views on the 1.1km (.7-mile) Coho Loop Trail, which begins and ends at the hatchery.

A great detour on this route is to veer right at Pipeline Bridge, about halfway along the Coho Loop, and take the brief detour to the Giant Fir Trail on the west side of the river. There, you'll find a truly awe-inspiring evergreen, thought to be more than 500 years old, 2.4m (8 ft.) in diameter, and 61m (200 ft.) tall. It is the biggest tree in the park.

❷ Camp Capilano Just south of this loop is Camp Capilano. Weathered wooden cabins (that sleep 44) are snug in a gentle, wooded clearing and have been here for more than half a century, guarded by totem poles. (Call ✆ **604/432-6352** for rental information.)

Pick up the Capilano Pacific Trail at the Pipeline Bridge, at 7.5km (4.7 miles), the longest trail in the park. It winds its way south from the dam to the oceanside in West Vancouver. The river is never far away on this trail—misty, mysterious, and turbulent. Listen to it roar through narrow canyons and take the time to scramble down to the riverbed on one of the many side trails. At low water, explore the river-smoothed boulders. These trails should be navigated with care and are extremely slippery when wet. In places, the trail is rough and has some short climbs. Watch children carefully near the river. Thick underbrush of bracken and sometimes blackberries line the trail, and rotting logs are decorated with lichen and fungi. Bridges spanning the mountain streams rushing to meet the river are good viewpoints, and everywhere, the air is rich with the aroma of cedar and Douglas fir.

❸ Rabbit Lane Junction Capilano Park is wedge-shaped, and the widest section is at the dam. As this trail winds south, you become more aware of civilization, so where the trail meets Rabbit Lane just below the viewpoint, double back or pick up one of a network of 26km (16 miles) of trails to take you back to the dam, which is about 7.5km (4.7 miles) to the north.

3 LIGHTHOUSE PARK ★

Difficulty rating: Easy to moderate

Distance: 2km–6km (1.2 miles–3.7 miles) on a variety of trails

Estimated time: 1½–2 hr.

Elevation gain: 100m (328 ft.)

Costs/permits: None

Pet friendly: Yes (this is an off-leash park, but dogs must be controlled)

Best time to go: It's beautiful all year, but the park is particularly lovely in the fall.

Website: None

Recommended map: Pick up a trail map at the information board on the west side of the park.

Trail head GPS: N 49 20.277, W 123 15.795

Trail head directions: From Vancouver, go over Lion's Gate Bridge and go west on Marine Dr. Drive about 10km (6¼ miles), the latter part on a lovely oceanside route, until you see the Lighthouse Park sign. Go left on Beacon Lane into the large parking lot. The park can also be reached by bus (Blue bus #250) from Georgia Street in Vancouver or from Park Royal Shopping Centre in West Vancouver.

There are few places where you can walk among old-growth forest, watch the waves lap a rugged shoreline, and be close to a world-class city. Hello Lighthouse Park. This is an easy walk painted with illustrious shades of wilderness. The focal point of the hike is the picture-perfect lighthouse.

There are many trail heads. Enter the park on the west side by the information board. (There is also a board at the very end of the parking lot, which is where this hike will end.) The trails are well marked. Follow the Juniper Loop marker right. Within a few moments, you are following the yellow marker for Juniper Point and heading downhill.

❶ Juniper Point As you face the ocean, there are two areas to explore. Clamber up the boulders, breath the ocean air, and enjoy the view of Howe Sound. You may see a Bowen Island ferry, backdropped by this verdant, large island, and in the distance, the mountains of the Sechelt Peninsula. Hear the call of seagulls and oyster catchers that nest on some of the small islets. The smoothly worn granite shoreline you see is a good example of granodiorite. It was formed some 150 million years ago below the Earth's surface; over the last 50 million years, it was thrust upwards and forms much of the landscape of the West Coast.

If it is low tide, head back down the way you came and follow the short trail onto the flat granite tongue. Take care if it is damp. This is one of many favorite spots for sunbathing. There are also tidal pools to peek at the marine life.

Follow the Juniper Loop Trail (this is now the lower end of the loop) back to the main trail, then go right on Shore Pine Trail, uphill. Here, as in many places in this park, you will be in awe of the giant trees—groves of Western Red cedars and Douglas fir, some reaching 67m (220 ft.) in height and more than 6m (20 ft.) around. Make sure to find time alone and look way up to feel the magic of these trees, some more than 550 years of age! Heading downhill, you hear the lap—or crash, depending on the weather—of waves along the shore.

❷ Jackpine Point Another view spot, and one we can never visit enough. Look out to the distant Gulf Islands and the closer Bowen Island. Yes, there are Jackpines here, as well as lustrous, red-barked Arbutus. Should you wish an early lunch or late-morning java break, this is idyllic. If it is windy—Lighthouse Park is a dramatic walk in the rain or in blustery weather, as the quivering evergreens take on a mystical quality—you may see sailboats seemingly flying as sailors try to combat the winds that whip through Howe Sound. Here, you can also head down to the water, near a wooden footbridge that parallels the shoreline.

To continue, with the water at your back, follow the trail right. Soon, you are going uphill past moss-laden boulders, and at one point, you are in a grove of huge cedars. Pass trail markers to West Beach and, on your left, one to the interior of the park, the trail to Songbird Meadow.

Fun Facts Shining a Light

Captain Vancouver sailed past this rocky outcrop in 1792 and named Point Atkinson after a friend. Construction began on the lighthouse in 1874, and in 1881, the Dominion of Canada preserved the 65 hectares (161 acres) that surround the lighthouse. The dark green swath of old-growth rainforest, rich in towering Douglas fir, provides the perfect backdrop for the lighthouse's beacon light, which is why the surroundings have not been logged. The lighthouse we view today was built in 1912. During World War II, search lights and guns, as well as billeted soldiers, were here.

At this point, you are on a mission to see the famous lighthouse, so continue onward.

3 Lighthouse Look-Out Scramble up the large boulder and look down on Point Atkinson Lighthouse. A plaque gives some historical details.

As you leave the lookout, there are a couple of picnic tables; there is no view though, so even if you haven't taken a break, give these a pass. Go right on the trail and soon arrive at a clearing with several buildings, one a weathered log cabin. One building, the Phyl Munday Nature House, is used by girl guides; another is named Sk'iwitsut, after the First Nations' family who lived here in the mid 1800s. There is also a washroom here in one of the lower buildings. A marker tells the history of junior forest warden camps held here in the 1940s. Trail markers lead to other trails.

4 Head onto Valley Trail With buildings on your right, a wooden marker leads to the Valley Trail. Almost immediately, there is a short path to a picnic table; if you prefer to picnic at a table, this is a good bet, as it has a view out to Burrard Inlet and, in the distance, the cityscape of Vancouver. Shortly, another short trail diverts to Arbutus Knoll, another viewpoint. When taking in the panorama of Vancouver and Lion's Gate Bridge, notice the large green space that is Stanley Park. Follow the trail, occasionally looking down on small, picturesque bays. The last viewpoint on Valley Trail before it leads inland is Starboat Cove. If you don't need a table, but still want city and bridge views, this is the place. Continuing on the Valley Trail, it is uphill and past some mammoth maple and cedar trees.

5 Divert along Arbutus Trail As you tramp this beautiful, woodsy trail, you have the option here to turn right on Arbutus Trail. It leads uphill first and then out to Eagle Point, another view spot above the water. From there, you follow another loop trail, Valley of the Giants.

Then, you veer left on Summit Trail to reach the highest point of the park, 115m (377 ft.). You loop back onto Valley Trail right near the exit gate. This diversion adds about an hour to your hiking time.

If you don't divert and continue on the Valley Trail, you go uphill over some inset wooden steps and bridges. Notice the Barred Owl Path on the left (there are toilets and picnic tables close by), but continue on the Valley Trail, past mossy and fern-laden boulders. Eventually, it opens up, and you are soon through the gates at the end of the parking lot.

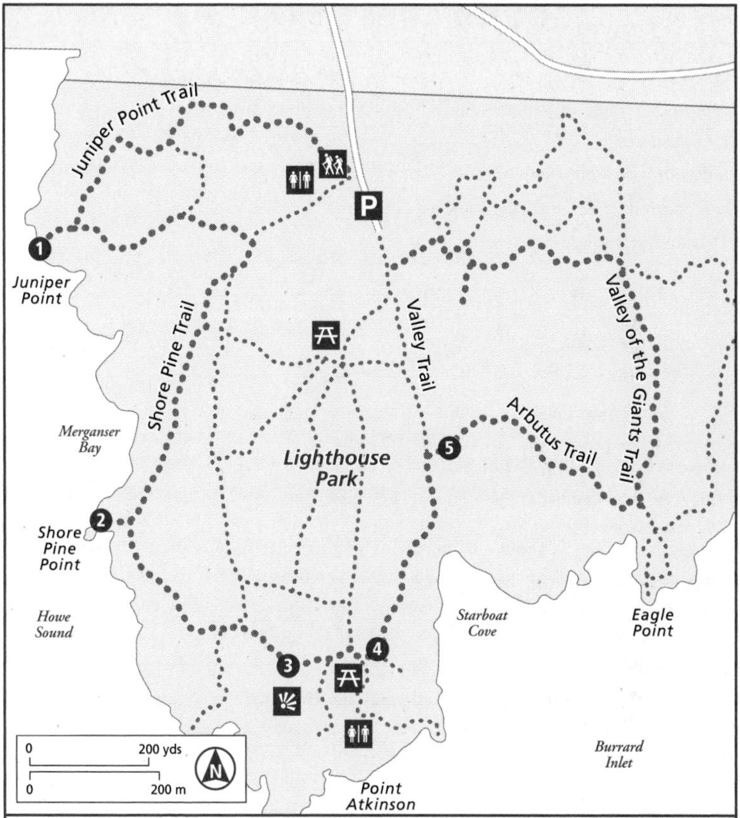

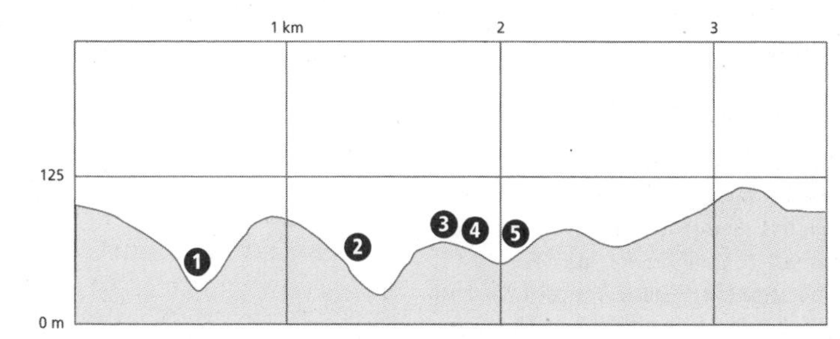

- N 49 20.277, W 123 15.795 (0 km): Trail head
- ❶ N 49 20.209, W 123 16.136 (0.6 km): Juniper Point
- ❷ N 49 20.020, W 123 16.098 (1.3 km): Enjoy views of Gulf Islands and Bowen Island at Jackpine Point
- ❸ N 49 19.886, W 123 15.871 (1.7 km): Point Atkinson Lighthouse
- ❹ N 49 19.913, W 123 15.788 (1.8 km): Follow wooden marker to Valley Trail
- ❺ N 49 30.778, W 123 55.653 (2.1 km): Turn right for diversion along Arbutus Trail

4 ST. MARK'S SUMMIT, HOWE SOUND CREST TRAIL ★★

Difficulty rating: Moderate

Distance: 11km (6.8 miles) round trip

Estimated time: 5–7 hr.

Elevation gain: 330m (1,083 ft.)

Costs/permits: C$3 for daily parking

Pet friendly: Yes (dogs must be leashed)

Best time to go: Sept–Oct

Website: www.env.gov.bc.ca/bcparks

Recommended map: North Vancouver 92G/6

Trail head GPS: N 49 23.776, W 123 12.153

Trail head directions: This hike is in Cypress Provincial Park. From Vancouver, go over Lion's Gate Bridge onto Marine Dr. W., turn right on Taylor Way, and go uphill to access Upper Levels Highway (Hwy. 1) W. Head towards Horseshoe Bay, turning right at exit 8 and driving the 15km (9¼ miles) up the Cypress Parkway to the downhill ski area at the top. The trail head is at the northwest corner of the parking lot.

This is an opportunity to hike a scenic section of the famed Howe Sound Crest Trail, a sometimes rugged 30km (19-mile) trek that departs from Cypress Bowl and comes out on the Sea-to-Sky Highway just south of Porteau Cove. St. Mark's Summit is a challenging day hike due to some rooted uphill sections—you can easily spend 7 hours, setting a leisurely pace—but it shows off gorgeous groves of large evergreens and subalpine meadows. This day hike may inspire you to plan an overnight trip to The Lions, mountain peaks that are a famous Vancouver landmark, and are accessed by continuing past St. Mark's Summit.

Check out the information board, then follow the signs for Howe Sound Crest Trail, heading past service buildings and chair lifts. Follow the rocky service road uphill to an opening.

❶ Start of Howe Sound Crest Trail A brown-and-white Howe Sound Crest Trail sign leads you onto the trail. (The elevation here is 972m/3,189 ft.) Follow the rocky, narrow path uphill to enter the forest; snack on wild blueberries if it is late summer or early fall. On one of our hikes, a group of botanists showed us tiny, orange fungi called Apricot Jelly that is apparently an unusual find. They also pointed out veins of glittering quartz in the granite boulders that sometimes edged the trail.

❷ Trail Opens to Service Road After about 30 minutes of traversing uphill—you are following orange-triangle markers on trees—the trail opens onto a wide, gravel road, and a Howe Sound Crest Trail sign points you left. This spacious section is fringed by forest on both sides; enjoy bright pink fireweed that stands tall here, and above the forest on your left is Black Mountain. It would probably be unusual not to see bear scat here! This is also your first view of Howe Sound—on a clear day, you can see the mountains of Vancouver Island across the water. The trail eventually narrows, and you are among the glorious giants of the West Coast. On this hike, you'll find yellow cedar (some are more than 1,000 years old), Western hemlock, mountain hemlock, and Amabilis fir. The latter grows to heights of 47m (154 ft.). One yellow cedar in this park is more than 2,000 years old.

❸ Information Sign and Bowen Lookout At this board (that, among

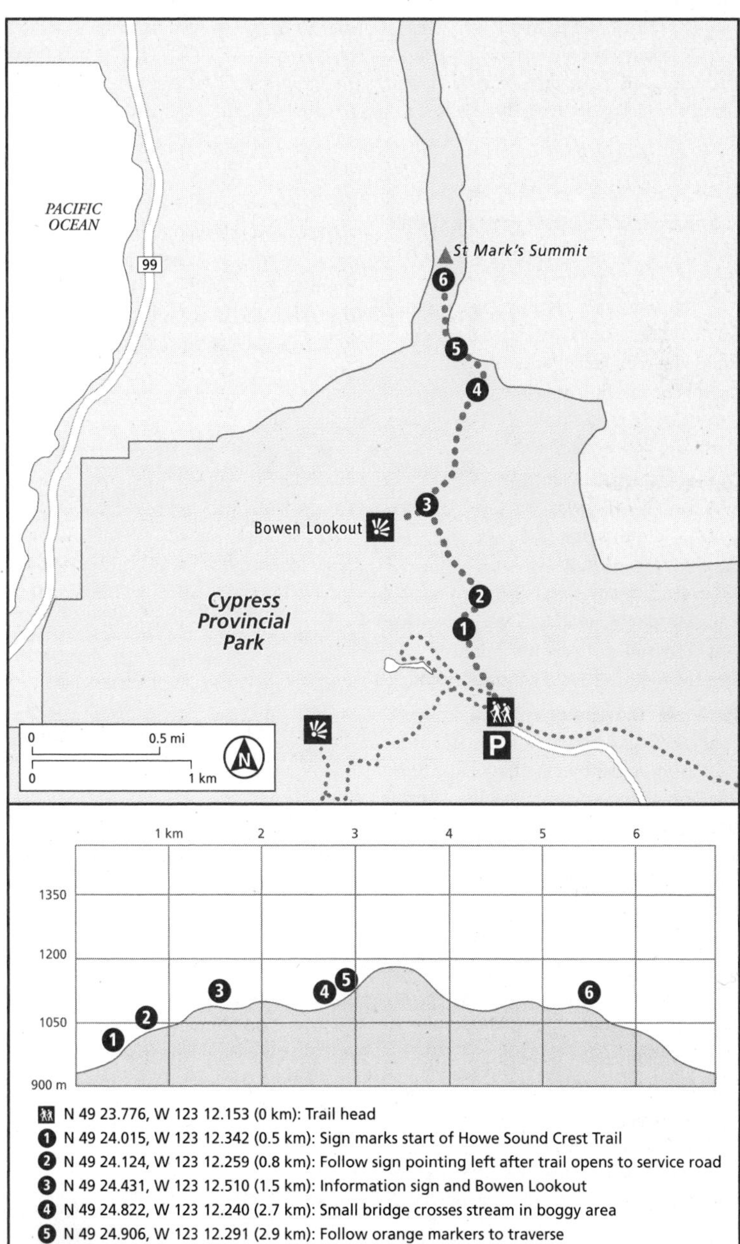

N 49 23.776, W 123 12.153 (0 km): Trail head
1. N 49 24.015, W 123 12.342 (0.5 km): Sign marks start of Howe Sound Crest Trail
2. N 49 24.124, W 123 12.259 (0.8 km): Follow sign pointing left after trail opens to service road
3. N 49 24.431, W 123 12.510 (1.5 km): Information sign and Bowen Lookout
4. N 49 24.822, W 123 12.240 (2.7 km): Small bridge crosses stream in boggy area
5. N 49 24.906, W 123 12.291 (2.9 km): Follow orange markers to traverse
6. N 49 25.695, W 123 12.381 (5.5 km): St. Mark's Summit

other items, cautions against going into backcountry unprepared), there is a trail on your left to Bowen Lookout. (We prefer to do this section on our way down when the afternoon sun gives the scene of Bowen Island a golden glow. It's a 10-minute walk, thick with blueberry bushes.) The main trail undulates here, goes over a stream, and again boasts some of the gorgeous old-growth trees made famous by painter Emily Carr. After 10 to 15 minutes, there is a clearing on your left that showcases the coastline; you can even see the ferry terminal on the Sunshine Coast if it is a clear day. Along the trail, you spot the red berries of mountain ash and, in places, spangles of blue-flowered fleabane, small yellow blooms of arnicas, and white foamflowers.

❹ The Meadow A rustic, small bridge leads over a stream in a boggy area. An opening on the right takes you to a narrow meadow, unofficially dubbed Strachan Meadow, as it is overlooked by the two peaks of Mount Strachan. Notice the lacy deer fern and heather in this region. Go over the footbridge and continue uphill.

❺ Trail Markers As you traverse uphill, keep checking for the orange markers. In this particular spot, the trail appears to go straight, and you can easily miss the traverse. Your hint that you have missed the trail is that you are soon going downhill over fallen trees. Backtrack to continue the uphill traverse. After perhaps 30 minutes of steady uphill, the trail levels and veers right along a ridge. Enjoy the soft forest fragrances, as well as (through sparse, large trees) views of Howe Sound dotted with islands.

TAKE A BREAK
Along this wooded ridge is a good place to settle into a sunny spot, have a snack, and enjoy the distant view, as well as the forest. And rest before the 30 to 45 minutes remaining to the summit.

The trail leads downhill for a bit, but soon, you are again traversing uphill. Take care, it is heavy with tree roots and, in places, very steep. Go over a rickety, short ladder and small bridge spanning muddy patches. After one large muddy section, you are facing a boulder which is easily scaled.

❻ St. Mark's Summit You'll arrive in a boggy area (black mud!), but it is easy to scoot around it. Then, follow a rocky route on your left. There is no official sign that this is the summit, but once you carefully head out to the ledge, there is little doubt.

SPECTACULAR LOOKOUT
Take in the breathtaking view: You look down to Horseshoe Bay with its miniature ferry terminal, and you can follow the Sea-to-Sky Highway off into the distance. Directly below is a carpet of dense forest; on a sunny day, you easily see Vancouver Island and the Sunshine Coast. Turn to look north to the snowcapped mountains near Whistler. If you haven't had lunch earlier, there is room for two or three people to nestle near the edge of the summit. Vertigo sufferers will not be interested.

Don't rush retracing your route down the mountain; take care on both the wet and rooted sections. On the lower section of the mountain, when walking along the gravel road, watch carefully for the entrance into the forest after following the gravel road. You will see the Howe Sound Crest sign on your left; on your left is the trail that leads into the forest. If you miss this, follow the service road down the ski hill; however, the wooded route, which you came up, is much more pleasant.

5 THE GROUSE GRIND

Difficulty rating: Strenuous

Distance: 2.9km (1.8 miles) one way

Estimated time: 1½ hr.

Elevation gain: 928m (3,045 ft.)

Costs/permits: Parking is C$3 for 2 hr., C$5 all day. You're also required to buy a C$5 ticket to ride the tram down from the summit.

Pet friendly: No

Best time to go: Open mid-May to mid-Sept. Depending on the weather, July and Aug are the safest times to hike.

Website: www.grousemountain.com

Recommended maps: Not really necessary, but there's a good map of the chalet area when you get there.

Trail head GPS: N 49 22.345, W 123 05.881

Trail head directions: From Vancouver, go over Lion's Gate Bridge into North Vancouver. Exit right (east) onto Marine Dr. Turn left (north) on Capilano Rd. It turns into Nancy Greene Way after about 4km (2½ miles). Follow Nancy Greene Way to the parking lots at the bottom of Grouse Mountain. Park in one of the three pay-parking lots. There are washrooms and places to purchase water in the guest services building.

The Grouse Grind is really more of an endurance test than a hike. The short but intense incline, however, is incredibly popular. In fact, if you are a sports enthusiast visiting Vancouver, it is a must-do. Locals sometimes refer to it as God's Stairmaster and love to brag about their times. For a recreational hiker, it takes about 1½ hr. At the top are places to eat, picnic, attractions—and sweet, sweet bragging rights.

The hike will elevate the heart rate of even the fittest climber, and sometimes people do bite off more than they can chew with the Grind, so know your limits. It is recommended that people with high blood pressure, or heart or breathing problems, not attempt the hike.

Keeners, those who are really keen and plan to hike the Grind more than once, can purchase a Grind Timer card for C$20, plus tax, which you swipe before starting the Grind and swipe again when you reach the top; it records your exact time. The card lasts for one full season (late May–late Sept) and can be purchased at Guest Services at the base of the mountain.

Be sure to wear comfortable hiking shoes and weather-appropriate clothing—it is likely there will be snow at the top in late spring and early fall. The route is well marked, including one sign featuring photos of grizzly bears with the slightly disconcerting caption, "We're waiting for you."

Before you start the climb, take a look at the wolf habitat at the north end of Parking Lot A under the tram. Also, check out the impressive woodcarvings in front of the main guest services building.

The trail head starts immediately to the east of the information center and parking lots. You will know you are there when you reach a gated area with signs detailing the rules of Grouse Mountain, as well as safety tips. There will likely be numerous people around stretching before the hike. As you begin the climb, which has terrain ranging from rocks and roots to mud to makeshift stairs, realize that on a warm day or a weekend, at any given time, you will likely have a view of the derrières of about 15 people in front of you. Since the trail is well-marked and beaten down, you cannot get lost. As one climber remarked:

Fun Facts **Building the Grind**

As you huff and puff, think of the sweat that must have gone into this trail when, in 1981, an enthusiastic group of mountaineers in need of a challenging aerobic workout followed a route first cut by the British Columbia Mountaineering Club. Today's trail, completed in 1983, was upgraded and named the Grouse Grind in the early 1990s. More than 110,000 hikers climb the Grouse Grind each year.

"If you get lost on this trail, you are either an idiot or you are following an idiot."

About 5 minutes into the trail there is a fork—the Grouse Grind trail leads north, and the Baden-Powell Trail heads east. Stay left.

For the first 10 minutes of the climb, you are likely to hear conversations in many languages, but things tend to quiet down as people economize their breath.

Approaching the 200m (656-ft.) mark of the uphill, there is a sign warning the trail is about to become very steep and difficult. There is no doubt the trail becomes more challenging, but take heart: The sign makes it seem more ominous than it really is. At the halfway sign, you find crowds of people taking a well-deserved rest, sipping water and laughing as others reach the sign and nearly collapse as they cry out, "Only halfway?"

There are few opportunities to get a view of anything other than the lush forest as you climb. Near the 3/4 mark of the trail on the way up, there is a small opening in the trees where you get a peek at Capilano Lake, but it is best to save your landscape gazing for the top, where it is far more impressive.

1 Peak Chalet When you reach the top of the Grind trail, you will find other climbers collapsed on the flat rock surface outside the Peak chalet, thanking the heavens for completing the hike. Just outside the building, there is a tap with fresh water. Try not to be discouraged when you enter the chalet and see the record climbing times posted on the Grind Timer display screen, including those posted by adolescent girls and people in their 80s. The record time as of 2008 was just over 24 minutes.

SPECTACULAR LOOKOUT Grouse offers some of the best views of the city. The first good viewpoint you come to is just a few meters to the west of the trail end, in front of the chalet. Gasp in wonder (if you have any breath left) at the panorama of North and West Vancouver, Downtown, Burrard Inlet, Stanley Park, Point Grey, and English Bay. Walking east of the chalet to just beyond the Screaming Eagle chair lift, you can find a great view of Mount Baker in Washington State, as well as East Vancouver, Burnaby, and the rest of the Fraser Valley.

2 Grouse Mountain Peak If you have it in you, climb for another 30 minutes or so up to the peak of Grouse Mountain for vistas of the North Shore Mountains, as well as the distant cityscape. The trail to the peak is just north of the Grizzly Bear Habitat.

To get back down to the parking lot, purchase a C$5 tram ticket from Alpine Guest Services in the chalet. Trams run every 15 minutes. It is verboten to climb down the mountain.

Free attractions at the top include two young grizzly bears, Grinder and Coola, both found orphaned in the summer of 2001. Coola is named for Bella Coola, where he was found, and Grinder for his mountaintop home. The cubs play outside

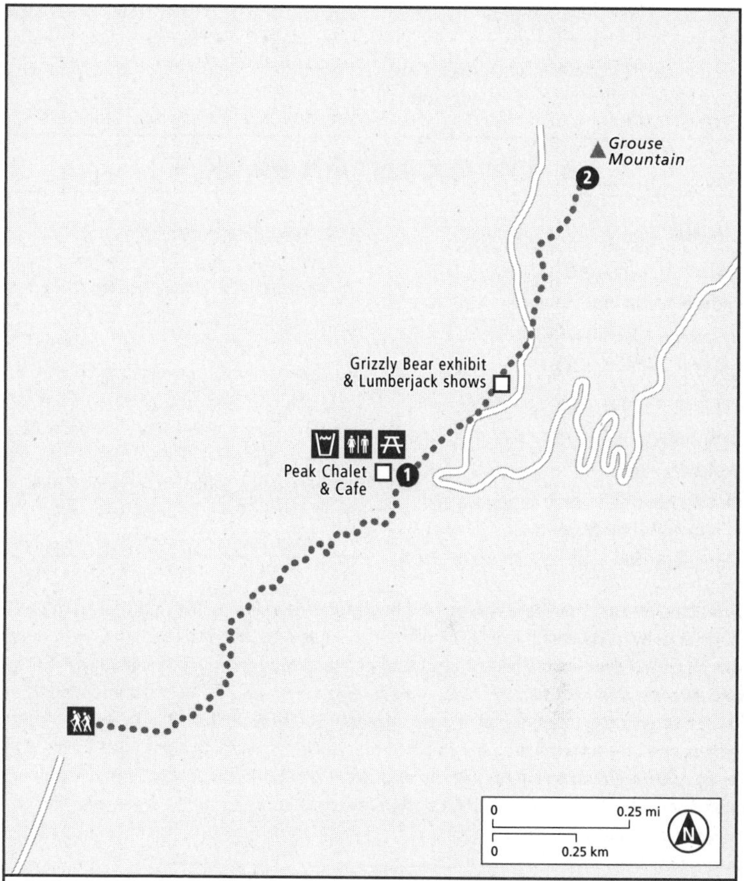

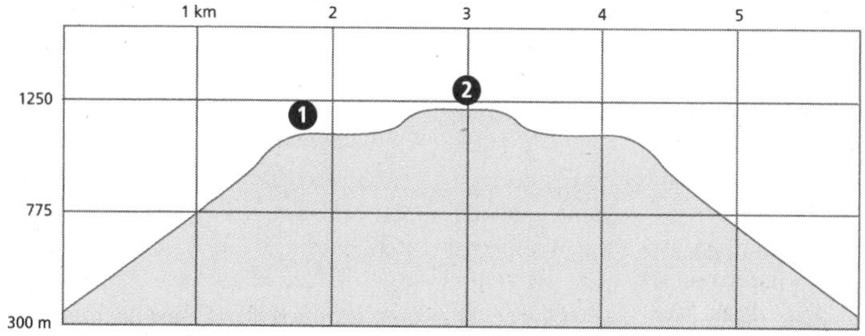

Grouse Mountain
Grizzly Bear exhibit & Lumberjack shows
Peak Chalet & Cafe
0 0.25 mi
0 0.25 km
N

1 km 2 3 4 5
1250
775
300 m

N 49 22.345, W 123 05.881 (0 km): Trail head
1 N 49 22.753, W 123 04.999 (1.8 km): Chalet at top of Grouse Grind Trail
2 N 49 23.243, W 123 04.522 (2.9 km): Grouse Mountain peak

in their 2-hectare (5-acre) pen, sometimes neck deep in their pond. A camera inside their den pictures them during their 3- to 4-month hibernation period.

You can also take in a lumberjack demonstration, a bird-of-prey show, and a theater showing educational films about the mountain. If you want to splurge, you can go for a helicopter tour, do tandem hang gliding, or ride the newly installed zip-line.

6 LYNN CANYON PARK ★

Difficulty rating: Easy to moderate

Distance: Up to 2km (1.2 miles)

Estimated time: Up to one hour per hike

Elevation gain: 50m (164 ft.)

Costs/permits: None

Pet friendly: Yes (dogs must be leashed)

Best time to go: Fall for misty atmosphere

Website: www.britishcolumbia.com/parks

Recommended map: Pick up map at Lynn Canyon Ecology Center

Trail head GPS: N 49 20.642, W 123 01.047

Trail head directions: From downtown Vancouver, cross the Lion's Gate Bridge into North Vancouver and follow signs to the Upper Levels Highway (Hwy. 1). After about 7km (4¼ miles), take the Lynn Valley Rd. exit near the Second Narrows Bridge and follow the signs to Lynn Canyon Park (not Lynn Headwaters Park). Turn right on Peters Rd. The park entrance is 1km (½ mile) along Peters Rd. All trails begin at the suspension bridge.

Lynn Canyon Park may be small, but it is mighty. Surrounded by the roar of the river as it hurls and swirls its way through the deep, rocky canyon, this lush second-growth forest has short but challenging hikes because of its steep topography. The suspension bridge has awe-inspiring views of the river and plunging waterfalls. We've recommended three trails that give you a sense of all the park has to offer. They are rarely busy, and the entire park is one of the prettiest on the North Shore. However, warning signs must be heeded, as people have died trying to climb up or down out-of-bounds sections, and it is slippery along both the canyon and the river's edge. Watch children carefully. Wear sensible footwear at all times.

The Lynn Canyon suspension bridge is free (not to be confused with the commercial Capilano Suspension Bridge), and the interpretive center and a delightful café are beside the parking lot, as well as a grassy picnic area with tables beside the trees.

This is a wonderful place for kids, and the information panels are full of information about animals you may see in the park, their tracks, and their place in the food chain, as well as how we can co-exist with them. The center also has slide shows, films, interpretive displays, and guided nature walks to help you identify birds and some of the common trees and shrubs in the park.

The suspension bridge is beside the parking lot. It replaced the original bridge constructed by a Mr. J. W. Crawford in 1912, who charged visitors C10¢ to cross. His bridge lasted only a few years. On today's bridge, mesh sides and wooden slats on the walkway make this a safe crossing, although it may not be for everyone. The bridge is narrow, with just enough room for two people to pass each other, and it bounces and sways gently beneath your feet. Most days, you'll have company

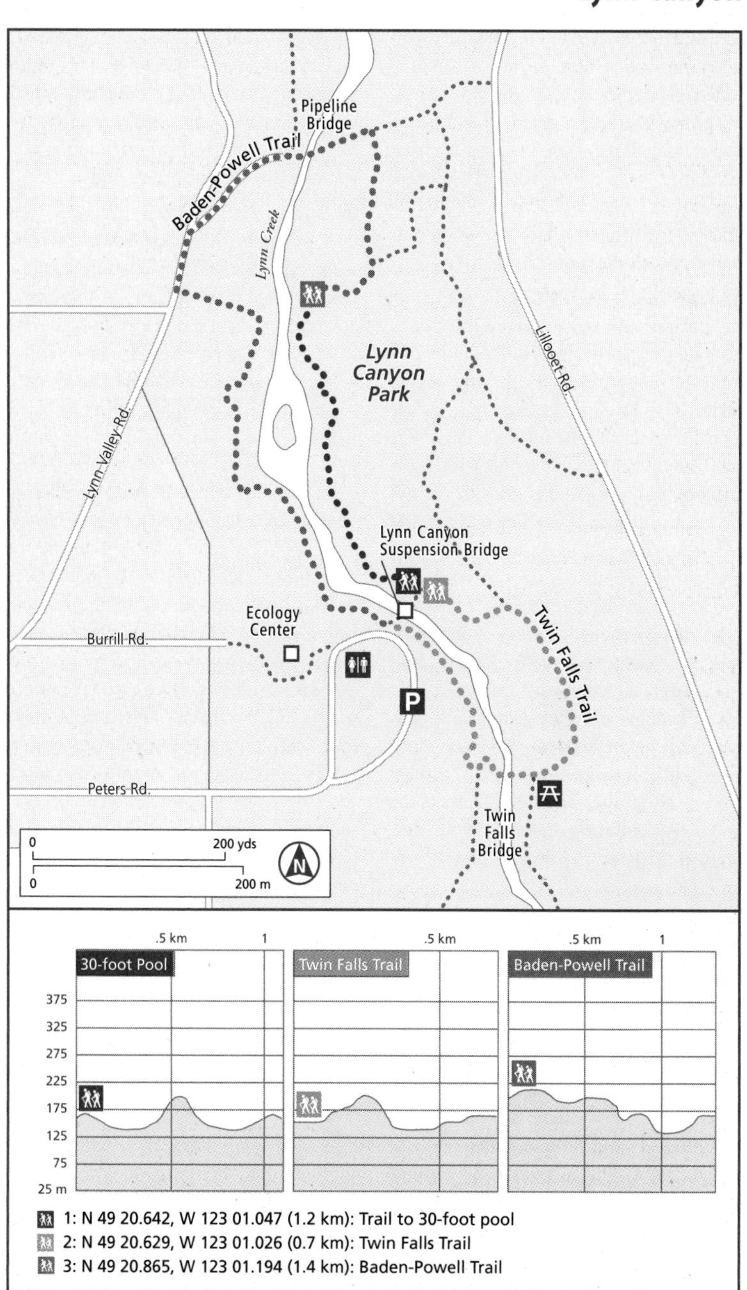

1: N 49 20.642, W 123 01.047 (1.2 km): Trail to 30-foot pool
2: N 49 20.629, W 123 01.026 (0.7 km): Twin Falls Trail
3: N 49 20.865, W 123 01.194 (1.4 km): Baden-Powell Trail

on the crossing. Fifty meters (164 ft.) below you rush the waters of Lynn Canyon and its waterfalls, which hurl themselves into Lynn Creek; there, the mercurial waters change from vivid green to churning whitewater in an instant. The impressive gorge, edged with Douglas firs that loom over western hemlock and red cedar, was carved by glacial action some 20,000 years ago. On the bridge, you are almost eye level with the tops of the trees.

❶ **Trail to 30-Foot Pool** Once across the bridge, turn left and take the downward-sloping path that, after about 15 minutes of wandering up and down between forest and creek, ends at the emerald waters of the 30-Foot Pool. The trail can be muddy, it's rough with rocks and exposed roots, and is close to the river's edge in places. Huge Douglas firs and cedars are along the trail. In this lush second-growth rainforest, trees grow swiftly, and these massive trees are only 80 to 100 years old. Because of the all-prevailing mist and dampness, many boulders and trees are thickly clothed in moss. At least 40 different species of moss have been identified here. The pool water is icy, but a small pebble beach is a good place to get close to the water. Be careful because the boulders are slippery. Take care with children, as the river is swift with undertows.

❷ **Twin Falls Trail** If you like bridges, after crossing the suspension bridge, take the boardwalk to your right. Where the trail forks, go right and follow the Twin Falls Trail for about 10 minutes to the Twin Falls Bridge, where a dramatic waterfall plunges into the canyon. This .5km (¼-mile) trail has many stumps of huge cedars, which were logged more than a century ago. Swaths of bracken fill in the undergrowth, along with shiny salal bushes and salmonberries. This bridge is much closer to the water than the suspension bridge, and it's often mysteriously misty and always beautiful. Also here is the ultimate wishing well, as a heap of pennies gleam in a depression in one of the riverside boulders. A notice board tells about the Pacific salmon spawning cycle, although the fish are rarely seen in the frothing water. A series of stairs (more than a hundred of them), along with boardwalks and rocky trail surfaces, lead you up more than 50m (164 ft.), back to the canyon rim and the suspension bridge.

❸ **Baden-Powell Trail** Built in 1971 by Girl Guides and Boy Scouts to commemorate the British Columbia Centennial, the trail is named for the founder of Scouts Canada, Lord Baden-Powell. This short section is part of a longer trail that winds its way from Horseshoe Bay to Deep Cove. The annual 48km (30-mile) Knee Knacker Run is also run along this entire trail, usually in July (www.kneeknacker.com). Pick up this trail beside the 30-Foot Pool, where a daunting flight of stairs (more than 160 of them) takes you up to the canyon rim. Head right on the trail back to the suspension bridge (it is well marked and will take about 30 minutes) or take a left to the Pipeline Bridge, which (with a brief detour on Rice Lake Road) will take you to the Baden-Powell Trail. This 1km (.6-mile) trail, marked with blue and white signs, is rough, with rocks and exposed tree roots; there are many long and short sections of stairs, with boardwalks over the muddiest sections. As you walk though this dense, aromatic forest—with its thick canopy of trees overhead and dense, flourishing bracken and ferns beside the trail—the roar of the river is always in the background, and there is the feeling of stepping back in time. The trail ends on the west side of the suspension bridge.

Lynn Canyon Park is the delicious filling in a double-decker park sandwich. The park is only 250 hectares (618 acres), but it is bracketed by Lynn Headwaters Regional Park to the north, Inter River Park to the south, and the Lower Seymour Conservation Reserve to the east. Trails in all four parks cross borders for longer, more strenuous hikes or cycling routes.

7 MOUNT SEYMOUR TRAIL ★★

Difficulty rating: Strenuous

Distance: 9.5km (5.9 miles) round trip

Estimated time: 4–5 hr.

Elevation gain: 350m (1,150 ft.)

Costs/permits: Parking C$3/day

Pet friendly: Yes (Dogs must be leashed on main trail. Dogs should not be taken on the back country trails.)

Best time to go: September for the warm late summer weather.

Website: www.env.gov.bc.ca/bcparks

Recommended map: North Vancouver 92G/6

Trail head GPS: N 49 22.009, W 122 56.879

Trail head directions: To get to Mount Seymour Provincial Park, take the Second Narrows Bridge (Hwy. 1 W.) across Burrard Inlet. Turn off on exit 22A, east to Mount Seymour Parkway. Follow Mount Seymour Parkway for 4.5km (2¾ miles) and turn north (left) on Mount Seymour Road. Follow the road to the top parking lot and park at the north end near the information board.

Mount Seymour is one of the best hiking locations within a short drive from Vancouver. The top peak—there are three high summits—offers an expansive panoramic view of the Lower Mainland, Indian Arm, Mount Baker in Washington State, and the North Shore Mountains. There are many trails of varying length and difficulty here. Start with a short hike to Mystery Lake and peak, then continue on to the Mount Seymour Trail to take in the spectacular views.

A few meters north of the information board is a marker for Mystery Lake. Turn right as you exit the parking lot at the north end, go underneath the chair-lift, and cross the small foot bridge. The trail itself is surrounded by dense vegetation and can be quite muddy; follow the yellow markers on trees. The large growth includes Amabilis fir, yellow cedar, and mountain hemlock; the higher you hike, the smaller the trees.

❶ Mystery Lake After 45 minutes, you reach Mystery Lake, a picturesque jewel of blue reflecting the boulders and deep green trees surrounding it. In summer, swim if you dare, but be prepared—it is chilly. On a cloudy day, the lake glows through the mist. The trail does not go up Mystery Peak but leads to the base of it on the north. However, it is an easy climb to the top, where the chair-lift ends, and there is a raised wooden platform you can get to via a slightly precarious wooden plank. This is a great spot to take photos.

❷ Following the Mount Seymour Trail To continue the hike to the summits, follow the trail northwest. Here, you connect with the Mount Seymour Trail, which heads northeast—to your right. The trail is well-marked, and you will likely have company on this popular hike. After following the trail that leads down into a meadow, you head up a steep section to Brockton Point.

❸ Brockton Point This wooded bluff is the first vista of the hike. To the east, you may see the waters of Indian Arm through the trees, and north is the first peak of Mount Seymour. There is a camping and picnic area just north of Brockton Point.

After Brockton Point, a side trail leads to First Peak, known as First Pump Peak. This is a long, steep section of the trail, and most people choose to stay on the main trail and continue to the Second Peak. Continue on the main trail, which goes downhill through meadows—in summer, enjoy the spray of color from fireweed, paintbrush, and lupins. The twisting trail is easily followed, thanks to orange markers; ignore the side trails you

Mountain Safety

Hiking in the mountains should never be taken lightly. Even on a warm summer day, the weather can change quickly, and the high trails may be snow-packed and dangerous. Do not attempt to complete the hike if there is snow on the trail. Always stay on the trail, and carry raingear and a warm jacket. There is no cell phone reception, so advise someone ahead of time where you are hiking. Although there are bears, you are in more danger from stepping in bear scat than you are of being attacked by one. See the Safety section of the planning chapter (p. 16) for more tips on staying safe in the mountains.

see and, at the junction, keep left to traverse up the east side of the Second Peak. The trail on the right leads to Elsay Lake, a rugged 7km ($4^{1}/_{4}$-mile) one-way route that is best suited to backcountry aficionados. The next trail mark after this trail split leads to Second Peak.

4 Second Pump Peak As you approach the Second Pump Peak along a rocky route, you have views of the First Peak straight ahead. There is a steep scramble here where you have to take extreme care, as there is a sharp drop-off on the left, then you reach the Second Peak.

SPECTACULAR LOOKOUT Savor the 360-degree view—the impressive Coast Mountains; the Fraser Valley, where the river winds a serpentine route; the snowy and showy Mount Baker; and the sprawling communities clustering the landscape. It's wonderful, if your group happens to be alone at this point, to quietly take in the wondrous view and congratulate yourselves on a great hike. This is an idyllic lunch spot, but you may be joined by pesky Steller's Jays and Whiskey Jacks, who love to share your food. You'll probably be amazed at the size of the shiny black ravens that also arrive at the sight of a meal. For many hikers, this is the end of the trail. It's been a satisfying day, and many choose to retrace their steps back to the parking lot.

Be very cautious as you descend this peak. More than a few people have had bad accidents here. To continue, return to the main trail and follow it down; again, it is steep, so tread carefully, especially if there is any snow. You end up between the Second and Third peaks, where you have the option to then follow the trail up the other side. The undulating trail, some of it over boulders, arrives at a high spot, from which you can see the higher peak ahead. Follow the steep trail for 200m (656 ft.) to arrive at the Third Peak. While you can indeed "see more" from your vantage point 1,455m (4,774 ft.) above sea level, the mountain's name actually comes from Frederick Seymour, who was governor of the province from 1864 to 1869. If you didn't have your lunch break earlier, this is the place. In any case, have a rest before heading back the way you came.

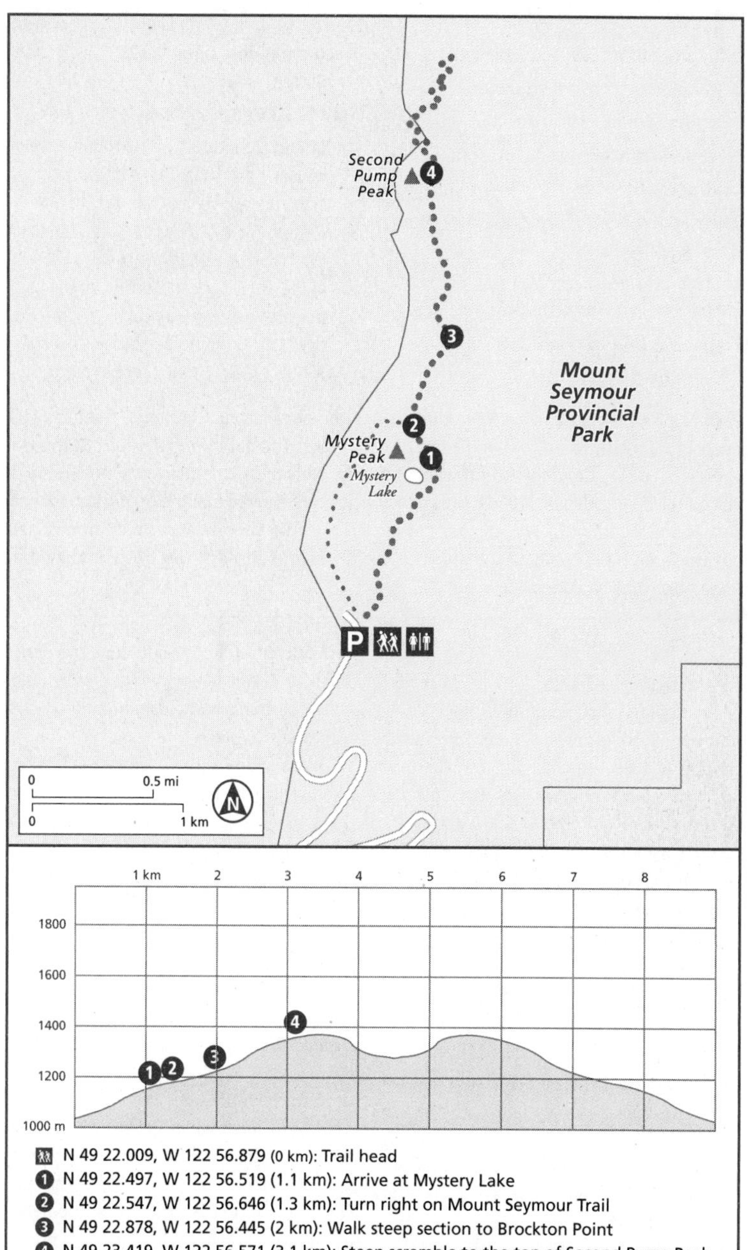
Second Pump Peak
Mystery Peak
Mystery Lake
Mount Seymour Provincial Park
0
0.5 mi
0
1 km
N
1 km
2
3
4
5
6
7
8
1800
1600
1400
1200
1000 m
N 49 22.009, W 122 56.879 (0 km): Trail head
1 N 49 22.497, W 122 56.519 (1.1 km): Arrive at Mystery Lake
2 N 49 22.547, W 122 56.646 (1.3 km): Turn right on Mount Seymour Trail
3 N 49 22.878, W 122 56.445 (2 km): Walk steep section to Brockton Point
4 N 49 23.419, W 122 56.571 (3.1 km): Steep scramble to the top of Second Pump Peak

8 PACIFIC SPIRIT PARK

Difficulty rating: Easy to moderate

Distance: 5km (3 miles) round-trip

Estimated time: 1½ hr. minimum

Elevation gain: Minimal

Cost/permits: None

Pet friendly: Yes (dogs must be leashed on all but a few trails)

Best time to go: Spring and summer for the new growth and birdsong

Website: www.metrovancouver.org

Recommended map: Available at the park office

Trail head GPS: N 49 15.541, W 123 13.337

Trail head direction: From downtown Vancouver, head south along Burrard St., cross the bridge, and take the 4th Ave. turnoff. Follow 4th Ave. for about 5.4km (3¼ miles) to Blanca and turn left (south) at the traffic light on Blanca and then at (to) 16th Ave. and Blanca St., (then) turn right (on 16th Ave.) and proceed about 500m (1,640 ft.) to the park center.

Pacific Spirit Park nestles between the city and the ocean, a vast, tranquil, diverse swath of second-growth forest with a mosaic of leafy trails. The park, formerly part of the University of British Columbia's Endowment Lands, surrounds the university on the tip of Point Grey Peninsula; its 800 hectares (1,977 acres) are a joy to explore at any time of year and in any weather. In winter, rain patters on the tree canopy and small brooks rush beside some trails, while in the summer, the sun slants through the trees, highlighting leaves and grassy glades.

The Cleveland Trail begins behind the park center. Head north, to be immediately enfolded in the forest, where tree branches form a dense, green overhead canopy. Spindly vine maples, towering firs and cedars, salal, salmonberry, and bracken surround you. Woodpeckers leave a legacy of lacy wooden stumps along the trails, and birds are everywhere. Raccoons, squirrels, and coyotes live here, safe in the dense bush, but are rarely seen.

Within a few minutes, there's the junction of Cleveland and Heron; stay on Cleveland until you reach the Lily of the Valley Trail.

❶ Lily of the Valley Detour Take a 5-minute detour east along the Lily of the Valley Trail, named for miner's lettuce, which looks a little like the Lily of the Valley plant. You will come back to this intersection, but detour to explore a cluster of magnificent hollow trunks of lightening-killed cedars, at least 5m (16 ft.) in circumference. Step inside these blackened giants and look up—way up—to the sky, visible through a circular opening. It is a very peaceful place.

Beyond the stumps, there's a brief open area on this trail and, where the trees begin again, look carefully to your right at a huge stump, where there's the remains of a deer-head carving, missing its face but with ears and face outlined. On the back of this trunk is a carving of a bear, clothed in moss, possibly done by a member of the Musqeam band. Look around and you might spy an eagle's head on another stump, although it's thickly covered in moss.

Retrace your steps to the Cleveland Trail and, through the trees, you can see the manicured lawns of the University Golf Course. This trail skirts the golf course for about 10 minutes and emerges on University Boulevard at St. Anslem's Church.

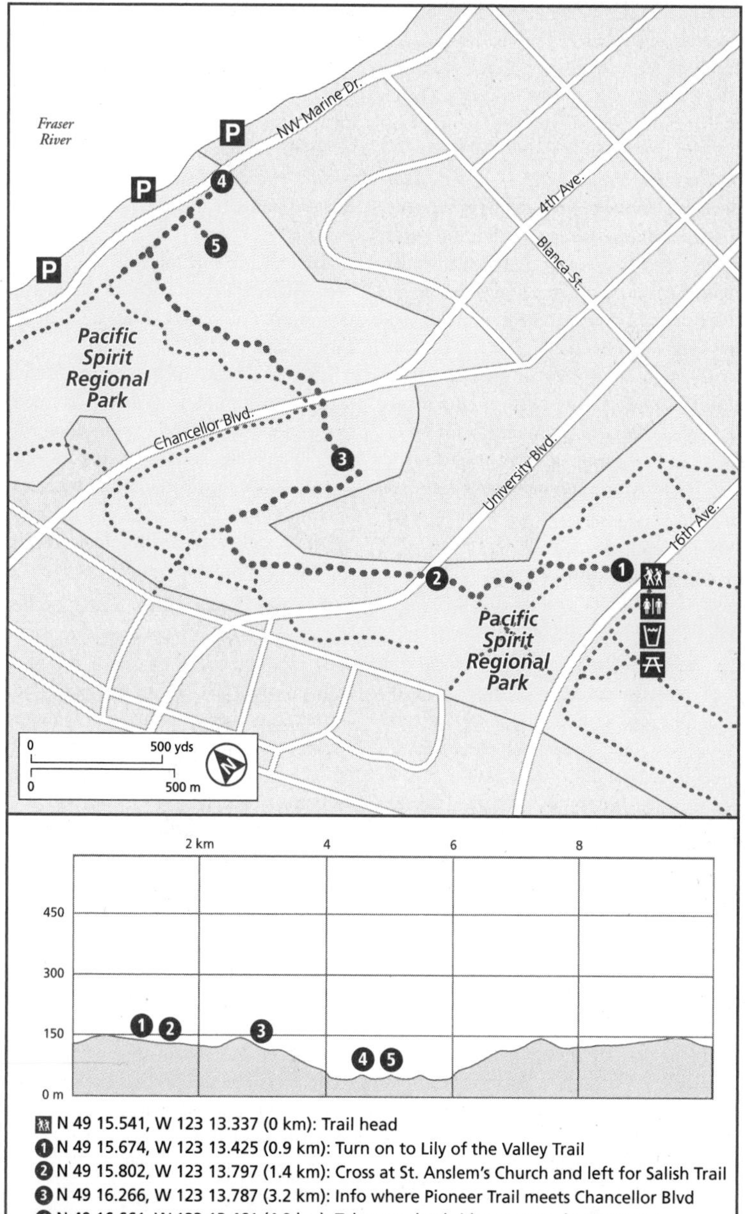

N 49 15.541, W 123 13.337 (0 km): Trail head

❶ N 49 15.674, W 123 13.425 (0.9 km): Turn on to Lily of the Valley Trail

❷ N 49 15.802, W 123 13.797 (1.4 km): Cross at St. Anslem's Church and left for Salish Trail

❸ N 49 16.266, W 123 13.787 (3.2 km): Info where Pioneer Trail meets Chancellor Blvd

❹ N 49 16.661, W 123 13.461 (4.9 km): Take wooden bridge across salmon stream

❺ N 49 16.587, W 123 13.572 (5.1 km): Right on Admiralty Trail to enter Plains of Abraham

2 St. Anslem's Church Cross the road, and to your left (just past the entrance to the University Golf Club) is the start of the Salish Trail, which plunges you back into a world of tranquil greenery. Thick blackberry bushes edge this wide trail as it parallels the golf course for about 10 minutes before turning right (north) onto the winding Spanish Trail as it heads downhill. At the bottom of this brief, steep hill is a swampy area and pond, the result of busy beavers. The beaver dam is to the right of the little wooden bridge. Although the beavers are undoubtedly around, it's unlikely you'll see them. The rising water is drowning alder trees in this area, and skunk cabbage—or swamp lanterns—flourish in the damp ground. This is also home to a profusion of frogs, salamanders, and toads, whose summer songs ring out loud and clear. The water's rusty red color is caused by iron.

The Spanish Trail slopes gently uphill now to meet Pioneer Trail, which you follow to Chancellor Boulevard.

3 Information Board Cross the road, and Pioneer Trail will be in front of you. But first go left a few meters to a notice board with maps and park information. If you are in a rush, park here and walk just this section of the park. Take the East Canyon Trail, and you'll soon be viewing the deep, leafy canyon, but take care near the edge, as the ground is crumbling away; watch children carefully. Look for a huge cedar stump with trees growing on top, their convoluted roots twisting creatively down to the ground.

A short distance on, a split rail fence guards against an unwary fall and protects the fragile canyon edges. Just to your right is a serene, open clearing in the trees, a perfect rest or picnic spot. The trail slopes gently downhill to where, for a few meters, the path is broken up and steep.

4 Wooden Bridge Over a Stream Admiralty Trail borders the cliffs east and west above Spanish banks, and you can go left (west) to where the trail, and steep steps set in the earth, head down to the beach. Across the road and beach parking lot is a salmon stream that heads into the ocean. From a wooden bridge across the stream, you might see the tiny fish in the shallow water. Signs have information on the salmon.

Back on the cliff top, you can take the West Canyon Trail back to Chancellor Boulevard and retrace your steps to the park center.

Or stay on the cliff top and turn right (east) on Admiralty Trail. Salmonberry bushes are thick here, pretty in spring with their deep pink flowers. The berries make a great snack in early summer, but you'll have to beat the birds to them. You can see Spanish Banks Beach, Burrard Inlet, and the North Shore through the trees.

5 Plains of Abraham Take the first turnoff on your right and emerge into a wide clearing called the Plains of Abraham. More than a century ago, John Stewart ran a dairy farm here. Fireweed, nettles, blackberry, and salmonberry bushes, plus a handful of donated trees, have taken over most of this clearing. It's a wonderful spot to settle on a log for a rest or a picnic. Pioneer Trail, which crosses this clearing, was originally the road built and used by Stewart to haul goods to the main road.

On the south side of the clearing is a stile; go through here to Pioneer Trail, which wanders gently along though the trees back to Chancellor Boulevard. Retrace your steps back to the park headquarters, or pick up Pioneer Trail across the road and follow it to its junction with the Spanish Trail to University Boulevard to get back on the Cleveland Trail.

9 POINT GREY FORESHORE, FROM SPANISH BANKS TO WRECK BEACH ★

Difficulty rating: Easy

Distance: 10km (6.2 miles) round trip

Estimated time: 4 hr.

Elevation gain: None

Costs/permits: None

Pet friendly: Yes (dogs are allowed off leash from Oct–Feb)

Best time to go: July and Aug for swimming and sunbathing

Website: www.wreckbeach.org

Recommended map: Edge of the Pacific Spirit park map (At Pacific Spirit Park park centre on 16th Ave., see Pacific Spirit Park for centre directions.)

Trail head GPS: N 49 16.595, W 123 12.881

Trail head directions: From downtown Vancouver, head south on Burrard St., cross the bridge, and turn right (west) on W. 4th Ave. for about 5km (3 miles). Turn right onto N.W. Marine Dr.

The beaches that fringe the northern edge of Vancouver's West Side offer something for everyone, from the long, sandy stretches of Spanish Banks to Wreck Beach, the biggest nude beach in Canada. Between these two scenic spots are 5km (3 miles) of rocky beach and a colorful slice of history.

Don't let the sandy beaches here deceive you—it's important to wear shoes with good support. Begin your walk at Spanish Banks (below Blanca St.), an ideal family beach. A 1.5km (1-mile) stretch of golden sand, a gently sloping beach, lifeguard protected swimming areas, and concession stands provide all you need for a day in the sun. At the lowest of low tides, the water recedes more than 400m (1,312 ft.), giving the illusion that you could walk across to English Bay, skirting the freighters and sailboats in the harbor as you go. Watch for soaring eagles, herons waiting in the shallows, and gulls and crows eager for handouts.

❶ Dog Beach Walking west, as the beach narrows, the grass verge widens; this is a popular area for BBQs and volleyball. Follow the hard-packed beachside path approximately 2.5km (1½ miles), sharing it with other walkers, runners, and cyclists. This is also a popular dog-walking path; at the western end is a doggy beach, always lively with cavorting canines.

Here also is a stylized concrete anchor commemorating the 1791 visit of Spanish explorer Joe Maria Narvaez, the first European to sail these waters. The beach is named for him. It was 1 year later than Capt. George Vancouver sailed these waters, exploring Burrard Inlet. He named Point Grey after Colin Grey, the son of Earl Grey, of tea fame.

Now, the beach becomes narrow and rocky, rounding a point to widen out into two sandy, protected bays.

If you enjoy exploring tidal pools or trying to imagine faces in pieces of driftwood, you are in the right place; the beach here is strewn with downed tree trunks, large pebbles, and rocks, many of which are encrusted with barnacles and draped in seaweed. Short sandy stretches offer some respite from scrambling; at low tide, walking is easier. Envy the people who walk this route daily, as at any time, the views are sublime. To the west lies Vancouver Island and the Sunshine Coast, while

Fun Facts Get Wrecked

Wreck Beach Day, usually held in mid-July, celebrates this unique beach, a nude beach for more than half a century.

Equally famous is the Bare Buns Run in August, a 5k (3-mile) run/walk to raise money for the Wreck Beach Preservation Society (www.barebuns.ca).

across the bay, the North Shore Mountains provide a stunning skyline.

❷ **Acadia Beach** Starting at Acadia Beach, dogs are allowed from October to February, and don't be surprised to see nude sunbathers here, as clothing is optional at anytime. While most are at Tower and Wreck beaches, a few prefer to sunbathe in sheltered nooks created by piles of driftwood.

❸ **Tower Beach** At the bottom of the #3 Trail looms the first of two towers, giving this stretch the name Tower Beach. Backed by dense blackberry bushes, these structures were built during World War II as searchlight towers when people feared the possibility of attack by Japanese submarines. Now, they are canvasses for graffiti artists. Scramble along a rocky berm and watch for the shiny black heads of harbor seals, seen year round but most frequently in winter. These berms are more than just pretty rocks; they are helping to slow down the erosion of the cliffs behind the Museum of Anthropology, although not always successfully, as proven by the downed trees and exposed tangles of tree roots. Hear the surf crash on windy days, drowning out all other sounds, even that of the music of the pebbles sliding in and out with the waves.

In summer, cruise ships head out on the tide, huge white confections against the emerald green of the North Shore Mountains.

❹ **Trail #4** Join this path to make your way to a quiet beach, a great place to watch the sunset; it is also where families and couples swim in the clear ocean (clothing optional). You can also reach it from the Museum of Anthropology on N.W. Marine Drive. Walk down the 390 steps—someone counted!

❺ **Wreck Beach** The beach becomes progressively sandier, and it's a 20-minute walk to the wide, sandy swath of Wreck Beach. It's named for the three barges that were sunk near here to provide a breakwater for the log booming grounds around the corner. Log booms, huge rafts of logs, are moored here before being taken to the lumber mills.

In all but the most inclement weather, lots of people of all ages—from babies to the elderly—sunbathe, play games, swim, and even tend flower gardens in the nude. Other people sell cold or hot drinks, snacks, and treats. Members of the Royal Canadian Mounted Police (fully clothed) often visit the beach, checking for drugs or alcohol.

In the early evening, watch the herons flying home; the largest heronry in Vancouver is deep in the forest behind Wreck Beach.

❻ **Trail #6** At Trail #6, you can leave the beach and climb up the steps (more than 400 of them), with several much-needed resting spots, that snake up the cliff to Marine Drive. Or retrace your steps. Remember your clothes!

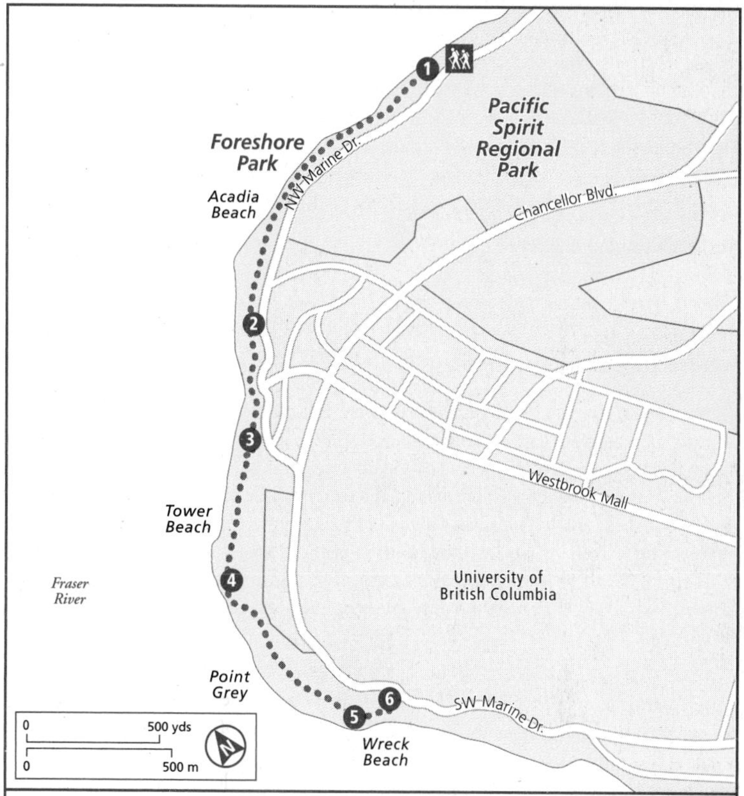

Pacific
Spirit
Regional
Park
Foreshore
Park
NW Marine Dr.
Acadia
Beach
Chancellor Blvd.
Westbrook Mall
Tower
Beach
Fraser
River
University of
British Columbia
Point
Grey
SW Marine Dr.
Wreck
Beach
0
500 yds
0
500 m

2 km
4
6
8
10
250
200
150
100
50
0 m

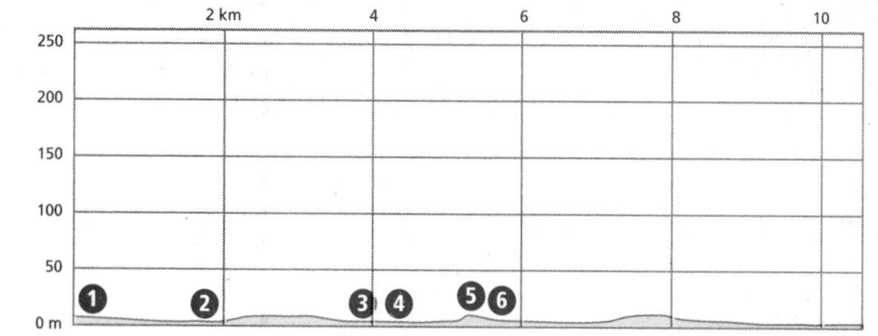

- N 49 16.595, W 123 12.881 (0 km): Trail head
- ❶ N 49 16.595, W 123 12.881 (0 km): Follow beach path past commemorative anchor
- ❷ N 49 16.752, W 123 14.029 (1.5 km): Dogs and nude sunbathers at Acadia Beach
- ❸ N 49 16.396, W 123 15.443 (3.5 km): First tower at bottom of Trail #3
- ❹ N 49 16.254, W 123 15.718 (3.9 km): Join Trail #4 and follow steps down to the beach
- ❺ N 49 15.674, W 123 15.695 (5.1 km): Pass nude bathers at Wreck Beach
- ❻ N 49 15.773, W 123 15.522 (5.4 km): Leave beach and climb long stairway at Trail #6

10 IONA BEACH REGIONAL PARK ★

Difficulty rating: Easy

Distance: 9km (5.6 miles) round trip

Estimated time: 2 hr.

Elevation gain: None

Costs/permit: None

Pet friendly: Yes (dogs must be leashed)

Best time to go: Arrive in the early morning to see eagles perched along the jetty or at sunset for spectacular ocean views

Website: www.metrovancouver.org

Recommended map: Maps available at the parking area by the washrooms

Trail head GPS: N 49 13.105, W 123 12.808

Trail head directions: From downtown, go south along Granville and follow signs to Vancouver International Airport. Go over Arthur Laing Bridge and after a further 1.8km (1 mile), take the Templeton St. turnoff. Follow the signs 5.7km (3½ miles) to Iona Beach Regional Park. Park at the beginning of the jetty walk.

In this unique park, a border between land and sea, you stroll far out into the Strait of Georgia without ever getting your feet wet. The source of this feat is the remarkable 4.5km (2.8-mile) South Jetty, formed by the outtake pipes of the Iona Island sewage treatment plant. While the idea is unromantic, the water and beaches are pristine. Stretching to the southwest, the jetty forms a flat, uninterrupted gravel walkway that is excellent for enthusiastic walkers as well as those with strollers or wheelchairs. Mere minutes from the airport, if you flew in, you may have spotted it just before landing. This is a bird watchers paradise, both from the jetty and surrounding marshland, as well as a Wildlife Watch site.

You depart from the parking lot: This area has washrooms and picnic tables, as well as a tap with drinking water. Once you start walking, it's a whole new world stretching to the horizon, surrounded by tidal flats at low tide and the ocean at high tide. Cyclists, who enjoy exploring the 12km (7½ miles) of quiet, country roads around this area, have their own parallel cycle path along the jetty.

You will probably start off at a brisk pace, breathing deeply of the crisp, ocean air, but gradually the peaceful surroundings work their magic, and you'll slow down to stop and stare. There is nothing to distract you from the scenery, or as one walker put it, "If I wasn't here, I wouldn't believe it."

❶ First Bench To help you believe, there are three areas to protect you from the frequent wind along the jetty. The first bench, 1.3km (¾ mile) along, is an excellent place to watch birds flitting around the water's edge and, at low tide, count their myriad tracks in the mud. A rest at the second bench, at 2.5km (1½ miles), provides the opportunity to watch the procession of tugs, log booms, scows, and other boats. The principal shipping lanes for freighters and, in summer, passenger liners are just to the west.

❷ Viewing Tower When you reach your goal, the viewing tower, at the end of this digit of land—a favorite, if breezy, picnic spot—there's a bird's-eye view of the ocean, stunning at sunset, fascinating at anytime.

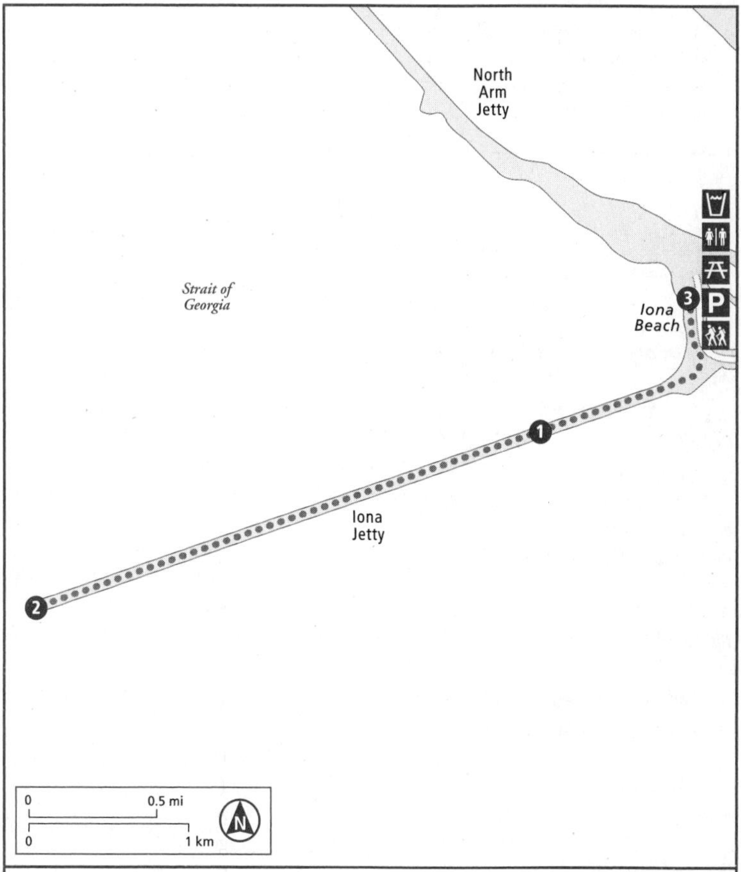

North
Arm
Jetty
Strait of
Georgia
Iona
Beach
Iona
Jetty
0
0.5 mi
0
1 km
N

1 km
2
3
4
5
6
7
8
50
0 m

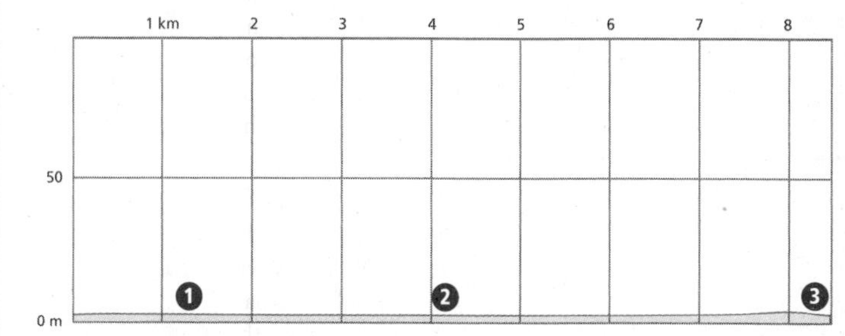

N 49 13.105, W 123 12.808 (0 km): Trail head
❶ N 49 12.805, W 123 13.573 (1.3 km): Stop to watch birds at first bench
❷ N 49 12.346, W 123 15.758 (4.1 km): Viewing tower at end of jetty
❸ N 49 13.174, W 123 12.766 (8.4 km): Boardwalk and ponds behind the parking area

Stargazing

Park gates close at dusk, but if you are into stargazing, leave your vehicle at the park entrance and walk in 1.9km (1¼ miles). Here, far from the lights of the city, the night sky is a black velvet backdrop to myriad stars. The **Greater Vancouver Regional District** has occasional star gazing evenings (✆ **604/224-5739**).

SPECTACULAR LOOKOUT To the east soar the impressive slopes of Mount Baker, and the Coast Mountains form a backdrop to the north for planes taking off and landing at the airport. Looking west across the Strait of Georgia, you may see the mountains that form the backbone of Vancouver Island.

As you stroll back to shore along the jetty, you see why the park's exceptional position at the mouth of the Fraser River's north arm, where fresh and salt water mingle—combined with the influence of the shoreline, ponds, marshes, and a freshwater slough—makes it one of the best bird-watching areas in Canada. The park area protects the breeding habitat of local birds and also protects the foreshore areas of the Fraser River delta, used by thousands of migratory shorebirds and waterfowl (more than 300 species of birds have been recorded here). Many shorebirds also winter on Iona Island. In chillier months, the bird population is the largest on the West Coast (north of California), luring birders from across Canada and the United States. You will likely see loons, herons, ducks, blackbirds, plovers, gulls, and sandpipers, along with falcons, eagles, and possibly even owls.

❸ Bird Ponds After your windy walk, visit the ponds behind the parking area, lush with golden broom in early summer, and also rich in bird life. Take a stroll around the short boardwalk here, overlooking bustling bird breeding areas.

For beachcombing and more birds, head northwest along the beach from the main parking area. The Iona Island Sandspit, which is not officially part of the park, has its own pleasures. At low tide, the flats are great for exploring, and above the flats are sandy beaches, littered with heaps of bleached driftwood, offering sheltered perches for a rest or a picnic. About 1.5km (1 mile) farther along the beach are wonderful wind-ridged sand dunes, the ultimate children's sandbox.

Northwards is a backdoor glimpse of the city. Across the river, the thick stands of trees are part of Pacific Spirit Park beside the University of British Columbia, and the manicured lawns of several golf clubs border the river.

To the east is MacDonald Slough, another excellent birding area. Migrating birds spangle the sky on their journey to and from Arctic breeding grounds, and the area teems with bird life. Mergansers, harlequin ducks, oldsquaw, kestrels, canvasbacks, sandpipers, and black-bellied plovers are just some of the birds you might see.

11 SKOOKUMCHUCK NARROWS PROVINCIAL PARK ★★

Difficulty rating: Easy

Distance: 8km (5 miles) round trip

Estimated time: 2½–3 hr.

Elevation gain: 7km (4.3 miles)

Costs/permits: None

Pet friendly: Yes (dogs must be leashed)

Best time to go: In winter, to see the highest tides

Website: www.env.gov.bc.ca/bcparks or www.sunshinecoastparks.com

Recommended map: 92G/12

Trail head GPS: N 49 44.996, W 123 56.180

Trail head directions: Take the ferry from Horseshoe Bay in West Vancouver to Langdale on the Sunshine Coast. Follow signs to the Sunshine Coast Highway and head north towards Sechelt, approximately 27km (17 miles). Continue past Sechelt on the highway approximately another 53km (33 miles) to Egmont Rd., turn right, and drive about 5.5km (3½ miles) to the parking lot of the park.

View a natural phenomena—one of the world's largest saltwater rapids. Skookumchuck, a Chinook word, means "turbulent water," and when you see the change of tide that takes place twice daily at the narrows connecting the Sechelt Inlet to the Jervis Inlet, that will seem an understatement. The easy hike into Skookumchuck is a rite of passage for locals and visitors on the Sunshine Coast.

Depart from the parking lot along a gravel road. There is a pit toilet here. This is a residential road; do not enter any of the driveways. Notice the Green Rosette, up a driveway on your right, and decide when you wish to treat yourself to a sweet. At one point, you come to an information sign that is put up by locals, noting if there is a bear or cougar around and also mentioning a few landmarks. There is a rustic look-out up a few stairs.

❶ Wooded Trail After walking about 750m (2,461 ft.), you enter the wooded trail. You are instantly in tall trees, luxuriant ferns, moss-draped logs, trees, and boulders. All along this trail, you'll see areas with many fallen trees. This park used to be much denser in growth; however, ferocious storms in November 2006 and 2007 have thinned these woods.

❷ Hollowed-Out Tree After walking about 15 minutes, notice the massive stump hollowed out, probably by a lightning strike. You'll see the gouge out of the side of this giant cedar, where loggers placed a springboard to stand on while cutting down the tree. Soon, you see a lake glimmering through the trees.

❸ Brown Lake If you are hankering for a rest, stop at this opening that shows off Brown Lake, backed by Mountain Drew in the Coast Mountain Range.

TAKE A BREAK
On the shoreline, read the interpretive board with details about the trout found in the lake. In summer, enjoy the showy flowers on the bush commonly called a Butterfly bush and watch for waterfowl. You also see clear-cuts on the mountains backdropping the lake. The nearby community of Egmont has occasionally been a hotbed of controversy when developers clear their scenic mountainscapes.

Fun Facts Tide in Knots

On a 3m ($9^3/_4$-ft.) tide, some 200 billion gallons of water churn through the narrows. To view the most exciting action, a park's guide recommends: "The higher the knots [water speed], the better the view." Both websites listed above, as well as the Sechelt Visitor Info Centre and the Sunshine Coast Tourist Guide, provide good information on tides. The maximum speed is about 17 knots. Big waves are viewed on a "flood tide;" whirlpool action is found during an "ebb tide."

Continuing on, you'll find a section where fallen down trees resemble pick-up sticks. This is an undulating trail with nothing too extreme. There is plenty of time to take in nature. Notice the huge "mother" or "nurse" stumps and logs that have a wealth of growth on them—everything from huckleberry shrubs to Salal and small evergreens.

❹ **First Glimpse of Ocean** You have walked about 2.8km ($1^3/_4$ miles) and probably met other hikers, when you pass through a lovely downhill section, lush with ferns, to catch your first glimpse of the ocean through the trees. In this area, an interpretive board explains how the giant trees were logged in the early days. If the trail isn't too busy, this is a nice spot to enjoy as you hear the call of the ocean. From here, the trail meanders uphill.

❺ **Signpost to North Point and Roland Point** This signpost gives warnings about taking precautions near the shoreline. It doesn't matter which point you visit first, but we prefer to go left to North Point. You arrive at a viewpoint above the rapids, where a wire fence protects sightseers from getting too carried away; below is the rushing whitewater. Chances are you won't be alone at either one of these viewpoints. Since this has a fence, it is relaxing to sit and have a picnic and watch the mesmerizing water.

However, when you backtrack to the sign and head to Roland Point, it is far more enchanting. (There is a pit toilet along this trail.) The narrow trail that leads up and down is pretty, spangled with ferns and huckleberries, and past a small bay with kelp beds and waterfowl—it's a nice build-up to reaching slabs of granite that lead you down right beside the rushing tides. Hopefully, there will be entertainment—this is where whitewater kayakers play. We've seen as many as 30 kayakers take on the rapids. In wetsuits, they hop into their stubby kayaks and battle the whitewater, sometimes doing 360s in the foaming water.

This is a fabulous place to hang out. Check out the tidal pools, rich in colorful marine life—sponges, sea anemones, sea stars, a variety of crabs, and more. (An interpretive board will fill you in.) In fact, that's the only reason to arrive in a low tide, as there are more tidal pools to explore. Don't forget your camera. Retrace your steps to return, making time for a bakery stop.

TAKE A BREAK

We like to save our visit to the **Green Rosette** for the return trip. On a hot day, enjoy an iced coffee and killer cinnamon bun—or a healthy muffin—on the outdoor deck. In season, don't miss a piece of blackberry cake. Open July and Aug daily; in late spring and Sept, on weekends.

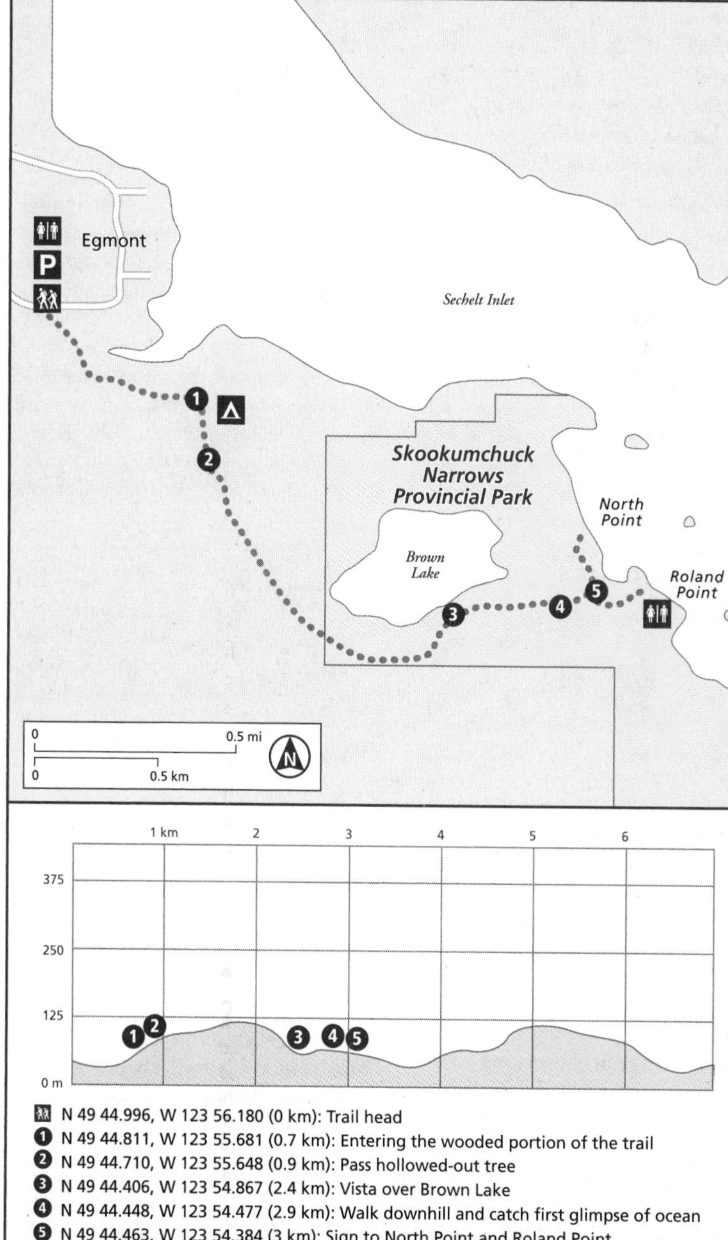
Egmont
P
Sechelt Inlet
Skookumchuck Narrows Provincial Park
Brown Lake
North Point
Roland Point
0
0.5 mi
0
0.5 km
N
1 km
2
3
4
5
6
375
250
125
0 m
N 49 44.996, W 123 56.180 (0 km): Trail head
1 N 49 44.811, W 123 55.681 (0.7 km): Entering the wooded portion of the trail
2 N 49 44.710, W 123 55.648 (0.9 km): Pass hollowed-out tree
3 N 49 44.406, W 123 54.867 (2.4 km): Vista over Brown Lake
4 N 49 44.448, W 123 54.477 (2.9 km): Walk downhill and catch first glimpse of ocean
5 N 49 44.463, W 123 54.384 (3 km): Sign to North Point and Roland Point

12 SMUGGLER COVE PROVINCIAL PARK ★

Difficulty rating: Easy

Distance: 2.5km (1.6 miles) round trip

Estimated time: 1 hr.

Elevation gain: 3.5km (2.2 miles)

Costs/permits: None

Pet friendly: Yes (dogs must be leashed)

Best time to go: Summer is best to enjoy the waterfront

Website: www.env.gov.bc.ca/bcparks

Recommended maps: Sechelt Inlet 92G/12

Trail head GPS: N 49 30.684, W 123 56.947

Trail head directions: Take the ferry from Horseshoe Bay in West Vancouver to Langdale on the Sunshine Coast. Follow signs to the Sunshine Coast Highway (Hwy. 101) and head north towards Sechelt, approximately 27km (17 miles). Continue past Sechelt another 16km (10 miles) and turn left on Brooks Rd. Drive about 5km (3 miles) to the entrance to the park.

This is where Sunshine Coasters take their visitors, as it typifies the beauty of the region with its phenomenal ocean views, rich growth, stands of Arbutus, great birding opportunities, and interpretive boards with tidbits about the natural and First Nations history. If you love swimming in the ocean, wear your swimsuit under your hiking gear. However, be aware that while hardy locals swim most of the summer, these waters are not considered warm!

Check the information board in the parking lot; the map will give you the lay of the land (this hike is straightforward with a loop at the end) and may have wildlife notices posted, for example, if there are bear—or very occasionally, cougar—in the area. The wide trail leads into the woods downhill and is suitable for families; however, since there are many viewpoints above the water, care must be taken. Small children have to be watched carefully. Within minutes, you arrive at the first of five boardwalks. This park is home to pesky beaver, and the parks' people are constantly upgrading trails. The trail weaves through a forest of cedar, hemlock, fir, and Arbutus. Enjoy the waterfowl, blackbirds, and (of course) beaver as you view marshy areas from boardwalks.

❶ Smuggler Cove After about 20 minutes, you arrive at a clearing for your first view of the ocean. This is the end of the island-spangled Smuggler Cove; especially at high tide, it is picture perfect, fringed by forest, granite boulders with golden lichen, and often, several yachts. One trail goes left and can be explored later; there is a pit toilet here. Another trail also leads left from this clearing to a few cleared spots for wilderness campers. (It is popular with cyclists during summer months.) Follow the trail that leads uphill into the trees. It is a short distance to uphill stairs, eventually a few steps set into the earth going downhill. Enjoy the undergrowth of ferns, Salal, and Oregon grape. Keep watch for woodpeckers—we've spotted both downy and Pileated species here.

❷ First Viewpoint Keep watch for a trail that heads right towards the water. Clamber up the rocky route to look down on the beautiful inlet below—the blue-green of the water and deep green of the woods are dazzling. In summer, it is unusual not to see boats anchored here. Kayakers also love this space.

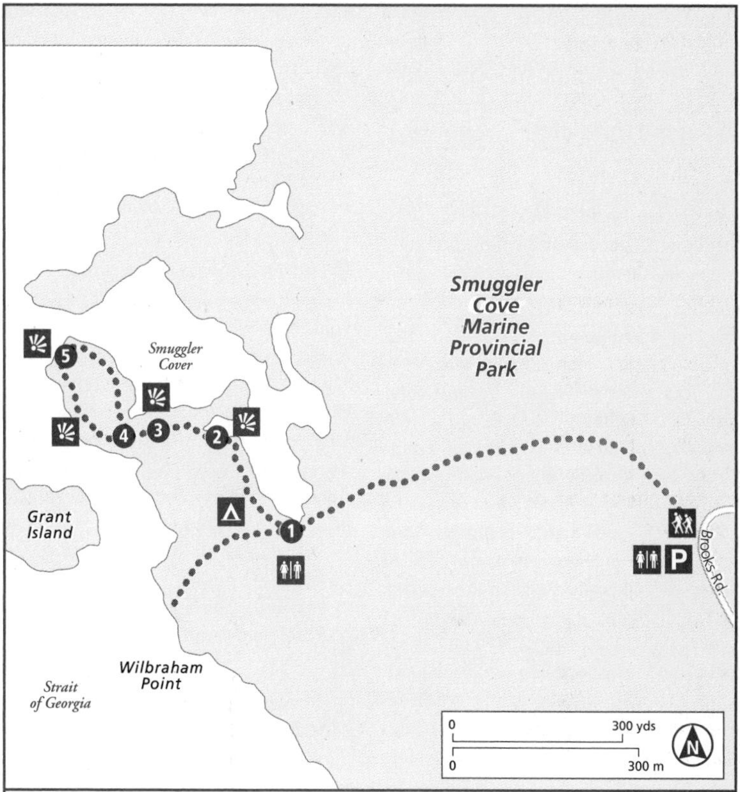

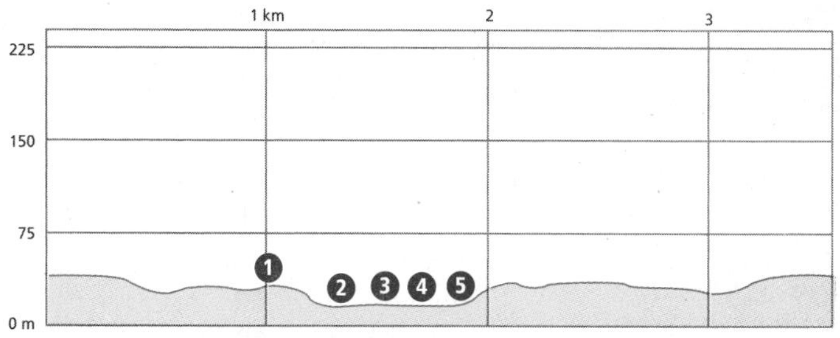

- N 49 30.684, W 123 56.947 (0 km): Trail head
- ❶ N 49 30.676, W 123 57.671 (1 km): Arrive at clearing and first glimpse of the ocean
- ❷ N 49 30.761, W 123 57.831 (1.3 km): Go right and follow rocky route towards the water
- ❸ N 49 30.809, W 123 57.916 (1.5 km): Second viewpoint and interpretative board
- ❹ N 49 30.777, W 123 57.976 (1.6 km): Follow trail to large mossy bluff
- ❺ N 49 30.885, W 123 58.087 (1.8 km): Take second trail on your right on return journey to visit Mi-La Miwala viewpoint

Back to the trail, noticing the variety of mosses that carpet the boulders and trees. The water is on your right. Through a clearing, view a lone cabin on an island. A short trail leads down to a rocky beach where you can swim in high tide.

3 Second Viewpoint The trail meanders above the shoreline, where you overlook a gentle, shallow bay. Here, an interpretive board shows how the First Nations people fished by constructing a net across the bay's mouth and then spearing the rock cod and herring.

4 Third Viewpoint Follow the trail to a large mossy bluff adorned with Arbutus trees. Take a seat on a log and enjoy your surroundings. The small isle to your left often has colonies of Oystercatchers—easily identified by their bright orange beaks—while the larger island boasts an old cottage tucked into the trees. Look across Welcome Passage to the verdant island of Thormanby dotting the horizon. It has a community of summer cottages and one of the region's best sandy beaches—a favorite playground for locals who boat over for the day or weekend. (Buccaneer Bay, on Thormanby, is one of the best places to drop anchor, dine, and watch the sunset.) The large island to the north is Texada Island. Looking directly down and left from your perch on the boulder is a driftwood strewn beach—this is where you will arrive if you take the short trail that passes the pit toilet.

From here, go right, with the large Arbutus on your left; you have started the loop at the end of the trail. The configuration of this hike is linear with a short circuit that skirts the shoreline at the end. With the water on your left, you soon come to an interpretive board with interesting facts about the Arbutus tree that each summer loses its shiny red bark. Stroll the edge of the park, enjoying the sound of gentle waves (or crashing ones, depending on the day) and ocean views. Don't forget to look up—it's not unusual to see soaring eagles, hawks, and vultures. There are several small bays that invite you to scramble down the boulders and check out tidal pools.

5 Mi-La Miwala Viewpoint Head back to the trail, keeping the water on your left. One more viewpoint has an interpretive board on the eagle (called Kaykw, the lord of the sky, by the Sechelt people.) Then, follow the trail to retrace your route. Back at the clearing, take the second trail on your right (past the outhouse) for a 5-minute walk down to a beach. If you prefer to picnic right beside the ocean, this is the place. It is tucked away, has lots of interesting driftwood, and is usually vacant. Return to the original trail and go right to the parking lot.

TAKE A BREAK

The trail leads onto a granite bluff, above the narrow opening of Smuggler Cove. If this is a summer day, enjoy the boat traffic—sailboats, pleasure yachts, small motor boats, catamarans, and kayaks. Clearly, this is a slice of boater heaven. (Sometimes, you see yachts the size of small hotels, complete with a heli landing pad.) An interpretive board says the Sechelt Nation welcomed other tribes here; *Mi-La Miwala* is the Sechelt word for welcome. This is an excellent spot to have a snack or picnic before your return.

13 KILLARNEY LAKE, BOWEN ISLAND

Difficulty rating: Easy
Distance: 9km (5.6 miles) round trip
Time: 2–3 hr.
Elevation gain: 8km (5 miles)
Costs/permits: None
Pet friendly: Yes (dogs must be leashed)
Best time to go: Spring and fall
Website: www.bowen-island-bc.com
Recommended map: North Vancouver 92G/6

Trail head GPS: N 49 22.792, W 123 20.032
Trail head directions: Travel via Upper Levels Highway to Horseshoe Bay in West Vancouver to catch the ferry to Bowen Island. Park the car or arrive by bus and go as a foot passenger on the small car ferry (C$8). Arrive 20 minutes later at picture-perfect Snug Cove, Bowen Island.

Bowen Island is a perfect day trip. The charming village and historic buildings of Snug Cove harken back to more peaceful days. Formerly a resort in the 1920s, today you can kayak, swim, fish, and (of course) hike. This idyllic hike will not challenge but will charm you, not to mention provide an awesome ocean view near its completion. Pack a picnic, as there is the perfect bench along the way.

Upon arrival, walk up Bowen Trunk Road (also called Government Rd.) and enjoy the quaint village. The restored Union Steamship Company store today houses a parks office where you can pick up a map of Crippen Regional Park (Killarney Lake is within the park). If you need a morning java fix, there are opportunities here. Continue up the road to Miller Road and turn right. Pass houses and green space until you see a sign across the road on your left.

❶ Sign to Killarney Lake Follow the green and yellow signs to the Fish Hatchery, Meadows, and Killarney Lake into the woods. The wide, even trail goes through open forest and ferns. Notice springboard markers on huge weathered cedar trees. In early fall, the trail is crunchy and thick with maple leaves. Pass a huge stump carved out by a lightning burn and soon take a footbridge over Terminal Creek. Salmon spawn in this stream, and a hatchery is tucked away to your left.

The trail comes to a T and points you right to Killarney Lake. Within minutes, you are in an open meadow, with a large equestrian ring on your right. Walk through the grassy field and into the alder forest. Go over another footbridge at a swampy area where skunk cabbage and grasses thrive. In about 20 minutes, you intersect another trail. Go left.

❷ Killarney Creek Trail Follow the trail left uphill. On a sunny, early autumn day, the sun filters through the trees—maple, cedar, hemlock, and occasionally groves of alder. Killarney Lake is located in Crippen Regional Park. Keep watch for herons, ducks, kingfishers, and deer. Follow the trail over Magee Road (a narrow road, there is a yellow gate here), and soon you sight the lake through the trees.

❸ Beginning of Killarney Lake Loop This is the beginning of the 4km (2½-mile) loop around the lake. You can go right or left, but take the right fork.

Finds Grab a Paddle!

For a "pinch me, it's perfect" moment, get in a kayak here. Rent if you have experience or take the full-day guided trip to the Pasley Islands, a cluster of eight wilderness gems off the west coast of Bowen. Rentals and lessons are available from Bowen Island Sea Kayaking (✆ **800/947-9266;** www.bowenislandkayaking.com). Rentals are C$45 for 3 hours, and tours range from C$65 to C$130.

The trail narrows and begins to rise and fall, but there is still easy footing. In a few places, you get views of the lake, surrounded by woods with a few cabins nestled into the hillside. You continue on the mostly uphill route, viewing some large stumps and tall trees. Cross another footbridge and continue uphill.

At a marker, you can divert left over a wooden bridge to a viewpoint that overlooks the lake. It is a marshy lake, with bulrushes and stands of dead trees giving it a somewhat eerie beauty even in the sunshine. This lake was once the water supply for Bowen.

Back on the main trail, it is only a few minutes before a boardwalk takes you across the northern end of the lake.

TAKE A BREAK If you are the only hikers here, a rustic bench in the middle of the boardwalk is a perfect spot for lunch. It rests in the sun, and the only sound is the whisper of the breeze through the marsh grass and perhaps the chatter of a saucy kingfisher as it dives for lunch.

From here, you follow the shoreline of the lake. There are a few boardwalks and footbridges; in places, the lily pad scenes on your left appear to have jumped off a Monet canvas. Just over a wooden bridge, stop at a rocky beach—the best place to let dogs swim if you have them along! In about 10 minutes, you arrive at the south end of the lake.

This is the Killarney Lake Picnic Area, and if you didn't have your lunch earlier, there are picnic tables and pit toilets here, although it is beside the road. There is also an information board with details about Crippen Regional Park and a map showing the wide variety of trails available. Continuing to walk with the lake on your left, you will see the tiny dam, built in the 1920s, just before you get back to where the loop trail began.

To return, with the lake at your back, go back on the main trail. However, when you get to Miller Road, cross the road and continue through the park to Bowen Memorial Garden (on the Crippen Regional Park map, this is called the Alder Grove Trail).

❹ Ocean Viewpoint Go through the large, wooden archway, which has memorial plaques on it, and climb out to the viewpoint. This lakeside trail now shows off a gorgeous ocean view! You are looking upon Deep Bay, which is dotted with pleasure boats, and then across Georgia Strait to the towering Coast Mountains. Down from the viewpoint, go through a second wooden archway and left to where the trail soon deposits you onto the road. Turn right to go back to the ferry terminal.

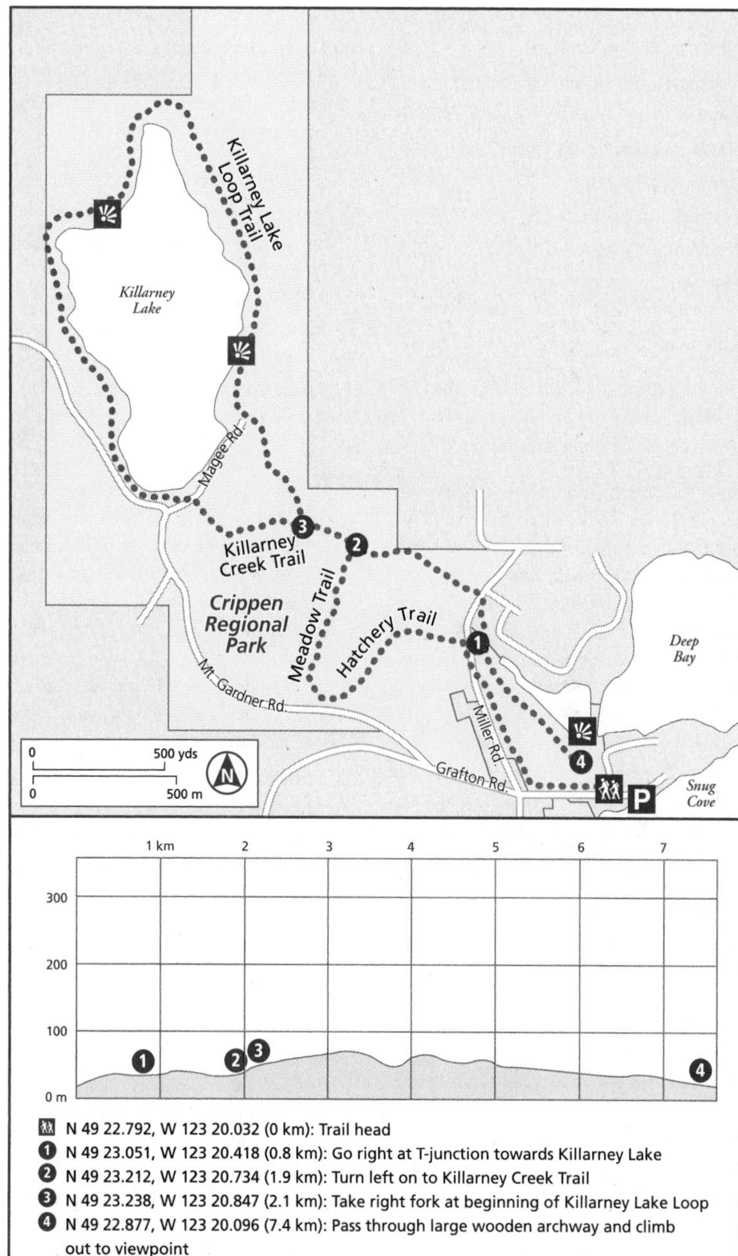

N 49 22.792, W 123 20.032 (0 km): Trail head

❶ N 49 23.051, W 123 20.418 (0.8 km): Go right at T-junction towards Killarney Lake

❷ N 49 23.212, W 123 20.734 (1.9 km): Turn left on to Killarney Creek Trail

❸ N 49 23.238, W 123 20.847 (2.1 km): Take right fork at beginning of Killarney Lake Loop

❹ N 49 22.877, W 123 20.096 (7.4 km): Pass through large wooden archway and climb out to viewpoint

14 MOUNT DANIEL ★★

Difficulty rating: Moderate

Distance: 2.5km (1.6 miles) round trip

Time: 1–1½ hr.

Elevation gain: 5km (3.1 miles)

Costs/permits: None

Best time to go: Spring or fall

Recommended map: NTS 92G/12

Website: www.sunshinecoasteh.com/penderharbour/parks/mt_daniel.htm

Trail head GPS: N 49 31.859, W 123 57.545

Trail head directions: Take the ferry from Horseshoe Bay in West Vancouver to Langdale on the Sunshine Coast. Follow signs to the Sunshine Coast Highway and head north towards Sechelt, approximately 27km (17 miles). Continue through Sechelt (the highway winds through the town) and drive about 38km (24 miles) to turn left on Garden Bay Road and drive just over 3km (1¾ miles) to the trail head on your left.

This hike is all about the view at the top. Most often, a panorama like this can only be enjoyed after hours and hours of hiking. This is a bonus after an hour's uphill; however, in places, footing may be slippery.

Thanks to the Rotary Club of Pender Harbour, there is information on the hike posted beside the road. Park here and walk (for about 10 min.) along the rough road known as the Old Dump Road; bear left where the road forks and continue along the trail where it narrows. Keep going uphill through a bit of clearing and spot the brown-and-white trail sign. After about another 5 minutes, the trail gets steep. You are surrounded by luxuriant ferns and mossy maples and evergreens. This traversing trail leads steadily uphill, occasionally leveling off for short sections. There are rocky areas where footing is tricky, especially if wet. Also, tree roots pepper this trail, in some places making natural stairs, but in other spots, they can be treacherous if wet. In a few places, you see blue sky through the trees and feel you are near the top. Don't get excited, you have another 30 to 40 minutes of climbing.

❶ **First Summit** You come to a spot, beside a large boulder, where it looks like you have lost the trail. Climb up the large boulder and, on your right, follow up another boulder. This spot is often noted as the First Summit of Mount Daniel; however, due to growth, there isn't much of a view anymore. Go back down and continue down the boulder—it is narrow footing—to a flat area for a short section before climbing again. (As you go down the boulder, the trail is obvious below.) Then, you follow the trail straight ahead for the "wow" moment.

❷ **Summit with a View** Walk out, carefully, towards the edge of a high cliff or settle on a ridge above the drop-off to take in the gorgeous panorama. You are looking down at Irvine's Landing and Madeira Park, a hodgepodge of islands and peninsulas in a natural harbor. Although not pristine, it is dotted with small communities, neighborhoods, and marinas, tucked into the greenery. It's a beautiful sight, especially when you look beyond to the deep blue Pacific Ocean and the coastline of the Sunshine Coast that fades into the horizon. Looking west, the large island is Texada. On a clear day, you feel like you can see forever, but we've been up here in drifting cloud, which is also beautiful in a mystical way.

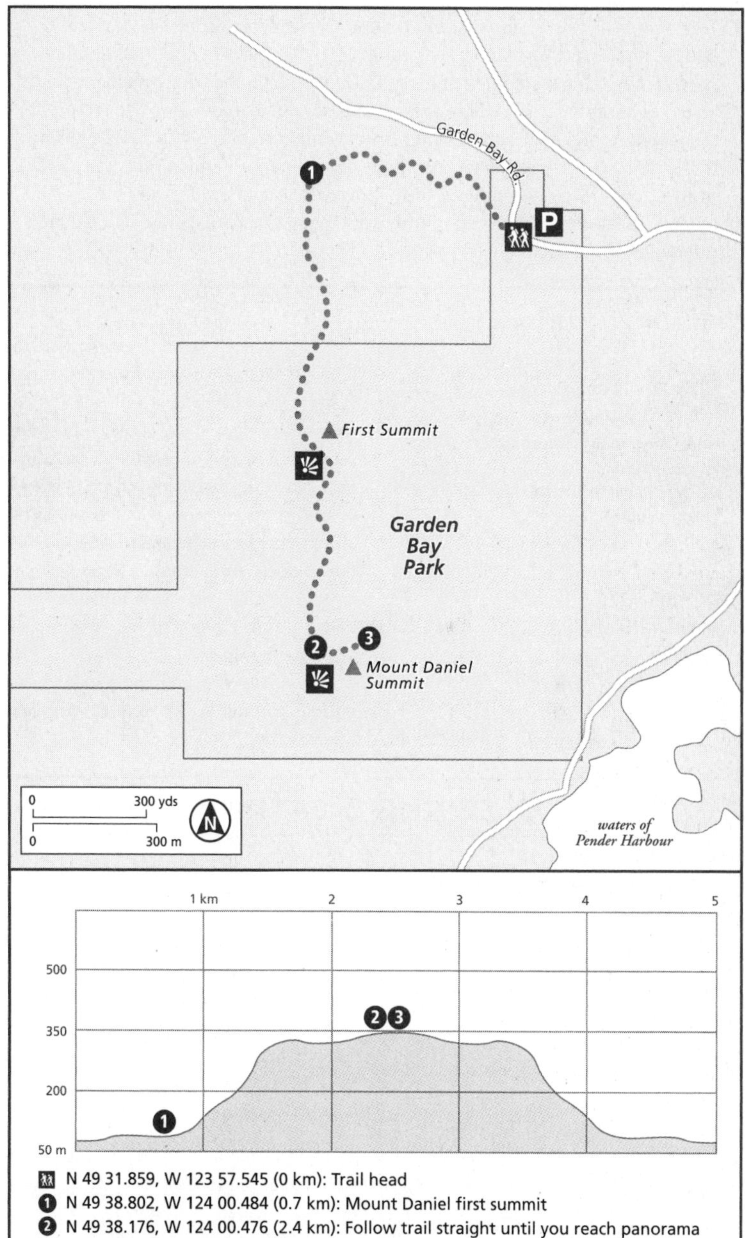

N 49 31.859, W 123 57.545 (0 km): Trail head

❶ N 49 38.802, W 124 00.484 (0.7 km): Mount Daniel first summit

❷ N 49 38.176, W 124 00.476 (2.4 km): Follow trail straight until you reach panorama

❸ N 49 38.185, W 124 00.353 (2.5 km): Take trail on your right on journey back down

Fun Facts **Moonstruck**

Take a moment and realize that this is a special place for Sechelt First Nations people. Known as *Kwiss Cham,* the peak of Mount Daniel was known as a rite of passage for young women. At puberty, the legend says, the young maidens would arrive at this peak, where stones were laid out in "moon rings" to represent the moon. As night fell, each young woman would caress every stone as if talking to the moon in a sacred lunar ritual. Some say remnants of moon rings can be spotted, but we've never noticed them. However, should you feel you see a moon ring, the First Nations people here ask that you do not disturb it; it is considered sacred to them.

SPECTACULAR LOOKOUT If you don't suffer from vertigo and love that "edge of the world" feeling, sit on the edge of the cliff for your snack or picnic, and enjoy looking way down at the toy-size boats and buildings below.

3 Ridge Trail To explore further, go back down the hill and watch for the trail going right.

Walk along it for 5 to 10 minutes and then climb up to a clearing. You are looking out on the Caren Mountain Range; there are a few *inukshuks* constructed by hikers. Up here, you watch eagles, turkey vultures, and hawks soar—they are beside you, rather than above—and, on a warm summer day, the click-click of grasshoppers has a mesmerizing effect. There is plenty of space here to climb around—adventurers like to scramble up and down the boulders, but always be aware that you are near a cliff edge. It is usually easy to find an isolated perch and bask in the scenery on your own.

Return the way you came, taking care on the roots and rocky sections, especially if it is damp.

SLEEPING & EATING

ACCOMMODATIONS

Capilano RV Park If you are an RVer, sites don't come any better than these. Located beside the Capilano River, close to Park Royal's 200 shops, within walking distance of beaches and parks, there is a swimming pool, green spaces, a Laundromat, free showers, paved roads, travel information and assistance, plus Internet connections.

295 Tomahawk Ave., North Vancouver, V7P 1C5. ✆ **604/987-4722.** www.capilanorvpark.com. 208 sites. C$25–C$52 per site. MC, V. **Close to:** St. Mark's Summit, Lighthouse Park, Grouse Grind, Capilano Regional Park.

Finds **The Eco-Shed** This sustainably designed studio, a 10-minute walk from Snug Cove, has many treats, including a bottle of chilled BC wine in the small fridge. Island-roasted coffee, homemade muffins, and fruit are delivered for breakfast. Your accommodation is the subject of a much-lauded eco-memoir, *Almost Green* (Greystone/Skyhorse), by James Glave, your host.

985 Seaview Place, Bowen Island, VON 1G0. ✆ **604/947-9268.** http://eco-shed.ca. 1 unit. C$150 double. **Close to:** Killarney Lake.

★ **Harbourview Retreat B&B** There really is a harbor view here, as well as views of Stanley Park, downtown, and the North shore mountains, all seen from your private deck, as well as from each serene, elegant room. Make yourself a snack anytime or relax in the hot tub in the lush garden.

4675 W. 4th Ave., Vancouver, V6R 1R6. ✆ **866/221-7273** or 604/221-7273. www.ahvr.com. 3 units. High season C$220–C$240 double; low season C$170–C$190 double. MC, V. **Close to:** Point Grey Foreshore, Pacific Spirit Park.

(Kids) **Holiday Inn Hotel & Suites** Great views, comfortable rooms (some with kitchenettes), and proximity to many of North Vancouver's attractions, as well as downtown, this hotel has friendly helpful staff and many amenities.

700 Old Lillooet Rd., North Vancouver, V73 2H5. ✆ **877/985-3111** or 604/985-3111. Fax: 604/985-0857. www.hinorthvancouver.com. 162 units. C$150–C$360 double. AE, DC, DISC, MC, V. **Close to:** Lynn Canyon Park.

(Finds) (Kids) **Hostelling International Vancouver-Jericho Beach** Sleep at the beach surrounded by expansive lawns beside Jericho Beach. Formerly a military barracks, accommodation is spartan but well-maintained. Dorms, and also private rooms (book well ahead), have shared washrooms and shared kitchen facilities. A cafeteria serves breakfast and dinner. Open May to September only.

1515 Discovery St., Vancouver, V6R 4K5. ✆ **888/203-4303** or 604/224-3208. Fax 604/224-4852. www.hihostels.ca. High season C$24–C$68 members, C$28–C$76 non-members; shoulder season C$20–C$60 members, C$24–C$68 non-members; youth (6–11) C$10; children 6 and under stay free. MC, V. Closed Oct–Apr. Reservations essential. **Close to:** Point Grey Foreshore, Pacific Spirit Park.

★ **A Lakeside Retreat** Three B&B suites and three self-contained cottages are snuggled into the woods around North Lake. Enjoy the tranquility of a paddle on the lake, fishing, or quiet time on a private deck. The cottages have full kitchens and are perfect for families.

6054 Egmont Rd, Egmont, VON 1NO. ✆ **866/883-9234** or 604/883-9234. www.alakesideretreat.com. 6 units. C$159–C$179 B&B suite; C$189–C$299 cottage; weekly rates available. MC, V. **Close to:** Skookumchuck Narrows Provincial Park, Smuggler Cove Provincial Park.

★ **Lighthouse Park B&B** Tucked down a lane right near the park entrance, fringed by forest, surrounded by gardens, is this West Coast home with two suites. Each has a private entrance and lovely touches like robes and sherry; both are cozy and tastefully appointed. You'll love the breakfasts, served in a dining room that opens to a large deck.

4875 Water Lane, West Vancouver, V7W 1K4. ✆ **800/926-0262** or 604/926-5959. www.lighthouseretreat.com. 2 units. C$175–C$195 suite. AE, MC, V. **Close to:** Lighthouse Park, St. Mark's Summit.

★★ (Finds) **Listel Vancouver** The work of well-known artists decorates this delightful, inviting boutique hotel in the heart of the bustling West End. Accommodation is quietly elegant, soothing in its sophistication and includes literary masterpieces for bedtime reading between top-quality bedding.

1300 Robson St., Vancouver, V6E 1C5. ✆ **800/663-5491** or 604/684-8461. Fax 604/684-7092. www.listelvancouver.com. 129 units. C$220–C$359 double; C$399 suite. AE, DC, DISC, MC, V. **Close to:** Stanley Park.

(Value) **Lodge at the Old Dorm** This lovingly restored heritage inn—it dates to the 1940s, when it housed staff of the Union Steamship Company—conveys comfort with every detail. Enjoy the archival photos and art deco touches, and become enamored with the down duvets, comfy armchairs, and in some rooms, soaker tubs.

460 Melmore Rd., Bowen Island, VON 1GO. ✆ **604/947-0947.** www.lodgeattheolddorm.com. 7 units. C$95-C$140 double. MC, V. Closed over Christmas. **Close to:** Killarney Lake.

★ Kids Value **Oceanside Hotel** Minutes from the seawall, Stanley Park, and the pleasures of the West End, this comfortable, friendly hotel quickly feels like home. Spacious units all have separate bedrooms and living rooms, as well as a full kitchen, all recently renovated.

1847 Pendrell St., Vancouver, V6G 1T3. ✆ **877/506-2326** or 604/682-5641. Fax 604/687-2340. www.oceanside-hotel.com. 24 units. C$120–C$150 double; extra person C$20 per night; children 5 and under stay free. AE, MC, V. **Close to:** Stanley Park.

★★ **River Rock Casino Resort** A little luxury occasionally is good for you, and whether you like gaming or not, you will love all the action. Everything here has great style: from top entertainers, to the choice of restaurants, to the spas, to watching the river traffic, to the elegant suites.

8811 River Rd., Richmond, V6X 3P8. ✆ **866/748-3718** or 604/247-8900. Fax 604/207-2641. www.riverrock.com. 222 units. C$169–C$289 double. AE, MC, V. **Close to:** Iona Beach.

Finds Kids **Ruby Lake Resort and Rainforest Spa** Comfy cottages border a wildlife bird sanctuary; a deluxe, romantic suite opens to the lake; and safari-style tents are tucked into the woods. This family-run resort has been around for decades but keeps changing with the times. Cottages all have kitchen facilities, decks, and country pine furnishings. Two tents are family style with bunks.

Site 20, Camp 25, RR#1 Hwy. 1, Madeira Park, VON 2HO. ✆ **800/717-6611** or 604/883-2269. www.rubylakeresort.com. 23 units. C$149–C$177 cottage; C$238 deluxe suite; C$89–C$99 tent. MC, V. **Close to:** Mount Daniel, Skoomchuk Narrows Provincial Park.

★ **Sunshine Coast Resort Hotel & Marina** This hillside resort overlooking Garden Bay exudes the ambience of a West Coast Riviera as lawns terrace down to the picturesque marina. All rooms have views of the ocean and Mount Daniel, as well as kitchen facilities, fireplaces, and soaker tubs. It is peaceful, yet close to outdoor adventures.

12695 Sunshine Coast Highway, Madeira Park, VON 2H0. ✆ **604/883-9177.** www.sunshinecoast-resort.com. 16 units. C$150-C$495 double. AE, MC, V. **Close to:** Mount Daniel.

★ **Thistledown House Bed and Breakfast** A gracious 1920s heritage home that combines the woodsy feel of the mountains with the elegance of the finest of inns. Indulge yourself, as the touches of private garden patios, Persian rugs, stained glass windows, and European pastries served at afternoon tea make this a holiday in itself.

3910 Capilano Rd., North Vancouver, V7R 4J2. ✆ **888/633-7173** or 604/986-7173. www.thistle-down.com. 6 units. C$165–C$295 double. MC, V. Closed Dec and Jan. **Close to:** Capilano River Regional Park, Grouse Grind.

Value **University of British Columbia Conference Centre** Family groups or individuals can both find clean and comfortable (although not luxurious) one- to six-bedroom suites. All have kitchens and private bathrooms, and some suites have sweeping views of the city. Luxury suites and hostel accommodation also available. About 20 minutes from downtown, surrounded by a lush campus near beaches and many attractions.

5961 Student Union Blvd., Vancouver, V6T 2C9. ✆ **888/822-1030** or 604/822-1000. Fax 604/822-1001. www.ubcconferences.com/accommodation. 1,900 units. C$50–C$150 suite. AE, MC, V. **Close to:** Pacific Spirit Park, Point Grey Foreshore.

★ (Kids) **West Coast Wilderness Lodge** The location overlooking ocean, islands, and mountains, plus the friendliness of the owners, makes this a special stay. The cottages hidden in the woods maintain a rustic feel, but with first-class amenities, including a three-room spa. The lodge is a hub for adventure tours such as heli-hiking.

6649 Maple Rd., Egmont, V0N 1N0. ✆ **877/988-3838** or 604/883-3667. www.wcwl.com. 20 units (40 by the end of 2010). C$195-C$310 ocean-view suite; C$155-C$258 forest-view suite. AE, MC, V. **Close to:** Skookumchuck Narrows Provincial Park, Mount Daniel.

RESTAURANTS

★ (Value) **Arm's Reach Bistro** WEST COAST/FUSION Everyone loves this friendly eatery with an upscale menu. Expect to find fresh seafood, great Italian, and what about that—shades of India—butter chicken? Service is down-home friendly, and the view of Indian Arm from the huge deck makes this a memorable visit.

4390 Gallant Ave., Deep Cove. ✆ **604/929-7442.** www.armsreachbistro.com. Brunch/lunch C$5–C$18; dinner C$24–C$30. AE, MC, V. Daily 11am–11 pm. **Close to:** Mount Seymour.

★ **Capilano Heights Chinese Restaurant** CHINESE This restaurant has been across the road from Capilano River Park since 1972, and one bite of their lemon chicken will help you understand why, or fill your hungry hiking stomach with Chow Mein. Eat in the attractive atrium with views of the garden.

5020 Capilano Rd., North Vancouver. ✆ **604/987-9511.** www.capheights.ca. Reservations recommended. Main courses C$10–C$20. AE, MC, V. Mon–Fri noon–9pm; Sat & Sun 4:30–9pm. **Close to:** Capilano River Regional Park, Grouse Grind.

Crave Beachside FUSION This is the second location of a very popular Vancouver restaurant that boasts trendy ambience and friendly service with lots of intriguing options. Head for the back deck on a warm day. A great sampler is the ahi tempura rolls. For dinner, be decadent and have the short rib *poutine.*

1362 Marine Dr., West Vancouver. ✆ **604/926-3332.** Brunch $2–$13; lunch $5–$24; dinner $9–$26. AE, MC, V. Tue–Fri 11am–10pm; Sat and Sun 9am–10pm. **Close to:** Lighthouse Park, St. Mark's Summit.

★ **The Fish House** SEAFOOD/WEST COAST Once a sports pavilion, this charming restaurant retains the peaceful ambiance of bygone days. Set amid trees with views of the tennis courts and a heronry, the restaurant is famous for its fresh oysters and flaming prawns, but the ahi tuna Diane brings many patrons back for more.

8901 Stanley Park Dr. (by the tennis courts). ✆ **604/681-7275.** www.fishhousestanleypark.com. Reservations recommended. Main courses C$12–C$30. AE, MC, V. Daily lunch 11:30am–2:30pm; afternoon tea from 2–4pm; dinner from 5pm. **Close to:** Stanley Park.

(Finds) (Kids) **The Flying Beaver Pub** CANADIAN This kid-friendly pub perches beside the Fraser River, where float-plane traffic provides uniquely West Coast entertainment. From the patio, you get views of Vancouver Island, the Gulf Islands, and the Straight of Georgia. Kids are allowed on the patio and in one dining section. Friendly service. Excellent fish and chips, and Cobb salad.

N. end of No. 2 Road Bridge, Richmond. ✆ **604/273-0278.** www.markjamesgroup.com/flyingbeaver.html. Main courses C$10–C$20. AE, MC, V. Daily 11am–midnight. **Close to:** Iona Beach.

(Kids) **The Galley Patio and Grill** This popular spot at Jericho Beach is utilitarian, but with its wraparound scenery, decorating would be a waste. The panoramic view from the patio is awe inspiring—from Vancouver Island, the mountains, Stanley Park, and downtown Vancouver, the views just keep on going. Angus beef burgers and the wild salmon burger are superb, along with the sunsets.

1000 Discovery St., Vancouver. ✆ **604/222-1331.** www.thegalley.ca. Main courses C$7–C$12; kids menu available. AE, MC, V. Spring–fall daily 11am–sunset; summer daily 9am–10pm; winter Sat & Sun only 11am–sunset. **Close to:** Point Grey Foreshore, Pacific Spirit Park.

Garden Bay Pub & Restaurant WEST COAST/PUB FARE Nestled into a sleepy community at the end of the road overlooking the bay, this has been a treasure since 1932! Sit on the sunny deck for lunch, enjoy live jazz in the pub come nightfall, or chat with locals. Try the rack of lamb for dinner.

4958 Lyons Rd., Garden Bay. ✆ **604/883-9919.** www.gardenbaypub.com. Brunch and lunch C$9–C$12; dinner C$12–C$32. AE, MC, V. Daily 11am–2pm and 5–9pm. **Close to:** Mount Daniel.

★★ **Inlets** WEST COAST/SEAFOOD Located at West Coast Wilderness Resort, go for the view, then rave about the fare. For breakfast, everything from intriguing granolas to seafood eggs Bennie; when in season, have the huge spot prawns for lunch and the pumpkin seed crusted halibut for dinner. In warm weather, have a nightcap on the deck with, arguably, one of the world's best vistas.

6649 Maple Rd., Egmont. ✆ **877/988-3838** or 604/883-3667. www.wcwl.com. Breakfast C$12; lunch C$12–C$18; dinner C$28–C$38. AE, MC, V. May–Oct 31 daily 7:30am–8:30pm, Nov–Apr Sat and Sun 7:30am–8:30pm. **Close to:** Skookumchuck Narrows Provincial Park, Mount Daniel.

(Finds) (Kids) **Lynn Canyon Café** CANADIAN You must visit this wonderful wood and glass structure, designed by architect David Nairn. Sit in or out, enjoy the view, and feast on a Canyon Burger for lunch or Thai curry prawns on rice for dinner. Or do takeout and find a pleasant picnic spot.

Inside Lynn Valley Park, near parking lot. ✆ **604/984-9311.** www.lynnvalleycentre.ca/Lynn%20Canyon%20Cafe.htm. Lunch C$7–C$10; dinner C$12–C$20. MC, V. Mon–Tues 9am–5pm, Wed–Sun 9am–9pm; dinner served on Fri and Sat 5–9pm. **Close to:** Lynn Canyon Park.

Ruby Lake Resort Restaurant NORTHERN ITALIAN In summer, reserve a table on the sunny deck to view wildlife around the lagoon—we've seen eagles swoop by and a bear on the shoreline. The owner/Italian chef presents local products at their best, from freshly caught fish to just-picked produce. Have the *penne con fungi* when Chanterelles are in season.

Site 20, Camp 25, RR#1 Hwy. 1, Madeira Park. ✆ **800/717-6611** or 604/883-2269. www.rubylakeresort.com. Lunch C$5–C$17; dinner C$17–C$35. MC, V. May–Oct lunch noon–3pm, dinner 5–9pm; Nov–Apr Sat and Sun, dinner 5–9pm. **Close to:** Mount Daniel, Skoomchuk Narrows Provincial Park.

Salmon House on the Hill BC SEAFOOD Although it occasionally gets mixed reviews—it has been around since 1976—the alder grilled salmon is renowned, and the views are astounding. After a hike, go for the Coho Room tapas—we recommend the Gulf Island mussels. Or get gussied up for dinner and imbibe in BC fresh fare and a great wine selection.

2229 Folkestone Way, West Vancouver. ✆ **604/926-3212.** www.salmonhouse.com. Reservations recommended. Lunch C$14–C$22; dinner C$28–C$32. AE, MC, V. Mon–Sat lunch 11:30am–2pm, dinner after 5pm; Sun brunch 11am-2pm, dinner after 5pm. **Close to:** St. Mark's Summit, Lighthouse Park.

★ **Savary Island Pie Company** CAFE Located in the cheerful village of Ambleside, this café exudes the atmosphere of a New York coffee house, but has much more than coffee. People drive for miles to purchase a pie, but you can have a light lunch or early dinner, as well.

1533 Marine Dr., West Vancouver. ✆ **604/926-4021.** spico@telus.net. Whole pies C$20–C$24; meals C$8–C$15. MC, V. Daily 5:30am–7pm. **Close to:** Lighthouse Park, St. Mark's Summit.

★★ **Sequoia Grill** WEST COAST Dress up and revel in this picture-perfect setting. Perched above the ocean, backed by towering trees, this elegant grill personifies West Coast, featuring mainly local ingredients. Sunsets are spectacular, as is the cedar plank salmon with a maple whisky glaze or, on a cooler evening, braised short ribs.

Stanley Park Dr. at Ferguson Point. ✆ **800/280-9893** or 604/669-3281. www.vancouverdine.com/sgrill/home.html. Reservations essential. Lunch C$7–C$28; dinner C$17–C$36. AE, MC, V. Lunch Mon–Fri 11:30am–2:30pm; dinner daily from 5pm. **Close to:** Stanley Park.

★ **The Snug Café** ORGANIC/FRESH CASUAL FARE Plop down at a picnic table, chat with locals, savor organic coffee (or tea), and perhaps pick up a boxed lunch for the hike. A sandwich, salad, and juice costs about C$10 to C$12. Everything here is freshly made; the chocolate chip cookies are to die for. The service is quick and friendly.

443B Bowen Trunk Rd., Bowen Island. ✆ **604/947-0402.** Breakfast C$8; lunch C$7–C$12. MC, V. Mon–Fri 5am–4pm; Sat and Sun 7am–4pm. **Close to:** Killarney Lake.

(Kids) **The Stanley Park Pavilion** CANADIAN Set in the Rose Garden at the park entrance, this is a popular, relaxing place to lunch on the large, flower-filled deck. The menu features burgers, fish and chips, and salads. The Canuck Beef Burger is a worthy star feature if you are really hungry.

610 Pipeline Rd., Stanley Park. ✆ **604/602-3088.** www.stanleyparkpavilion.com. Main courses C$8.50–C$15. AE, MC, V. Daily 11:30am–5pm. Summer only. **Close to:** Stanley Park.

(Kids) (Value) **University Golf Club** CANADIAN Eating here is like dining in the park, surrounded by huge cedars and rolling lawns. Sit by the window or, in summer, on the patio overlooking the flower gardens. Try the creamy wild mushroom ravioli to complete your park experience, with lots of wild mushrooms in Pacific Spirit Park.

5185 University Blvd., Vancouver. ✆ **604/224-7799.** www.universitygolf.com/dine. Main courses C$15–C$24. AE, MC, V. Daily 7:30am–11pm. **Close to:** Pacific Spirit Park, Point Grey Foreshore.

5 Vancouver Island Hikes

by Amanda Castleman

Fringed by the wild Pacific Ocean and pierced by snow-capped peaks, Vancouver Island offers some of the coast's best hiking. Roughly the size of Holland, it weighs in as the largest island on the western side of North America, so there's plenty to explore.

The bottom of this long otter-shaped land mass fits into the notch of Washington State. Its Mediterranean-type climate—Canada's mildest—encourages dense tangles of rare temperate rainforest. Among the arbutus and red cedar stalk one of the world's densest concentrations of cougars and black bears. But Vancouver Island isn't all wilds: The chic provincial capital anchors its southeastern tip. Famous for high teas and British pubs, Victoria packs a lot of sophistication into a small city center.

An interurban path begins there, then stretches 55km (34 miles) to the opposite coast. Part of the Trans-Canada Trail, the Galloping Goose traces an old Canadian National rail line that originated in the 1920s and is named for one if its noisy, gas-powered cars.

North lies the country's most popular path: the legendary West Coast Trail. This tricky 75km (46.6-mile) route features cable cars, suspension bridges, and ladder complexes that can soar 25 to 35 stories. But it rewards trekkers with waterfalls, eagles, surf, seals, sandstone bluffs, and tide pools brimming with sea stars, urchins, and sponges—not to mention serous bragging rights! The nearby Juan de Fuca Marine Trail offers a taste of the same landscape at a fraction of the price, time, and fuss.

From the sharp fang of Mount Finlayson to flat, cove-pocketed Newcastle Island, the terrain varies wildly. More hardcore hikers head inland to the steep, snowy ridges of Strathcona Park, often compared to the Alps or Norwegian fjords. Those who like to mix in kayaking, fine dining, and storm watching gravitate towards the Tofino area. Known for its wildcat cold-water surfers, the artsy town provides a base for exploring the Pacific Rim National Park. Just south of the reserve, the Wild Pacific Trail provides easy access to stunning views of Barkley Sound and the Broken Group Islands. North of Tofino curls Meares Island, where the largest act of civil disobedience in Canadian history saved ancient groves. The Big Cedar Trail's star is a tree known as The Hanging Garden. Estimated to be 2,000 years old, it has an 18m (59-ft.) circumference.

A similar upscale-bohemian vibe dominates the 200-strong Gulf Island archipelago, and its southern extension: Washington's San Juan Islands. Eclectic Salt Spring Island even issues its own currency. Explore its pioneer history with a hike through Ruckle Provincial Park, where turkeys still flock in the homestead's orchard. Or dip down into the States to the maritime prairie that hosted the non-violent Pig War: American Camp on San Juan Island.

Some pleasures remain constant, happily, throughout the Vancouver Island area. Intensely "foodie," the region boasts an unusual number of top-notch restaurants, many of which source local, organic, seasonal ingredients. Take a page from their book at a roadside "honesty stand": drop cash in the jar and walk away with honey, flowers, veggies, and jams. Even clocks slip into an easy groove here, as "island time" takes over. Things may not run to schedule, but most visitors are too charmed to care.

ESSENTIALS

GETTING THERE

By Plane

Most visitors arrive via a connecting flight from either **Vancouver International Airport** (✆ **604/207-7077;** www.yvr.ca) or **Sea-Tac International Airport** in Seattle (✆ **206/433-5388;** www.seatac.org). Airlines flying into the rapidly expanding **Victoria International Airport** (✆ **250/953-7500;** www.victoriaairport.com) include **Air Canada** (✆ **888/247-2262;** www.aircanada.ca), **Horizon Air** (✆ **800/547-9308;** www.alaskaair.com), and **WestJet** (✆ **888/937-8538;** www.westjet.com). Planes land near the BC Ferries terminal in Sidney, 26km (16 miles) north of Victoria off Hwy. 17. This route heads south to Victoria, becoming Douglas St. where it enters downtown.

Airport bus service, operated by **AKAL Airport** (✆ **877/386-2525** or 250/386-2526; www.victoriaairportshuttle.com), takes about 45 minutes to get into town. Buses leave from the airport daily, every 30 minutes from 4:30am to midnight. The adult fare is C$15 one way. Drop-offs and pickups are made at most Victoria area hotels. **Yellow Cabs** (✆ **800/808-6881** or 250/381-2222) and **Blue Bird Cabs** (✆ **800/665-7055** or 250/382-4235) make airport runs. It costs about C$50 one way, plus tip.

Several car-rental firms have desks at the Victoria International Airport, including **Avis** (✆ **800/879-2847** or 250/656-6033; www.avis.com), **Budget** (✆ **800/668-9833** or 250/953-5300; www.budgetvictoria.com), **Hertz** (✆ **800/654-3131** or 250/656-2312; www.hertz.com), and **National (Tilden)** (✆ **800/227-7368** or 250/656-2541; www.nationalcar.com). Car reservations are recommended from June to September and during peak travel times on holiday weekends.

Float planes service terminals in Victoria's Inner Harbor, connecting to Seattle, Vancouver, and far-flung points on the island, such as Tofino, Bamfield, and Campbell River. Carriers include **Hyack Air** (✆ **250/384-2499;** www.hyackair.com), **Kenmore** (✆ **866/435-9524** or 425/486-1257; www.kenmoreair.com) and **Harbour Air** (✆ **800/665-0212** or 250/384-2215; www.harbour-air.com).

By Train

Trains arrive at Victoria's **VIA Rail Station,** 450 Pandora Ave., near the Johnson Street Bridge (✆ **888/842-7245;** www.viarail.com).

By Bus

The **Victoria Bus Depot** is at 700 Douglas St. (behind the Fairmont Empress Hotel). **Pacific Coach Lines** (✆ **800/661-1725** or 250/385-4411; www.pacificcoach.com) offers daily service to and from Vancouver, and includes the ferry trip across the Georgia Strait between Tsawwassen and Sidney. **Greyhound Coach Lines/Island Coach Lines** (✆ **800/661-8747** or 250/385-4411; www.greyhound.ca) connects travellers up-island daily to Nanaimo, Port Alberni, Campbell River, and Port Hardy. The **West Coast Trail Express** runs from Victoria and Nanaimo to the Juan de Fuca and West Coast trail heads from May 1 to September 30 (✆ **888/999-2288** or 250/477-8700; www.trailbus.com).

By Ferry

BC Ferries offers crossings from the mainland to various points on Vancouver Island (✆ **888/BCFERRY** [888/223-3779] in BC outside the Victoria dialing area or 250/386-3431; www.bcferries.com). For more information, see the section "Getting There" in chapter 3.

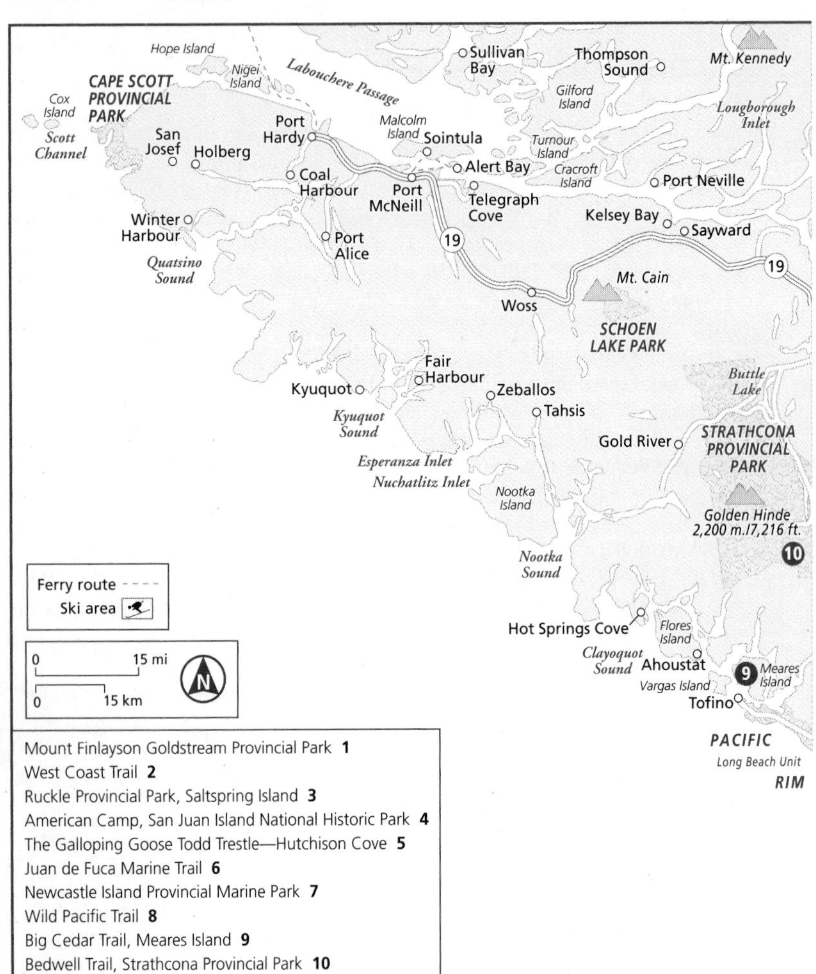

VISITOR INFORMATION

The **Tourism Victoria Visitor Information Centre,** 812 Wharf St., Victoria, BC V8W 1T3 (✆ **250/953-2033;** www.tourismvictoria.com) is an excellent resource for maps, brochures, and ideas for itineraries. Tourism Victoria also operates a **reservations hotline** (✆ **800/663-3883** or 250/953-2022) for last-minute bookings at hotels, inns, and B&Bs. The center is open September through April daily from 9am to 5pm, May and June daily from 8:30am to 6:30pm, and July and August daily from 9am to 9pm. Bus nos. 1, 27, or 28 to Douglas and Courtney streets.

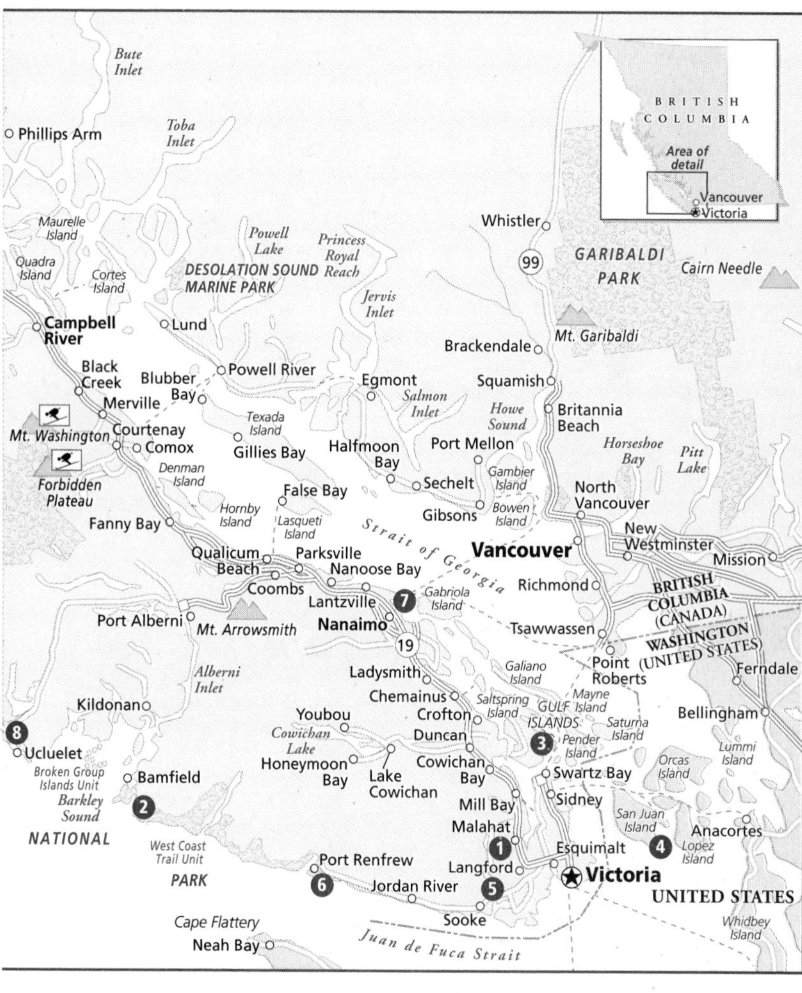

1 MOUNT FINLAYSON GOLDSTREAM PROVINCIAL PARK

Difficulty rating: Moderate to strenuous

Distance: 7.4km (4.6 miles) round trip

Estimated time: 4 hr.

Elevation gain: 420m (1,378 ft.)

Costs/permits: C$3 parking

Pet friendly: Yes, but only for agile animals

Best time to go: The trail is best in spring or autumn to avoid overheating on the steep, exposed sections. Ice and snow can make the winter months uncomfortable.

Website: www.goldstreampark.com

Recommended map: The Visitor Centre hands out good trail maps.

Trail head GPS: N 48 28.732, W 123 32.758

Trail head directions: From Victoria, drive 16km (10 miles) north on the Trans-Canada Highway (Hwy. 1): Just past the Route 14 junction to Langford and Sooke, signs indicate Goldstream Provincial Park. Ignore the campground on the left. Instead, turn right at Finlayson Arm Rd. into the parking lot. Cross the bridge to the trail head, marked with a notice board.

Just outside the provincial capital, this trail rises through second-growth Douglas fir, passes arbutus groves—a species exclusive to BC in Canada—and involves some fun, light scrambling. Though steep, the peak rewards hikers with a 360-degree panorama of sea and mountains . . . only slightly diminished by the subdivision, golf course, and other urban elements that litter the landscape.

Traditionally, tribes fished this area: small wonder, as some 50,000 chum salmon spawn here each autumn, attracting hundreds of bald eagles. The park's old mining shafts and tunnels remind visitors of the gold rush era. Today, locals train on Mount Finlayson: Adventure racers speed upward with CamelBaks, and mountaineers toil under heavy loads to build muscle endurance. The trail grinds upward, often dwindling to reflective arrows on raw rock. At the summit, trekkers can pivot and descend the same route for a shorter hike—or rest inflamed knees with a gentler descent through the forest, our recommended route.

Warm up with a stroll to the wildlife viewing platform and Freeman King Visitor Centre, 300m (984 ft.) north of the left-hand parking lot.

From roughly mid-October to early December, an indoor "salmon cam" tracks fish in the Goldstream River. Returning to spawn and die, the male chum salmon develop reddish-purple vertical bars and hooked jaws to fight off rivals. The species dominates these waters, though visitors may also glimpse coho and chinook salmon, as well as steelhead, a sea-going rainbow trout.

Come spring, the salmon eggs hatch. In recent years, the government, park, and local anglers have worked hard to protect the fish, which are multiplying. Help them by approaching the banks slowly and quietly, keeping dogs leashed. Avoid wearing bright clothing, especially reds, pinks, and purples, which can distract the salmon.

TAKE A BREAK

Open 9am–4:30pm, the Visitor Centre's snug chalet often keeps a fire blazing, and serves hot coffee and baked goods in its bookstore. Weekend activities include *Gyotaku* (Japanese fish printing), salmon slide shows, videos, and interpretive programs. Animals—marine and avian—are the real draw, however, making Goldstream Provincial Park worth a stop, even when the Finlayson trail's snowed out.

In winter, wardens turn the cameras skyward. Bald eagles gather to feed on the chum carcasses from early December until the end of February. In 1990, the park created a quiet zone—no people allowed—on the river's lower stretch during the salmon run. Since then, the number of eagles has soared from a yearly high of 12 per day to 276.

Retrace your steps back to Finlayson Arm Road, between the two parking lots, then turn left and cross the bridge. Follow the pavement about 150m (492 ft.). As the road starts to curve to the left, the signposted trail head appears to the right.

❶ **Trail Head** Take the left-hand path east here: The right leads to the Prospector's Trail. The Mount Finlayson route switchbacks (zigzags) in the shade for the first 20 to 30 minutes, climbing steadily. Among the second-growth Douglas firs sprout blueberries and arbutus, also known as madronas or Strawberry Trees. Distinctive for their ruddy trunks and peeling barks, they're Canada's only broad-leafed evergreens, found exclusively in British Columbia.

After roughly a kilometer (1/2 mile), roots begin to furrow the trail, which weaves around stones, then boulders. The fun is only beginning.

❷ **The Cliff Face** After a staircase-steep stretch, the route levels out briefly as it emerges from the wooded slopes. Then, it pounds upward without mercy for the next half a kilometer (1/4 mile). Bring plenty of water in hot weather. Clamber among the slick rocks, following the orange metal markers. Despite these, many hikers veer off course and simply scramble for the false summit, where the trail resumes in earnest. Avoid such "off-roading," which damages the terrain. Plus, the blazes mark the safest route over the slippery stone.

❸ **The False Summit** Hikers switchback, picking back and forth across the cliff. The trail straightens out, evoking sighs of relief, and heads into a patch of trees. But you're not quite at the top yet. Continue onward and upward about 300m (984 ft.).

❹ **The Summit** At 1.8km (1 mile), Finlayson's peak unfurls some spectacular views of Victoria's Inner Harbour and Finlayson Arm (as well as Bear Mountain Golf Club and its development, directly below). Clear days even reveal Washington State: the Strait of Juan de Fuca, Olympic peaks, and the snow cone of Mount Baker set among the North Cascades. The Nooksack Indians called this dramatic volcano *Koma Kulshan* (white steep mountain), while Spanish explorer Manuel Quimper poetically christened it *La Monta del Carmelo* (the great white watcher). But a 1792 expedition, led by Britain's George Vancouver, gave the mountain its modern name, after third lieutenant Joseph Baker, who spotted it.

❺ **The Back Loop** Hikers in a hurry can now retrace the route, but be warned: This makes for a fierce workout. If you boomerang back along the familiar path, you face those steep 420m (1,378 ft.) in reverse—often more challenging.

A gentler descent lies on the northern slope, however. Turn your back on the golf course and walk towards the tree line, veering slightly left: Signs indicate the path down. Heavily forested, this longer trail shelters deer and the odd cougar or black bear. After 2.4km (1 1/2 miles), it passes the Gowland Todd information board and emerges onto the Finlayson Arm Road. Turn left.

❻ **Finlayson Arm Road** Stroll downhill 3.1km (2 miles) on this paved road, which offers a peek into Malahat culture, like big-rig trucks outside family barbecues blaring heavy metal. While not the most atmospheric conclusion, this route is recommended for those with vertigo or wonky knees.

Mount Finlayson Goldstream Provincial Park

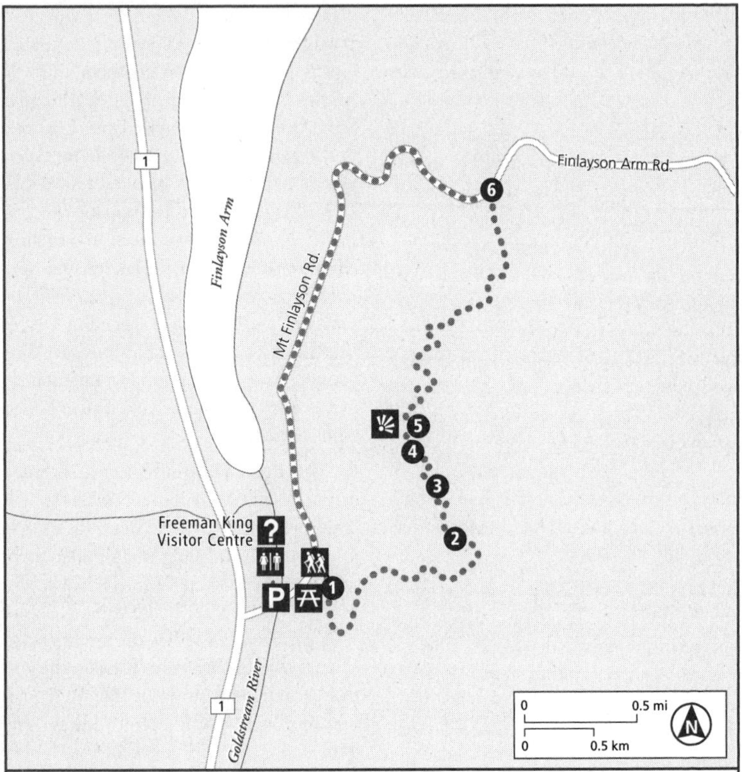

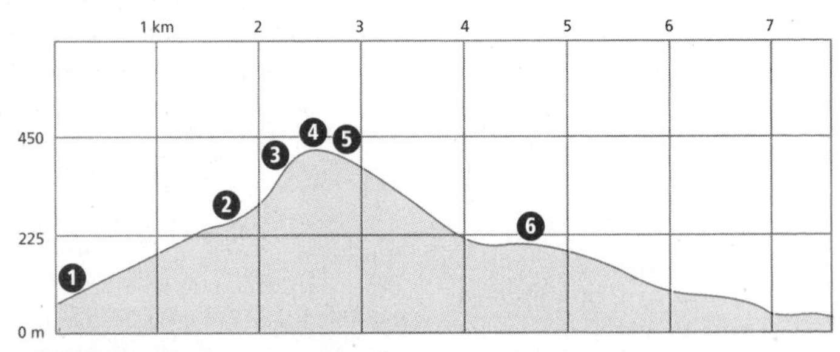

- N 48 28.732, W 123 32.758 (0 km): Trail head
- ❶ N 48 28.732, W 123 32.741 (0.1 km): Go left at signposted trailhead
- ❷ N 48 28.761, W 123 32.195 (1.7 km): Route levels out briefly as it emerges from woods
- ❸ N 48 28.891, W 123 32.236 (2.2 km): Trail straightens and goes into patch of trees
- ❹ N 48 28.978, W 123 32.344 (2.5 km): Summit of Mount Finlayson
- ❺ N 48 29.029, W 123 32.279 (2.8 km): Turn your back to view of golf course and follow signs downhill
- ❻ N 48 29.562, W 123 32.020 (4.6 km): Turn left at Finlayson Arm Road

2 WEST COAST TRAIL ★★★

Difficulty rating: Very strenuous

Distance: 75km (46.6 miles) round trip

Estimated time: 6–8 days

Elevation gain: 190m (625 ft.)

Costs/permits: C$127.50 trip fee and C$30 for the two private ferry crossings, all bundled into the permit. C$24.50 reservations; advisable for those on a tight schedule

Pet friendly: No

Best time to go: Open May 1–Sept 30, the trail's best weather usually falls in Aug or Sept.

Website: www.pc.gc.ca/pacificrim

Recommended map: The Pacific Rim National Park hands out its own water-resistant West Coast Trail maps with registration. Otherwise, NTS Maps 92 C/10, 92 C/15. Most parties also carry a dedicated guidebook, either Tim Leadem's *Hiking the West Coast Trail* or David Foster and Wayne Aitken's superior *Blisters and Bliss.*

Trail head GPS: N 48 47.602, W 125 06.929

Trail head directions: The Parks Canada Information Centre lies 5km (3 miles) down a dirt road from West Bamfield (hikers starting on the east side should factor in the water-crossing). The town has just one taxi service, often reserved for "scheduled emergencies." So be prepared to walk or hitch this dull stretch.

Canada's most popular hike traces Vancouver Island's southwestern edge. This wild strip of coastline earned the nickname "the Graveyard of the Pacific," as more than 50 ships foundered here in the last century. In 1906, the American steamship *Valencia* smashed onto a rocky reef north of Klanawa River: 136 people died about 18m (59 ft.) from wave-battered cliffs. This tragedy spurred the federal government to transform an old telegraph-line route into the Life Saving Trail, now the legendary West Coast Trail (WCT) and part of the Pacific Rim National Park. These rugged 75km (46.6 miles) require some serious infrastructure: elaborate bridges, ferry crossings, cable cars, and ladder complexes that can stretch 50 stories. Despite such aids, the route remains dangerous, often clocking an evacuation per day, mainly due to sprains, breaks, and hypothermia. Only experienced hikers should attempt the WCT, and they must learn to read tide tables, essential to coastal navigation. The risks pay off with huge rewards, however. The trail weaves through rare temperate rainforest thick with ancient cedars, firs, and Sitka spruce, where bears and cougars prowl. It dips onto sandy beaches, traces stony shoals where shipwrecks rust, and climbs sheer sandstone bluffs battered by the Pacific. This world-class trail attracts hikers for its haunting beauty, but also for its extremity: Those who finish earn some serious bragging rights.

The park limits the number of trekkers on the WCT (only 30 start from each trail head daily: Reservations are essential from mid-June to mid-Sept). Our recommended route begins on the north end, at Pachena Bay near Bamfield. This allows hikers to adjust to the trail's unique demands on the easier stretches—and shed pack weight before the tough sections south of Walbran Creek. We've divided the trip into 6 days, a challenging but comfortable pace for an active, fit person. This also takes advantage of the two snack spots and many of the best campsites, including spectacular Tsusiat Falls, where many spend several nights, gathering strength.

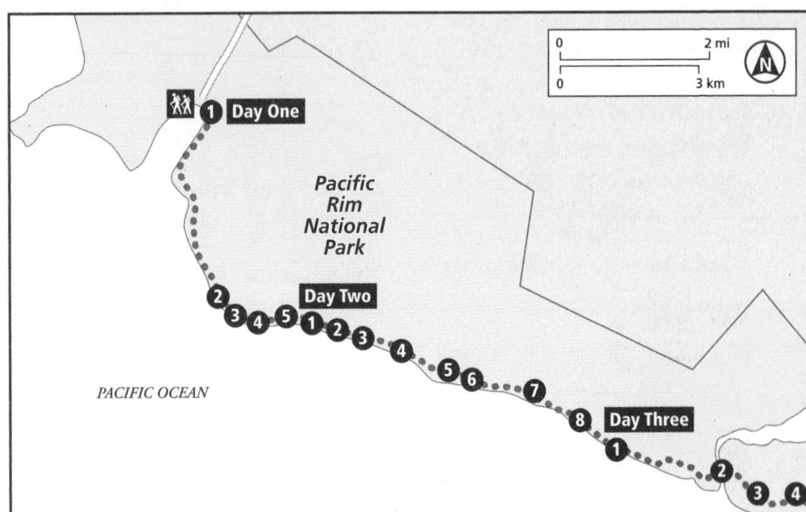

N 48 47.602, W 125 06.929 (0 km): Trail head

Day one

1 N 48 47.579, W 125 06.958 (0 km): A three-tier ladder ten minutes beyond trail head
2 N 48 47.588, W 125 06.951 (8.2 km): Bridge over Black River
3 N 48 43.502, W 125 06.265 (9.5 km): Flat rocks at edge of ocean
4 N 48 43.352, W 125 05.809 (10 km): Pachena lighthouse
5 N 48 43.402, W 125 04.330 (12 km): Michigan Creek campground

Day Two

1 N 48 43.387, W 125 04.240 (11.8 km): Remains of the steamship Michigan
2 N 48 43.218, W 125 03.244 (13.2 km): Darling River campsite
3 N 48 43.130, W 125 02.657 (13.9 km): Cross Orange Juice creek
4 N 48 42.805, W 125 01.091 (15.9 km): Tsocowis Creek warden cabin
5 N 48 42.386, W 124 59.507 (18.2 km): Take right-branching path to lookout over
6 N 48 42.326, W 124 59.109 (18.7 km): Trail crosses beach past anchor
7 N 48 42.028, W 124 56.897 (21.6 km): Cable car across Klanawa River
8 N 48 41.475, W 124 55.555 (23.7 km): Turn right at trail fork and descend steep ladder

Day Three

1 N 48 40.890, W 124 54.605 (25.4 km): Pass through natural arch on Tsusiat Point
2 N 48 40.432, W 124 52.012 (29 km): Follow path through rainforest past patrol cabin
3 N 48 40.468, W 124 51.219 (30.4 km): Take ferry across Nitinat Narrows
4 N 48 39.748, W 124 48.674 (35.1 km): Take suspension bridge across Cheewhat River
5 N 48 38.312, W 124 47.284 (38.6 km): Dare Beach campsite

Day Four

1 N 48 37.740, W 124 46.166 (40.4 km): Cribs Creek campsite
2 N 48 36.706, W 124 45.073 (42.9 km): Carmanah lighthouse
3 N 48 36.635, W 124 44.136 (44.4 km): Chez Monique's eatery
4 N 48 36.320, W 124 43.592 (45.4 km): Cross Carmanah Creek
5 N 48 34.861, W 124 39.313 (52.2 km): Take cable car across Walbran Creek

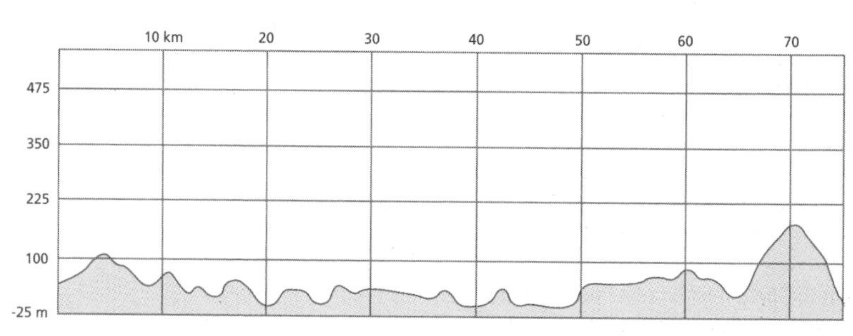

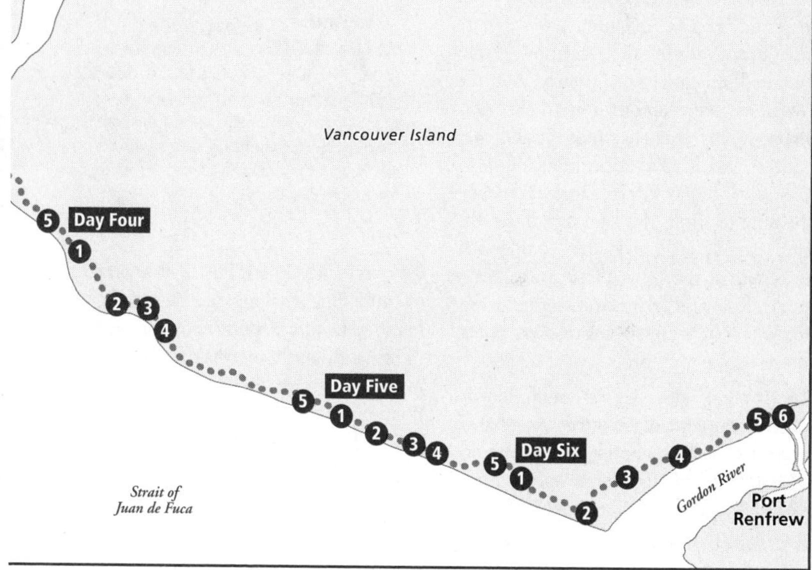

Day Five

1. N 48 34.583, W 124 38.154 (54 km): Boardwalk
2. N 48 34.268, W 124 37.024 (55.6 km): Cross Logan Creek via the suspension bridge
3. N 48 34.020, W 124 35.849 (57.3 km): Cable car at Cullite Creek
4. N 48 34.000, W 124 35.381 (57.9 km): Waterfall and swimming hole at Sandstone Creek
5. N 48 33.495, W 124 33.040 (61.7 km): Camper Bay

Day Six

1. N 48 33.499, W 124 32.960 (62.2 km): Cross Camper Creek in cable car
2. N 48 32.753, W 124 30.565 (66.2 km): Beach Access B
3. N 48 33.451, W 124 29.345 (68.7 km): Turn off for Thrasher Cove campsite
4. N 48 33.842, W 124 27.719 (71 km): Pass old donkey engine
5. N 48 34.670, W 124 24.979 (75 km): Gordon River boat crossing
6. N 48 34.651, W 124 24.730 (75.6 km): Information center for sign-in

Day One

Pachena Bay–Michigan Creek; moderate; 12km (7.5 miles)

❶ Pachena Bay Trail Head The half-hour mandatory orientations start at 9:30am, 1:30pm, and 3:30pm, though nothing runs quite on the clock here. The registration process takes roughly 90 minutes: Most hikers prefer to attend the later session a day before departure, overnighting in the superb Pachena Bay campground. Those without reservations should do the same, then queue early.

Trail veterans claim the first 12km (7½-mile) day is easy. And sure, it was, before the dread storm of December 2006 rerouted much of this stretch. But the WCT no longer ambles over an old lighthouse-supply road: It grinds up and over root-snarled headlands, introducing newbies to its architecture in a big way. In fact, 10 minutes from the launch pad lies the trail's second highest ladder—a three-tier monster unloved by those with heavy packs. Salal and other shrubs sprout a few feet under the rungs: below trekkers' boots, however, the drop-off is several stories.

❷ Black River Expect mud, blown-down trees with dirt-clotted "root balls," and spider webs spanning puddles the size of hot tubs. The first views open at 4km (2½ miles), then again at 6km (3¾ miles), just before the waterway at 8.2km (5 miles). A high bridge spans the Black River, but don't scramble to refill here. The mineral content is unsavory, and the lighthouse supplies fresh water up ahead.

❸ Flat Rocks South 1.5km (1 mile), a right-branching spur leads travelers to sun-warmed rocks, where they can bask and often watch caramel-colored sea lions do the same below. They twist like bratwurst in a hot pan, then shuffle across the sandstone. The ocean smacks through the surge channel and churns the sea foam sky high.

> **TAKE A BREAK**
> Sea lions often sun on the Flat Rocks, drawing hikers down the short right-branching spur at 9.3km (5¾ miles) along the trail. Despite the mesmerizing display, hikers can doze off in the cliff's craters. Keep an eye on the clock.

❹ Pachena Point A half-kilometer (¼ mile) further along, the Pachena lighthouse welcomes visitors: Look for another right-hand spur. Grey whales often surface in the waters here, though the quirky multinational signpost is a more reliable photo op. Built after the 1906 wreck of the SS *Valencia,* this remains one of the oldest beacons on the island's treacherous Pacific coast.

Tips — Things That Go Bump in the Night

Vancouver Island has one of the world's densest concentration of cougars and black bears, not to mention a smattering of wolves. Always make noise in areas frequented by *ursus americanus:* Talk, sing, clap, or wear bells. Store all food and toiletries in bear canisters (sleek plastic tubes), the caches (metal lockers) at popular campsites, or hung on a tree limb away from camp. If you encounter a black bear, back away slowly. In case of attack, fight back, unless the aggressor is a mamma bear protecting her cubs, then play dead. Should a cougar appear, try to look big (stand tall, face it head on, throw back your shoulders, and so on). Maintain eye contact and never turn your back on the wild cat. The same goes for wolves, though they're rarely spotted on the West Coast Trail.

❺ Michigan Creek The trail pounds 2km (1¼ miles) to Michigan Creek, a popular campsite and our recommended first-day finale (at 12km/7½ miles from the start). Sing down the knee-wobbling switchbacks or haul out the bear bells: Cub sightings are common here. At the ocean's edge stands a monolithic composting outhouse, nicknamed the "Cadillac of toilets." The window's second-story view is famous, but taller guests should be wary of flashing fellow travelers who wash pots and pump water on the cobblestone beach below.

The campground also has two food caches (bear-proof lockers) and enough buoys to refloat the Graveyard of the Pacific's wrecks. Originally, these signaled beach access points: Now, great shaggy bouquets of them double as the trail's graffiti medium. Words gouge deep into their once-bright Styrofoam cores. *John + Adele. Troop 786. Bamfield or bust.*

Sunset stains the evening mists here pastel, as driftwood campfires crackle on the beach. Why push on to Darling River, unless northbound hikers have hogged all the prime spots?

Day Two

Michigan Creek–Tsusiat Falls; moderate; 13km (8 miles)

❶ The Michigan's Boiler About 150m (492 ft.) south of the creek, the surprisingly intact boiler of the steamship *Michigan* rusts into the Pacific (best viewed at lower tides). The 1893 wreck lost no lives.

❷ Darling River Follow the beach 1.5km (1 mile) to the next campsite on the banks of the Darling River. Low tides expose the tidal shale: sometimes offering good traction, other times snotty with algae. Hikers tend to race along this beach stretch, but hold back and save energy: The day will be long.

Scan the waves for grey whales, often spotted feeding on kelp here. They also rub on the sand, scratching themselves. The wreck at the river's mouth is the SS *Uzbekistan,* a Russian steamship carrying war supplies that sunk in 1943. At 14km (8¾ miles) ford the river, then continue along the beach when tides are under 3.7m (12 ft.). Otherwise, take the upland path.

❸ Orange Juice Creek At 15km (9¼ miles), shallow caves pierce the cliff, alongside a rough campsite only accessible at tides below 2.7m (8¾ ft.). Cross Orange Juice Creek, then continue 1.8km (1 mile) to Tsocowis Creek, another overnight spot with good amenities (bear caches and a composting toilet).

❹ Tsocowis Creek Navigation can get a bit tricky between 16km and 17km (10–10½ miles). For starters, most hikers have easily doubled their inland pace on the beach. Those not watching the map closely can overshoot Tsocowis Creek (at 17km/10½ miles) and its clearly labeled warden cabin, plowing unwittingly into the impassable headlands that wrecked the SS *Valencia* and kick-started this very trail.

Tips — Getting a Foot on the Ladder

The WCT has some serious infrastructure: boardwalks, bridges, ferries, cable cars, and ladder complexes (Thrasher Cove's rises the equivalent of 50 stories). Though the trail peaks at a mere 230m (754.6 ft.), these vertical hauls can challenge even seasoned hikers. Only one person at a time should ever be on a ladder section: wait off to the side on the platforms, away from the potential fall line. Balance weight evenly within your pack and tighten all straps. Always face inward and watch for loose or missing rungs.

Don't make the same mistake: The terrain is far too deadly. Stop, look, and listen. Read the tide charts. Talk to the seasoned northbound hikers, who pool here during high tides. Then, ascend the Tsocowis Creek ladders and cross the dramatic suspension bridge over Billy Goat Creek.

TAKE A BREAK The Valencia Bluffs remain a popular snack spot at around 18km (11¼ miles). Pitch-sticky roots jam the vantage point, so watch where you sit.

❺ **The Valencia Lookout** Opposite an old donkey (steam-powered) grader around 18km (11¼ miles), a right-branching path leads to a lookout. Beneath these bluffs, the SS *Valencia* sunk in 1906, killing 136 of the 173 people aboard in a horrible, prolonged fashion. Known as "the most shameful incident in Canadian maritime history," the wreck inspired the Pachena Point lighthouse and a life-saving trail that evolved into the West Coast Trail.

❻ **Trestle Creek** The trail dips onto the shore at 20km (12½ miles), where an anchor rusts on the cobblestones. The next 3km (1¾ miles) trace the beach and are only possible at tides below 2.7m (8¾ ft.). Hikers can make good time, thanks to the stone shelf's traction.

❼ **Klanawa River** Slow and fat, the Klanawa River sprawls at 23km (14¼ miles). Here, hikers encounter their first cable car. On the north side lie some campsites. However, the brackish, tidal Klanawa is a bad bet for drinking water, so push on to Tsusiat and scenic glory. The trail grinds up and down hills for 3km (1¾ miles), before hitting the monster ladders that descend to Tsusiat Falls, generally considered the route's highlight.

❽ **Tsusiat Falls** At 25km (15½ miles), the trail forks. Turn right and descend the steep ladders to the ocean-side campsite, which sparkles with energy, thanks to the surf, the great sheet of waterfall, and shrieking bathers in its pool below. Tents brighten the soft, grey sand here, often cozy behind windbreaks of driftwood.

The Sinking of the SS *Valencia*

In 1906, the SS *Valencia,* on a run from San Francisco to Seattle, strayed north and smashed onto rocks in the "Graveyard of the Pacific." For 2 days, the crew and passengers clung to the wave-thrashed iron steamship. Land was tantalizingly close—18m (59 ft.), at most—but for the deadly breakers, reefs, and cliffs. Scheme after scheme failed them: The lifeboats, deployed accidentally in the dark, largely capsized, drowning at least 40 souls in the disaster's first half-hour. Lines shot to shore missed, frayed, or were simply ignored by those who had struggled to safety. "Why did you run away? Why didn't you come back to help us?" survivor Charles Allison asked this first group's spokesman at the inquiry. "We prayed for the sight of a man up there! Just one man to catch the end of a rope and make it fast to a tree! We were so close!"

Ultimately, blame fell on the lack of lighthouses, fog signals, wireless stations, and equipment like ocean-going tugs. These 161km (100 miles) of coast, deemed the most dangerous on the continent's western rim, didn't even have a life-saving station.

The net result: creation of the Pachena Point lighthouse and a trail with shelters for shipwrecked mariners, now the WCT.

> **Tips** **Cable Car Comportment**
>
> Load packs into the center and never more than two people at a time. Tuck in all straps, hair, and limbs before releasing the line. The car hauls on the down slope: Then the pulling begins. Companions on the platforms can really help with this, if not glued to their cameras. Do not rock the cars; they have been known to disengage from the cable.

Hikers have stacked surf logs into benches, chairs, pavilions—even a penthouse once. Full of beachy, carnival charm, Tsuisiat (pronounced *Sue-see-at*) often persuades folks to stay 2 nights or more.

The only downsides are the crowds and the long slog to the composting outhouse and food lockers, set on the bay's north end. Trekkers have to ford a creek, then cross another stream on logs: no fun in the dark. Put food in the available cache early, since attempts to haul bags into the cliff's few trees are more amusing than effective. Happily, mice are more likely to plunder supplies here than bears.

Day Three

Tsusiat Falls–Dare Beach; strenuous; 15km (9.3 miles)

❶ Hole in the Wall From Tsusiat, hikers can boogie down the sand, at tides below 2.7m (8¾ ft.), or crawl back up the steep ladders and resume the forest trail. The spectacular coastal route really shouldn't be missed, however: Fir-fringed cliffs rear back from the silky sand. Sail down the beach through Hole in the Wall, a natural arch on Tsusiat Point (at 27km/ 17 miles). Here also is an access point for the inland route; another lies at 28km (a little over 17 miles). Sea levels permitting, stay on the shore until you're at 29km (18 miles), where the route plunges into the woods.

❷ Tsuquadra Point Inland, the route weaves through stunning rainforest: small wonder the Ditidaht (pronounced *Diitiid-aa-tx* or *Dee-tee-daht*) tribe kept this as the Tsuquanah Reserve 2 (pronounced *Tsuxwkwaad-aa-tx*). Stay on the path and don't tamper with the guardians' patrol cabin around 30km (19 miles). Back in park lands, the WCT crests up to bluffs with dramatic sea views, then winds down to a petite wharf on the Nitinat Narrows, just past the 32km (20-mile) point.

❸ Nitinat Narrows Tidal currents smash through here at speeds up to 8 knots: The resulting whirlpools and standing waves have drowned many. Never attempt to swim. Instead, wait among the blown-down trees for the sporadic ferry: an open fishing boat that tootles across the river when the operator notices patrons. His fee's bundled into the cost of the permit, which he'll ask to see. So, keep the paperwork handy—and maybe some cash too for the snacks on the other side in the Wyah Indian Reserve.

During the season, the water taxi (✆ **250/745-3509**) runs between 9am and 5pm. It's also the escape hatch for hikers who've had enough: The boat can run them 45 minutes up the lake to the Ditidaht Reserve for C$25. An overnight stay may be required in the village.

> **TAKE A BREAK** On the south dock of Nitinat Narrows, the ferry operator and his family serve up seafood, boiled potatoes, and drinks, including C$5 cans of iced beer. Order up a slab of salmon or ling cod, depending on the catch. Lucky patrons might score a C$20 Dungeness crab, selected from a trap hauled out of the chill waters.

❹ The Cheewhat River A kilometer (1/2 mile) south flows the brackish Cheewhat. Its name translates as "river of urine"—warning enough not to fill water bottles here. Cross the suspension bridge and cruise the wide, level trail to the 37km (23-mile) mark. Here, a feeble spring drips at the southern end of the beach.

❺ Dare Beach South 1.2km (3/4 mile) looms Dare Point, then around the bend, Dare Beach (at 40km/25 miles) and its primitive campsite: no cache, no toilet. But the quiet can be a welcome respite on this popular trail. With plenty of accessible trees to hang food, why not enjoy a solitary campfire on the beach?

Day Four

Dare Beach–Walbran Creek; strenuous; 13km (8.1 miles)

❶ Cribs Creek Tides permitting (under 2.1m/7 ft.), blast 1.4km (3/4 mile) down the beach to Cribs Creek: The popularity of this campsite results in a shameful amount of trash but some exceptional driftwood furniture. Turn inland or continue down the shore (again, only at tides below 2.1m/7 ft.). About 1.5km (1 mile) along is another beach access point, where you can revisit the decision. The coastal route may offer a glimpse of California sea lions, just southwest of the point, but the staircase up to Carmanah lighthouse is a killer. On the other hand, the path through the forest contains some old-school West Coast Trail obstacles: blow-downs, a swaybacked bridge, and ropes spanning churned-mud pits and inclines. Pick your poison.

❷ Carmanah Lighthouse At 44km (27 miles), a short path diverges right to the 1891 lighthouse. The bones of a gray whale and a cobblestone labyrinth liven up the lawns. If you've been involved in any accidents or predator encounters, report them to the keepers here.

❸ Chez Monique's Regain the WCT, which plunges down steep ladders to the beach. The driftwood and tarp shack houses Chez Monique's, a grocery and eatery. The owner—Monique Nytom—is equally famous for her frank talk and far-ranging beagle Charlie Parker, who mastered the ladders and roamed dozens of miles north and south, until his death in 2008.

> **TAKE A BREAK**
> Chez Monique's, just south of Carmanah lighthouse, specializes in beachside burgers. While the chatty proprietor's frying, settle into the hammock with a beer or glass of Chilean Malbec. She even has a vegetarian option, though it's just a Denver omelet on a bun. Monique also sells chips, oranges, and candy bars. While the treats here and at Nitinat delight hikers tired of freeze-dried rations, park officials warn not to rely on them. Carry food supplies for 2 to 3 days more than your anticipated itinerary.

❹ Carmanah Creek Two kilometers (1 1/4 miles) down the beach flows Carmanah Creek. Cross by cable car or simply ford—easiest where the stream broadens and meets the sea. Remember to unfasten your chest strap and waist belt: otherwise the pack could pin you underwater, should you slip. Campsites snuggle close to both banks. Up this valley grow some of the world's tallest Sitka spruce (one soars almost 32 stories).

❺ Walbran Creek The trail hugs the shore for 2.1km (1 1/4 miles) to Bonilla Point (look for the large red navigation triangle above the beach), then another 1.2km (3/4 mile) to the Cullite Indian Reserve, pierced by Kalide Creek. From here to Vancouver Point, the beach is only passable at tides below 3m (10 ft.). Just before the headland stands an intersection: Turn left when the water's high (2.7m/9 ft.), then take the cable car across Walbran Creek. Otherwise, continue along the

Dining Out

Save the snack attacks for the Nitinat ferry crossing and Chez Monique's: Never harvest mussels, clams, or other sea life. Red tides here can induce paralytic shellfish poisoning, fatal to humans.

beach (a more direct route) and ford the broad, cold river to the campground at 53km (33 miles). Pitch your tent among the tangle of driftwood or in spaces sheltered by the rainforest.

Day Five

Walbran Creek–Camper Bay; very strenuous; 9.3km (5.8 miles)

❶ The Bog Ignore the left-hand spur, which leads northbound to the cable car, and follow the path 3km (1³/₄ miles) to Adrenalin Creek, then another kilometer (¹/₂ mile) to Logan Creek. A boardwalk takes the edge off the bog, but hikers still slip and claw through plenty of mud pits riddled with roots. The WCT shows its grit here and will remain challenging until the very end.

❷ Logan Creek At 56km (35 miles), intense ladders book-end a skinny suspension bridge. The waterway's named for David Logan, a telegraph lineman who tried to rescue passengers during the 1906 wreck of the SS *Valencia.* A tough and eccentric coot, he allegedly walked the trail barefoot from time to time. Ignore the right-hand spur on the south side, which leads to a campsite known for good beachcombing.

❸ Cullite Creek More ladders, more mud: The next 6km (3³/₄ miles) pass in slow motion. The cable car at Cullite Creek breaks up the monotony (at 58km/36 miles). Again, ignore the southern campsite spur and continue to Sandstone Creek.

TAKE A BREAK

Sandstone Creek—at the 58km (36-mile) point—flows in shallow sheets but occasionally pools deep into smooth, circular basins: natural tubs. The easiest access is via the bridge's trestle supports: a simple two-move climb, but still, be careful. Range upstream for privacy and avoid polluting with soaps or shampoos, even biodegradable ones. ***Note:*** The park discourages bathing and dishwashing in fresh water: a suggestion many hikers defy here and at Tsusiat Falls.

❹ Sandstone Creek A grueling descent lands trekkers at this sweet spot at 58km (36 miles) along the trail, known for its waterfalls and swimming holes. Downstream lies a crude campground, accessible only via a half-kilometer (¹/₄-mile) bushwhack when the water is low. Avoid this and head 2.3km (1¹/₂ miles) for the splendid site with a cache and an outhouse at Camper Bay.

❺ Camper Bay Tribal carvings peer down from the Quu'as guardian's hut at this popular campground. Be mindful of the tides while pitching your tent: that prime ocean-view property could result in a night-time soaking.

Day Six

Camper Bay–Gordon River; very strenuous; 13km (8 miles)

❶ Camper Creek Cable Car Fording can be tricky, so most hikers whiz across in the cable car. Stick to the forest route past the first beach access point at 64km (40 miles),

Tips: Who You Gonna Call?

The WCT averages an evacuation a day some years, mainly due to sprains, breaks, and hypothermia. Cell phones work on most beaches, tapping into a nearby American network. However, do not call 911, as the U.S. Coast Guard charges for international assistance. The park (✆ **250/726-3604**) removes injured hikers by boat for free but may levy a fee for situations that require a helicopter.

where the descent is steep and usually slippery. Instead, at tides below 2.4m (7¾ ft.), hit Beach Access A at 65km (a little over 40 miles) and check out the surge channels and colorful sea caves between there and the next access point at 66km (41 miles).

❷ Beach Access B Time for a hard decision: a dramatic shore-side dash or a slog through the forest, riddled with blown-down trees? Owen Point to Quartertide Rocks requires tides under 1.8m (6 ft.). Littered with slimy boulders, this stretch is the trail's most evacuation-prone—both due to slips and tidal miscalculations (foolhardy hikers get stranded against the cliffs or on sea stacks). Due to the tricky coastal conditions, we recommend the inland route for less fit or experienced travelers.

❸ The Turn-Off to Thrasher At 70km (43 miles), a right-hand spur leads 1km (½ mile) down to the campsite at Thrasher Cove, a trail head until 1998 and now a pleasant campsite. Heavy with ladders, this descent—the equivalent of 50 stories—is a monster. And you'll have to climb back up the next morning. For this reason, many prefer to simply push on the tough, last 5km (3 miles) to the journey's end.

❹ Donkey Engine Logging debris litters the area at around 72km (45 miles): Cables thread through the trees, looping around stumps, and an old donkey engine (steam-powered hoist) rusts in the rainforest.

❺ Gordon River The WCT's second boat crossing concludes the trail. Pull the rope to hoist the buoy, signaling the ferryman, who works daily 9am to 5pm. A few tent sites dot the woods near the trail head sign, for those who arrive late. As at Nitinat Narrows, do not attempt to swim the channel, no matter how brightly Port Renfrew's lights shine.

❻ Information Center From the landing, turn right and walk a half-kilometer (¼ mile) to the information center: Wardens monitor arrivals and departures. The complex has bathrooms and a shower, though most prefer the plusher facilities in town. The West Coast Trail bus stops at the center and also in Port Renfrew at the intersection by the Lighthouse Pub sign, kitty-corner from the Port Renfrew Hotel. Otherwise, take a taxi or walk the last 5km (3 miles) south from the Gordon River trail head to Port Renfrew.

3 RUCKLE PROVINCIAL PARK, SALTSPRING ISLAND

Difficulty rating: Easy to moderate

Distance: 6.7km (4.2 miles) round trip

Estimated time: 3–4 hr.

Elevation gain: Minimal

Costs/permits: C$3 parking fee. Camp sites cost C$10–C$24 per group each night.

Pet friendly: Yes (only in the campground and lower day-use area, due to livestock conflicts)

Best time to go: Mid-Sept for the fall fair

Website: www.env.gov.bc.ca/bcparks/explore/parkpgs/ruckle

Recommended map: Ruckle Provincial Park map, available by download at the website above, or from the Park's headquarters.

Trail head GPS: N 48 46.405, W 123 22.587

Trail head directions: Ferries connect the Island to Tsawwassen on the mainland, and Schwartz Bay and Crofton on Vancouver Island. From the Fulford Harbour terminal, turn right onto Beaver Point Rd. and continue for 10km (6¼ miles). Car-free travelers can book a taxi (✆ 250/537-2006) or the shuttle (✆ 250/538-9007).

Largest of the Southern Gulf Islands, this area first drew farmers in 1859: Later settlers included African-Americans and Hawaiians, then back-to-the-landers (squatters and commune members). Artists followed, then the inevitable gentrification—today, laid-back locals struggle to embrace tourists, celebrities, and wealthy boomer retirees. Our recommended route explores the historic homestead, dodges its lively turkeys, and dips down to a driftwood-laden bay. Then, it traces sea cliffs through the campground and north along Swanson Channel, before skirting the active farm and returning to the trail head. Terrain ranges from rocky headlands to sheltered coves, wetlands to mossy forests and sun-soaked meadows.

From the parking lot, walk southwest 200m (656 ft.) to the historic farm. "A man who understands farming and has a little capital will do as well or better here than any place in North America," Henry Ruckle declared in 1895. The Irish emigrant began homesteading here in 1872 and flourished. One hundred and two years later, his family sold the 484 hectares (1,196 acres) to the provincial government, creating the Gulf Island's largest protected zone. But the Ruckles still maintain a foothold here, grazing sheep inland on BC's oldest continually operating farm. The barn dates back to 1900. Though off-limits, it hints at the pioneer landscape.

❶ Old Ruckle Homestead About 75m (246 ft.) along the path, peer inside the windows of the candy-cane-colored farmhouse. Inside, dust and sunlight slant across period tableaus: straight-backed chairs, a cast-iron stove. In its heyday, this orchard contained 600 fruit trees and was a major player until the irrigation of the Okanogan Valley.

❷ Turkey Time Several dozen turkeys lurk in the pen just 15m (49 ft.) south of the homestead. At least, they're supposed to lurk there . . . but these gobblers sometimes make bids for freedom through the snaggletoothed fence. Judging by the slick of guano on the porch, this happens with some regularity. They also seem accustomed to handouts—and will peck at visitors' rings, cameras, and clothing labels (either to bully food or through abject confusion). Tread carefully.

❸ Grandma's Bay After roughly 150m (492 ft.), a trail spur to the right dips down to a sandy cove, thick with driftwood. During America's Prohibition, rum runners would frequent the coast's nooks and crannies like this before smuggling booze into the San Juan Islands across the border.

❹ The Campground The route follows the coastline for about .7km (½ mile) until it hits a road: Take the right fork, which leads back to the trail. The Gulf Islands' largest campground offers picnic

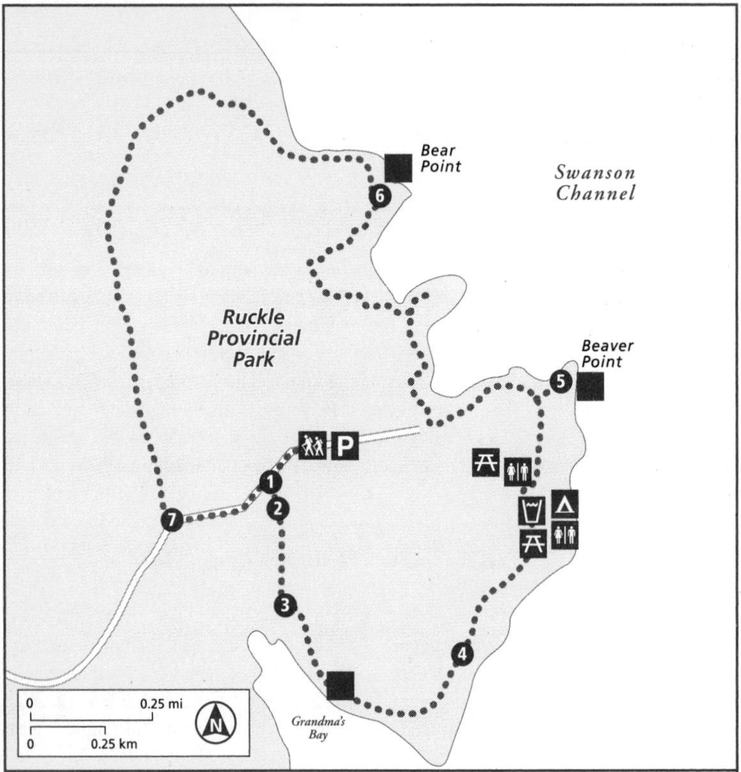

Bear Point
Swanson Channel
Ruckle Provincial Park
Beaver Point
Grandma's Bay
0 0.25 mi
0 0.25 km

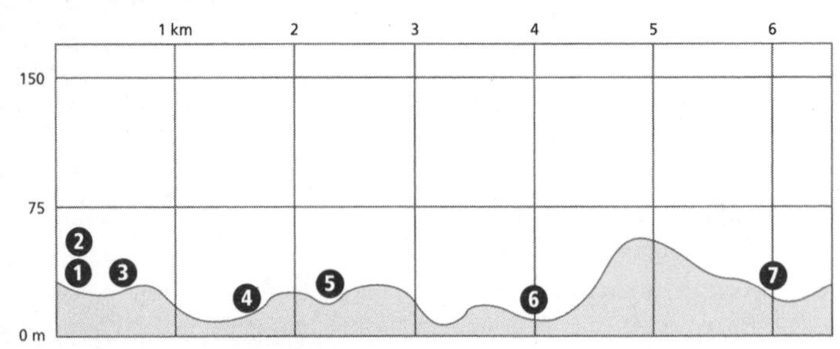

N 48 27.884, W 123 01.466 (0 km): Trail head
1 N 48 46.335, W 123 22.673 (0.2 km): Old Ruckle farmhouse
2 N 48 46.324, W 123 22.669 (0.2 km): Turkey pen
3 N 48 46.161, W 123 22.700 (0.6 km): Trail spur on the right goes down to Grandma's Bay
4 N 48 46.202, W 123 22.208 (1.6 km): Take right fork at road, proceed to campground
5 N 48 46.507, W 123 22.022 (2.3 km): Beaver Point wharf
6 N 48 46.755, W 123 22.424 (4 km): Bear Point
7 N 48 46.301, W 123 22.909 (6 km): Turn left and follow pavement past working farm

Fun Facts Funny Money

This outpost boasts its own currency. Local artists designed the colorful bills and silver coins, which honor white, black, and Hawaiian settlers. Issued by the Salt Spring Island Monetary Foundation, these dollars are perfectly legal and exchange at a one-to-one rate with their Canadian counterparts. Find out more about them at www.saltspringdollars.com.

tables, water stations, pit toilets, and even communal fire pits. Fir and arbutus frame views of Swanson Channel, where ferries bustle. Its 78 walk-in sites are a short, level stroll from the parking lots, opening up this pleasant spot to folks with impaired mobility. The footpath forks repeatedly: Always take the right, clinging to the shore.

Signs here warn about an invasion of carpet burweed *(Soliva sessilis)*. This South American native grows in winter, edging out other plants and creating a dense mat on lawns, roadsides, and hard-packed trails. Respect the patches marked "off limits" here: Conservationists have been working since 1997 to ban the weed and protect the four blue-listed plants it threatens.

The campground, however magnificent, hurts the remote, back-in-time vibe. But its views are among the trail's best—and just northwest of Beaver Point, the trail gnarls up with roots and overgrowth, returning the romantic mood. Keep an eye out for owls along this stretch: Some even emerge in daylight.

TAKE A BREAK The route's best snack spot lies about 150m (492 ft.) northwest of Beaver Point. The views rival the campgrounds', but these picnic tables are reserved for day users.

5 Beaver Point Before steamer service, islanders would row to Vancouver Island for supplies. Henry Ruckle built a wharf here in 1889, which eventually housed a general store, post office, and residence. The ferry service shifted to Fulford Harbour in the 1950s. The shore and trail turn west (left) here. At 2.7km ($1^3/_4$ miles), just past the day-use picnic area, lies junction 1. Tired trekkers can go straight here, returning another 250m (820 ft.) to the parking lot. Others should turn right, bound for the next point, atmospherically known as 2A on the park maps, 750m (2,461 ft.) away. Again, stick to the right-hand forks.

6 Bear Point From peninsula 2A, retrace your steps to the last intersection, then turn right and proceed for 850m (2,789 ft.). The route swoops along the cove out to Bear Point (labeled 2 on the park map). Sea lions and orcas ply these waters, along with mink and river otters. Ruckle remains popular among divers for its ornate caves. Peer into tide pools for a glimpse of the rich marine life here, which includes crabs, sculpins, and gaudy sea stars. The rich offshore kelp forests attract fish; these, in turn, draw birds, including eagles and cormorants.

Take the left-hand junction here, skirting the farm's edge, unless you plan to extend the hike. The trail cuts inland (west), the terrain changing almost at each turn: mossy rocks here, blow-downs there, even a sty (fence ladder) leading into pastureland. Six hundred meters (1,969 ft.) on lies the next intersection. Turn left and continue 1.2km ($^3/_4$ mile) to where the trail hits the entry road.

7 The Farm Turn left and follow the pavement along the working farm for about 300m (984 ft.) back to the parking lot. Stop at the "honesty stand," selling cookies, lemonade, bouquets, *courgettes* (zucchini), fresh greens, or whatever else is in season that week.

The Ruckle family contributed most of its land to the park, but descendants still raise sheep opposite the campground's entrance, thanks to a "tenancy for life" clause. As Michael Kluckner, artist and illustrator of *Vanishing British Columbia*, wrote, "Ruckle is a combination of restoration, contemporary recreational access, and working farm that would be the pride of any National Trust in the world, and yet it is a park run by the BC Parks Service."

4 AMERICAN CAMP, SAN JUAN ISLAND NATIONAL HISTORIC PARK ★★★

Difficulty rating: Moderate

Distance: 14km (8.7 miles) round trip; shorter options available

Estimated time: 5 hr.

Elevation gain: 88m (289 ft.)

Costs/permits: None

Pet friendly: Yes (dogs must be leashed)

Best time to go: Open year-round, this park dazzles most in early autumn sunshine. Families also flock to the Encampment, 3 days of period cooking, blacksmithing, fiddling, dancing, and gaming in late Aug.

Website: www.nps.gov/sajh

Recommended map: Detailed maps available in box beside the trail head

Trail head GPS: N 48 27.884, W 123 01.466

Trail head directions: The Sidney ferry is the most painless route from BC to Washington State's San Juan Island (Vehicle reservations recommended: ✆ 888/808-7977 or 206/464-6400; www.wsdot.wa.gov/ferries). Disembark at Friday Harbor, then drive west on Spring to Mullis St. and turn left. This wiggly artery changes name twice until it's Cattle Point Rd. American Camp lies 9.6km (6 miles) from town. Turn right on the visitor center entrance road after the park entrance sign.

Some enjoy cycling to the site. Contact Island Bicycles for a rental (✆ 360/378-4941; www.islandbicycles.com). San Juan Transit—a private shuttle service—runs from Friday Harbor to American Camp at 11:30am, 1:30pm, and 3:30pm (C$10 round trip, reservation required at least 30 minutes in advance; www.sanjuantransit.com; ✆ 800/887-8387 or 360/378-8887).

In 1859, this maritime prairie hosted the peaceful Pig War, where the U.S. and Great Britain squared off over a dead swine (not to mention border disputes). The island's joint occupation lasted 12 years, during which time, the troops began picnicking, partying, and horse racing together. Except for suicides and accidents, this war shed no human blood.

Snow-capped mountains peer over the tawny grasses of American Camp. Start on the interpretive trail, descend to Grandma's Cove for some beachcombing, then trace the bluffs down to Pickett's Lane. Here, hikers can loop back to the interpretive center for a shorter trek or continue to the Jakle's Lagoon Trail, a 4.8km (3-mile) circuit that climbs 88m (289 ft.) up Mount Finlayson.

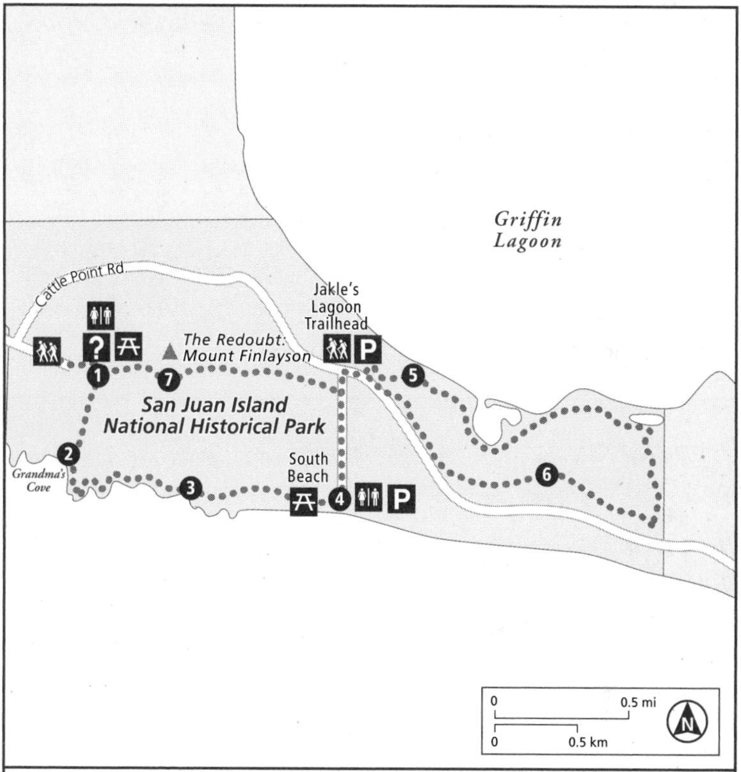

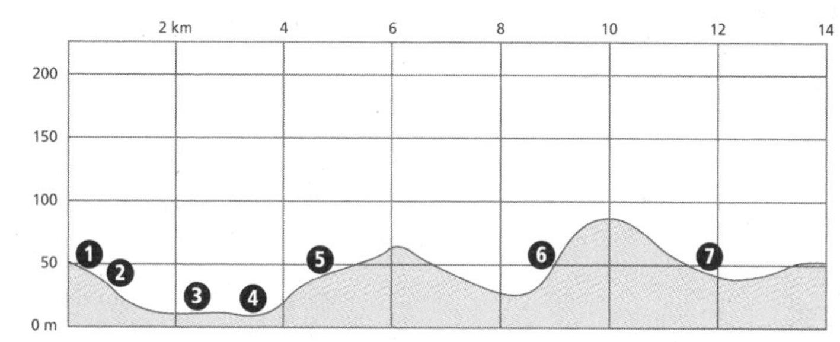

N 48 27.884, W 123 01.466 (0 km): Trail head

❶ N 48 27.828, W 123 01.273 (0.3 km): Belle Vue Farm Site

❷ N 48 27.559, W 123 01.409 (0.9 km): Follow spur on the right to beach

❸ N 48 27.465, W 123 00.773 (2.3 km): Turn right at unmarked junction

❹ N 48 27.405, W 123 00.092 (3.4 km): Left at restrooms, follow Pickett's Lane

❺ N 48 27.800, W 122 59.656 (4.7 km): Jakle's Lagoon

❻ N 48 27.515, W 122 59.028 (8.9 km): Summit of Mount Finlayson

❼ N 48 27.823, W 123 00.962 (11.9 km): Redoubt fortifications

Fun Facts Free Willy

Around 86 orcas—the endangered species often called "killer whales"—summer in this area, hanging out in three pods (social groups). Sometimes visible from American Camp, they more frequently spout and splash off Lime Kiln Point on the island's west side. Many consider this state park the best land-based whale-watching outlook in the Lower 48, if not the world.

The resident orcas feast on fatty chinook salmon and other fish, drawn by the brisk currents and upwelling nutrients here. Their transient kin—just passing through—hunt marine mammals like seals and the Stellar sea lions that winter in these waters. Each orca consumes 227 kilograms (500 lb.) of food each day on average. Largest of all the dolphins, *orcinus orca* sports a tall dorsal fin and a distinctive black-and-white pattern: Think *Free Willy.* But you might be already, since the hit's sequel was filmed right here in the San Juan Islands, incorporating local sights and faces.

A small visitor's center dispenses maps and screens a video on the area's history. Remember to scan the skies and treetops as you set out: The San Juan Islands boast the largest concentration of bald eagles in the continental United States, and two have nested here.

❶ Belle Vue Farm Site The trail winds through a grove, then opens onto the rare and stunning prairie of American Camp. Gold-brown grasses ripple high above the sea, framed by snow-capped peaks on the horizon. Even on overcast days—for which Washington is justly famed—the view remains tremendous.

History buffs may enjoy detours to the officers' quarters (left), laundresses' cabin (right), and the ruins of Belle Vue Farm (on the left about 500m/1,640 ft. down from the visitor center). The Hudson's Bay Company's Charles John Griffin imported four Hawaiian herdsmen and 1,369 sheep there, plus a few pigs. One of these hogs repeatedly rooted in a potato patch, until neighboring American farmer Lyman Cutlar shot him. The squabble quickly mushroomed, and soon the U.S. and Great Britain both garrisoned soldiers on Cattle Point peninsula.

The animosity ran beyond spuds and bacon, of course: This was a bigger backfence issue. The two countries had fought 40 years over the Pacific Northwest—and the San Juans were the last disputed area.

For 12 years, the soldiers jointly occupied the island and began to share whiskey and cigars amid the games, races, and parties. Finally, arbitrator Kaiser Wilhelm I of Germany awarded the territory to America. The war's only casualty was the wayward pig.

❷ Grandma's Cove Continue south, descending a short right-branching spur to a beach jammed with driftwood. Visitors sometimes build impromptu shelters here, ideal for picnicking near on a blustery day.

Wrist-thick ropes of seaweed crowd the shore further: bull kelp, often complete with float bulb and long, ruffly fronds. Like all marine flora here, *nereocystis luetkeana* is edible and hugely nutritious. None of the seaweed in Puget Sound is dangerous, just a little yucky.

But don't tuck in: Traffic offshore may have polluted this patch. Plus, Washington State requires a shellfish and seaweed permit (C$11 for residents, C$25 for nonresidents; www.wdfw.wa.gov/fishing).

❸ The Bluffs Ascend the bluff, then turn right at the unmarked junction, threading along the sea cliffs. Blackberries line the trail in late summer: The rules permit snacking, but not take-away. Along the jig-sawed coastline, watch for raptors, songbirds, and rare Island Marble butterflies. Thought to be extinct from 1908 to 1998, *Euchloe ausonides insulanus* re-colonized American Camp. A mottled white and pale green, they feed on the wild mustards.

Native Americans would burn the prairies every year to encourage camas, once common to the islands. This purple-bloomed plant has bulbs with a taste akin to creamy potato and baked pear, long prized by local tribes. Wildflower enthusiasts should also search for chocolate lilies, taper-tip onions, seashore lupins, and few-flowered shooting stars. Western bluebirds (reintroduced in 2007) flit over the prairie, which is being restored to support native species like the Townsend's vole and streaked horned lark.

Step carefully: Rabbit warrens undermine the bluffs.

❹ Pickett's Lane The path narrows, then descends slightly to South Beach. Take a left at the restrooms, following Pickett's Lane—named for an army officer stationed here, who later led an infamously stupid and bloody charge at the Battle of Gettysburg.

TAKE A BREAK Gravely South Beach contains fire pits and picnic tables, as well as restrooms. After fuelling up, wander the island's longest public coastline, a 3.2km (2-mile) stretch.

At the street's end, tired trekkers can take another left, looping back to the visitor's center via the redoubt (waypoint #7). Energetic travelers should push onward, however: A few minutes ahead on the right lies another trail head.

❺ Jakle's Lagoon Decide between the 2.4km (1½-mile) woodland route and the recommended 4.8km (3-mile) loop that "summits" Mount Finlayson. At 88m (289 ft.), this peak doesn't offer much in the way of bragging rights—but its views are superb, spreading beyond the lighthouse to Puget Sound.

Either way, plunge into the hushed, shadowy forest—a great contrast to the prairie. Here, hemlocks and cedars sprout on fallen firs (known as "nurse logs"), alongside delicate mosses and orchids. Ferns, Salal, and other shrubberies crowd the understory, while pileated woodpeckers hammer above. A short path leads down to Jakle's Lagoon and Griffin Bay. Turn right and head up the hill, climbing past the main trail.

❻ Mount Finlayson The trees and shrubs thin towards the top of Finlayson, where the grassland reasserts itself. Small Rocky Mountain junipers dot this arid plateau, also home to mice and voles, which attract owls, hawks, and other predators. Those include red fox, whose color may range from auburn to black, always crowned by a white-tipped brush tail, though. On the mainland, the species has a more coyote look: Locals speculate that English soldiers released this invasive strain to hunt.

At the summit, scan the Strait of Juan de Fuca for orcas, otters, or sea lions. To the southwest, the Olympic Mountains may be visible. This range pushes the clouds high, pouring all their moisture over the temperate rainforests. This creates the "banana belt": a dry zone girded by damp. In fact, another inch of rain falls for each mile west you travel from Port Angeles, Washington. Thanks to this rain shadow, American Camp enjoys a relatively balmy climate.

Loop down the open hillside, passing through the trail head parking lot. A brief stretch of road reconnects with Pickett's Lane, and the track to the redoubt and interpretive center lies straight ahead.

7 The Redoubt Here, the hopelessly outgunned U.S. Army could survey all the water approaches to the island. Little remains of their fortifications, except the earthworks of the redoubt (fort). When the "mountains are out," as Washingtonians say, Baker gleams to the east, past the old Parade Ground with its white picket fence. The Olympic and Cascade ranges are also visible on clear days, with Mount Rainier—a volcanic snow cone 209km (130 miles) away—making guest appearances. From the redoubt, follow the self-guided trail a half kilometer (1/3 mile) west back to the parking lot.

5 THE GALLOPING GOOSE TODD TRESTLE—HUTCHINSON COVE

Difficulty rating: Moderate

Distance: 20.5km (12.7 miles) round trip

Estimated time: 5–6 hr.

Elevation gain: None

Costs/permits: None

Best time to go: Open year-round, this trail is especially pleasant when autumn ignites the foliage.

Website: www.crd.bc.ca/parks/galloping-goose/index.htm and www.gallopinggoosetrail.com

Recommended map: CRD Parks produces a Galloping Goose Regional Trail Guide, which can be downloaded from www.crd.bc.ca/parks/galloping-goose/index.htm

Trail head GPS: N 48 25.686, W 123 42.647

Trail head directions: Drive north of Victoria on the Trans-Canada Highway (Hwy. 1), then turn west on Rte. 14 towards Sooke. Just past the transit center and strip of stores, take a right onto Sooke River Rd. The trail head is 6km (3¾ miles) north with outhouses, information boards, and a parking lot.

From downtown Victoria, the 55km (34-mile) Galloping Goose Trail traces an old Canadian National Rail line from the 1920s and is named for one if its noisy, gas-powered cars. It's part of the Trans-Canada Trail, which traverses the country. The more rustic western stretches have many moods, like a vaudeville show. Our recommended route centers around the Sooke River Road parking lot at 43km (27 miles). First, head north to explore the trestles, falls, and fantastical limestone formations at Sooke Potholes Provincial Park. Then, backtrack towards the water, passing backyard forts and perhaps detouring for bacon-flecked, *poutine*-inspired fries at Homers Most Excellent Take Out. Finally, thread along the rocky headlands of the Sooke Basin until the turnaround point at Hutchinson Cove. Options abound to shorten, lengthen, or—for those who push daylight or dally too long at the Fuse Grill—just plain cheat the route (hurrah for the #61 bus!).

Head north from the 43km (27-mile) point, the Sooke River Road parking lot. The shady trail aims straight past riots of ferns at the outset, while olive- and sage-colored mosses coat the sci-fi rock formations. Ignore the strange creaking and squealing in the background: The path borders a working gravel pit.

1 Ridgeline View The forest thins, opening up views of the ridgeline. Tawny grasses creep beside the trail—and suddenly, it's easy to picture Butch Cassidy and the Sundance Kid hunkered behind the crags, waiting to ambush the train's payroll, though the outlaws never wandered this far north (not to mention that

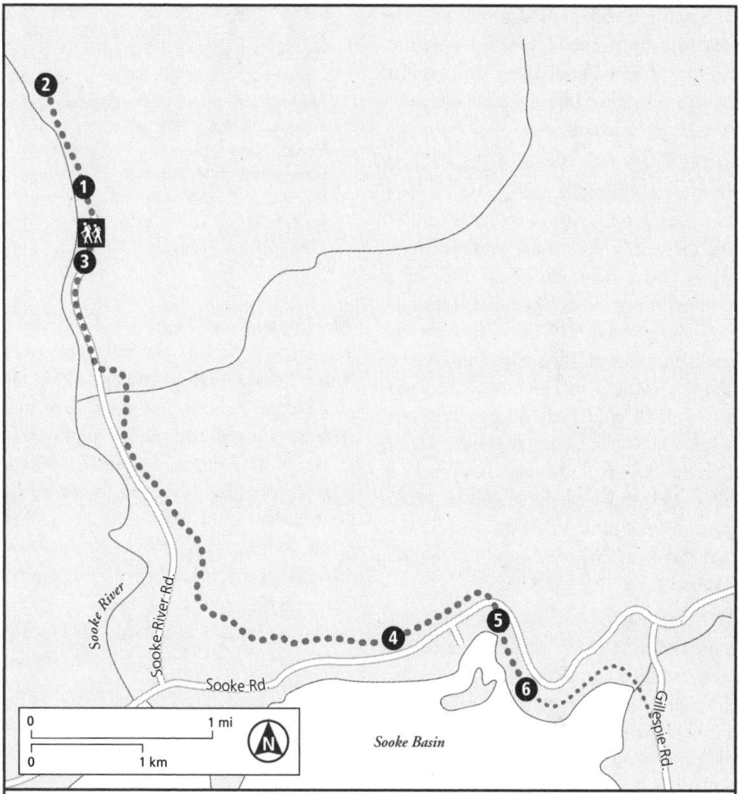

Sooke River
Sooke River Rd.
Sooke Rd.
Gillespie Rd.
Sooke Basin
0 1 mi
0 1 km

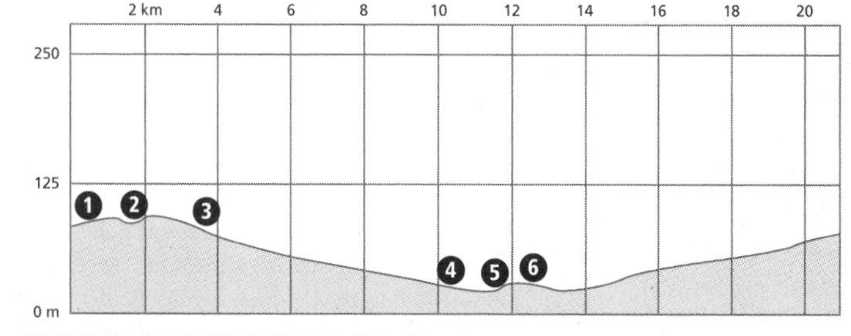

- Trail head: N 48 25.686, W 123 42.647 (0 km): Trail head
- ❶ N 48 25.914, W 123 42.753 (0.5 km): Views of ridgeline appear as forest thins
- ❷ N 48 26.428, W 123 43.160 (1.8 km): Entrance to Sooke Provincial Potholes Park
- ❸ N 48 25.558, W 123 42.656 (3.8 km): Head past Sooke River Road trail head to water
- ❹ N 48 23.478, W 123 40.031 (10.2 km): Path crosses Harbourview Road
- ❺ N 48 23.635, W 123 39.154 (11.6 km): Hutchinson Cove
- ❻ N 48 23.271, W 123 38.960 (12.4 km): Turnaround point

the Wild Bunch flourished in the 1890s, while the Goose's heyday was the 1920s). The two railroad trestles further into the trek seal the fantasy. Curving high above bourbon-colored pools, they still smell of creosote—and a whiff of gun smoke, with enough imagination.

❷ The Potholes Between Charter Creek Trestle (at 45km/28 miles) and the one spanning Todd Creek (at 46km/29 miles) lies the Sooke Provincial Potholes Park. Water and wind sculpted the rock here, eroding limestone into gargoyle lumps.

Those enchanted by the Wild West vibe could continue on the same route another 9km (5½ miles) to Leechtown, an abandoned 1864 gold rush village: Bears and cougars now lurk among the ruins, weeds, and wildflowers. However, the scenery is more spectacular to the south, so beat a hasty retreat back to Sooke River Road trail head—then keep heading for the water.

❸ Coastward Bound South of this route's starting point, maple gives way to arbutus and Douglas fir. The trail winds through fields and back yards, full of forts and rope swings. The interurban nature of the route grows clearer. Once part of the Canadian National Railway, this stretch connected Sooke and Victoria. The Galloping Goose commuter carriage that traveled this section ferried mail and 30 passengers daily.

❹ Harbourview Road Water vistas blossom at around 40km (25 miles). The trail hugs close to Sooke Road for 300m (984 ft.). Where the Goose intersects with Harbourview Road is a pleasant bench. Queen Anne's lace frames bobbing boats and a distant water tower. A kilometer (½ mile) on, the path crosses Sooke Road and veers steadily east, tracing the rocky shoreline of Sooke Basin.

TAKE A BREAK

Where the Goose crosses Sooke Road stands **Fuse Waterfront Grill,** a chic eatery with a waterfront patio. Its dishes range from predictable (chowder) to imaginative (mint edamame). Standouts include seared polenta and Sooke trout with tricolor confit potatoes. (5449 Sooke Rd., Sooke. ✆ **250/642-0011.** www.fuse-waterfrontgrill.com. Open Mon–Thurs 11am–9pm, Fri–Sat 11am–10pm.)

❺ Hutchinson Cove Bed-and-breakfast signs punctuate the trail, but otherwise, trekkers can daydream along the land's edge. Benches line the narrow shelf between the cliff and the sweep of water.

At 38km (24 miles) unfurls Hutchinson Cove. Here, hikers can begin backtracking (our recommendation) or extend their jaunt another 4km (2½ miles) to Roche Cove Regional Park, where there is another car-accessible trail head, useful to parties with two vehicles. (The no. 66 bus also runs down here, but not with helpful regularity.)

❻ Turnaround Point Too tired to retrace your steps all the way back to the Sooke River Road parking lot? Turn inland at Manzer Road, then left on Sooke Road. The no. 61 Victoria-Sooke bus runs along this stretch roughly on the hour until 5:44pm (more often during morning and evening commutes; ✆ 250/382-6161; www.bctransit.com). Just past the high school, disembark at the transit center—near the convenience store and Homer's Most Excellent Take Out, renowned for burgers and poutine-inspired fries—then walk north up the Sooke River Road. This shortcut eliminates about 6km (3¾ miles) from the hike.

6 JUAN DE FUCA MARINE TRAIL

Difficulty rating: Moderate

Distance: 10km (6.2 miles) round trip

Estimated time: 3–4 hr.

Elevation gain: The trail undulates over hilly terrain, but no climbs exceed 60m (200 ft.).

Costs/permits: C$3 parking fee, C$5 per person overnight fee if you extend the hike

Best time to go: Pods of gray whales often draw close to shore May–Aug.

Website: www.env.gov.bc.ca/bcparks/explore/parkpgs/juan_de_fuca

Recommended map: 92C09

Trail head GPS: N 48 31.976, W 124 26.637

Trail head directions: Drive north of Victoria on the Trans-Canada Highway (Hwy. 1), then turn west on Rte. 14 through Sooke. Past the Jordan River lies the China Beach trail head, then Sombrio Beach's and Parkinson Creek's. Continue west beyond these and the town of Port Renfrew. Turn left before the Port Renfrew Hotel and government dock, then drive 3.5km (2¼ miles) down a gravel road to the Botanical Beach parking lot. The West Coast Trail Express (✆ 888/999-2288 or 250-477-8700; www.trailbus.com; C$25) also serves this area.

Orca pods sometimes cruise close to shore here. Southern Vancouver Island's best tasting menu also features waterfalls, eagles, surf, seals, sandstone bluffs, and tide pools brimming with sea stars, urchins, and sponges. Not as rigorous as the nearby West Coast Trail, the Juan de Fuca hints at the same landscape—and doesn't require expensive permits, hard-to-score reservations, or nearly as much time.

Like its more glamorous cousin, this trek has roots in the 1889 telegraph line that linked Victoria to Bamfield, where the transpacific cable flowed out to the British Empire. Volunteers renewed the overgrown, long-neglected trail to mark the 1994 Commonwealth Games in Victoria.

While the Juan de Fuca stretches 47km (29 miles), we recommend day-hikers tackle its westernmost tip. Like a Zen koan, begin at the end: Botanical Beach. There, the trail threads through temperate rainforest, flirting with the coastline. At around 42km (26 miles), the area west of Providence Cove provides a good turnaround and picnicking point. Mix up the return trip with the loop to some of the richest tidal areas along the west coast.

Jammed in summer, the Botanical Beach Trail head draws all types, from toddlers to backpackers tackling the entire 4- to 5-day route. Volunteer attendants sometimes watch the parking lot during high season since break-ins have become all too common.

The Botanical Beach Trail descends steeply through a shady forest. After 1.2km (¾ mile), it passes an outhouse and reaches the water. Turn left here for the Juan de Fuca Trail.

❶ Juan de Fuca Trail Head Thread among hemlock, Sitka spruce, and western red cedars as the route mirrors the coast. Step carefully. Gnarled roots booby-trap the trail—and boardwalks can tilt at strange angles, not to mention grow slick with moss and rain.

Vancouver Island shelters one of the world's largest remaining stands of old-growth temperate rainforest, yet two-thirds of its old trees are now gone, mostly due to pulp and paper production.

❷ The Spit About a half-kilometer (1/4 mile) from the Juan de Fuca's trail head, a peninsula juts into the strait. Sandstone flows into the sea: on a calm day, it resembles velvet spilling onto a mirror. Drift logs, weathered bone-white, jumble like pick-up-sticks in the cove. Here buoys—once-bright tubes and bells of Styrofoam—in the trees mark the points where the path traverses the beach, as elsewhere on this route and the nearby West Coast Trail.

❸ Soule Creek The path swerves inland after 1.5km (1 mile) to cross its third stream. Listen for staccato rhythms: both downy and pileated woodpeckers inhabit this forest. The heights might also reveal the tree-climbing clouded salamander: Vancouver Island is the only place to spot these agile creatures in all of Canada.

❹ Providence Cove Stunning, jagged coastline unreels between Soule Creek and Providence Cove. The third "beach" access point provides an atmospheric stop at 42km (26 miles)—and our recommended turn-around point (from here, the trail turns inland, crosses Yauh Creek, then descends to Payzant Creek campsite at 40km/25 miles and on to Parkinson's Creek trail head at 37km/23 miles, for those with two vehicles, trail bus reservations, or friends willing to play chauffeur).

TAKE A BREAK Sheaves of dark shale loom over the sea at 42km (26 miles), this hike's turnaround point—offering a fine view for anyone ready to break for a picnic.

❺ Botanical Beach Retrace your steps back to the Juan de Fuca Trail head, then mix things up with the Botanical Loop (straight ahead). This well-signed path returns hikers to the parking lot via an alternate 1.6km (1 mile) route, rather than the 1.2km (3/4-mile) path taken earlier.

A short spur branches to the left, revealing views of Botanical Beach. Ridges of shale and quartz jut through the black basalt, creating a dramatic tableau, often punctuated with wheeling osprey and eagles. But the landscape's true glory unfolds on a smaller scale. Sandstone shelves smoothed by surf cradle tide pools teeming with life. Anemones and gooseneck barnacles jostle for space, alongside sea stars in lurid hues of red, purple, and orange. Visitors have even found octopuses in the sun-warmed basins. Here biologists have recorded more than 100 marine invertebrates and 231 plant species, including the discovery of the kelp *Laminaria ephemera.*

Be aware, however, that waves can smash this coast—known as the "Graveyard of the Pacific"—like Mac trucks. This fickle, ever-changing environment attracted the Northwest's first marine research station back in 1901, where scientists from the University of Minnesota studied this strip. The rainforest long ago reclaimed its ruins, however.

❻ Bonsai Tree Wind, water, and thin topsoil conspire to dwarf and twist trees here. A particularly fine specimen is signposted 500m (1,640 ft.) down the trail.

Fun Facts **Time and Tides**

Sea levels below 1.2m (4 ft.) showcase the shore best, especially the legendary tide pools at Botany Bay. Consult the Canadian Tide Tables "Port Renfrew section," adding 1 hour to calculations from May to October, when Daylight Saving Time kicks in (www.lau.chs-shc.gc.ca).

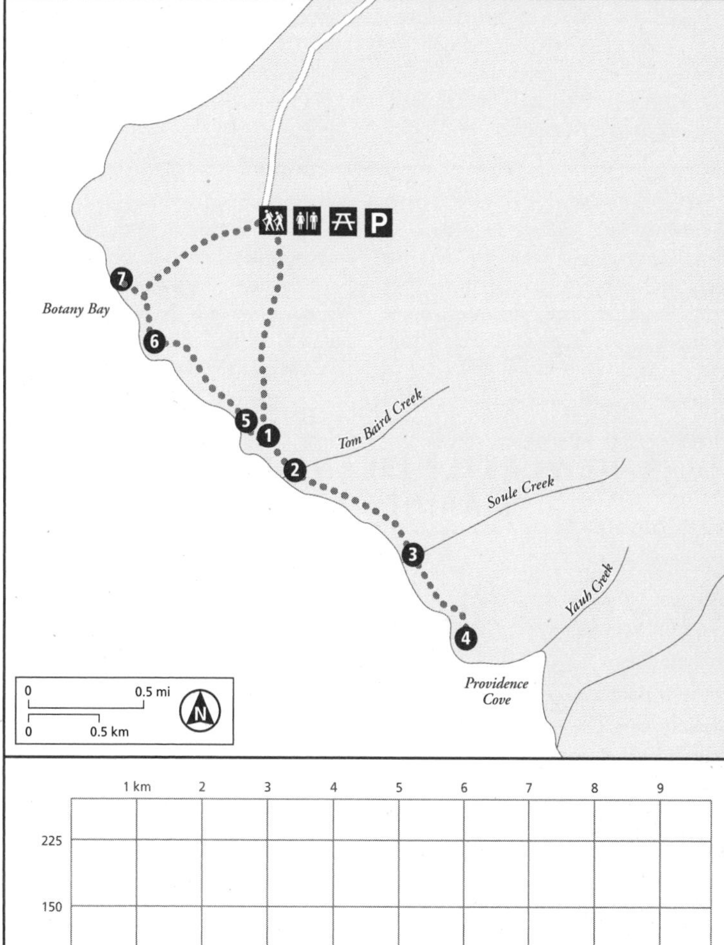

N 48 31.976, W 124 26.637 (0 km): Trail head

1. N 48 31.590, W 124 26.575 (1.2 km): Turn left at Juan de Fuca trail head
2. N 48 31.542, W 124 26.250 (1.7 km): The Spit
3. N 48 31.470, W 124 25.135 (3.2 km): Cross Soule Creek
4. N 48 31.105, W 124 24.340 (4.5 km): Providence Cove access point
5. N 48 31.593, W 124 26.693 (8 km): Turn on to Botanical Loop
6. N 48 31.747, W 124 26.992 (8.4 km): Pass Bonsai tree
7. N 48 31.832, W 124 27.157 (8.7 km): Arrive at Botany Bay

Kids Play Nice

The Botanical Beach–Botany Bay loop remains popular with families. The 3km (1¾-mile) route descends through forest to the tide pools. Curtail the splashing, however: Even touching the water with sunscreen could kill vulnerable creatures. Also, keep children away from the surf line, as rogue waves can drag people out to sea, even on calm days.

7 Botany Bay After 300m (984 ft.), the trail emerges into Botany Bay, home to sandy and pebbled coves protected by rocky headlands and platforms. Some small sea caves dot the shoreline. From here, the trail hooks inland, following an old road that leads trekkers 1km (½ mile) back to the north end of the parking lot. Anyone complaining of tired legs should be reminded of adventure racer Shawn Nelson, who holds the record for traversing the entire 47km (29-mile) trail: 6 hours and 15 minutes!

7 NEWCASTLE ISLAND PROVINCIAL MARINE PARK ★★

Difficulty rating: Easy

Distance: 7.5km (4.7 miles) round trip; shorter options available

Estimated time: 2–3 hr.

Elevation gain: 60m (200 feet)

Costs/permits: C$8 return ferry ticket

Best time to go: Accessible year-round, Newcastle Island's ferries run most frequently from mid-May to early Sept.

Website: www.env.gov.bc.ca/bcparks/explore/parkpgs/newcastle or www.newcastleisland.ca

Recommended map: Ferry operators dispense a free Newcastle Island pamphlet with map.

Trail head GPS: N 49 10.825, W 123 55.720

Trail head directions: The Nanaimo Harbour Ferry trundles passengers from Maffeo Sutton Park to Newcastle Island. Drive north from downtown Nanaimo on Terminal Ave. (19A). Turn left after the Civic Arena into the parking lot. The dock lies past the playground.

Accessible by a 10-minute pint-sized ferry, this island once sheltered Salish villagers: Some shell middens remain. Mining and Japanese herring salteries once thrived here, too. In 1941, the Canadian Pacific Steamship Company bought Newcastle as a tourist destination. Its pavilion now houses a snack shop and cultural venue.

The perimeter trail ambles past marshes, lakes, coastal caves, and an old sandstone quarry. Altogether, this history-rich park contains 22km (14 miles) of trails, so hikers can extend or shorten their explorations.

Various paths blossom from the dock on the southern tip, overlooking Nanaimo, Bate Point, and nearby Protection Island. Totemic carvings greet visitors, along with the amenities: marina, phone, playground, restroom, snack shop, historical exhibit, and on any given day, a mess of school children dorking around with push carts

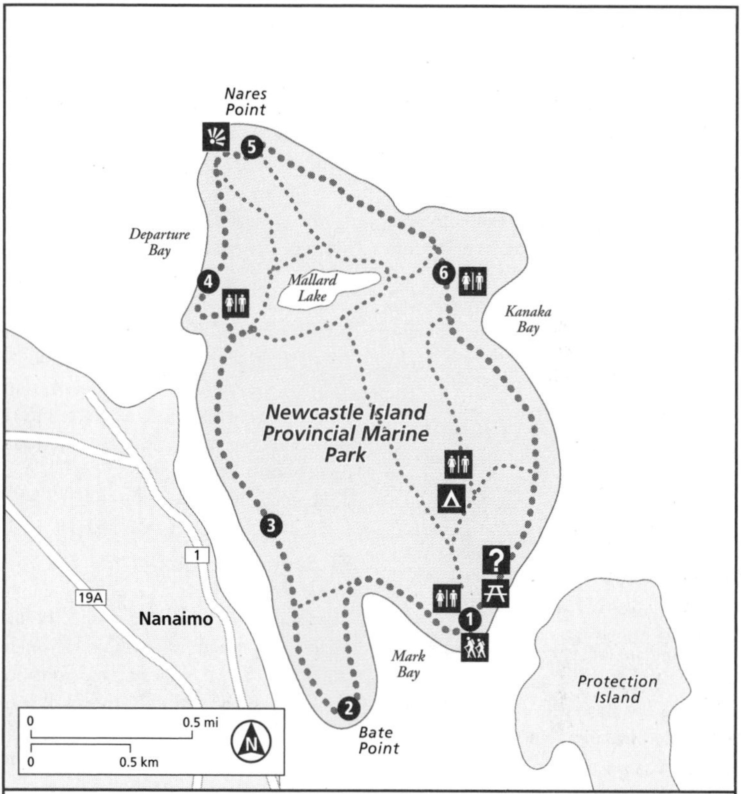

Nares Point
Departure Bay
Mallard Lake
Kanaka Bay
Newcastle Island Provincial Marine Park
1
19A
Nanaimo
Mark Bay
Protection Island
Bate Point
0 0.5 mi
0 0.5 km
N

1 km
2
3
4
5
6
7
150
75
0 m

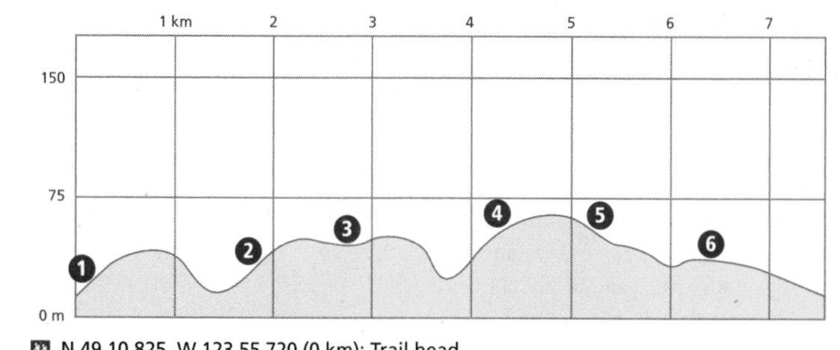

N 49 10.825, W 123 55.720 (0 km): Trail head
❶ N 49 10.849, W 123 55.700 (0.1 km): Totem pole northeast of the dock
❷ N 49 10.701, W 123 56.200 (1.8 km): Small wharf at Bate Point
❸ N 49 11.186, W 123 56.533 (2.8 km): Old Sandstone quarry
❹ N 49 11.749, W 123 56.744 (4.3 km): Turn left on Shoreline Trail
❺ N 49 12.122, W 123 56.560 (5.2 km): Turn left at intersection towards Nares Point
❻ N 49 11.798, W 123 55.868 (6.4 km): Trail skirts north end of Mallard Lake

full of camping gear. Veer left along Mark Bay to circumnavigate the island.

❶ Totem Pole Immediately northeast of the dock, a totem demonstrates the Snuneymuxw's presence, which dates back thousands of years. Here, these coastal Salish people hunted deer, fished for salmon, and gathered clams, crabs, and shellfish. They also trained youths in spiritual ways, as well as foot racing and canoe pulling. One of their legends claims Haals, the transformer, turned animals and people to stone. Along the island's western side, look for the unusual shapes in the shoreline sandstone that inspired this tale.

TAKE A BREAK The old dance pavilion houses an exhibit space and a small café selling fresh dairy products from local farms. A long, brick-red building, it stands about 500m (1,640 ft.) north of the docks.

The abundant fish later attracted *issei*, first generation Japanese-Canadians, who built the Nanaimo Shipyards and herring salteries facing Brechin Point and Departure Bay. The government confiscated these properties during the WWII internment sweeps. No ruins are visible, as these businesses were stripped of their assets, then razed and burned after the war.

Keep an eye out for rare purple martins *(progne subis arboricola),* which dwell in nest boxes. Nearly exterminated in the mid-80s, these medium-sized songbirds battled back from a low of five breeding pairs. By 2006, BC reduced their status from "threatened" to "vulnerable." Newcastle alone has over 30 couples now, most often spotted near the docks around dawn or dusk. About 100m (328 ft.) north of the docks, the trail forks. Veer left and either continue northwest for 500m (1,640 ft.) or thread along the less formal trails at the edge of Mark Bay. Both routes converge at the junction for the Bate Point Trail. Turn left, following the bay's other flank south.

❷ Bate Point Trees bow towards the water, curved by years of wild winds. The Canadian Pacific Steamship bought Newcastle in 1931, creating a resort complete with a "boatel." The *Charmer* (later replaced by the *Princess Victoria*) allowed visitors to overnight in the cove. Popular for company picnics, this destination drew ships from Vancouver, sometimes attracting 1,500 people per day. When the war diverted many of the vessels, the area's star sank.

Boats still moor in the shelter of Mark Bay, and another small wharf stands at Bate Point, a sandy spit. Here, the route curves north again, following the Channel Trail along the water. After 400m (1,312 ft.), a junction appears. Go straight.

❸ Sandstone Quarry A half-kilometer (1/4 mile) on, a tumble of rough-hewn boulders stack in a basin: the old quarry. From here, the U.S. government purchased 8,000 tons of sandstone for the San Francisco Mint. Others followed suit, since Newcastle's rock is unusually strong, flawless, and water-resistant. Check it out at Nanaimo's Post Office and Court House, Victoria's Oddfellows Hall, and the BC Penitentiary.

Follow a short spur to the water, where a monumental column sprawls before a view of Nanaimo. Bound for the mint, this sank along with the barque *Zephyr* near Mayne Island during an 1872 snowstorm. A diver discovered the wreck more than 100 years later. It became a BC Historic Site, while some of the cubes and one 40-ton pillar returned home.

Backtrack to the quarry. At press time, the park had closed the stairs on its northern end: the usual route. So, retrace your steps about 250m (820 ft.) to the south, where mountain goat types can bound up

Fun Facts Blondes Have More Fun

Newcastle Island shelters an unusual number of champagne raccoons—pale yellow mutants who lack black pigment in their fur, but otherwise are normal.

the left-hand slope—and mere mortals can burn 2 or 3 minutes on a gentler detour.

4 Mine Shaft Continue north, turning left, then immediately left again towards Shaft Point on the Shoreline Trail. The rich coal seams here earned the island its name (in honor of the famous mining town Newcastle-upon-Tyne, England). Danger and racism led to strikes in 1862, shortly before the Hudson's Bay Company sold its stake. The industry halted here 2 decades later, but traces still remain near Midden Bay.

5 Nares Point About 700m (2,297 ft.) north, the trail curves at Tyne Point, then reaches an intersection. Turn left, reaching Nares Point in a few minutes. Just east of here, a short diversion leads to the Giovando Lookout, offering views of the Strait of Georgia and Coastal Mountains.

6 Mallard Lake The perimeter trail skirts to the north of this lake, home to beavers, ducks, mergansers, and tiny pumpkin seed sunfish.

Tired hikers can turn left and cut south 3km (1¾ miles) to the docks here on the Mallard Lake Trail, saving about 1km (½ mile). This route winds through a mature forest of arbutus, Douglas fir, and Garry oak. Otherwise, continue 4km (2½ miles) along the shoreline, past Kanaka Bay and Brownie Bay on the Shoreline Trail. The latter is named for *Kanakas,* Hawaiian immigrant laborers who worked throughout the British colonies. The channel between Newcastle and Protection Islands narrows just before the amenities. During summer low tides, visitors can walk across "the gap" without submerging their ankles.

8 WILD PACIFIC TRAIL

Difficulty rating: Easy

Distance: 7.8km (4.8 miles) round trip

Estimated time: 2–3 hr.

Elevation gain: Minimal

Costs/permits: None

Pet friendly: Yes

Best time to go: Delightful year-round, the trail provides superb storm-watching opportunities in winter.

Website: www.longbeachmaps.com/wildtrail.html

Recommended map: The 8.4km (5.2-mile) trail head on Peninsula Road stocks free maps. Pick one up on the way into Ucluelet.

Trail head GPS: N 48 56.242, W 125 33.028

Trail head directions: Take Hwy. 4 across the island. At the coastal T-intersection, turn left towards Ucluelet on Peninsula Rd. Turn right onto Matterson Dr. just past downtown. The unmarked parking lot lies on the right, third block down. Cross Marine Dr. to reach the 4.5km (2.8-mile) trail head.

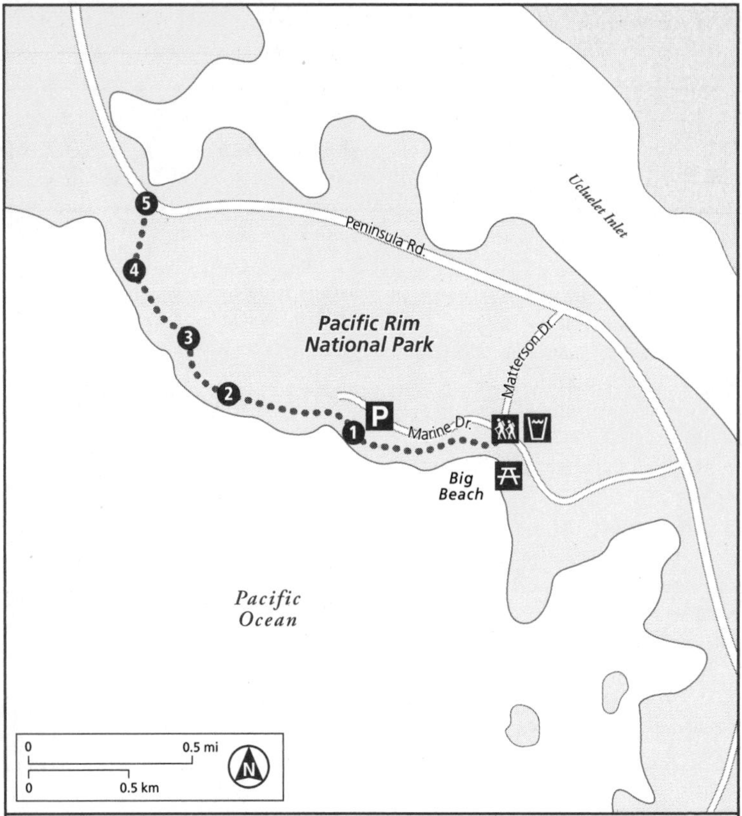

Uclulet Inlet
Peninsula Rd.
Pacific Rim National Park
Matterson Dr.
Marine Dr.
Big Beach
Pacific Ocean
0 0.5 mi
0 0.5 km
N

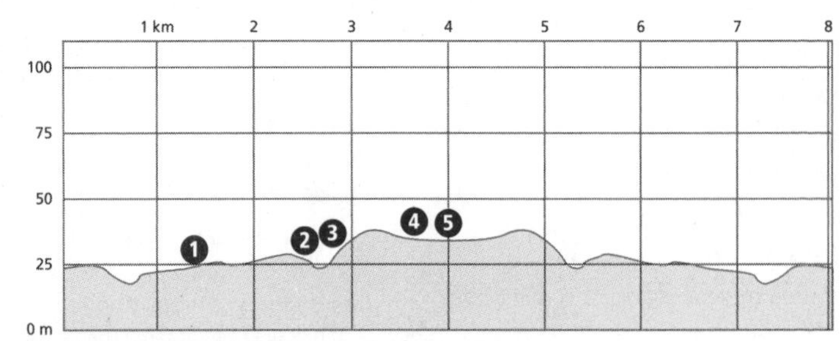

N 48 56.242, W 125 33.028 (0 km): Trail head

❶ N 48 56.284, W 125 33.661 (1.4 km): Oceanwest development

❷ N 48 56.396, W 125 34.246 (2.5 km): Ahluwalia memorial bench

❸ N 48 56.505, W 125 34.246 (2.8 km): Skirt gorge

❹ N 48 56.695, W 125 34.563 (3.6 km): Follow short spur left down to marsh

❺ N 48 56.859, W 125 34.436 (4 km): Trail end at Peninsula Road

Gray whales migrate past this route late Feb–late May. Surfers, seals, and sea lions often play in the whitewater. The views of Barkley Sound and the Broken Group Islands are most spectacular when storm-tossed in winter. Gales here strip all color from the sea, which spits foam and fog. Spruce and cedars shelter hikers, however, and numerous benches invite daydreaming. But don't zone out too much: Bears, cougars, and wolves prowl this area, no matter how manicured the walkway.

Still under construction, the Wild Pacific Trail (WPT) has two unconnected segments: a 2.5km (1.6-mile) loop at Amphitrite Lighthouse and a longer 4.4km (2.7-mile) stretch to the west. Two kilometers (1¼ miles) of pavement separate them (Peninsula Rd. and Marine Dr.). Our recommended route begins at Big Beach, home to the 4.4km (2.8-mile) trail head. Bleached bone white, driftwood logs—indeed, whole trunks with root systems—mass along this sandy cove. The path dips and weaves through the rainforest. Examine the fungi, mosses, and ferns that first sprout on fallen timber. Some of these "nurse logs" boost mature trees high in the canopy.

TAKE A BREAK The first headland, 15m (49 ft.) west of Big Beach, boasts an appealing wood-slab picnic table. Pack treats from Tofino's **Breakers Deli** (430 Campbell St.; ✆ **250/725-2558;** www.breakersdeli.com; open daily 7am–10pm), like a falafel wrap, smoked salmon burrito, or chevre and roasted tofu salad.

1 Oceanwest The WPT becomes difficult to follow after 1.5km (1 mile), due to a real estate development going by the name Oceanwest.

The developer claims the route will be improved and brought closer to the water. Until that occurs, hikers should hug as close to the water as possible and remain attentive (the signposts are more obvious on the way back).

2 Ahluwalia Bench Another kilometer (½ mile) down the trail, especially fine 180-degree views open up from this memorial bench. To the east is Barkley Sound and the Broken Group Islands. To the west, the Pacific Ocean unfurls. There's nothing out there except Hawaii, Japan, and Australia.

Rest here and scan for gray whales during their spring migration. Seals, mink, river otters, and sea lions also ply these waters.

3 Gorge A half-kilometer (¼ mile) down the trail, signs warn hikers away from the crumbling edges of a chasm. Remember to wrench your gaze away from the pounding surf occasionally: Bald and gold eagles may coast overhead.

4 Marshland A short spur—the trail's only one—runs left down to a boggy area, excellent for bird watching. Expect to log ducks, herons, and oystercatchers along the Wild Pacific Trail.

5 End Trail Head At 8.4km (5¼ miles), the trail dead-ends on Peninsula Road. Either follow the bike path back into town or, preferably, pivot and experience it all again eastbound.

Fun Facts **Need to Park a Canoe?**

Ucluelet's tongue-twisting syllables derive from the Nuu-chah-nulth First Nation phrase *Yu-clutl-ahts:* the people with a good landing place for canoes. Struggling with you-*clue*-let? Call it "Ukee," like the locals do.

9 BIG CEDAR TRAIL, MEARES ISLAND

Difficulty rating: Easy

Distance: 1.2km (.7 miles) or 2.6km (1.6 miles) round trip

Estimated time: 1 hr. or 2 hrs. (plus water transit)

Elevation gain: Minimal

Costs/permits: Water taxi (C$25) or guided paddle trip (C$75)

Best time to go: Hike-able year-round, this trail appeals most in summer, when more light pierces the thick rainforest canopy.

Website: www.longbeachmaps.com/wildtrail.html

Recommend map: NTS 92C, but the route is very clearly marked

Trail head GPS: N 49 9.020, W 125 52.118

Trail head directions: Take Hwy. 4 across the island 156km (97 miles) from its start near Parksville. At its other end, the coastal T-intersection, turn right. Pass through Pacific Rim National Park en route to Tofino. Meares Island is across Browning Passage: Arrange a water taxi or boat excursion.

A water taxi or paddle tour ferries hikers to this Tla-o-qui-aht tribal park, created after a 1984 logging controversy. Groves of giant trees reward the extra travel effort, especially the Hanging Garden Cedar, estimated to be 2,000 years old, with an 18m (59-ft.) circumference. Clayoquot Sound (pronounced "Klak-wot") sprawls over about eight percent of Vancouver Island. Rivers and lakes meet the wild Pacific Rim here, fringed with temperate rainforests both rare and ancient. Parks preserve only one-quarter of this terrain. While not a significant leg-stretcher, Meares Island's Big Cedar Trail remains a BC highlight for its eagle nests, extraordinary old growth, and the lengths Canadians took to preserve it. The chance to easily combine hiking and boating—by kayak or traditional canoe—adds even more allure.

The **Tofino Water Taxi** departs from the 1st Street Dock by arrangement, although it doesn't always honor confirmed reservations (C$25 per person, C$50 minimum fare; ✆ **877/726-5484;** www.tofinowatertaxi.com). **Ocean Outfitters** provides a more reliable service at the same price (#5-421 Main St., Tofino; ✆ **877/906-2326** or 250/725-2866; www.oceanoutfitters.bc.ca). Trips begin below the company's office on Main Street, between 3rd and 4th streets.

Even better: Paddle out to Meares Island. The **Tofino Sea Kayaking Company** offers a 4- to 5-hour excursion that includes gear rental and is suitable for all active travelers, regardless of boat experience (C$75; 320 Main St., Tofino; ✆ **800/863-4664** or 250/725-4222; www.tofino-kayaking.com). Boats launch from below its office, and the package includes a guided hike on the Big Cedar Trail. **Tla-ook Cultural Adventures** offers similar half-day tours by canoe: paddling or sailing, depending on the winds. Their Wild Grocery Walk concentrates on the edibles of Meares Island (C$64; ✆ **250/725-2656**; www.tlaook.com).

❶ **Meares' Island Dock** Disembark onto a boardwalk of cedar shakes. At the junction, 81m (266 ft.) up, turn left (the right branch leads to the high-tide kayak pull-out spot). Salal and salmonberries line the path, providing sweet trailside snacks in late summer. Salal is a leathery-leaved shrub that produces purple-black berries, usually in August. It may look familiar, as the plant's a florist staple, often paired with long-stemmed roses.

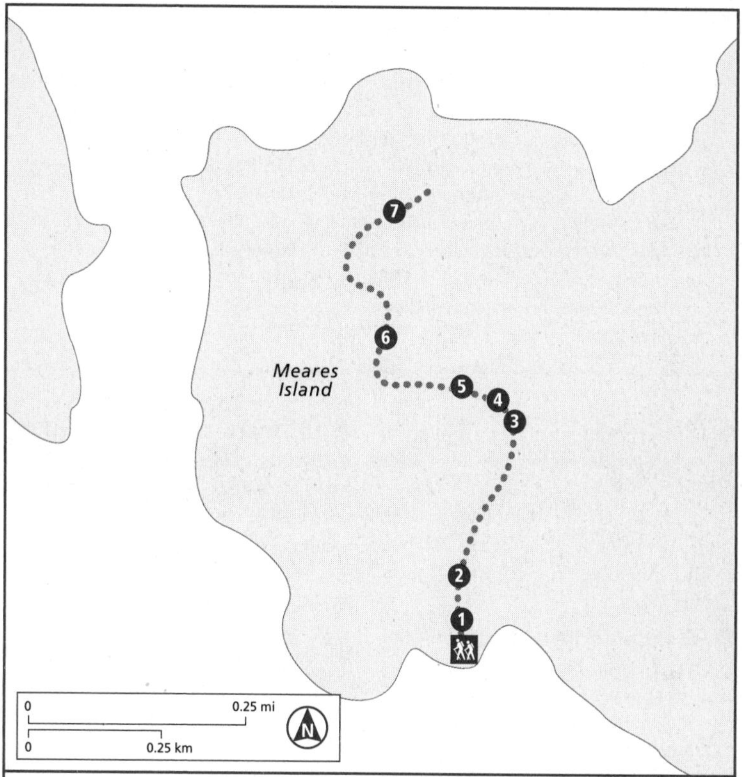

Meares
Island
0
0.25 mi
0
0.25 km
N

.5 km
1
1.5
2
200
150
100
50
0 m

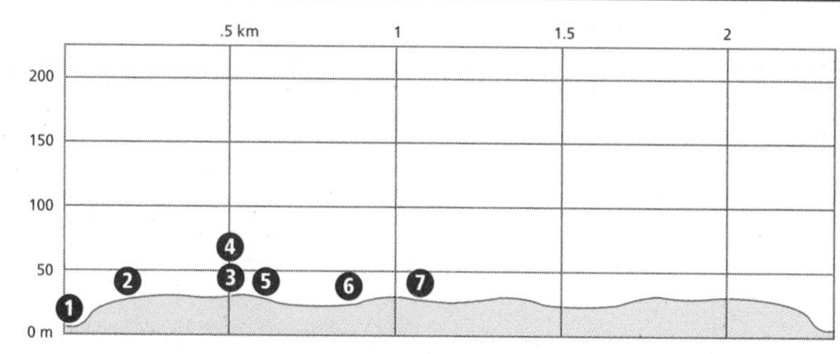

- N 49 9.020, W 125 52.118 (0 km): Trail head
- ❶ N 49 9.018, W 125 52.090 (0 km): Turn left at junction 80m beyond the dock
- ❷ N 49 9.081, W 125 52.098 (0.2 km): Giant rootball of fallen tree
- ❸ N 49 9.235, W 125 52.005 (0.5 km): Bald eagle nest
- ❹ N 49 9.247, W 125 52.039 (0.5 km): Giant cedar to left of trail
- ❺ N 49 9.259, W 125 52.090 (0.6 km): Boardwalk forks at shake-making place
- ❻ N 49 9.303, W 125 52.206 (0.8 km): Two-thousand-year-old red cedar tree
- ❼ N 49 9.411, W 125 52.201 (1.1 km): Sidewalk ends

Hang Ten in Tofino

Serious Canadian surfers all eventually wash up in Tofino, British Columbia. They pool in this funky end-of-the-road town, surrounded on three sides by Clayoquot Sound, a UNESCO Biosphere Reserve. Vietnam draft dodgers may have inspired locals to carve boards, even if they were uncertain which side to wax. The sport gained momentum in the '80s, when environmentalists lobbied to save old growth in and around this hamlet. In the last decade, local kids began going pro.

The famous Bruhwiler brothers each anchor a school: Raph (**Bruhwiler Surf;** ✆ **250/726-5481;** www.bruhwilersurf.com) and Sepp (**Westside Surf;** ✆ **250/725-2404;** www.westsidesurfschool.com). **Surf Sisters** is Canada's only women's wave-riding academy (✆ **877/724-7873;** www.surfsister.com). Summer camps combine waves with yoga and mother-daughter getaways, despite water temperatures from 9°C to 16°C (48°F–61°F).

Salmonberry fruit resembles a raspberry, but ranges in color from yellow to orange-red.

Spruce and hemlock blast high into the rainforest's canopy, while cedar—"the tree of life," according to many tribes—lurks just underneath.

❷ Giant Rootball Roughly 150m (492 ft.) down the trail, a fallen tree exposes its rootball (a bulb of limbs and dirt). In the hot-tub-sized space it bared, duff—decaying leaf matter—begins to collect. In 50 years, vegetation will grow here again. This slow pace is because 3m (9¾ ft.) of rain bathe the island each year, flushing nutrients from the soil. But the rainforest is resilient: Plants dog-pile each other, growing in the crooks of limbs and atop downed trees (sweetly known as "nurse logs"). These epiphytes—such as mosses, lichens, and ferns—don't directly harm their host plants: They simply boost themselves higher in the canopy.

❸ Bald Eagle Nest At 458m (1,503 ft.), a vast twig haystack—weighing as much as 450kg (992 lb.)—occupies a leaning treetop just off the trail. Winter is the best time to spot America's national bird. The boardwalk offers a few vantage points on the nest: The last is marked with an oar.

❹ The Poster Tree Sixty meters (197 ft.) past the nest, a lofty cedar looms to the left. This giant fronted the successful 1984 campaign to rescue the ancient grove from logging. Environmentalists and local tribes blockaded timber crews and won victory by bringing out the original land treaty with the First Nations people that promised to respect "their gardens."

The Tla-o-qui-aht people declared the island a tribal park—Canada's first. Success here fueled the "War of the Woods" protest a decade later. Over 12,000 people demonstrated against logging in Clayoquot Sound: The RCMP arrested 857 during the summer of 1993 alone. It remains the largest act of civil disobedience in Canadian history.

❺ Make a Shake Continue 75m (246 ft.). Where the boardwalk forks, look left at its birthplace: the shake-making spot. Volunteers hammer a wedge into the natural cracks in logs. The rough-hewn slices become treads on the Big Cedar Trail's elevated walkway.

❻ The Hanging Garden Dead ahead lies the province's fourth-largest red cedar, encircled by boardwalk. Estimated to be 2,000 years old, it has an 18m (59-ft.) circumference. The top is dead, but the lower portions continue to grow. At least 11 hemlocks sprout from its flanks, along with hundreds of epiphytes.

7 Where the Sidewalk Ends The elevated trail ends down a short 58m (190-ft.) spur. Avid bushwhackers can follow flagging tape to the Pipeline Trail, which begins a longer 2.6km (1.6-mile) circuit. Otherwise, retrace your steps back to the dock or high-tide kayak landing.

10 BEDWELL TRAIL, STRATHCONA PROVINCIAL PARK

Difficulty rating: Strenuous

Distance: 12km (7.5 miles) round trip

Estimated time: 7 hr.

Elevation gain: 300m (984 ft.)

Costs/permits: C$3 parking fee; C$5/person each night for overnight hikers

Best time to go: The trail is only passable from late Mar to mid-Nov. Late summer provides the warmest treks in this alpine environment.

Website: www.env.gov.bc.ca/bcparks/explore/parkpgs/strath

Recommended map: Topo 92F/12

Trail head GPS: N 49 31.089, W 125 35.548

Trail head directions: From Victoria, drive on Hwy. 1 to Nanaimo, then take Hwy. 19 north 153km (95 miles) to Campbell River. Stock up on gas and provisions there (next opportunity: Gold River). Turn west on Hwy. 28, winding upland for 48km (30 miles). Cross the channel between Upper Campbell Lake and Buttle Lake, then turn right onto Westmin Rd. At the lake's southern end, just past the scenic pullout, go left onto the unmarked Jim Mitchell Lake Rd. Blast 6.8km (4¼ miles) over gravely washouts—4WD is advisable—to the signposted trail head.

British Columbia's first provincial park rises in sharp, snowy ridges along the island's spine. Waterfalls froth into snake-thin Buttle Lake, 32km (20 miles) long. Often compared to the Alps or Norwegian fjords, this landscape couldn't be more startling (or pleasing), smack in the middle of a coastal island.

The Bedwell Trail rises quickly above the elk-haunted valley at Buttle Lake's southern tip. In fact, the access road does most of the heavy lifting. This rutted, dusty slalom climbs 660m (2,165 ft.) before depositing hikers at a parking lot. The path winds a further 300m (984 ft.) upward, passing Douglas firs and Western red cedar as it threads among the mountain hemlock and creeping juniper upslope. Flowers explode here in summer: heather, violets, and lupins, to name a few. By autumn, turkey tails and other fungi rule the roost.

Mountaineers frequent this trail, en route to summit Tom Taylor. Avid backpackers also connect this route with the multi-day Bedwell River Trail. Our recommended day hike pivots at the outlook above Bedwell Lake. We advise travelers to pause beside Buttle Lake at the intersection of Westmin and Jim Mitchell Lake roads. Here, half-submerged stumps bear witness to the logging permitted in this region, both to make room for the Strathcona Dam reservoir and in "timber swaps" to protect forest elsewhere. Rumor has it that the government traded the upper Bedwell watershed to preserve swathes of what became the Pacific Rim National Park. Roosevelt elk often browse among the reeds at dusk: Scan the marshy area south

Jim Mitchell Lake Rd.
Jim Mitchell Lake
Thelwood Creek
Strathcona Provincial Park
Baby Bedwell Lake
Bedwell Lake
0 1 mi
0 1 km

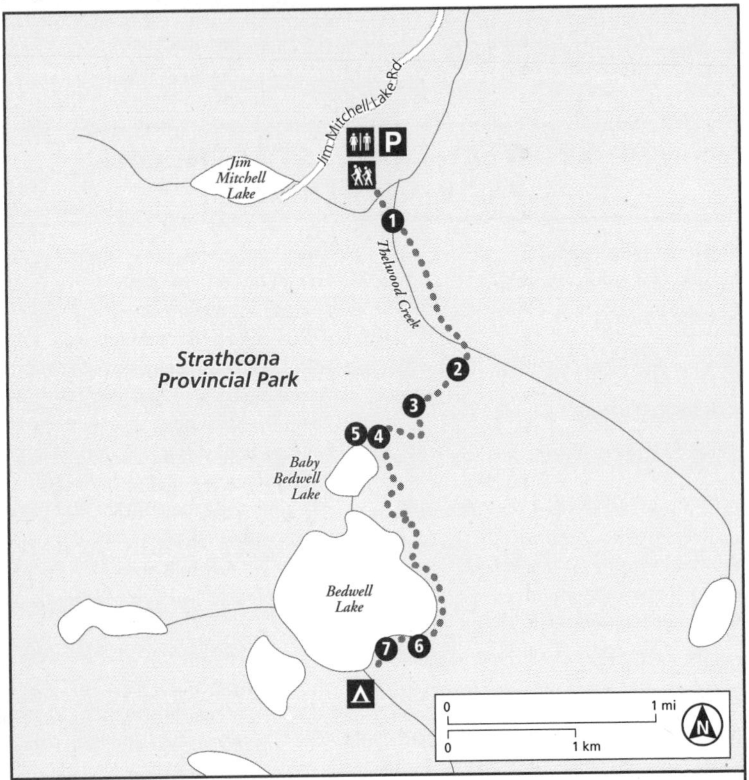

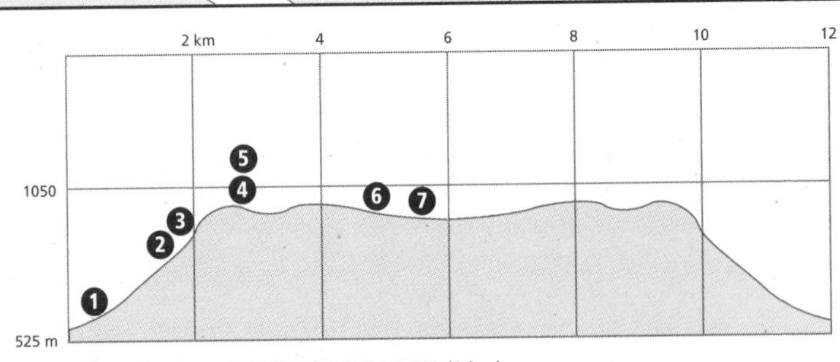

Trail head GPS: N 49 31.089, W 125 35.548 (0 km)

❶ N 49 30.884, W 125 35.322 (0.5 km): Cross bridge over Thelwood Creek.

❷ N 49 30.411, W 125 35.096 (1.6 km): Majestic views appear through forest.

❸ N 49 30.287, W 125 35.307 (1.9 km): First metal ladder.

❹ N 49 30.137, W 125 35.518 (2.6 km): Tent platforms to right of junction.

❺ N 49 30.157, W 125 35.603 (2.7 km): Pass outhouse.

❻ N 49 29.379, W 125 35.376 (4.8 km): Views over Mount Tom Taylor and Taylor Glacier.

❼ N 49 29.402, W 125 35.489 (5.4 km): Descend right-hand spur to Bedwell Lake.

Tips: Fuel Up

Few amenities exist between Campbell River and Gold River: Stock up on gas and groceries before heading inland. Ill-prepared hikers should drop into the Strathcona Park Lodge shop for snacks (40km/25 miles west of Campbell River on Hwy. 28). Or better yet, book a cabin and tuck into the superb buffets, which even cater to vegan and gluten-free diets (✆ **250/286-3122;** www.strathcona.bc.ca).

of Westmin Mine Road, also renowned for bird-sightings. A handful of trumpeter swans overwinter here. Watchers might also spot their cousins, whistling and mute swans, too.

❶ Thelwood Creek A springy bridge spans Thelwood Creek, about 500m (1,640 ft.) down the trail. Spare a thought for James Scott Mitchell, who gave his name to the trail's access road and adjacent lake. During a 1937 survey, he fatally struck his head crossing this stream. *The Comox Argus* reported that the victim was "a six-foot youngster of quiet habits and a good bushman."

Formerly known as "Oinimitis" (Bear River), this area still houses black bruins, as well as cougars, Vancouver Island wolves, and marmots. Also unique are the white-tailed ptarmigan, currently being studied along this route.

A series of switchbacks blast upward from the next bridge. The trail veers into the forest, where lichen-padded logs and stones muffle sound.

❷ Forest Viewpoint About 2.5km (1½ miles) in, the trail begins to play peek-a-boo with views, which are—on the whole—majestic. Except for the bald patches. Though established as a park in 1911, Strathcona has scars from logging and mining. Boliden continues to run a mill, as well as open pit and underground ore excavations. But the real problems may begin when the company pulls out, critics suggest, wondering about maintenance of the tailings (waste by-product) left behind, that could potentially leak toxins into the local environment for many decades.

❸ Metal Staircase A half-kilometer (¼ mile) along, the first metal ladder appears. Some smile upon these kelly-green helpers bolted to various rock faces. Not only do they ease the climbs, but they protect fragile ecosystems. Others find such artificial elements jarring: mountains with handrails. The trail rolls through a marsh after the first set of stairs, passing whiskey-colored pools and then snowy vales.

❹ Baby Bedwell Lake Nine tent platforms preen to the right of the junction. Large and luxurious, they overlook this alpine lake, better suited to swimming than Bedwell proper. Continue ahead for the lake or turn right to witness one of hiking's more curious restrooms—the zippered cocoon toilet—about 100m (328 ft.) down.

❺ Outhouse Made of rubberized canvas flaps atop a PVC frame, it's suspended over a port-a-loo tank. At the end of the season, a helicopter swoops in to whisk the tank away.

❻ The Outlook Retrace your steps to the junction, then continue straight, climbing the craggy knoll. Views of Mount Tom Taylor and Taylor Glacier unfold—when poor weather doesn't envelop the ridge. On misty days, clouds can completely mask the lake (never mind the peaks behind it).

7 Bedwell Lake Descend the right-hand spur to the larger lake, home to another toilet, 12 tent platforms, and a food cache (a bear-proof locker for campers). Mountaineers often overnight here before summiting Tom Taylor and Big Interior Mountain. Avid backpackers could continue to the Pacific Ocean via the Bedwell River Trail (a 2- or 3-day trek). While The Friends of Strathcona Park cut this trail 2 decades ago, it's not formally maintained. If venturing further, be prepared to navigate by topo map and compass here—and to bushwhack, where needed. We recommend day hikers turn around at the outlook or bigger lake.

SLEEPING & EATING

ACCOMMODATIONS

Bamfield's Trails Hotel This cheerful red structure offers its outdoorsy guests a wealth of choice, from a C$39 bunk to a C$170 one-bedroom suite. Set on Bamfield's east side, the affordable option is also closest to the West Coast Trail's launch pad. Its complex includes the Hawk's Nest Pub, often the town's only open restaurant.

226 Frigate Rd., Bamfield. ✆ **877/728-3474** or 250/728-3231. www.hawkeyemarinegroup.com. 35 units and a 10-person bunkhouse. C$39 bunkhouse per person; C$120–170 suite. MC, V. **Close to:** West Coast Trail (start).

★★ **Buccaneer Inn** Nanaimo's highest-rated motel since 1998, this marine-themed gem shines amid the port town's neon-drenched chains. From goose-down duvets to wood-burning fireplaces, quality rules here quietly. Owners Dave and Marlene Ilyn go the extra mile, from real cream to eco-friendly paper products—and all just 3 blocks from the Departure Bay terminal.

1577 Stewart Ave., Nanaimo. ✆ **877/282-6337** or 250-753-1246. www.buccaneerinn.com. 13 units. C$59–C$199 double. MC, V. **Close to:** Newcastle Island.

★★★ **Hastings House** A member of the exclusive Small Luxury Hotels of the World, this upscale inn stands in a magnificent garden and orchard overlooking Ganges Harbour. First a trading post, it was reborn as a Tudor-style manor house thanks to an eccentric heiress. The cottages and suites are all charged with character and filled with original art and antiques.

160 Upper Ganges Rd., Ganges, Salt Spring Island. ✆ **800/661-9255** or 250/537-2362. www.hastingshouse.com. 18 units. June–Sept C$360–C$910 double; Mid-Mar to May and Oct to mid-Nov C$295–C$800 double; extra person C$85. AE, DC, MC, V. Closed mid-Nov to mid-Mar. Children 16 and under not accepted. **Close to:** Ruckle Provincial Park.

(Finds) **Port Renfrew Hotel** Built in 2006, this resort spruced up the town's options with a bar, restaurant, and waterfront cabins beside the community wharf. Heavy on the varnished wood, the rooms range from simple ("motel-style") to the two-bedroom Alcatraz Cabin with a BBQ, kitchenette, hot tub, and private deck. Reserve early.

17310 Parkinson Rd., Port Renfrew. ✆ **250/647-5541.** www.portrenfrewhotel.ca. 11 units. C$199–C$399 double. MC, V. **Close to:** Juan de Fuca Marine Trail, West Coast Trail (end).

★★ (Kids) **Roche Harbor Resort** A village unto itself, this grande dame offers a variety of lodging, plus a 337-berth marina. The century-old Hotel de Haro is the gem: all antiques, lace-trimmed beds, and roaring fireplaces. Originally a log bunkhouse, the hotel evolved into a distinctive three-story structure, which once hosted President Theodore Roosevelt.

4950 Reuben Tarte Memorial Dr., Roche Harbor, WA. ✆ **800/451-8910** or 360/378-2155. www.roche harbor.com. 72 units, some w/kitchens. US$70–US$450 double. Children 18 and under stay free in parent's room. AE, MC, V. **Close to:** American Camp.

Spinnaker's Guest House Overlooking the entrance to Victoria Harbour, Spinnaker's remains most famous for its brewpub. But the rooms are also noteworthy, with queen-size beds, soft earth-toned West Coast furnishings, in-room hot tubs, and even some wood-burning fireplaces. Just beware the trek downtown: 15 minutes on foot or 5 minutes by ferry.

308 Catherine St., Victoria. ✆ **877/838-2739** or 250/384-2739. www.spinnakers.com. 10 units. C$179–C$249 double (includes breakfast). AE, DC, MC, V. **Close to:** Mount Finlayson, Galloping Goose, Juan de Fuca Marine Trail.

★★★ Kids **Strathcona Park Lodge & Outdoor Education Centre** This superb property contains cabins, chalets, and lodge rooms on Upper Campbell Lake. From the hydroelectric power to gluten-free menu options, it's one of the nation's most thoughtful—and principled—resorts, as evidenced by the numerous eco-friendly awards. Families are especially drawn to the Adventure Unlimited package, which lets them explore with the lodge's excellent guides.

25 miles west of Campbell River on Hwy. 28. ✆ **250/286-3122.** www.strathcona.bc.ca. 39 units. C$40–C$88 chalet double with shared bathroom; C$136–C$160 double with private bathroom; C$175–C$480 cabin (2- to 3-night minimum stay). Adventure packages and off-season discounts available. MC, V. **Close to:** Bedwell Trail.

★★★ **Swans Hotel** One of Victoria's best-loved heritage restorations, this 1913 warehouse now contains 30 huge, distinctive suites rich with art. Accommodating up to six, they feature equipped kitchens, private patios, and separate living and dining areas. Big spenders can splurge on a three-level penthouse with a Roy Henry Vickers totem pole.

506 Pandora Ave., Victoria. ✆ **800/668-7926** or 250/361-3310. www.swanshotel.com. 30 suites. C$199–C$299 double (includes breakfast); extra person C$30; children under 13 free. AE, DC, MC, V. **Close to:** Mount Finlayson, Galloping Goose, Juan de Fuca Marine Trail.

★ Kids **Terrace Beach Resort** Set high on pilings, this dramatic wood and metal lodge contains lofts and suites. Oceanfront cabins nestle closer to the shoreline, set among 350-year-old evergreens. Candles and local stones dot the chic rooms: Most have kitchenettes, hot tubs, electric fireplaces, and propane barbecues outside. The Wild Pacific Trail (accessible via a staircase) makes this a good choice for families.

1002 Peninsula Rd., Ucluelet. ✆ **866/726-2901** or 250/726-2901. www.terracebeachresort.ca. C$99–C$349; children 12 and under stay free; extra person C$10; pets C$20. MC, V. **Close to:** Big Cedar Trail, Wild Pacific Trail.

Value **Travellers Inn** The "three and a half stars" sign often provokes laughter, but for hikers stranded unexpectedly in the city, no deal is sweeter. Friendlier, cleaner, bigger, and better-furnished than its competitors, this local chain also boasts free Wi-Fi, parking, and a harbor shuttle, plus some pools. Check for online booking deals.

Various locations; 1850 Douglas St. is closest to downtown Victoria. ✆ **888/872-83556** or 250/381-1000. www.travellersinn.com. C$69–C$169 double. AE, DC, MC, V. **Close to:** Mount Finlayson, Galloping Goose, Juan de Fuca Marine Trail.

★★★ **Wickaninnish Inn** On a rocky promontory, this standard-setting hotel presides between old-growth forest and the Pacific Ocean. A member of the renowned

Relais & Châteaux network, it claims "rustic elegance." Expect handmade driftwood furniture and local artwork alongside fireplaces, large-screen TVs, en suites with double soakers, and breathtaking views of the ocean.

Osprey Lane at Chesterman Beach (P.O. Box 250), Tofino. ✆ **800/333-4604** or 250/725-3300. www.wickinn.com. 75 units. High-season C$480–C$680 double, C$600–C$1,500 suite; low-season C$280–C$480 double, C$400–C$975 suite. Storm-watching, spa, and other packages available. AE, MC, V. **Close to:** Big Cedar Trail, Wild Pacific Trail.

RESTAURANTS

Baan Thai THAI This great spot would dazzle amid any urban environment: In the boonies, it's near miraculous. The 40-seat saffron-colored restaurant lies over a storefront on Shoppers Row (Campbell River's main drag). The entrance is easy to miss, but let the aromatic smells be your guide. There's also a rooftop patio.

1090 B Shoppers Row, Campbell River. ✆ **250/286-4853.** Reservations recommended. Main courses C$12–C$15. MC, V. Mon and Sat 5–9pm; Tues–Fri 11:30am–2pm and 5–9pm. **Close to:** Bedwell Trail.

★★ **Breakers Deli** NORTHWEST FUSION/DELI The line can grow long at this informal eatery, which has a handful of stools. Rather than linger amid the bustle, take away treats like a falafel wrap, smoked salmon burrito, chevre and roasted-tofu salad, wasabi *verdelait,* or beet-pecan pesto and potato-rosemary loaf.

430 Campbell St., Tofino. ✆ **250-725-2558.** www.breakersdeli.com. Main courses C$6–C$12. MC, V. Open daily 7am–10pm. **Close to:** Big Cedar Trail, Wild Pacific Trail.

★ Value **Cafe Brio** WEST COAST This award-winning restaurant serves Tuscan-inspired, West Coast fare, based on what's fresh, organic, and available. Expect items like peppered duck breast, nutmeg gnocchi with roasted squash, and red-wine-poached pig's ear. Ask about the bargain C$29 early bird *table d'hote* menu. Wood floor planks and ochre walls—with local art—add warmth.

944 Fort St., Victoria. ✆ **250/383-0009.** www.cafe-brio.com. Reservations recommended. Main courses C$26–C$45. AE, MC, V. Daily 5:30–10:30pm. **Close to:** Mount Finlayson, Galloping Goose, Juan de Fuca Marine Trail.

Coastal Kitchen NORTHWEST FUSION Pacificana dominates this laid-back eatery: a saw, wooden surfboard, and stuffed-animal moose head keep company with the foosball table. The menu ranges from the BC buffalo burger to a coastal berry salad, drizzled in blackberry vinaigrette. This could be the most unpretentious purveyor of Northwest cuisine—heavy on fusion and fresh, local ingredients—in the world.

17245 Parkinson Rd., Port Renfrew. ✆ **250/647-5545.** Main courses C$8–C$16. MC, V. Daily 9am–9pm. **Close to:** Juan de Fuca Marine Trail, West Coast Trail (end).

★★ Finds **Fox & Hounds** ENGLISH PUB Easily recognized by its bright red phone booth, this Brit pub lies two blocks uphill from the Old City Quarter. Expect tap beers, Sunday roasts, countryside oil paintings, and a cozy fireplace mantle. Plates are heaped with hearty pub grub like chicken curry, and cod and chips: none of that frozen rubbish.

247 Milton St., Nanaimo. ✆ **250/740-1000.** Main courses C$10–C$24. MC, V. Daily noon–10pm. **Close to:** Newcastle Island.

Hawk's Nest Pub PUB A stone fireplace dominates this laid-back bar inside the Bamfield Trails Hotel on the east side: the town's only dining-out option many nights. It serves stick-to-your-ribs hungry-hiker fare like burgers, fries, and mozzarella sticks, but also offers one last Caesar salad before the trail head. A patio area accommodates families.

226 Frigate Rd., Bamfield. ✆ **877/728-3474** or 250/728-3422. Main courses C$7–C$15. MC, V. Nov–Mar Thurs–Sat 5pm–midnight; Apr–Oct daily 8am–midnight. **Close to:** West Coast Trail (start).

★ Value **Homer's Most Excellent Take Out** DINER A 1950s throwback, this shake shack serves burritos, fish and chips, BBQ "beer bottle" beefwiches, Thai chicken wraps, and Tex Mex burgers oozing jalapeños, mozzarella, and guacamole. *Poutine* aficionados should opt for the Pot Hole Fries: home-cut potatoes smothered in cheese, sautéed onions and mushrooms, real bacon bits, and homemade gravy.

6250 Sooke Rd., at the corner of Rte. 14 and Sooke River Rd. ✆ **250-642-7456.** Main courses C$6–C$11. No credit cards. Tues–Sat 11:30am–8pm; Sun 3:30–7:30pm. **Close to:** Galloping Goose, Juan de Fuca Marine Trail.

★★ **Maloula's** SYRIAN Heat lamps warm diners on a terrace overlooking the harbor. Chef-owner Adnan Nassrallah sources organic and hormone-free food for this superb restaurant, which would shine in any city. The falafel is a menu standout, along with the lamb kabobs, grilled eggplant, and kibbeh (mixed ground lamb and bulgur).

445 Carter Ave., Friday Harbor, WA. ✆ **360/378-8485.** www.maloula.com. Main courses US$15–US$34. AE, MC, V. Apr–Oct Tues–Sun 11:30am–3:30pm and 5:30–9:30pm. Closed Nov–Mar. **Close to:** American Camp.

★ **rebar Modern Food** Kids VEGETARIAN This bright and funky basement restaurant is likely the coast's best vegetarian cafe. The stress-busting Soul Change juice—a blend of carrot, apple, celery, ginger, and Siberian ginseng—is a winner. The menu ranges from Thai curries to hummus and fresh shrimp quesadillas. A small wine cellar offers predominately BC wines.

50 Bastion Sq. (downstairs), Victoria. ✆ **250/361-9223.** www.rebarmodernfood.com. Main courses C$8–C$16. AE, MC, V. Mon–Thurs 8:30am–9pm; Fri–Sat 8:30am–10pm; Sun 8:30am–3:30pm. Reduced hours in winter. **Close to:** Mount Finlayson, Galloping Goose, Juan de Fuca Marine Trail.

★★ **Rock Salt** NORTHWEST FUSION This sassy hotspot sources local, organic ingredients whenever possible and even makes its own baked goods. Playful dishes include roasted yam quesadilla, miso-crusted salmon, and Saigon chili chicken on slaw. Bold and bright, the interior features funky stained-glass panels, while the patio overlooks the Fulford harbor.

2921 Fulford Ganges Rd., Salt Spring Island. ✆ **250/653-4833.** www.rocksaltrestaurant.com. Reservations recommended. Main courses C$12–C$24. AE, MC, V. Daily 6am–9pm. **Close to:** Ruckle Provincial Park.

★★ **Shelter** PACIFIC NORTHWEST WWII airplane-hangar post and beams grace this trend-setting eatery. Fish is the specialty, from macadamia-crusted halibut to Thai yellow curry seafood with sticky rice on a banana leaf. Other standouts include Angus rib-eye with *panko* onion rings and the char-grilled vegetable ratatouille. Most wines are award-winning whites from BC vineyards.

601 Campbell St., Tofino. ✆ **250/725-3353.** www.shelterrestaurant.com. Reservations recommended. Main courses C$11–C$32. MC, V. Daily 11am–10pm. **Close to:** Big Cedar Trail, Wild Pacific Trail.

SoBo ECLECTIC The name is short for "Sophisticated Bohemian"—a spirit reflected in the imaginative cuisine and décor: lots of glass, high ceilings, and colorful art. Because chef-owner Lisa Ahier started in a tiny catering truck, she still favors hand-held eats such as "gringo" soft chicken tacos and crispy shrimp cakes.

311 Neill St., Tofino. ✆ **250/725-2341.** www.sobo.ca. Main courses C$9–C$28. MC, V. Wed–Sun 11am–9pm; Mon–Tues 11am–5:30pm. **Close to:** Big Cedar Trail, Wild Pacific Trail.

6

Whistler & Sea-to-Sky Country Hikes

by Chloë Ernst

Traveling north along the Sea-to-Sky corridor will leave you marveling at the monumental and isolated surroundings that border the route. Although Hwy. 99—which runs through Squamish, Whistler, Pemberton, and on to Lillooet—presents itself as tranquil wilderness, this 200km (124-mile) stretch hides an explosive history.

Ice, lava, and shifting tectonic plates sculpted this section of the Coast Mountains over thousands and millions of years, creating today's outdoor wonderland of strangely shaped peaks, waterfalls, natural dams, and brilliant aqua lakes. With incalculable kilometers of charming and hikeable terrain, this region contains some of the best trekking in BC for its dramatic landscapes, outstanding viewpoints, and proximity to Vancouver.

The most diverse Sea-to-Sky hikes lie in Garibaldi Provincial Park. This park covers nearly 2,000 sq. km (772 sq. miles) and stretches from north of Squamish to south of Pemberton. The world-famous ski runs on Whistler and Blackcomb mountains lie just outside the northwestern edge of the park, while the impressive Mount Garibaldi rises 2,678m (8,786 ft.) in the southwest. The eastern portion of the park rarely welcomes visitors and remains a remote sanctuary for wildlife, including grizzly bears.

From the park's five western trail heads (Diamond Head, Black Tusk/Garibaldi Lake, Cheakamus Lake, Singing Pass near Whistler Village, and Wedgemount Lake), you'll find options for day hikes through to multi-day excursions.

On the opposite side of the Squamish Valley, the Tantalus Range poses both a challenge and an expense to access, but destinations with names like Lake Lovely Water will woo you into the outdoors. Currently, six companies provide air-taxi service to the park—a list of them is available on the BC Parks website (www.env.gov.bc.ca/bcparks).

Many parks, however, are in easy striking distance of the Sea-to-Sky Highway. Shannon Falls, Alice Lake, and Nairn Falls provincial parks border the road and offer pretty, leg-stretch-length trails. Just south of Whistler, Callaghan Lake is a popular area for snowshoeing and cross-country skiing. The park lies in the Callaghan Valley, which will host the Nordic events for the 2010 Olympic Games.

For those with limited time, Peak Adventures delivers easy access to alpine hikes via the Whistler Village Gondola. The lift whisks you to elevations greater than 2,000m (6,561 ft.), where a network of developed trails wends from panoramic mountain look-offs to glacier viewpoints and wildflower meadows.

Continue north of the village, and you will enter a less-visited region of glacial beauty. Joffre Lakes and Birkenhead Lake provincial parks offer tranquil lakeside hikes off the regular tourist loop.

With all hikes in this region, large tracts of protected and undeveloped land make for prime wildlife watching. Black bears, deer, hoary marmots (the whistling creatures that gave Whistler village its name), cougars, bald eagles, and peregrine falcons roam the mountains and soar over the valleys.

While trip planning, keep in mind that with the lead-up to the 2010 Winter Games, some trail heads are closed and there may be a lack of signage due to ongoing highway construction. Check the BC Parks website (www.env.gov.bc.ca/bcparks) for trail updates.

As you discover the stunning lakes, impressive mountain peaks, dramatic waterfalls, and awe-inspiring lookouts of the Sea-to-Sky corridor, remember that you are walking over the lands stewarded by the local First Nation communities, the Squamish and the Lil'wat peoples. Tread lightly and admire the splendor of Sea-to-Sky country.

ESSENTIALS

GETTING THERE

By Car

Head north from Vancouver towards Horseshoe Bay and then travel the awe-inducing Hwy. 99—dubbed the Sea-to-Sky. At the head of Howe Sound, 65km (40 miles) from downtown Vancouver, Squamish sits in a network of channels. Whistler sits at the foot of its namesake mountain at 120km (75 miles) from Vancouver, while a further 32km (20 miles) past Whistler lies Pemberton. To reach Lytton, take Hwy. 99 to Lillooet (250km/155 miles), then travel south on Hwy. 12 for 63km (39 miles) to Lytton. Alternately, travel north from Hope 110km (68 miles) along the Trans-Canada Highway.

By Bus

Perimeter's **Whistler Express** runs from Vancouver International Airport and Vancouver hotels to Whistler and Squamish 8 times daily during the summer, and 11 times during the winter. Cost is higher than Greyhound, but it's the most convenient option, particularly if you're traveling to a private condo, as the bus provides a door-to-door service option. Trip length is nearly 3 hours. One-way adult fare is C$55, C$63 for door-to-door. Children under 5 travel free; fare for children 5 to 12 is C$30, C$38 for door-to-door. Call ✆ **877/317-7788** or visit www.perimeterbus.com.

Regular **Greyhound** service to Whistler serves many points between the resort town and Vancouver, as well as beyond (including Squamish, Pemberton, and Lytton). Express and local buses leave the Vancouver terminal, 1150 Station Street (near Main St. and Terminal Ave.), eight times daily and arrive 2½ hours later in Whistler Creekside at 2029 London Lane. A more convenient stop, however, is on Gateway Drive, across from the Whistler Visitor Information Centre. One-way fare is C$21.40, or C$42.80 roundtrip. Weekend surcharges apply. Call ✆ **800/661-8747** or visit www.greyhound.ca.

By Train

The 3-hour trip of the **Whistler Mountaineer** offers the scenic route along Howe Sound to the resort town. While the train offers less schedule flexibility than bussing, the rails eliminate the Sea-to-Sky traffic headaches. Trains leave late April to mid-October at 8:30am from North Vancouver (at Philip Ave. and W. 1st St.) and arrive in Whistler

Whistler and the Olympics

Whistler was born to host the Olympics—and that's no exaggeration. Back in the 1960s, a group of businessmen formed the Garibaldi Olympic Development Association and set about developing a potential site for the 1968 games. The community, then known as Alta Lake, had long been a summer-resort destination, boasting famous fishing and tranquility; however, the community lacked water, sewage, electricity, and even a road. Yet what the area needed in amenities, it compensated for in natural suitability for skiing.

London Mountain—as Whistler Mountain was called before being renamed after the whistling alpine marmot in 1965—featured terrain to interest all levels of winter-sport enthusiasts. With unmatchable slopes and the ambition of a ski-development company called Garibaldi Lifts Limited, Whistler Mountain was soon open.

In February 1966, Whistler Mountain featured six runs, a four-passenger gondola, a chairlift, and two T-bars. Blackcomb Mountain, Whistler's twin, opened in 1980.

Despite Whistler's multiple failed bids for the Olympics, it quickly built an impressive snow base as a top-rated ski resort.

Fast-forward to 2003 and the International Olympic Committee meeting in Prague, Czech Republic to consider the bids for the 2010 Winter Olympic Games, for which Vancouver–Whistler submitted a joint bid.

Although trailing Pyeongchang, South Korea on the first round of voting, Vancouver gained support and won the bidding process in the second round.

Ever since, construction teams have been busy in Vancouver and Whistler, undertaking extensive building and improvements (on the Sea-to-Sky Highway, in particular) to make the region Games-ready.

And so, in 2010, this once-remote community will finally have its dream of an Olympics on Whistler Mountain. The mountain resort will host bobsled, luge, and skeleton events at the **Sliding Centre** on Blackcomb Mountain; alpine events on **Whistler Mountain;** and at the **Whistler Olympic Park** in the Callaghan Valley, cross-country, Nordic, biathlon, and ski-jumping events.

If you arrive outside the window of the Olympics (Feb 12–28, 2010 for the Winter Olympics and Mar 12–21, 2010 for the Paralympics), visit www.whistlersliding centre.com and www.whistlerolympicpark.com for availability of venue tours.

Creekside on Lake Placid Road. One-way fare is C$110 to C$185, round-trip C$199 to C$309. Enquire by calling ✆ **888/687-7245** or 604/606-8460, or go to www.whistler mountaineer.com.

By Plane

There is no major airport serving Whistler; however, **Whistler Air** flies to the resort village May through October from Coal Harbor in Vancouver. Two flights leave Vancouver daily at 8am and 5:30pm. The 35-minute flight costs C$159 one-way. Call ✆ **888/806-2299** or 604/932-6615, or visit www.whistlerair.ca.

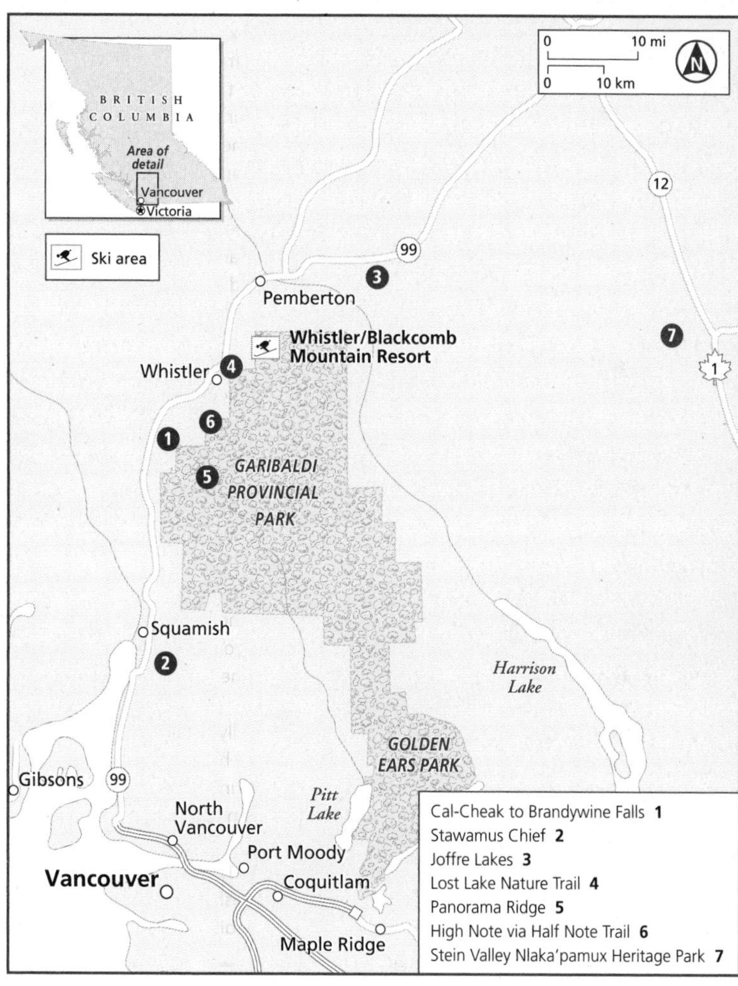

VISITOR INFORMATION

The **Whistler Visitor Info Centre** operates a busy location at 4230 Gateway Dr. (Village Bus Loop), Whistler, BC V0N 1B4. Call ✆ **877/991-9988** or 604/935-3357, or visit www.whistlerchamber.com. It's open daily 8am to 8pm. Also, **Whistler Activity and Information Centre** offers lots of insight at 4010 Whistler Way, Whistler, BC V0N 1B0. Call ✆ **877/991-9988** or 604/938-2769, or visit www.tourismwhistler.com. You can visit daily between 10am and 6pm.

The **Squamish Adventure Centre** is easy to find when the towering lumberjack statue named Sam (the Squamish Axe Man) is in his summer residence. Find Sam and the center at 38551 Loggers Lane, Squamish, BC V8B 0H2. Call ✆ **866/333-2010** or 604/815-4994, or check out www.squamishchamber.com. This center is open daily 9am to 5pm.

The **Pemberton and District Visitor Info Centre** is at the busy junction of Hwy. 99 and Portage Road, Pemberton, BC V0N 2L0. You can get information by calling ✆ **604/894-6175** or visiting www.pembertonchamber.com. From mid-May to September, the center is open daily from 9am to 5pm.

For Stein Valley Provincial Park information and maps, visit the **Lytton Visitor Centre,** 400 Fraser St., Lytton, BC V0K 1Z0. Call ✆ **250/455-2523** for friendly help or visit www.lytton.ca. Hours vary by season and volunteer availability, but generally the center is open daily 10am to 4pm.

GETTING AROUND

Whistler was designed to accommodate skiers and, as a result, is a pleasurable village for pedestrians. The main drag, known as the Village Stroll, will guide you to most bars, restaurants, and shops. The Whistler Village Gondola lies to the south of the village and is a good landmark. The village center lies between the Sea-to-Sky Highway and Blackcomb Way. Watch for yellow signs that direct you to key areas of the village, such as the gondolas and washrooms. Easy parking abounds in the large day lots just off Blackcomb Way.

In Squamish, the tight-knit town center lies to the northwest of the towering granite gatekeeper, the Stawamus Chief. Although the Sea-to-Sky Highway runs east of downtown, many facilities are clustered along Hwy. 99 to tempt the thousands who venture to Whistler along the route.

Pemberton sits amidst the lush agricultural region in the Pemberton Valley. Most amenities can be found on Prospect Street, Frontier Street, and Portage Road—the latter is the route into town from the highway.

Although not on the Sea-to-Sky route, Lytton is the main gateway to Stein Valley Provincial Park, which lies to the south of Hwy. 99 and Lillooet. The quaint and quiet town sits on the eastern bank of the Fraser River, where the Thompson ends. Hwy. 12 leaves town to the northwest toward Lillooet, Hwy. 99, and the Lytton Ferry. The Trans-Canada Highway lies to the east of the town center.

By Bus

In Whistler, an excellent selection of more than a dozen routes will quickly whisk you around the area on the WAVE transit system. Routes also travel to Squamish and Pemberton. Fare within the village is C$2. Find details by calling ✆ **604/932-4020** or visiting www.busonline.ca/regions/whi for maps and schedules.

By Taxi

Whistler Taxi offers fast and friendly service to Whistler and Vancouver International Airport. Call ✆ **800/203-5322** or 604/938-3333 for pick up.

In Pemberton, contact **Pemberton Taxi** at ✆ **604-894-1111.**

Yellow Cabs Squamish provides 24-hour service from Squamish through to Whistler. Call ✆ **604/892-5995** for service.

By Car

Limos topped with ski racks are a common sight on the Sea-to-Sky Highway during winter. Car rentals are available in Whistler and Vancouver. In Whistler, try **Avis Car and Truck Rental,** 4315 Northlands Blvd., ✆ **604/932-1236.** Also, **Budget Rent A Car** operates from 1180 Hunter Pl., Squamish, ✆ **604/815-4686.**

1 CAL-CHEAK TO BRANDYWINE FALLS ★ Finds

Difficulty rating: Moderate

Distance: 8km (5 miles) round trip

Estimated time: 2½ hr.

Elevation gain: 60m (197 ft.)

Costs/permits: None

Best time to go: July–Sept

Website: www.env.gov.bc.ca/bcparks/explore/parkpgs/brandywine_falls

Recommended map: Available for download on BC Parks website (above)

Trail head GPS: N 50 05.976, W 123 10.173

Trail head directions: At 13km (8 miles) south of Whistler Village, look for signs for Cal-Cheak recreation area. About 1km (½ mile) along the logging road, pass the first camping area and make a right turn into the recreation site marked Cal-Cheak Confluence.

This short hike takes a step outside the bustle of Whistler to explore a less-visited region. The spectacular destination—Brandywine Falls—enhances the adventure of traversing a river, exploring small lakes, and trail hunting.

From the Cal-Cheak recreation site, cross the suspension bridge spanning Callaghan Creek and follow the serene needle-packed trail southeast along the creek bank.

Soon, you pass the confluence where the chalky green waters of Callaghan Creek meet the deep blue Cheakamus River.

❶ Station After walking 5 minutes, cross the double set of railway tracks. Note here that the left fork just before the tracks (sometimes overgrown) is where you will return. Although this first leg of the trail follows a car-width gravel road, greater wonders lie beyond.

After about 200m (656 ft.), make a left onto an all-terrain-vehicle-width path, then after another 300m (984 ft.) or so, make another left.

Here, the path narrows, and the scenery becomes beautiful in its melancholic grays of lichens, tree trucks, and boulders.

❷ Lava Lake The landscape wears the hallmarks of glacial erosion, with numerous small lakes and lily ponds, as well as scattered boulders throughout the terrain.

Continue straight along this clear path for 30 to 45 minutes, watching for the largest body of water, Lava Lake, about halfway through. When you reach signs marking the park boundary, you'll know that the falls are near.

Brandywine Falls lie in the northern end of the provincial park with Daisy Lake in the south. As the path begins to descend, the sound of rushing water grows louder. When the trail meets the manicured park trail to the falls, make a left down to the viewpoint and cross the train tracks again.

❸ Brandywine Falls Brandywine Creek pours off the cliff lip from 70m (230 ft.) up, creating a frothy horseshoe of white water in the pool below. Stand on the viewing platform and take in the full plunge of Brandywine Falls. The falls, it is said, are named as a result of a bet—two railway surveyors, Bob Mollison and Jack Nelson, wagered a bottle of brandy on the accurate height of the falls. Mollison won the brandy, and the falls won its name.

From the viewing platform, the Canyon Rim Trail continues a little further south to a second viewpoint, where you can savor views of Daisy Lake far below.

❹ Return Trail Halfway between the parking area and the falls, a trail branches off for the 3.3km (2-mile) return trek to Cal-Cheak Suspension Bridge. The trail ascends a rocky bluff and then follows infrequent markings north towards the bridge.

A mixed bag of flagging tape and orange diamonds mark the route. Be sure to watch carefully.

❺ Swim Lake An optional side tour includes a 5-minute walk to the small body of water called Swim Lake. As lovely as the name sounds, the mosquitoes here can be vicious and make for an unpleasant dip. We advise remaining clothed or chance becoming a feast for the insects!

On the upside, friendly Canada Jays (also called Whiskey Jacks)—BC's most avid ambassadors—perch around the water's edge and warmly welcome visitors who potentially have food.

❻ Blueberry Meadows Back on the main trail, after your quick visit to Swim Lake, make a left turn at this waypoint, even though the trail appears to head straight.

Climb a short slope, then follow the pretty path winding through a meadow and keep Swim Lake on your left. Here, the lichen, blueberry bushes, and small lakes make for a delicious panorama.

In BC, berries mean bears. If you are hiking through in berry season—generally in July, although it does vary—be sure to whistle and sing along the way so as not to surprise any lunching black bears. Carrying bear spray is also recommended.

The trail weaves through the forest and over makeshift bridges, always heading north. After 10 to 15 minutes of hiking through the forest, keep right at a slight fork in the trail. Again, watch carefully for flagging tape that marks the winding turns in the trail.

❼ Mile 66.5 When the trail pops out on the train tracks, look for the 66.5 mile marker on your right.

These rail lines reached Alta Lake (the former name for Whistler Village) in 1914 and played a large role in making the region accessible. Now, the line shuttles freight and the Whistler Mountaineer passenger trains from Vancouver through to the resort and beyond.

Look for the trail on the other side of the tracks, slightly to the left. Like much of the trail, it is not well-marked—but continue looking!

Back in the woods, a sign points right to Whistler Bungee, but continue to the left. At the next slight fork, veer right and down the dozen wooden stairs. Slowly, over the course of a log bridge and another set of stairs, the trail winds to a close at the familiar double set of railway tracks. From here, the route back to the suspension bridge will be familiar.

❽ Suspension Bridge Back at the Cal-Cheak recreation site, either picnic at one of the well-maintained spots or head further down the logging road for a full-force adrenaline blast at Whistler Bungee.

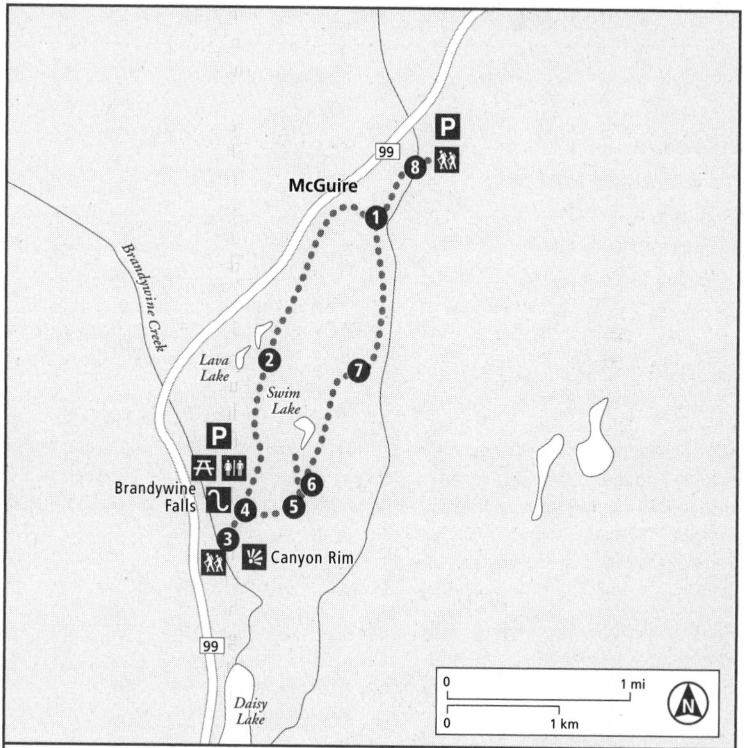

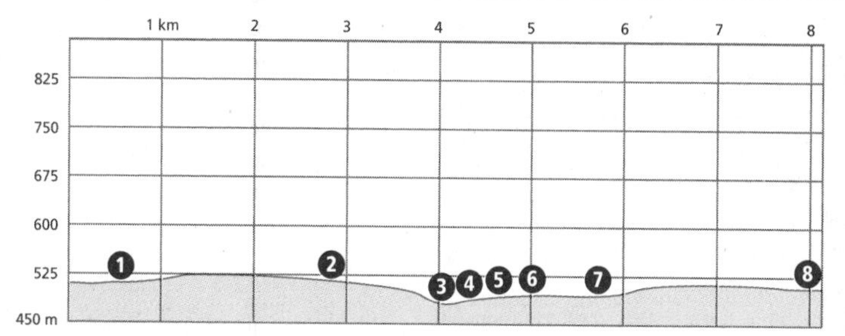

N 50 05.976, W 123 10.173 (0 km): Trail head

❶ N 50 05.580, W 123 10.645 (0.6 km): Cross railway tracks at the former McGuire Station

❷ N 50 04.407, W 123 11.863 (2.8 km): Pass Lava Lake

❸ N 50 03.579, W 123 11.854 (4 km): Survey the plunge of Brandywine Falls

❹ N 50 03.692, W 123 11.845 (4.3 km): Turn right onto the return path heading north

❺ N 50 03.738, W 123 11.470 (4.6 km): Make a detour to the shore of Swim Lake

❻ N 50 03.770, W 123 11.430 (5 km): Amble through blueberry meadows

❼ N 50 04.224, W 123 10.848 (5.7 km): Cross the train tracks at Mile 66.5

❽ N 50 05.976, W 123 10.172 (8 km): Return to the Suspension Bridge at the trailhead

2 STAWAMUS CHIEF (CENTRE & NORTH PEAKS) ★★ (Kids)

Difficulty rating: Strenuous

Distance: 5.5km (3.4 miles) round trip

Estimated time: 4 hr.

Elevation gain: 630m (2,067 ft.)

Costs/permits: None

Pet friendly: No

Best time to go: June–Oct

Website: www.env.gov.bc.ca/bcparks/explore/parkpgs/stawamus

Recommended map: Available for download on BC Parks website (address above)

Trail head GPS: N 49 67.591, W 123 15.322

Trail head directions: From West Vancouver, take the Trans-Canada Highway west toward Horseshoe Bay. At 11km (6¾ miles), take exit 1 onto Hwy. 99. Travel along the stunning ocean-side route for 40km (25 miles), then make a right turn at Stawamus Chief Provincial Park. From Whistler, travel south 62km (39 miles) along Hwy 99. The park is about 3km (1¾ miles) south of downtown Squamish.

More challenging and less popular than the hike to South Peak, the steady climb to Centre Peak and then on to North Peak will leave you breathless—first from the steep ascent, and second for the horizon-reaching views of the snowy Tantalus Range and hulking Garibaldi Mountain. Along the way, you'll see climbers scaling the world's second-largest granite monolith and a large peregrine falcon nesting area.

The trail head lies just beyond the camping grounds, where you'll see well-used climbing gear and tired rock climbers slumped around the tents. Huge numbers of avid climbers flock to the Squamish area to scale the Stawamus Chief—claimed to be the world's second largest granite monolith after the Rock of Gibraltar.

But you need not scale these sheer cliffs in order to reach fantastic views. Simply hike the trails that hide behind the great rock.

First, however, follow the gravel path towards the "test" climb that marks the start of your ascent. Strongly worded warnings regarding safety are aimed at the hoards (ranging from the unsuspecting to seasoned trekkers) that swarm up the steep trails, particularly on weekends. Climb on up and begin your ascent.

❶ Olesen Creek The trail, marked with orange diamonds, zigzags up stone steps, logs, roots, and hillside parallel to the gushing Olesen Creek. The terrain climbs steeply, so take plenty of breathers in the shade. And remember: The hike along these trails is undeniably easier that scaling one of the Chief's very vertical rock faces!

At the right fork to the lower Shannon Falls trail, BC's third highest waterfall, take a short detour onto the bridge to admire a sliver of Howe Sound. This sneak peek previews the grand show waiting at the summit. Be refreshed by the gentle breeze and then keep moving at a steady pace on this first (and most unforgiving) portion of the trail.

Keep left as trails to upper Shannon Falls and then North Peak branch off from the main Chief Peaks Trail.

❷ Balancing Rock A great boulder perched in a clearing marks the halfway point of your total ascent.

Before the Chief was visible above the earth's surface, it lurked as molten magma underground, slowly rising as it cooled. Meanwhile, natural forces (everything

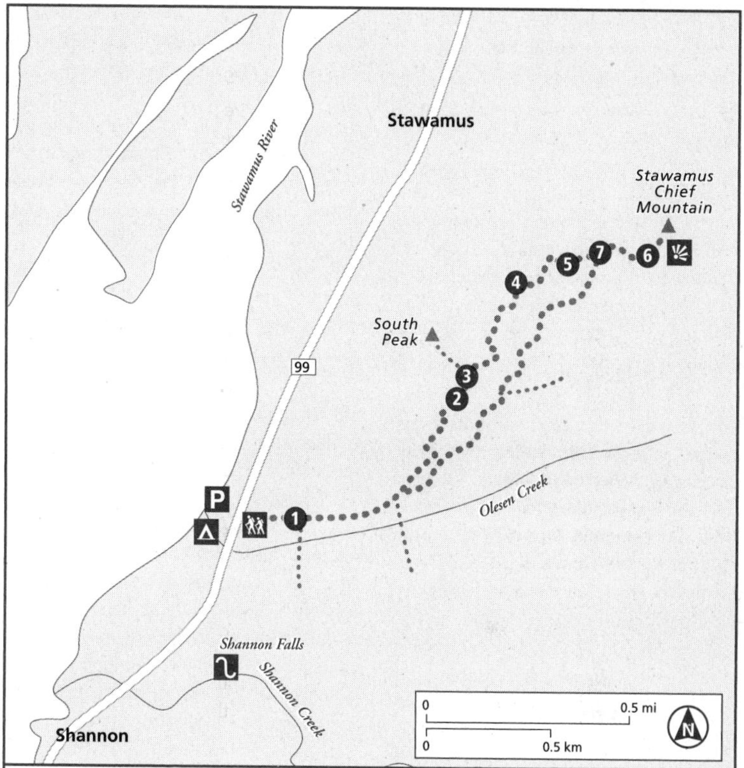

Stawamus
Stawamus River
Stawamus Chief Mountain
South Peak
99
Olesen Creek
Shannon Falls
Shannon Creek
Shannon
0 0.5 mi
0 0.5 km
N

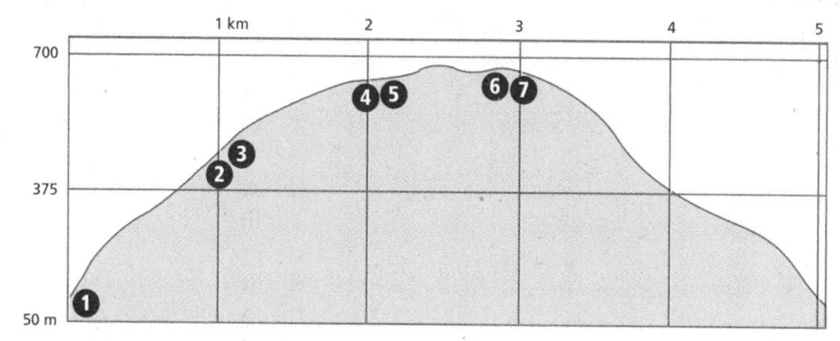

N 49 67.591, W 123 15.322 (0 km): Trail head

❶ N 49 67.569, W 123 15.242 (0.1 km): Begin following Olesen Creek

❷ N 49 68.026, W 123 14.507 (1 km): Reach a lookout at a large balancing rock

❸ N 49 68.081, W 123 14.458 (1.1 km): Left fork to South Peak and right to Center Peak

❹ N 49 68.459, W 123 14.127 (2 km): Take in the views from Center Peak

❺ N 49 68.510, W 123 13.892 (2.2 km): In North Gully, take a left to North Peak

❻ N 49 68.577, W 123 13.496 (2.8 km): Arrive at North Peak

❼ N 49 68.604, W 123 13.658 (3 km): Turn left North North Gully and return to trailhead

from weather to earthquakes and glaciers) scraped away the earth between the Chief and the surface, with the final stage in the Chief's formation being the receding of the glaciers about 10,000 years ago.

3 Centre and North peaks After 30 to 45 minutes, you arrive at the fork where the crowds turn left and head to South Peak. Continue straight towards Centre and North peaks along a woodland trail, watching now for white diamond trail markers with a smaller red square.

Notice the sudden quiet of the trail and perhaps the whistle of the train heading through Squamish. Mercifully, the gradient of the trail also lessens.

4 Centre Peak As the woodland path merges with the granite, keep to the right and watch carefully for the trail. Once you find the chains that offer you a hand up the steep slope, the path is easy to locate, despite the tricky footing. Keep your hands free as you slowly navigate this technical portion (including a ladder).

Up top, gnarly pines and scrubby brush cling to the crevices. Keep climbing until the view of Howe Sound stops you in your tracks.

From here, look down to the crowds on South Peak. Shifting your view clockwise, Howe Sound, the Tantalus range, the bulky grey Mount Garibaldi, and your final destination—North Peak—provide a stunning panorama.

TAKE A BREAK The flat granite of Centre Peak offers a serene spot for lunch. On a warm day, the rock radiates heat, but the wind can be chilly. With your muscles twitching from climbing nearly 600m (1,969 ft.) in elevation, a gentle stretch is also a good idea.

5 North Gully Walking north over the flattish top of Centre Peak, look for more white-and-red diamond trail markers to flag the descent into North Gully. The sharp drop requires careful footing and yes, unfortunately, you do have to go down before you go up.

Here in the gully, the sides of Centre and North peaks frame the ashy slopes and snowy hat of Mount Garibaldi. The dormant volcano formed quite uniquely: on top of the thick glaciers that once covered Howe Sound. As the glaciers melted, large portions of the volcano collapsed into the valley.

In the gully, the route to the left takes you to North Peak along a trail of yellow diamonds, while a right turn is the return trail.

6 North Peak Climbing up out of the gullies, stop briefly to peer over the edge of another sheer drop.

The Chief, as the locals call it, is home to a rebounding population of peregrine falcons. As nesting habitat crosses some of the rock's climbing routes, climbers have established self-regulated bans on certain routes from mid-March through July. Watch here for these birds of prey, with their meter-wide wingspans, soaring above Squamish and around the Chief.

Make the last climb of the day along more granite slopes with wind-swept trees. Here, from the 702m (2,303-ft.) summit, savor an unobstructed view northward.

7 North North Gully Descend the granite slope slowly, once again following the yellow diamonds. When the trail forks right back to Centre Peak, take the left arm downhill. Continue on the trail of the yellow markers as the trail twists downwards over rocks and red rot, and around large cedars (although not giant by BC standards). From the familiar signpost for the Peaks Trail, continue down the hill toward the trail head.

Once back to the trail head, celebrate that you've climbed the Chief. No need to elaborate that you didn't scale up those sheer cliff faces.

 Squamish Lil'wat Cultural Centre

Stories of the Squamish and Lil'wat first nations fill the halls and walls of the **Squamish Lil'wat Cultural Centre** (4584 Blackcomb Way, Whistler, BC V0N 1B0; ✆ **866/441-7522** or 604/964-0990; www.slcc.ca)—the newest option in Whistler for those seeking an authentic and fresh experience.

The modern glass-and-cedar building evokes the spirit of the longhouses of the Squamish nation and the sub-ground *istken* of the Lil'wat nation. The large, carved cedar doors welcome visitors and face east—as is tradition.

Inside the space (that smells deliciously of cedar), you will find a museum, craft area, café, and a Great Hall. Look up and all around for the exhibits—a 12m (39-ft.) canoe that was carved from a single cedar tree hangs from the ceiling, examples of traditional dress fill the walls, and the Squamish and Lil'wat hosts help retell beautiful stories.

Traditional arts are happily shared in the center. Try twisting your own cedar bracelet from supple strips of cedar bark (this same technique is used to make rope). The center also focuses on preserving the techniques of canoe carving, basket making, and blanket weaving.

Then, wrap your tongue around the language games that employ the unique Skwxwú7mesh language of the Squamish people—for which a written form developed only in the 1960s—and the St'at'imcets language of the Lil'wat people.

Outside, a forest walk follows a glacial creek and provides a deeper insight into the spirituality of the people who have lived in these valleys for millennia. On the walk, you can reflect on the deep connection these communities share with nature. And, as the center is built as a "doorway to the forest," the walk will be a living example of where the Lil'wat and Squamish people have traditionally sourced natural products for medicine, clothing, food, and art.

When all the cultural exploration leaves you hungry, visit the on-site café for a locally inspired lunch. Venison chili or fresh berry desserts are delicious ways to share in the culture of the Lil'wat and Squamish first nations.

Open daily 9:30am to 5pm. Admission for adults is C$18, youth 13 to 18 C$11, and children 6 to 12 C$8.

3 JOFFRE LAKES ★★★ (Moments)

Difficulty rating: Moderate

Distance: 11km (6.8 miles) round trip

Estimated time: 5½ hr.

Elevation gain: 375m (1,230 ft.)

Costs/permits: None

Best time to go: July–Sept

Website: www.env.gov.bc.ca/bcparks/explore/parkpgs/joffre_lks

Recommended map: Available for download on BC Parks website (address above)

Trail head GPS: N 50 36.946, W 122 49.863

Trail head directions: Drive about 40km (25 miles) from Whistler towards Pemberton and Mount Currie. Turn right onto Duffey Lake Rd., which heads along Lillooet Lake then climbs a steep series of switchbacks. After 23km (14 miles), look for Joffre Provincial Park, which will be on your right.

Feel the cool air massing from the Matier Glacier that perches above the brilliant turquoise waters of the three Joffre lakes. Hike one, two, or all three, and you will happily find your oasis at an elevation of nearly 1,600m (nearly a mile high!).

From the far end of the parking lot, take a gravel trail that quickly plunges into woodlands and splendor. Western hemlocks line the path, and glimpses of the first magnificent lake soon emerge.

❶ Lower Joffre Lake Just 2 minutes in, a fork in the trail leads left to Lower Joffre Lake or right to Middle and Upper Joffre lakes. On a busy day, continue right to the upper lakes or, if people are scarce, stop and savor the multitude of greens that cover and surround the lake.

Why such a hue of blue, you ask? The lakes are so brightly colored due to glacial sediment in the water. When the sediment refracts sunlight, the water appears shades of brilliant turquoise.

As you continue on, notice the rich yet fragile vegetation that flanks the trail. Keep your boots on the path as you start snapping photos of the truly picturesque lakes.

❷ Lower Joffre Creek Stop here on this well-maintained bridge to gaze upon the already towering Matier Glacier as Lower Joffre Creek flows quickly beneath your feet. Follow the trail as it skirts counter-clockwise around the lake and begins to climb.

An advance warning—the 5.5km (3½-mile) stretch between the first lake and upper lakes requires careful footing over boulder fields, log bridges, and rooty paths. Be sure to have good walking shoes or, the best option, a sturdy pair of hiking boots.

❸ Boulder Field Here begins the trickiest part of the trail—a slope of varying-sized boulders. A large boulder patch (about .5km/¼ mile across) requires slow navigation, although the footing is sound. Note that on wet and muddy days, the boulder surfaces can be slippery, so keep your hands free as you move with caution over mostly flat, bathtub-sized rocks. Those used to boulder hopping will enjoy this terrain.

Continuing along the woodland path, you soon begin to hear the rushing glacial creek that connects Middle and Lower Joffre lakes.

❹ Log Bridge The trail twists upwards into the forest where Old Man's Beard lichen grows long from the limbs of more hemlocks. Trees felled by the wind crisscross the slopes beside the path as you begin the steady climb to the middle lake.

Keep a moderate pace and avoid slippery roots as the trail zigzags up. When the trail follows a short section of carefully laid stone then crosses a log bridge (with hand railing), the second turquoise delight is just ahead.

❺ Middle Joffre Lake The wooded trail opens suddenly onto the serene waters of the second lake. As the trail winds clockwise along the eastern shore of the lake, stop frequently to capture some snapshots of the fantastic vantages.

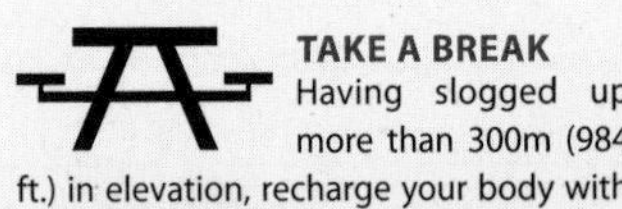

TAKE A BREAK Having slogged up more than 300m (984 ft.) in elevation, recharge your body with a snack break on the shore of Middle Joffre Lake. The smallest of the three lakes, Middle Joffre also marks the end of the day's heftiest climbs.

❻ Upper Joffre Lake Two more log bridges lead the way over the creek for the final time and up to the lakeshore of the third, final, and most picturesque lake.

From the northern end of the lake, the wooded trail arcs counter-clockwise around the western shore of Upper Joffre

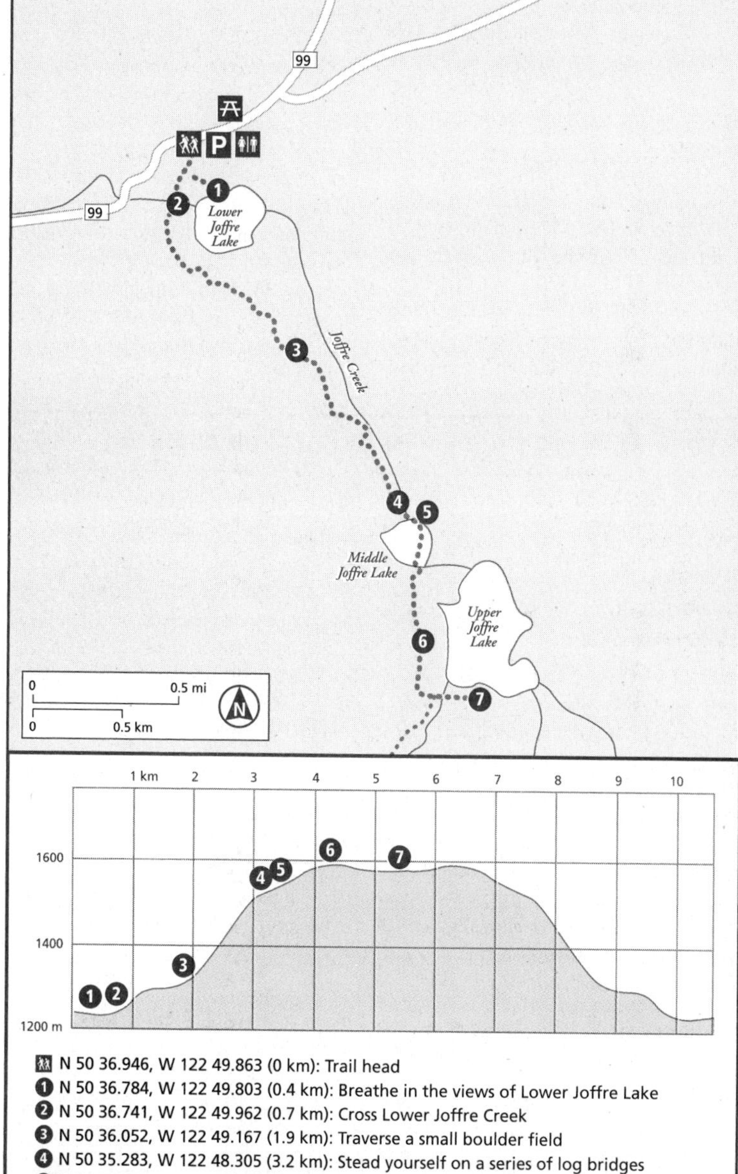

N 50 36.946, W 122 49.863 (0 km): Trail head

❶ N 50 36.784, W 122 49.803 (0.4 km): Breathe in the views of Lower Joffre Lake

❷ N 50 36.741, W 122 49.962 (0.7 km): Cross Lower Joffre Creek

❸ N 50 36.052, W 122 49.167 (1.9 km): Traverse a small boulder field

❹ N 50 35.283, W 122 48.305 (3.2 km): Stead yourself on a series of log bridges

❺ N 50 35.255, W 122 48.225 (3.3 km): Rest at Middle Joffre Lake

❻ N 50 34.671, W 122 48.003 (4.2 km): Trek counter-clockwise around Upper Joffre Lake

❼ N 50 34.428, W 122 47.756 (5.3 km): Reach the campground on the south lakeshore

Lake towards a campground and pit toilet.

The approach along the shore is relaxing and provides you ample time to gaze on the looming Matier Glacier, its pale blue slopes sharp against the blue sky. Look, too, for the miniature tents of the mountain climbers who frequent this spot for its accessibility and diversity.

Working around the lake, a right fork leads up to the Tszil Glacier; however, your destination lies on the left fork at the top of the lake.

Be prepared for all weather at these altitudes—even hail or snow in August. Toques, gloves, raingear, hiking boots, and fleeces can be essential equipment when the weather turns quickly.

7 Campground As close as the glacier looks from the campground, we don't recommend venturing nearer. Frequent icefalls are a danger to anyone in their paths.

Instead, scan the horizon, starting with Joffre Peak to the left of the Matier Glacier, shifting your gaze right to Mount Matier, Slalok Mountain, the Stonecrop Glacier, Tszil Mountain, and Mount Taylor.

As you sit, penned in by these towering icy peaks, simply enjoy the cool breeze drifting down and the views of the finest of the Joffre lakes.

4 LOST LAKE NATURE TRAIL Kids

Difficulty rating: Easy

Distance: 4km (2.5 miles) round trip

Estimated time: 1½ hr.

Elevation gain: 50m (164 ft.)

Costs/permits: None

Best time to go: Apr–Nov

Website: www.tourismwhistler.com/www/things_to_do/activities/profile/lost_lake

Recommended map: Available from the Whistler Visitor Info Centre

Trail head GPS: N 50 12.025, W 122 94.781

Trail head directions: From the Whistler Village Gondola, head north along Blackcomb Way. Look for the skateboard park on your right (hidden behind the sprawling parking lots), or pick up the Lost Lake trail signs along Fitzsimmons Creek Trail. Alternately, local transit runs a free summer shuttle to the park.

During the winter, cross-country skiers take advantage of Whistler's famous snowfalls on the more than 30km (19 miles) of trails in Lost Lake Park. And, in summer, mountain bikers make tire tracks on these routes. Amidst it all, the nature trail provides a short, reasonably secluded, and easy hike through the backyard of Whistler—a tiny piece of wilderness at your doorstep.

The trail ventures into the woods just to the right of the groomed gravel track beside the Cross Country Connection. The person-width forest path winds around trees and over roots and rocks, offering an isolated feeling in a popular recreation area.

The first leg follows Blackcomb Creek for about 10 minutes, passing large cedars standing silently in a quiet forest. The mood is peaceful—perfect for catching a glimpse or two of the local fauna.

1 Cairn Hill As the only climb in the hike, you will quickly ascend the steep but short hill with cairns bordering the path.

From here, the forest trail continues to twist through the trees for about 5 to 10 minutes. Twice, the nature trail meets the main gravel trail—simply cross the trail and rejoin.

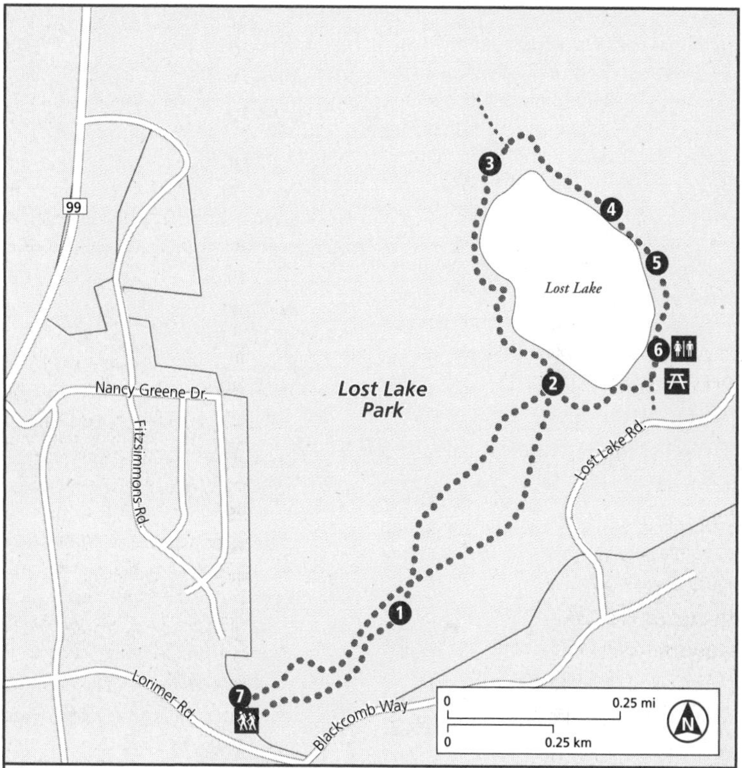

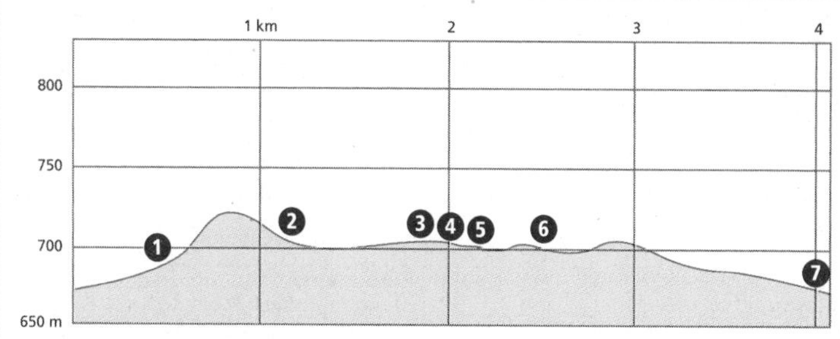

- Trail head icon: N 50 12.025, W 122 94.781 (0 km): Trail head
- 1 N 50 12.194, W 122 94.279 (0.5 km): Climb a route bordered by cairns
- 2 N 50 12.661, W 122 93.777 (1.2 km): Cross the main path and follow the lakeshore
- 3 N 50 13.100, W 122 93.966 (1.8 km): Rejoin the main gravel trail
- 4 N 50 13.008, W 122 93.585 (2 km): Watch for amphibians at the toad crossing
- 5 N 50 12.904, W 122 93.440 (2.2 km): Take a dip at Canine Cove
- 6 N 50 12.737, W 122 93.432 (2.5 km): Pass the popular beach
- 7 N 50 12.025, W 122 94.781 (4 km): Return to the Cross Country Connection

2 Lakeshore After 15 to 20 minutes of total hiking, the trail pops out of the woods just meters from the small body of water that once supported a mill.

Cross the main trail and follow the lakeshore clockwise along another section of the narrow nature trail. The lake is a magnet for activity—from swimming to fishing, you'll see plenty of Whistler residents out enjoying the sunshine.

Watch for Pileated Woodpeckers with their red crests knocking away at the trunks of the lakeside trees or slugs with the sheen of black licorice. Beavers, muskrats, and coyotes are also said to visit the park.

3 Main Trail The trail circles the lake, rejoining the main trail in places. Simply keep the water to your right to stay on course.

Finally, about halfway around the circumference of the lake, turn on to the main path for the last time and continue your lakeside walk.

4 Toad Crossing The Western Toad doesn't win any beauty titles, but healthy populations of these amphibians reflect the health of an ecosystem. For this reason, Whistlerites take their amphibians pretty seriously.

As park signs warn, watch where you tread along this portion of the trail as you scan the ground for the quarter-sized toads (particularly in Aug, which is baby toad season).

5 Canine Cove If there are four-legged pals in your hiking party, take a quick detour down to the doggie swimming area. As a side note, before the surrounding area was developed, this dock also doubled as Whistler's nude swimming area. If you're brave, take a dip with or without your suit.

6 Beach Access A popular spot for families, the beach is home also to Lost Lake BBQ, which sells typical concession food.

TAKE A BREAK The beach offers picnic tables, barbecue pits, toilets, and good swimming—perfect complements to a summer day trip. Sit and relax, or toss a Frisbee on the grassy area.

Continuing from the beach on the clockwise journey around the lake, cross the small bridge that spans Blackcomb Creek. Here, pause to watch for fish jumping, as the creek is a rearing area for Rainbow Trout, Dolly Vardon Char, and Kokanee Salmon.

7 Cross Country Connection From the bridge, take either the 1.2km (.7-mile) gravel trail back to Cross Country Connection and then Whistler Village, or return on the Nature Trail and look for more wildlife in this small backwoods escape so close to the heart of Whistler.

5 PANORAMA RIDGE ★★★ Moments

Difficulty rating: Strenuous

Distance: 31km (19 miles) round trip

Estimated time: 9 hr.

Elevation gain: 1,505m (4,938 ft.)

Costs/permits: Parking C$3 per day

Pet friendly: No

Best time to go: July–Aug

Website: www.env.gov.bc.ca/bcparks/explore/parkpgs/garibaldi

Recommended map: Available for download on BC Parks website (address above)

Trail head GPS: N 49 95.733, W 123 11.998

Trail head directions: About 95km (59 miles) north of Vancouver, or 25km (16 miles) south of Whistler, look for the provincial park signs for Black Tusk/Garibaldi Lake. Nearly 2km (1¼ miles) up the road is the Rubble Creek parking lot.

Hefty elevation gains pay off in unmatchable teal panoramas of shimmering Garibaldi Lake, landscapes crowned with glaciers, and views of the towering, volcanically formed cliff, The Barrier.

From the Rubble Creek parking lot, start the 6km (3¾-mile) climb that is the first test in this epic day hike. Although the switchbacks through the cedar and Douglas fir forests are well graded, the cumulative effect is unrelenting. Orange diamonds lodged in trees like ninja stars mark the way. Take it slow and steady, and listen as the rumble of Rubble Creek softens as you ascend.

❶ First Junction After 1½ hours or so, one of many detailed signposts points the way to Taylor Meadows. So far, over just 6km (3¾ miles), you've climbed more than 750m (2,461 ft.) in elevation.

Take the left fork to Taylor Meadows and appreciate as the trail eases and the trees thin out to lush meadows scattered with wildflowers.

❷ Taylor Meadows Here, 7.5km (4¾ miles) through the hike, Taylor Meadows campground sits in an entirely different world. Look for the red flowers of Indian Paintbrush, the dainty white petals of Sitka Valerien, the lilac-colored wild aster, the lush purple Arctic Lupines, or yellow of Mountain Arnica.

Also, gaze ahead at the monotone horn of Black Tusk that sits up and to the left of your destination: Panorama Ridge.

❸ Outhouse Junction At Outhouse Junction, 2km (1¼ miles) past Taylor Meadows, take the left trail to Panorama Ridge. This is where you will return to venture down to the shores of Garibaldi Lake later in the hike. Continue straight past the trail to Black Tusk viewpoint and keep heading east.

The path continues along the mountainside above Mimulus and then Black Tusk lakes. At 2km (1¼ miles) past Outhouse Junction, try to catch a glimpse of the hoary marmots that scamper over the rocks here as you take the right fork.

Head clockwise around Black Tusk Lake, looking in the meadow for the distinctive droopy shag of the Western pasqueflower.

❹ Helm Glacier As the trail climbs above Black Tusk Lake, look up to the false summit and the final rocky ascent to Panorama, which snakes up to the right of the Helm Glacier.

The way is marked with a series of cairns and orange flagging. When elevation gain leaves you breathless, pause and take in the lush green slopes and fantastic views of Black Tusk behind you.

❺ Panorama Ridge From your new height of 2,105m (6,906 ft.), the wind whips over the ridge and will quickly cool you down, even on the hottest of days.

SPECTACULAR LOOKOUT The views stretch out 360° from this rocky ridge. To the south, Mount Price and the Table sit off the far shore of Garibaldi Lake. Look west (to your right), and you will see the tiny Battleship Islands near the lakeshore of Garibaldi, along with Lesser Garibaldi Lake. To the north, Black Tusk is still visible. Below you lies Garibaldi Lake with its bright blue color—characteristic of a glacial-fed lake.

To descend from the peak, backtrack carefully down the rocky slopes and then around Black Tusk Lake. Return through the meadows—filling up water bottles from the creeks here, if need be (it is advisable to treat the water first)—and head west to Outhouse Junction.

At the junction, take the left fork that passes through a pretty area of meadow,

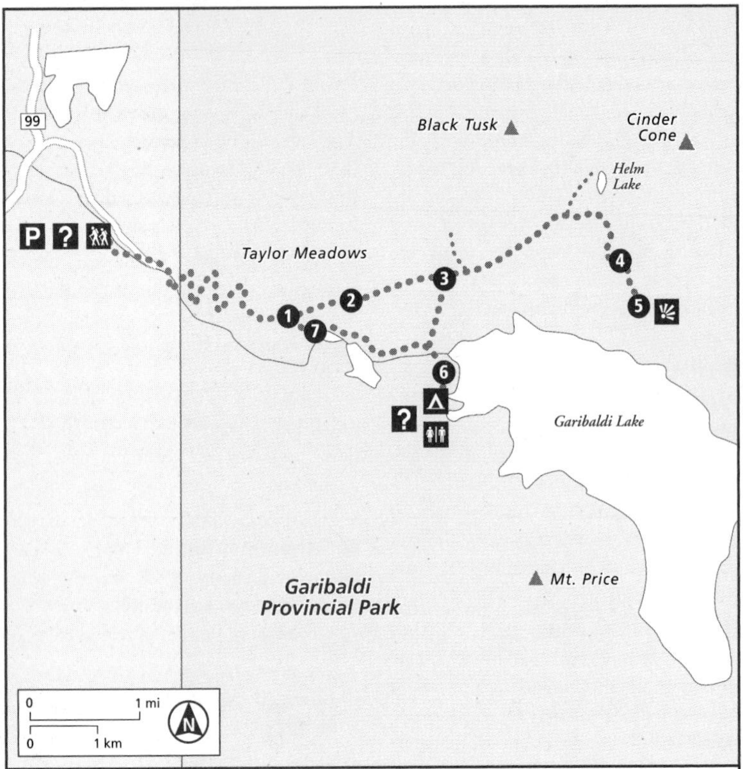

Panorama Ridge

99
P ?
Black Tusk
Cinder Cone
Helm Lake
Taylor Meadows
Garibaldi Lake
Garibaldi Provincial Park
Mt. Price
0 1 mi
0 1 km
N

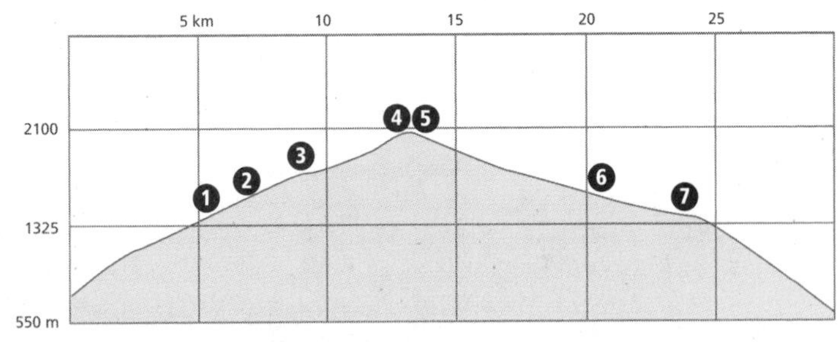

N 49 95.733, W 123 11.998 (0 km): Trail head

1 N 49 94.856, W 123 08.708 (5.5 km): Turn left at the first junction

2 N 49 95.136, W 123 07.576 (6.9 km): Reach Taylor Meadows campground

3 N 49 95.713, W 123 05.199 (8.9 km): Continue straight at Outhouse Junction

4 N 49 95.652, W 123 01.852 (12.9 km): Pass Helm Glacier

5 N 49 95.330, W 123 01.746 (13.6 km): Ascend the perfect lookout at Panorama Ridge

6 N 49 94.470, W 123 05.480 (20.7 km): Drop down to Garibaldi Lake

7 N 49 94.721, W 123 08.555 (23.9 km): Marvel at the geological history of The Barrier

ponds, and forest. Enjoy the slow decline to the lake.

❻ **Garibaldi Lake** A series of gentle switchbacks provide the first glimpses through the trees of Garibaldi Lake up-close.

Take the left fork that indicates .5km (1/4 mile) to the lake campground.

TAKE A BREAK Here on the shore, you are afforded an entirely different panorama: As fish splash on the surface (the lake was stocked with Rainbow Trout in the 1920s), the imposing Sphinx Glacier sits at the head of the lake. Note that the teal-colored waters now appear to have lost their bright hue.

Return to the main trail and continue left, following signs directing you along the final 9km (5 1/2 miles) to the parking lot.

❼ **The Barrier** Perhaps one of the most interesting formations in the park, The Barrier is truly like nothing else. Head down the short trail to the viewpoint and gaze upon this wonder of geology.

Formed 10,000 years ago when hot lava collided with a wall of glacial ice, the Barrier stands as a 455m (1,493-ft.) cliff retaining Garibaldi Lake. The area is unstable and susceptible to collapse from erosion, heavy rainfall, or seismic activity.

Now, with this new appreciation for the forces that shaped the park, head down the remaining path and switchbacks to the parking lot.

6 HIGH NOTE VIA HALF NOTE TRAIL ★★ Kids

Difficulty rating: Moderate

Distance: 5.5km (3.4 miles) round trip

Estimated time: 2 hr.

Elevation gain: 200m (656 ft.)

Costs/permits: Lift ticket for adult (19–64) C$32, youth (13–18) and senior (65+) C$22, child (7–12) C$11

Pet friendly: No

Best time to go: Late July–Sept

Website: www.whistlerblackcomb.com

Recommended map: Available from Guest Services near the Whistler Village Gondola

Trail head GPS: N 50 05.902, W 122 95.788

Trail head directions: From Whistler Village, take the Whistler Village Gondola up the mountain. At the Roundhouse lodge, follow the .6km (.4-mile) trail to the Peak Chair. Once at the top, head southeast towards the trail head marked High Note Trail.

This short yet high-elevation trail tours you through the most spectacular views of the region, with snowy peaks that stretch far into the horizon. The Peak Chair lifts you above 2,000m (6,562 ft.) to unobstructed views as you follow the trails circling the 2,181m (7,156-ft.) peak of Whistler Mountain.

Follow the loose rocky trail as it slowly descends from the trail head, and you immediately see the impressive horn of Black Tusk, a hardened volcano core after its sides have long eroded away. Along the entire horizon, coniferous forests reach up to the snow lines of mountains or the shores of tranquil lakes.

At the first fork in the trail, just 75m (246 ft.) in, head straight. When the trail

Whistler Adventures

Despite its mega-status as a winter resort, Whistler was originally established as—and remains—an epicenter of summer activity. With countless adventure thrills for those days off from hiking, here are a select few to get you started:

Backcountry Tours Whiz through the wilderness with a professionally trained driver as your chauffeur. **Barely Legal Motorsports** offers 2- to 4-hour tours in custom-built hotrods that whiz through the largely untouched off-road Whistler. And with the "environmentally sustainable hydrogen engine," you'll be minimizing your travel footprint, as well. These tours cost from C$129 to C$299. Call ✆ **877/932-9800** or 604/932-2222, or visit www.blhotrod.com for full vehicle specs.

Bungee Jumping Look down to the fast-flowing Cheakamus River from the 49m (161-ft.) bridge where **Whistler Bungee** takes its jumps. The crew is experienced with a flawless safety record. The first jump costs C$114, with discounts for subsequent plunges. Call ✆ **877/938-9333** or 604/938-9333, or visit www.whistlerbungee.com.

Mountain Biking Lift-serviced and gravity-fed: These are just two ways **Whistler Mountain Bike Park** delivers fabulous rides over more than 200km (124 miles) of trails. Take on a smooth, challenging, or hair-raising ride, depending on your level of daring. The park, with its base near the foot of the Village Gondola, opens at 10am from mid-May through mid-October. One-day lift tickets cost C$49, with rental bikes available. Call ✆ **866/218-9690** or 604/904-8134, or visit www.whistlerbike.com for park details.

Rafting From float trips for the timid to whitewater descents for the wild, rafting is more than a day on the water. **Sunwolf Outdoor Centre** offers a variety of half-day and full-day rafting trips, from C$99 to C$149. Call ✆ **877/806-8046** or 604/898-1537, or visit www.sunwolf.net for detailed tour packages.

Skiing/Snowboarding Visit Whistler in July, and alpine enthusiasts with snowboards over their shoulders stroll along next to patios filled with shorts-wearing sun-seekers. Yes, just because it's summer, don't think Whistler gives up on its true paramour. Through to late July, **Blackcomb Mountain** (Whistler Mountain's twin) is open for glacier riding. Call ✆ **866/218-9690** or 604/904-8134, or visit www.whistlerblackcomb.com/todo/summer/glacier for more information.

Trail Rides Feel like a cowboy when you saddle up with **Adventure Ranch.** During the summer, the 2-hour rides depart at 10am, 1pm, and 4pm near Pemberton. Off-season rides run at 1pm, weather dependent. C$69 per person. Call ✆ **604/894-5200** to reserve or check www.adventureranch.net for availability.

Zip-trekking Soar through the trees at heights of up to 61m (200 ft.). The famous 3-hour tours take visitors over a series of zip lines, trails, and suspension bridges to truly give a bird's eye view of Whistler's stunning natural surroundings. **Ziptrek Ecotours** operates year-round and runs a tour desk in the Carleton Lodge, 4284 Mountain Square. These tours cost C$100 to C$120. Call ✆ **866/935-0001** or 604/935-0001, or visit www.ziptrek.com.

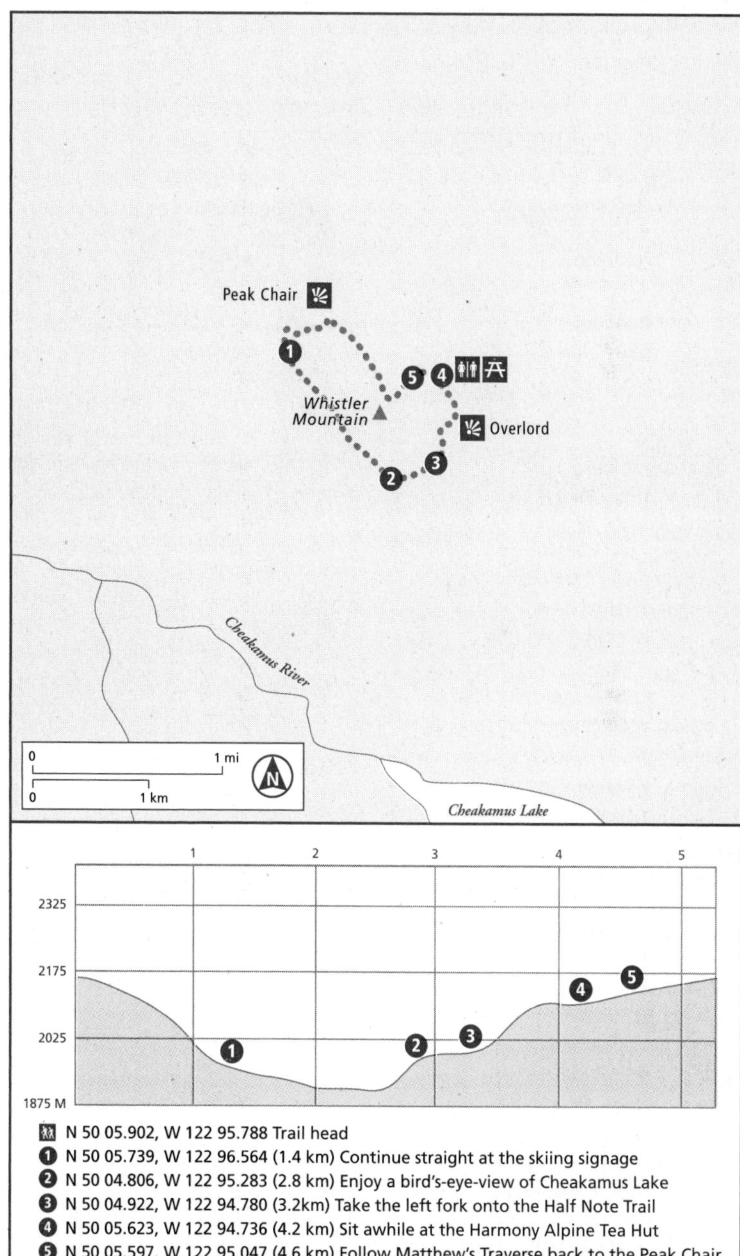

N 50 05.902, W 122 95.788 Trail head
❶ N 50 05.739, W 122 96.564 (1.4 km) Continue straight at the skiing signage
❷ N 50 04.806, W 122 95.283 (2.8 km) Enjoy a bird's-eye-view of Cheakamus Lake
❸ N 50 04.922, W 122 94.780 (3.2km) Take the left fork onto the Half Note Trail
❹ N 50 05.623, W 122 94.736 (4.2 km) Sit awhile at the Harmony Alpine Tea Hut
❺ N 50 05.597, W 122 95.047 (4.6 km) Follow Matthew's Traverse back to the Peak Chair

forks again, take the right fork up to a westerly lookout. After a few snapshots, follow the path down to a collection of interpretive signs that map out the horizon.

Take the trail that leads sharply downhill from the signs, over the rocky terrain with chains placed to ease your descent. As the switchbacks carve down the hill, alternate your gaze from the stunning landscapes to the narrow path.

1 On the Slopes Here, after about 1.3km (3/4 mile) and 30 minutes, is a hint of Whistler, the premier ski resort. Directional signs for skiers tower over you (remember that in winter, the snow pack reaches far above your head); however, the High Note Trail continues straight past.

Your descent has taken you to just the upper reaches of the tree line as the path follows the mountainside and the natural course of the land.

Scan the grasses for the lush wildflowers that are the antidote to Whistler's icy winters, including the deep purple of Arctic lupins and mop-heads of the Western pasqueflowers.

To the south, Black Tusk remains in view, along with the small oasis of Corrie Lake.

2 Cheakamus Lake About 2.5km (1 1/2 miles) in, and after about 1 hour of walking, the picturesque waters of Cheakamus Lake appear. As with many lakes in this region, glacial silt remains suspended in the water, creating a brilliant aqua color. From here, climb up the hill to your left.

3 Half Note Trail Another 15 minutes brings you to the junction of the High Note Trail (which continues for more than 8km/5 miles total hiking distance), and the Half Note Trail on the left.

Take the left fork and begin to regain your elevation as you navigate a boulder field.

On your right, look for the Symphony Express, frozen in the summer warmth, that climbs to the musical bump peak of Piccolo. The rather barren path crosses the Burnt Stew Trail, a vehicle-wide road, and continues up over the rocky climb.

SPECTACULAR LOOKOUT
The Overlord lookout features clear views of the sprawling snowy banks of its namesake glacier. The Overlord Glacier (you'll see it as the large, flat snowy area) covers more than 4 sq. km (1 1/2 sq. miles) and is currently retreating.

4 Harmony Alpine Tea Hut Tea may not be the first comfort that springs to mind after a summer alpine hike, but as the temperature is significantly cooler at Whistler Peak compared to the village, a hot cuppa becomes quickly appealing.

A small log-cabin tea hut sells snacks, as well as hot and cold beverages, and is well placed between the Peak Chair and the Harmony Express.

5 Matthew's Traverse From the tea hut, walk along the vehicle-width road that winds to the right of Symphony Amphitheatre and around the Saddle. Pause to listen for the boom of rocks falling from the cliffs below the peak, an area that remains permanently closed. The trail is well signposted: Simply head straight towards Matthew's Traverse—the final ascent of the day, leading back to the Peak Chair.

As you feel the high elevation tugging at your lungs, know the trip down on the chairlift will be smooth as can be.

7 STEIN VALLEY NLAKA'PAMUX HERITAGE PARK ★★ (Kids)

Difficulty rating: Easy

Distance: 9km (5.6 miles) round trip

Estimated time: 2½ hr.

Elevation gain: 105m (344 ft.)

Costs/permits: None

Best time to go: Year-round

Website: www.env.gov.bc.ca/bcparks/explore/parkpgs/stein_val

Recommended map: Available for download on BC Parks website (address above) or the Lytton Visitor Centre

Trail head GPS: N 50 27.289, W 121 63.553

Trail head directions: Travel 110km (68 miles) on Hwy. 1 north from Hope, or 64km (40 miles) south on Hwy. 12 from Lillooet. Take the exit for Lytton and follow Main St. through town, then turn onto 7th St. and cross the bridge (over the Thompson River). Look for Ferry Rd. on your left after about 1km (½ mile), where you'll find the reaction ferry that runs daily 6:30am–10:15pm, with breaks. Once across the Fraser, turn right and travel nearly 5km (3 miles) before making a left onto Stein Valley Rd. At the end of the single car-width road, you'll find the parking area.

Welcome to a sacred place. For several thousand years, the Lytton First Nation has revered this unlogged river valley, and the name Stein itself comes from the Nlaka'pamux word *Stagyn,* meaning hidden place. Yet, in most hiking books, this beautiful park remains absent. It could be the limited access points or the washouts at the Stein Divide trail head off Hwy. 99 that keep most people away—either way, you'll be glad you've found this park.

Descending the first 200m (656 ft.) or so of the trail quickly plunges you into the smells, sights, and sounds of the Stein Valley. The valley traverses multiple ecological zones and, as such, packs great diversity into one area.

The lush pines, roaring rapids, and scurrying wildlife all calm your senses through this low-difficulty hike.

The trail is easy to follow and well traveled, although there are no markers. At the first fork in the sandy path (about 5 min. in), take either, as both the high and low roads meet again in just a few meters.

❶ Stryen Creek Cross the plank bridge over the fast-flowing Stryen Creek and continue on the trail. This roaring sound of water will be the soundscape to your hike.

❷ Asking Rock Early on, the trail skirts the mini-bus-sized Asking Rock—which reveals a good introduction to the park's cultural significance.

Here, it is tradition to pray for safe passage through the Stein Valley. Inspect but don't touch the various charms embedded in the moss. From coins and fishing lures to tobacco and sage, the Nlaka'pamux people and visitors have made offerings and left small mementos here.

Stop to look up over the face of Asking Rock for the ochre markings of pictographs. Some of these depictions have existed for several thousands of years, according to BC Parks. The drawings represent dreams of the Nlaka'pamux people who came to this area on various spiritual quests, including puberty rituals. The rock is also believed to be a safe haven for women giving birth.

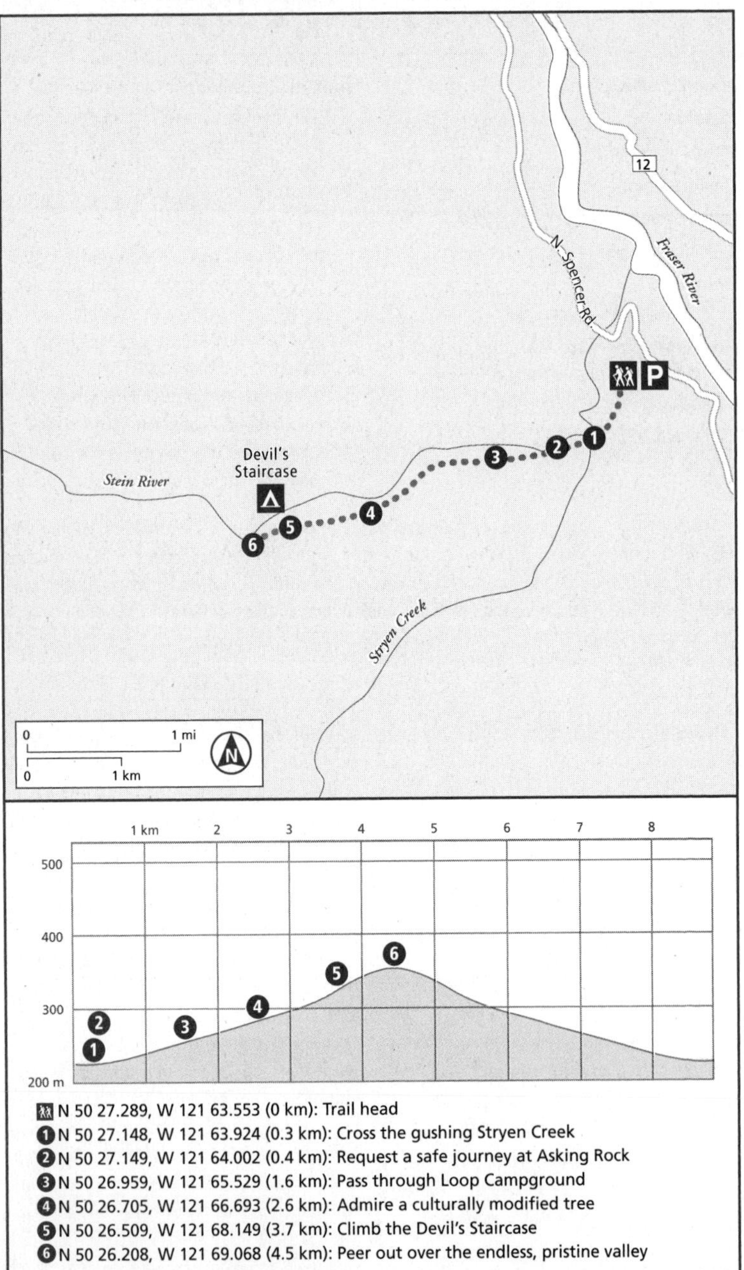
12
N. Spencer Rd.
Fraser River
Devil's Staircase
Stein River
Stryen Creek
0
1 mi
0
1 km
1 km
2
3
4
5
6
7
8
500
400
300
200 m
N 50 27.289, W 121 63.553 (0 km): Trail head
1 N 50 27.148, W 121 63.924 (0.3 km): Cross the gushing Stryen Creek
2 N 50 27.149, W 121 64.002 (0.4 km): Request a safe journey at Asking Rock
3 N 50 26.959, W 121 65.529 (1.6 km): Pass through Loop Campground
4 N 50 26.705, W 121 66.693 (2.6 km): Admire a culturally modified tree
5 N 50 26.509, W 121 68.149 (3.7 km): Climb the Devil's Staircase
6 N 50 26.208, W 121 69.068 (4.5 km): Peer out over the endless, pristine valley

Once you've surveyed the visible pictographs, continue west along the sandy trail that meanders over rocks worn smooth by the powerful currents.

❸ Loop Camp About 1.7km (1 mile) in, Loop Camp (also called Easy Camp) provides some basic facilities, including a pit toilet. Continuing from the camp, the trail requires you to carefully pick your way through small granite boulders.

❹ Culturally Modified Tree A kilometer (1/2 mile) past Loop Camp, a small trail on your left ventures over to a beautiful culturally modified tree.

The jigsaw bark of the Ponderosa pine features a number of plaques paying respects to members of the Lytton First Nation. Again, look with your eyes, not your hands, and remember you are a visitor in the valley.

From here through to Devil's Staircase, the trail slowly climbs in elevation, continuing on river right, and opens up to wider vistas of the valley.

❺ Devil's Staircase The narrowing of the path signals that the ominously named Devil's Staircase is nearing. At the signpost for the campground, either head right down to the camping area for a picnic or zigzag on the series of steep switchbacks en route to stunning views.

TAKE A BREAK

Large boulders near the river and log seats in the campground both afford a nice lunch spot. Just remember to pack up all your garbage: You are in grizzly and black bear country, so any garbage you leave (food or otherwise) will attract the curious mammals.

At the top of the climb, continue west over the talus slopes of tumbled debris. Move steadily through this area, which is the result of rock fall, as the area remains unstable.

Once you venture past the talus slope, the path returns to a wooded trail that winds along the mountain side.

❻ Look Off As you curve around the trail, the view opens up to long perspectives where rocky slopes of tree-covered mountains converge at the surging teal waters of the Stein.

Your destination is a cliff located just before the trail descends again and offers a serene vantage up the valley. Look here at the beauty of an unlogged valley, preserved for its ecological and cultural importance.

Although the trail continues on (for 9 days of hiking through to a trail head near Duffey Lake and Pemberton), take a few deep breaths overlooking it all before returning on the same path.

SLEEPING & EATING

ACCOMMODATIONS

Whistler

★★ (Value) **Golden Dreams Bed & Breakfast** A nice West-coast-themed alternative to the pseudo-European style throughout much of Whistler, this B&B offers three rooms with BC themes to enhance your stay. Guest kitchen, hot tub, and fabulous breakfasts complement the cozy residential location.

6412 Easy St., Whistler, BC V0N 1B6. ✆ **800/668-7055** or 604/932-2667. www.goldendreamswhistler.com. 3 units. Summer C$95–C$145 double; winter C$115–C$185 double; breakfast included. MC, V.

★★★ (Finds) **Nita Lake Lodge** This luxury boutique hotel is conveniently connected to the Whistler Mountaineer Train Station. Hidden just south of town on the shore of Nita Lake, the lodge offers high-class comforts in an understated way.

2131 Lake Placid Rd., Whistler, BC V0N 1B2. ✆ **888/755-6482** or 604/966-5700. www.nitalakelodge.com. 77 units. Summer suites starting at C$139; winter suites starting at C$239. AE, MC, V.

Pan Pacific Whistler Mountainside As all rooms are well-equipped with kitchenettes, this hotel offers ample flexibility for a family stay. Plus, the unbeatable location at the foot of the Village Gondola means the entire village is just a short stroll away.

4320 Sundial Crescent, Whistler, BC V0N 1B4. ✆ **888/905-9995** or 604/905-2999. www.panpacific.com/whistlermountainside. 121 units. Apr 27–Nov 19 C$129–C$1,499 studios through 2-bedroom; Nov 20–Apr 26 C$199– C$1,499 studios through 2-bedroom. AE, DC, MC, V.

★ **Riverside RV Resort & Campground** Whistler's only campground offers great diversity and even a dab of luxury: Heated shower floors, a café, and a putting course all elevate this campground far above roughing it. Backpackers will appreciate the free shuttle service to Whistler Village.

8018 Mons Rd., Whistler, BC V0N 1B8. ✆ **604/905-5533.** www.whistlercamping.com. 113 units (includes tent sites, RV sites, and cabins). Camping May–Sept C$35, Oct–Apr C$25; RV sites May–Sept C$55, Oct–Apr C$45; cabins C$135–C$215. AE, MC, V.

Squamish

(Kids) **Sunwolf Outdoor Centre** A comfy stay in secluded cabins, plus plenty of adventure opportunities, makes a great combination for all family members, including Rover. The nearby Tantalus mountain range beckons the avid hiker with lush slopes and snowy peaks.

70002 Squamish Valley Rd. (off Hwy. 99), Brackendale, BC V0N 1H0. ✆ **877/806-8046** or 604/898-1537. www.sunwolf.net. 10 units. C$90 cabin; C$100 cabin w/kitchenette. C$10 additional fee for pets. MC, V.

Pemberton

★ **Auberge du Pré B&B** This guest house offers quality and simplicity in its suites. Try the Ipsoot Room with its private access to the hot tub after 9pm, or the McKenzie Room with optional king-sized or twin beds.

7705 Pemberton Meadows Rd., Pemberton, BC V0N 2L0. ✆ **866/894-1471** or 604/894-1471. www.pemberton-bc-bb-whistler.com. 3 units. C$135 double. MC, V.

Lytton

★ **Totem Motel** Clean and cabin-like lodgings have a simple, rustic charm, plus a fabulous vantage overlooking the Fraser River. The main building once housed the local post office and is conveniently located close to the visitor center.

320 Fraser St. (at 3rd St.), Lytton, BC, V0K 1Z0. ✆ **250/455-2321.** www.angelfire.com/bc2/totemmotel. 15 units. C$75 double. MC, V.

RESTAURANTS

Whistler

★★★ **Araxi Restaurant & Bar** PACIFIC NORTHWEST With a long list of awards to its credit, Araxi draws on locally sourced ingredients to complement an extensive local and international wine list that features more than 1,000 labels. The restaurant's pretty garden patio makes this the perfect stop after a morning hiking the peak trails of Whistler Mountain.

4222 Village Sq. ✆ **604/932-4540.** www.araxi.com. Reservations recommended. Main courses C$30–C$45. AE, MC, V. Summer lunch 11am–3pm; year-round dinner 5–11pm.

★★ **Crêpe Montagne** CREPERIE Tasty crêpes served fast and hot—what a delicious taste of the Alps to start the day. Try a savory chicken and goat cheese crêpe, or a hearty bacon-and-egger. Bon appétit!

116–4368 Main St. (at Northlands Blvd.). ✆ **604/905-4444.** www.crepemontagne.com. Breakfast C$5.25–C$13; main courses C$15–C$33. AE, MC, V. Daily 8am–9:30pm.

★★ Value **Ingrid's Village Café** CAFE For an affordable and friendly quick bite to eat in a prime location, you can't beat Ingrid's. Get a veggie burger to go, or sit on the patio and watch Whistler walk by. Also, sample from a full breakfast menu.

4305 Skier's Approach. ✆ **604/932-7000.** www.ingridswhistler.com. Sandwiches C$5–C$7.25. MC, V. Daily 7am–6pm.

Squamish

★ **The Burrow** TAPAS This casual lounge atmosphere serves a variety of comfort foods with a twist. The baked pasta—with a variety of add-ons, from sausage and prawns to spinach and button mushrooms—is particularly filling.

11–40437 Tantalus Rd. ✆ **604/898-2801.** www.theburrow.ca. Reservations recommended. Tapas plates C$6–C$16. MC, V. Sun–Thurs 5–11pm; Fri–Sat 5pm–midnight.

★ Finds **Howe Sound Brewpub** PUB Since the 1890s, residents have grown hops in the rich agricultural lands around Squamish. This lively brewpub continues this tradition, offering a great combination of micro-brewed ales and simple eats. All beers are brewed on-site, and the selection changes regularly.

37801 Cleveland Ave. ✆ **800/919-2537** or 604/892-2603. www.howesound.com. Main courses C$12–C$22. AE, MC, V. Mon–Sat 11:30am–10pm; Sun 11:30am–9pm.

Pemberton

★★ **Wild Wood Restaurant & Bar** PACIFIC NORTHWEST A modern dining room serves up great service and quality meals. The same folks who established the popular restaurant of the same name in Whistler's Function Junction opened this location in 2004.

Suite 101, 1436 Portage Rd. ✆ **604/894-0114.** www.wildwoodrestaurants.ca. Main courses C$13–C$28. AE, MC, V. Sun–Thurs 9am–10pm; Fri–Sat 9am–11pm.

Lytton

Lytton Hotel Restaurant WESTERN/CHINESE TAKEOUT The basic-service dining room serves up a wide range of Western and Chinese dishes at reasonable prices. Dishes have no MSG added, and you'll be able to glean some local insight from the Lytton patrons.

538 Main St. ✆ **250/455-2239.** Main courses C$9–C$20. MC, V. Daily 6am–9pm.

7

Cariboo Country, Chilcotin, Coast & Northern BC Hikes

by Chloë Ernst

Cariboo Country stretches west from the Cariboo Mountains, drops into the ranchlands of the Chilcotin Plateau, and rises again as the snowy-peaked Coast Mountains.

In this region, undiscovered and largely unmarked hiking trails lie in the mazes of traditional First Nations trails, logging roads, and mining routes. As a result, this belt of BC attracts independent spirits who visit to explore panoramas of forest, isolated peaks, secluded lakes, and even a sand dune.

But to reach anywhere in Cariboo Country by land, you must first travel the old Cariboo Waggon Road from Yale. Dubbed the Eighth Wonder of the World, the route ferried supplies to gold-rushers starting in the 1860s.

The Waggon Road enters Cariboo Country where towns are named for their distance from Lillooet: 100 Mile House and 150 Mile House stand in as your odometer en-route to the larger centers of Williams Lake, Quesnel, and Prince George.

A number of hidden ghost towns stand as testament to the gold rush days. The best known (and least hidden) is Barkerville Historic Site, east of Quesnel. More than a living history lesson, Barkerville leads to the Mount Agnes Trail Network: an entanglement of hikes steeped in mining history. The trails offer a well-mapped introduction to BC hiking for all levels of enthusiasts.

Things get a little wilder heading west from Williams Lake on Hwy. 20. Passing through the tiny ranchland communities of the Chilcotin Plateau, cattle grids punctuate the road instead of stoplights, and the locals give passersby a polite wave.

For those seeking an off-road adventure, venture south from the Chilcotin Hwy. to Ts'il?os Provincial Park (beautifully pronounced *Sigh*-loss). If your shocks can take the 63km (39 miles) of gravel road, the challenging hikes climb above rivers of salmon to windy viewpoints overlooking picturesque Chilko Lake.

As the highway turns to gravel at Anahim Lake, so begin the Coast Mountains and then the raw wilderness of Tweedsmuir Provincial Park. The largest BC provincial park, Tweedsmuir boasts the most spectacular treks, including overnight expeditions to Hunlen Falls (Canada's third-highest free-falling waterfall) and the fiery slopes of the Rainbow Range. Tweedsmuir also safeguards the Canadian Shangri-La: the Bella Coola Valley.

While this lush valley is technically on the Pacific Ocean, it actually lies 100km (62 miles) inland in the North Bentinck Arm. Known for its large bear population, the Bella Coola Valley lies at the bottom of the brake-light burner descent called The Hill. In 1952, isolated and frustrated valley residents took highway construction into their own hands. Bulldozers started at the top and bottom and met in the middle by 1953. With grades up to 18 percent, The Hill tops the list of BC's most unique drives.

The more relaxing route to Bella Coola, however, remains the Discovery Coast Ferry from Port Hardy on Vancouver Island. At either end of your Cariboo Country, Chilcotin, and Coast tour, the scenic route perfectly accompanies the extraordinary hiking trails and grand wildlife of BC.

ESSENTIALS

Spanning lakes, grasslands, and rugged mountains, this stunning strip of the province promises a diverse and wild journey.

GETTING THERE

By Car

Hwy. 97 is the main vehicle artery twisting north from Cache Creek, an industrial town 345km (214 miles) from Vancouver via Hope and 340km (211 miles) north via Whistler.

The road continues north through towns built around roadhouses and onward to Williams Lake (200km/124 miles), Quesnel (325km/202 miles), Prince George (445km/277 miles), and the north.

From Williams Lake, Hwy. 20 branches 450km (280 miles) west to Bella Coola. To the east of Quesnel, Hwy. 26 connects the industrial city with the quaint town of Wells (81km/50 miles) and historic Barkerville (84km/52 miles).

By Bus

Greyhound (✆ **800/661-8747;** www.greyhound.ca) departs daily to Cache Creek, 70 Mile House, 100 Mile House, Williams Lake, Quesnel, and Prince George.

By Plane

Air Canada flies from Vancouver to Williams Lake, Quesnel, and Prince George (✆ **888/247-2262;** www.aircanada.com), while **WestJet** flies from Vancouver to Prince George (✆ **888/937-8538;** www.westjet.com).

A number of smaller airlines provide comprehensive service, including **Pacific Coastal Airlines,** which flies to Bella Coola, Anahim Lake, and Williams Lake (✆ **800-663-2872;** www.pacificcoastal.com). Charter operator **Bella Coola Air** serves the coastal region with transportation and tours (✆ **250/982-2545;** www.bellacoolaair.com).

By Train

Rocky Mountaineer Vacations' (✆ **877/460-3200** or 604/606-7245; www.rockymountaineer.com) Fraser Discovery Route departs from Whistler traveling to Quesnel (and then on to Jasper) on Tuesdays, Thursdays, and Saturdays at 7:10am between mid-May and mid-October.

VIA Rail (✆ **888/842-7245** or 604/640-3700; www.viarail.ca) travels from Vancouver to Prince George via Jasper on Tuesdays at 5:30pm. Fares vary based on seating.

By Ferry

Perhaps the most stunning way to reach Bella Coola is the Discovery Coast Ferry. Departing June through early September, the BC-Ferries-run route follows the Inside Passage, stopping at isolated coastal and island communities along the way. Visit www.bcferries.com for current scheduling and pricing, or call ✆ **888/223-3779** or 250/386-3431.

VISITOR INFORMATION

Situated on the Cariboo Highway, the **100 Mile House Visitor Centre** offers information on the South Cariboo region. You can find it at 422 Hwy. 97, 100 Mile House, BC V0K 2E0. Call ✆ **877/511-5353** or 250/395-5353, or visit www.southcaribootourism.com. The center is open Monday through Friday from 9am to 5pm.

The impressive **Williams Lake Visitor Centre** offers friendly local guidance from the shiny two-story building off Hwy. 97—at 1660 South Broadway, Williams Lake, BC V2G 2W4. Call ✆ **877/967-5253** or 250/392-5025, or check out www.williamslakechamber.com. It's open Monday to Saturday from 9am to 5pm.

Hidden inside the Coop Building, the **Bella Coola Visitor Information Booth's** trail maps remain on display year-round at 450 Mackenzie St., Bella Coola, BC V0T 1C0. Call ✆ **866/799-5202** or 250/799-5202, or visit www.bellacoola.ca. The booth is open early June to early September, from 9am to 5:30pm.

Located right off Hwy. 97 headed in to town, the **Quesnel Visitor Centre** provides insight on the northern region of the Cariboo. Find it at 703 Carson Ave., Quesnel, BC V2J 2B6. Call ✆ **800/992-4922** or 250/992-8716. You can also go to www.northcariboo.com. You can visit the center Tuesday to Saturday from 9am to 4pm.

The **Wells Visitor Centre** is located before the town at Jack O'Clubs Lake (11900 Hwy. 26, Wells, BC V0K 2R0) and offers advice on visiting Wells, Barkerville, and the Bowron Lakes. For information, call ✆ **877/451-9355** or 250/994-2323, or head to www.wellsbc.com. It's open mid-May to early September, daily from 9am to 5pm.

GETTING AROUND

100 Mile Taxi & Charter Services serves the 100 Mile District (✆ **250/791-5224**). Public transport is also available: One route serves 100 Mile House, while the second heads along Hwy. 97 to 108 Ranch. These services are available Monday through Friday for C$1.25 to C$1.75. Call ✆ **250/395-2834** or visit www.busonline.ca/regions/one.

Town Taxi runs a prompt and friendly 24-hour service in Williams Lake; call ✆ **250/392-4151.** Three local bus routes operate Monday to Saturday, and fares cost C$1 to C$2. You can call ✆ **250/398-7812** or head to www.busonline.ca/regions/wil.

Cariboo Taxi in Quesnel runs throughout the north Cariboo region and out to Barkerville. Call ✆ **250/991-0007.** Two bus routes run in town from Monday to Saturday; fare costs C$1.50. For information, call ✆ **250/992-1109.**

Scheduled bus service leaves twice daily from the village of Bella Coola to Burnt Bridge Creek at the bottom of The Hill. Otherwise, **Dial-a-Ride** service is available Monday to Saturday from 8am to 6pm for C$2. Exact change needed. Call 24 hours in advance, ✆ **250/799-0079.** Visit http://bct1.transitbc.com/regions/bel for more information.

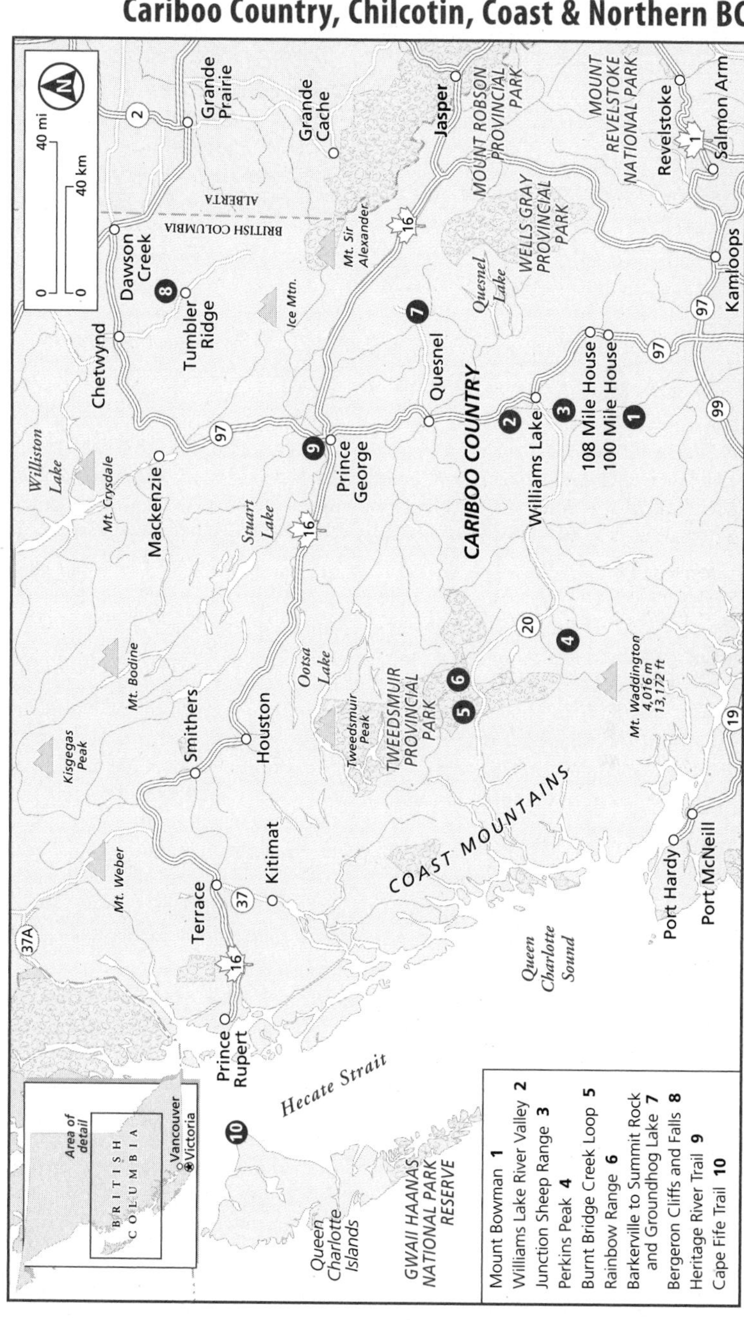
0 40 mi
0 40 km
N
BRITISH COLUMBIA
ALBERTA
Dawson Creek
Grande Prairie
Grande Cache
Jasper
MOUNT ROBSON PROVINCIAL PARK
MOUNT REVELSTOKE NATIONAL PARK
Revelstoke
Salmon Arm
Kamloops
WELLS GRAY PROVINCIAL PARK
Quesnel Lake
Mt. Sir Alexander
Ice Mtn.
Tumbler Ridge
Chetwynd
Quesnel
CARIBOO COUNTRY
Williams Lake
108 Mile House
100 Mile House
Prince George
Mackenzie
Williston Lake
Mt. Crysdale
Stuart Lake
Ootsa Lake
Mt. Bodine
Smithers
Houston
Kisgegas Peak
Tweedsmuir Peak
TWEEDSMUIR PROVINCIAL PARK
Mt. Waddington 4,016 m 13,172 ft
COAST MOUNTAINS
Kitimat
Terrace
Mt. Weber
Prince Rupert
Queen Charlotte Sound
Port Hardy
Port McNeill
Hecate Strait
Queen Charlotte Islands
GWAII HAANAS NATIONAL PARK RESERVE
Area of detail
BRITISH COLUMBIA
Vancouver
Victoria
2
16
97
99
20
19
37
37A
1
Mount Bowman 1
Williams Lake River Valley 2
Junction Sheep Range 3
Perkins Peak 4
Burnt Bridge Creek Loop 5
Rainbow Range 6
Barkerville to Summit Rock and Groundhog Lake 7
Bergeron Cliffs and Falls 8
Heritage River Trail 9
Cape Fife Trail 10

1 MOUNT BOWMAN ★★

Difficulty rating: Strenuous

Distance: 15km (9.3 miles) round trip

Estimated time: 5 hr.

Elevation gain: 890m (2,920 ft.)

Costs/permits: None

Best time to go: July–Sept

Recommended map: 92 P/4

Website: www.env.gov.bc.ca/bcparks/explore/parkpgs/marble_ran

Trail head GPS: N 51 16.778, W 121 94.455

Trail head directions: Take Hwy. 97 to Clinton—40km (25 miles) north of Cache Creek or 165km (103 miles) south of Williams Lake. Turn west onto Kelly Lake Rd. at the south end of the village. Travel for 16km (10 miles) and make a right onto Jesmond Rd.; follow Jesmond Rd. for 24km (15 miles). Look for a dirt road that starts the trail on your right, 1km (1/2 mile) past Circle H Ranch. Shortly after this road, a left turn provides a safe parking area.

This dry peak in the fairly unvisited Marble Range sits amidst a wild terrain of fabulous ridge hikes, unforgiving ascents, and undisturbed wildlife. Rolling ranges and defined ridges lie in all directions, with the scar of the Fraser River trench to the west.

From Jesmond Road, either hike or drive the first 2km (1 1/4 miles) of the dirt road towards Mount Bowman—which is immediately ahead. In dry conditions, the road may be 2WD accessible with careful driving, but road conditions shouldn't deter you from visiting this serene viewpoint.

The first trail section follows the road and traverses pretty glens of aspens that turn luminescent yellow in the fall. As the route heads under some large transmission lines, a number of branches split off from the main trail. Stay on the main and most traveled road.

After about 1.5km (1 mile), keep right at the fork. Another 100m (328 ft.) brings you to a pond and a large clearing. Continue straight here for another 350m (1,148 ft.) to an alternate parking spot.

❶ **Alternate Trail Head** For the walkers, continue on past this small clearing, and the trail shortly becomes a single-track sandy path. For drivers, park here and pick up the start of the trail.

The valley cuts through a thinly planted forest of pine and fir. To the right rises the canine-tooth peak of Mad Dog Mountain, with Lime Ridge behind it to the south and Bowman occasionally visible to the north.

At a fork in the path about 300m (984 ft.) after the alternate trail head, take the right branch. Trails in the Marble Range can be confusing, as they are wholly unmarked. In most cases, the most worn path is the best indication of the route.

Soon, the sounds of a stream down to your right begin to drift through the trees. Be sure to make plenty of noise throughout the hike, as the valleys around Mount Bowman are frequented by bears—both black and grizzly.

❷ **Valley Walk** Having quickly yet gently gained 100m (328 ft.) in elevation, the trail flattens out after 3.5km (2 1/4 miles) over slopes of juniper and blueberry bushes. In the initial approach, the western face of the mountain is visible from the road; however, this trail heads through a valley, then scoops around behind to ascend the eastern face.

❸ **Main Trail Fork** At 4.7km (3 miles), a fork in the trail veers left to Mount Bowman, and a right track climbs steeply uphill towards Wild Horse Ridge and on to

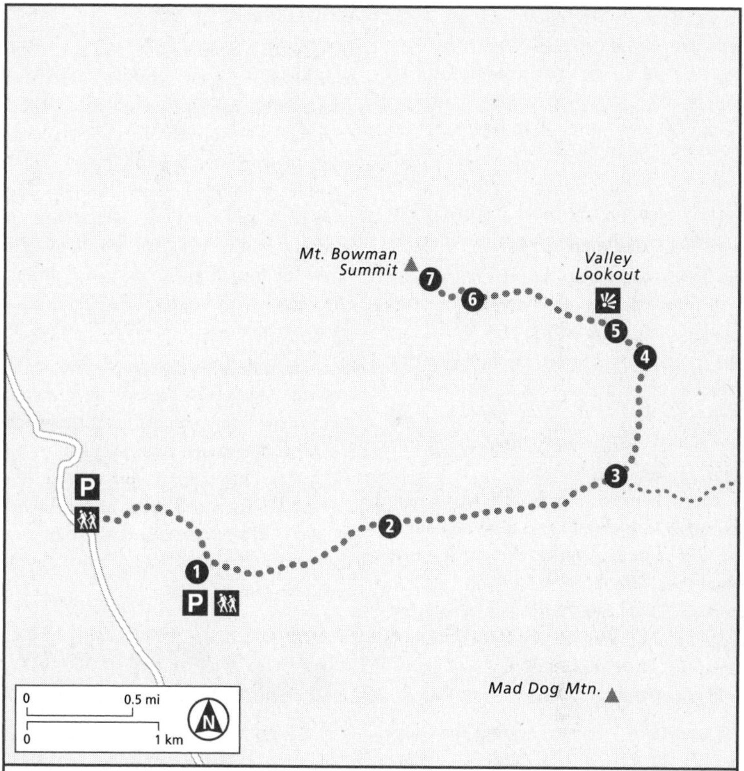

Mt. Bowman Summit
Valley Lookout
P
P
Mad Dog Mtn.
0 0.5 mi
0 1 km
N

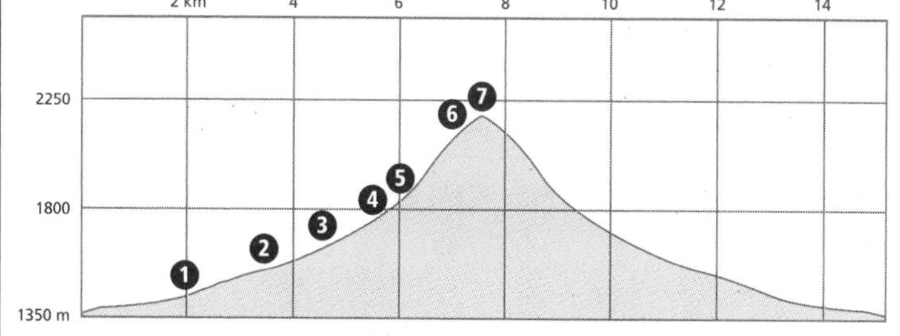

N 51 16.778, W 121 94.455 (0 km): Trail head
1 N 51 16.469, W 121 92.068 (2 km): Walk or drive to the alternate trailhead
2 N 51 16.881, W 121 90.366 (3.4 km): Proceed along the mountainside through the valley
3 N 51 17.028, W 121 88.646 (4.6 km): Take the left trail to Mt. Bowman
4 N 51 18.007, W 121 88.945 (5.8 km): Hike along a ridge leading to Mt. Bowman
5 N 51 18.112, W 121 89.133 (6 km): Admire the Marble Range from a rocky bluff
6 N 51 18.226, W 121 89.981 (7 km): Begin following cairns
7 N 51 18.271, W 121 90.571 (7.5 km): Scramble to the summit

Mount Kerr. Take the left fork and wend up through the lowest elevations of the valley. In wet weather, this trail quickly gets soggy with run-off slopes on either side. Fifty meters (164 ft.) after this main fork, a faint trail branches left, but continue straight on to the valley bottom trail to Bowman.

The unmarked trail follows the streambed, then veers up to a serene alpine meadow. Soon, the vegetation grows tighter around the path as the ascent continues.

❹ **Ridge Walk** At the next junction, the trail turns left and heads uphill. We advise marking this point with a rock so that, on the descent, you don't continue straight along a different trail. Hiking upwards, the path pops out of the trees, with the rocky lower slopes of Bowman ahead and narrow trails zigzagging up the face.

Pause here to look back over the surrounding forests: With a high portion of pine in the woodlands, many of the trees show the effects of the mountain pine beetle. Those trees with red needles are dead, having had their nutrient supply attacked. Next year, only the grey trunks will remain.

❺ **Lookout** Before tackling the trickiest portion of the trail, take in the views from this rocky outcrop high above the valley. Juniper bushes cover these lower slopes but thin out as you head up the scree slopes.

A few trees cling in patches and offer a more surefooted ascent. Head on up, keeping your hands free.

❻ **Cairns** None of the trail is marked, so fellow hikers have helpfully constructed a handful of cairns to mark the upwards scramble. Do not rely on these to determine your route, but do follow where possible as you navigate through sheer limestone and loose rock. Also, commit to memory where the trail passes notable limestone formations to ease your descent and keep you on track.

❼ **Summit** Here, at 2,243m (7,359-ft.) elevation, the landscape drops away to the west and rises up to the east. A final cairn and flag mark the peak, with a ridge stretching north to a second peak and cairn.

On our hike, we could hear a bear growling in the valley to the north. Take in the views before carefully descending over the scree slopes and through the valley on the same route.

SPECTACULAR LOOKOUT Scanning the view clockwise from the east, you'll see the fold of Wild Horse Ridge leading to Mount Kerr, Mad Dog Mountain, and Lime Ridge to the south; the Camelsfoot Range to the southwest; and where the Fraser River has eaten away a canyon in the land to the west.

2 WILLIAMS LAKE RIVER VALLEY TRAIL ★

Difficulty rating: Easy

Distance: 9.8km (6.1 miles) round trip

Estimated time: 2½ hr.

Elevation gain: Loss of 160m (525 ft.)

Costs/permits: None

Best time to go: July–Sept

Website: www.williamslake.ca/index.asp?p=80

Recommended map: Available from the visitor center

Trail head GPS: N 52 16.163, W 122 21.801

Trail head directions: Take Oliver St. (the town's main route) through town to its terminus at Mackenzie Ave. Turn right and follow the heavily trafficked road for 2.5km (1½ miles). Turn left onto Frizzi Rd., then make an immediate right. The dirt road takes you past the landfill and down some tight switchbacks. After 5km (3 miles), veer right at the cattle grid and leave your vehicle in the parking area.

This riverside amble crosses more than a dozen small bridges with lush, varied vegetation and fascinating glacial formations flanking the trail. At the confluence, watch the meek Williams Lake River meet the impressive force of the Fraser.

From the parking lot located just after the 7km trail marker, the unmarked path cuts west through marshlands of bulrushes. Here at the trail head, you'll likely see some black bear warning signs, so remain bear aware throughout the hike.

After 400m (1,312 ft.) of marsh, the trail enters a mixed forest, and the countryside blossoms with diversity while the path begins its gentle downward slope.

While vehicles previously frequented this trail, access is now limited to walkers, runners, horseback riders, and mountain bikers.

❶ Williams Lake River The path follows the route of the river as it connects the upstream San Jose watershed and Williams Lake to the downstream Fraser River. At 1.1km (3/4 mile), the banks of the Williams Lake River appear for the first (and certainly not the last) time.

On both sides of the river, the valley slopes reach high above the riparian zone—the rich area that offers a delightful diversity of trees, scrubs, plants, and animals. From wild roses and snowberries to groves of Douglas fir and cottonwood, be sure to walk slowly and identify the many species growing so close to your path.

For birdwatchers, the Williams Lake River valley features hundreds of species of birds, including goshawks, belted kingfishers, pygmy owls, and great blue herons. Watch, too, for a resident eagle, as she makes frequent trips from her nest (about 1.7km/1 mile along the trail) out to snag fish in the Fraser.

❷ Beaver Dam The dam, a collection of branches trying to hold back the river, shows a small portion of the wildlife diversity that lives in the banks of the Williams Lake River. Deer, muskrats, mink, and bear also frequent the valley.

The river connects to the San Jose watershed—an upstream network of lakes and rivers that feed into the San Jose River, which then drains into Williams Lake. Although these waters were once full of human and industrial pollutants, the river is rebounding and welcoming growing numbers of species.

Four species of salmon (Chinook, Coho, sockeye, and pink), as well as burbot, lake whitefish, rainbow trout, and peamouth chub, are said to rely on the Williams Lake River.

❸ Eroded Banks Throughout the trail, look up to see the massively eroded slopes that provide a rare cross-section of the surrounding lands.

The earth here built up layer by layer over untold years. Through 10,000 years of water flow, the Williams Lake River slowly dug away at the earth, dropping the riverbed more than 150m (492 ft.) into the valley and exposing colorful strata of minerals and sands.

Rain runoff also shaped the slopes by weakening the earth and causing large slides. Stop and listen carefully, and you may hear the course of erosion as small pebbles tinkle down the slopes.

Unfortunately, garbage is also very visible in this portion of the trail. Extensive restoration is on-going in this area, and nature and its protectors are progressively reclaiming the trail.

❹ Confluence The trail continues over narrow wooden bridges that provide a bird's eye view to the aquatic life of the river. Since livestock commonly graze along the path, do watch out for dung!

As the trail eases gently out of the forest, look up to see the muddy waters of the Fraser sliding by. Here, at the confluence of the Williams Lake River and the mighty

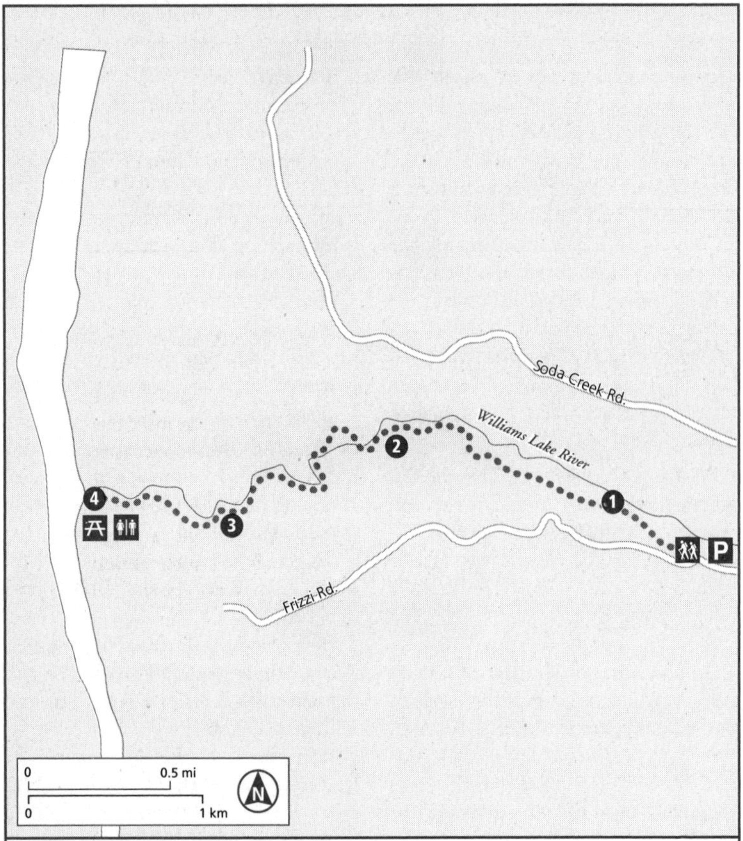

Williams Lake River Valley

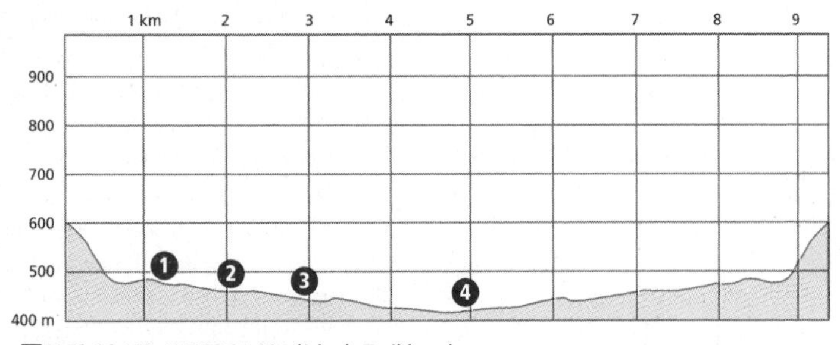

N 52 16.163, W 122 21.801 (0 km): Trail head
❶ N 52 16.479, W 122 23.124 (1.1 km): Cross the Williams Lake River
❷ N 52 16.724, W 122 24.188 (2 km): Pass a beaver dam
❸ N 52 16.552, W 122 25.105 (2.9 km): Admire the sand strata in the eroded banks
❹ N 52 16.366, W 122 27.175 (4.8 km): Arrive at the confluence

Fraser, you are far from roads yet still close to town.

The history of the Williams Lake River is inextricably tied to the Schuswap First Nation and industry in Williams Lake. Having supported sawmills and flourmills, supplied water to the Pacific Great Eastern Railway, and provided fishing grounds for the Schuswap, the river has played a large role in the area's history.

With all this history flowing past, sit on the sandy riverbank of the Fraser and examine the multi-hued pebbles, or watch for fish attempting to head upstream. And, if you ventured down on horseback, there are even hitchin' posts here for you to tie up.

Return to the parking lot over the now-familiar gravel road and bridges, gently regaining the lost elevation.

3 JUNCTION SHEEP RANGE ★★★ Finds

Difficulty rating: Moderate

Distance: 7km (4.3 miles) round trip

Estimated time: 2 hr.

Elevation gain: 275m (902 ft.)

Costs/permits: None

Best time to go: June, Sept–Oct

Website: www.env.gov.bc.ca/bcparks/explore/parkpgs/junction

Recommended map: Available on BC Parks website (address above)

Trail head GPS: N 51 77.234, W 122 40.630

Trail head directions: At 45km (28 miles) from Williams Lake, turn left off Hwy. 20 onto Farwell Canyon Rd. Travel just past the 15km (9¼-mile) mark, then turn left into a pull-out. A rollercoaster, rutted dirt road heads into the trees to the immediate left and winds 15km (9¼ miles) down to the sheep range. Keep right at the first three forks, following the worn road. Keep right at the information booth at 11km (6¾ miles), then pass a wildlife station and keep right again at the next fork. At 15km (9¼ miles), you reach a cairn and fence indicating the end of the road access. Park here.

This undiscovered portion of BC teems with astounding scenery. Wide-reaching grasslands slope down to the confluence of the snaking Chilcotin and Fraser rivers. Close to the park, you'll discover a canyon of hoodoos towering above Class IV rafting rapids, a shifting sand dune, an abandoned homestead, and ancient pictographs left by the ancestors of the local First Nations.

While it is possible to hike or bike the first 15km (9¼-mile) stretch, it makes for a long day over hot, dry terrain. Driving the road in dry conditions is possible with a high-clearance vehicle, with mountain biking being the second-best option. Note that the land on either side of the public road is the private property of Riske Creek Ranching. Frequent signs remind you to keep on the main route.

A cairn memorializing a biologist and a wildlife technician, who worked to protect this park and were killed in a 1981 helicopter crash, marks the lower trail head. Pass through the fence and follow the vehicle-width path down the slope.

The distant Fraser Canyon comes into view immediately and hints at the confluence where the bright blue Chilcotin meets the muddy but mighty river.

As water runs to the lower areas, this first section of the hike is also where you'll see the most vegetation. Here, the grasslands slope down towards a glade of Douglas fir—a good spot to watch for birds.

Cowboy Country

With the prevalence of quality ranchland in the Cariboo and Chilcotin, it's no wonder that the region evokes dreams of a cowboy lifestyle filled with campfires, tin-cup coffee, and stunning open landscapes seen from horseback. From stampedes to trail rides, here are some ideas for getting in on the fun:

Williams Lake Stampede This annual rodeo is the second largest in Canada. Each July 1 weekend, Williams Lake becomes a cowboy conference of sorts. Ranch hands square off in wild-cow-milking and chuck-wagon contests, as well as the usual rodeo and Canadian Professional Rodeo Association bull-riding feats. Book early to avoid missing BC's premier rodeo. Call ✆ **250/392-6585** or visit www.williamslakestampede.com.

Historic Hat Creek Ranch (Kids) Visit an 1860s roadhouse as it welcomes miners, wagoners, and pack-train riders from the Cariboo Waggon Road. The ranch provides historic insight on old-fashioned ranch life, as well as the traditions of the local First Nation communities. Try your hand at archery, take a trail ride, or pan for gold. Find it at the junction of Hwy. 97 and Hwy. 99, Cache Creek, BC. Call the ranch at ✆ **800/782-0922** or 250/457-9722, or check out their website at www.hatcreekranch.com. It's open May to June and September from 9am to 5pm; July and August from 9am to 6pm. Admission costs adults C$9, seniors (55+) C$8, children (6–12) C$6, and family passes C$20.

Guest ranches offer a deeper, hands-on cowboy experience, be it herding cattle, riding the range, or grabbing a fork to pitch some hay.

Chezacut Wilderness and Ranch Adventures This company guides horseback riding tours through the Chilcotin wilderness. See the bright starry skies of cowboy country from your base—a 1,619-hectare (4,000-acre) ranch. Visit www.chezacutwildernessadventures.com. Adventures run June through October.

Escott Bay Resort This resort runs pack trips to pre-established camp locations, as well as horse treks. The cowboy breakfasts and cool evenings are guaranteed to conjure up that Wild West feel. For the less wild, the resort leads horseback trips for beginner through advanced riders. Call ✆ **888/380-8802** or 250/742-3233, or check out www.escottbay.com.

Continue on the trail, looking also for the bright yellow and red crickets that leap out of the grasses; you may hear their chirp before you see them.

❶ **Aspen Grove** After 800m (2,625 ft.), the path plateaus and passes a small grove of aspens. On the southern hillside, across the Chilcotin River, the bright-leafed trees contrast the coniferous forest—particularly when the leaves turn their shade of autumn yellow.

Unlike trees that spread a seed, aspens send up new shoots from their roots. As the root network spreads, so does the copse of trees. Note the small suckers around the edge and the larger stand in the middle, as well as an offshoot to the south of the grove.

❷ **Grasslands** An incredibly easy-to-navigate trail runs across the grasslands and south towards the confluence. The Junction Sheep Range protects both the animals and plants of the region, including the important grasslands ecological zone.

Look for the hoof marks and droppings of the California bighorn sheep. If you're

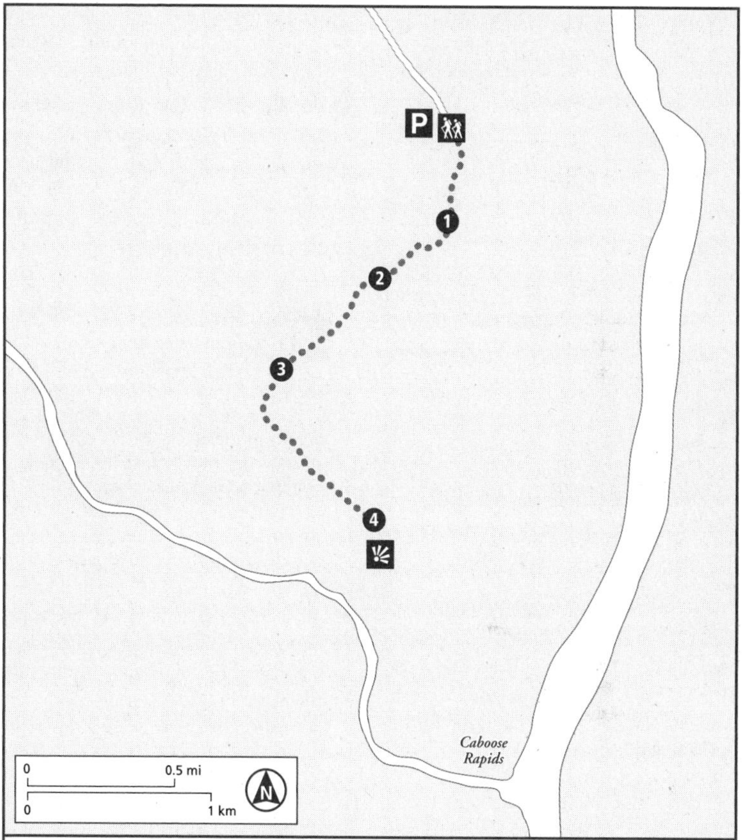

Caboose Rapids

0 0.5 mi

0 1 km

N

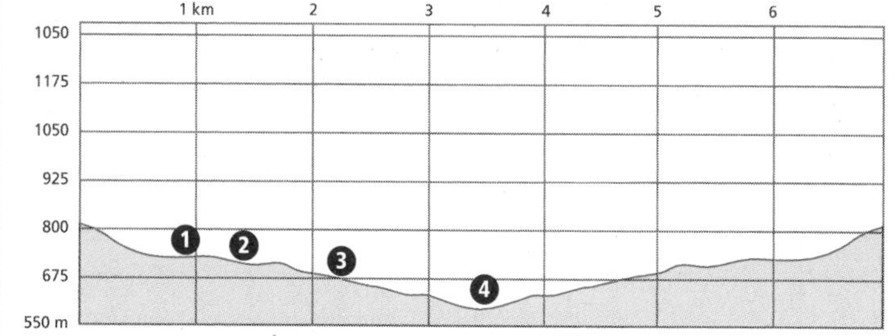

N 51 77.234, W 122 40.630 (0 km): Trail head

❶ N 51 76.724, W 122 40.752 (0.8 km): Pass an aspen grove

❷ N 51 76.519, W 122 40.998 (1.2 km): Cross the grasslands

❸ N 51 75.981, W 122 41.863 (2 km): Glimpse the views of the Fraser and Farwell canyons

❹ N 51 75.038, W 122 40.800 (3.5 km): Look out over the confluence

lucky, you may even catch a glimpse of the hoofed mammals. The herds in the junction range are the most stable and largest in North America, yet the species as a whole is at risk in BC, meaning it requires protection and stewardship.

The grasslands also contain many hardy species of flora, helping to stabilize the easily eroded soil. Rabbit brush, sagebrush, prickly pear cacti, and bluebunch wheatgrass all thrive in these dry conditions.

Staying on the path through the grasslands is essential to minimizing any impact on these fragile grasses. As a side benefit, you'll also better avoid the burrowing barbs of the cacti.

3 Canyon Views Look west to the hoodoos of Farwell Canyon and east to the Fraser Canyon. Although the best views of the hoodoos lie further along Farwell Canyon Road, the towering wind-whipped peaks still make an impression on the horizon.

Also in the west, near the end of the park, lies one of Canada's largest shifting sand dunes. The large desert-like peak, formed from the eroding sands of the hoodoos, is also best seen from further down Farwell Canyon Road.

The openness of the range here offers great wildlife viewing, with sightlines reaching kilometers in most directions. Watch for mule deer, eagles, and grouse, as well as the more rare cougars and black bears.

4 Confluence The rivers hold important heritage for the local First Nations communities. The Ts'ilqot'in (Chilcotin) and Secwepemc (Shuswap) people have camped and fished along these riverbanks for thousands of years.

SPECTACULAR LOOKOUT From the lookout atop a cliff, you have the perfect view of where the canyons and plains meet the confluence of the two rivers. While it is possible to scramble down the cliff to the lower altitudes, you're already seeing the most spectacular views.

The Chilcotin is a popular rafting route with sections of Class IV rapids (that's 4 out of 5 on the extreme scale). See where the upstream Railroad Rapids and downstream Caboose Rapids gush towards the confluence.

From this viewpoint overlooking it all, return over the same grasslands path to the memorial cairn.

4 PERKINS PEAK ★★ Finds

Difficulty rating: Moderate

Distance: 9.6km (6 miles) round trip

Estimated time: 3 hr.

Elevation gain: 430m (1,411 ft.)

Costs/permits: None

Best time to go: Aug–Sept

Website: none

Recommended map: 92 N/14

Trail head GPS: N 51 82.855, W 125 04.202

Trail head directions: Take Hwy. 20 west 220km (137 miles) from Williams Lake to Tatla Lake, then a further 23km (14 miles) from Tatla Lake to Miner Lake Rd. Alternately, the forestry service road is 5km (3 miles) from Rivers Edge Cottages. Head south on Miner Lake Rd. that, with all-terrain vehicle traffic, is barely 2WD passable in dry conditions; 4WD is best. Reset your odometer and head straight past the 7km marker, then veer right at 10km (6¼ miles). At 25km (16 miles), pass a lake and, shortly after, take the left fork. Pull off the road at the next fork and park.

The challenge of accessing this hidden hike makes it all the more lovely. Ascend the rocky bluff to the northeast of the unique Perkins Peak and look out over the bumpy, endless Chilcotin Plateau and west towards the Coast Mountains.

From the final fork in the road, head left uphill (the right ventures down to an abandoned gold mine). The forestry service road climbs past a pond ringed with black rocks. Keep right at the next two forks (after 850m/2,789 ft. and 1km/$^1/_2$ mile), and the loose, rocky road gets steeper.

1 Glacial Creek The road follows the right side of an unnamed creek for the first long elevation gain of the hike. Seemingly struggling pines and alpine firs edge the road, and patches of shrubs sprawl over the shaley slopes. In fall, look for the dime-sized scallop-edge leaves of the scrub birch that turn royal red.

2 Perkins Views After 3km (1$^3/_4$ miles), you see the full view of Perkins Peak, its couloirs still packed with snow and ice during the summer months. The peak is the northernmost in the Pantheon Range, part of the Coast Mountains, and marks the gateway between rugged icy mountains and dry dusty plateau.

The road is easily navigable as you pass two small ponds and continue climbing uphill. Soon after these ponds, the gradient evens out through to the lake.

3 Lake Follow the shore counter-clockwise around this unnamed lake and admire the up-close views of Perkins Peak. Note that arriving later in the afternoon will leave you in the chilly shadow of the 2,819m (9,249-ft.) mountain.

TAKE A BREAK For a gentler hike, make this pretty alpine lake, with the pristine beauty of Perkins and hints of the Chilcotin, your destination. Or simply rest alongside the quiet lake before proceeding to the awe-worthy panoramas that lie a little further up.

Start the second ascent of the hike, taking the lone set of switchbacks up the steep slope to the north of the lake. The footing shifts with each step—so proceed carefully.

4 Eastern Views About halfway, pause to catch your breath after the intense climb and look east at the diversity in the landscape. Eroding slopes, rolling hills, hidden lakes, thick forests, zigzagging roads, and scars of clear cuts mark the terrain.

The Chilcotin's main economic forces are ranching and logging. Large portions of the forests, however, are pine and show the devastation wrought by increased populations of the mountain pine beetle. The telltale signs are the huge patches of dead trees with rust-colored needles.

The beetles attack trees by laying eggs in the innermost layer of bark, cutting off the supply of nutrients to the tree. As the wood will be usable for a limited period and poses wild fire hazards while still standing, much of central BC is accelerating logging in order to harvest the dead wood.

5 Western Viewpoint Continue the trek up the switchbacks until you reach the snowline. Here, you can see the bank of Coast Mountains to the west and the far-reaching Chilcotin Plateau to the east with the long elegant Miner Lake, the Klinaklini River, Twin Lakes, and your return route to the highway in immediate view. In addition to forestry, miners also use these roads to explore ore claims. A number of iron and copper prospects surround the peak, as well as the abandoned gold mine to the north.

After some deep cool alpine breaths and many scans and photos of the panoramic horizon, return on the same route.

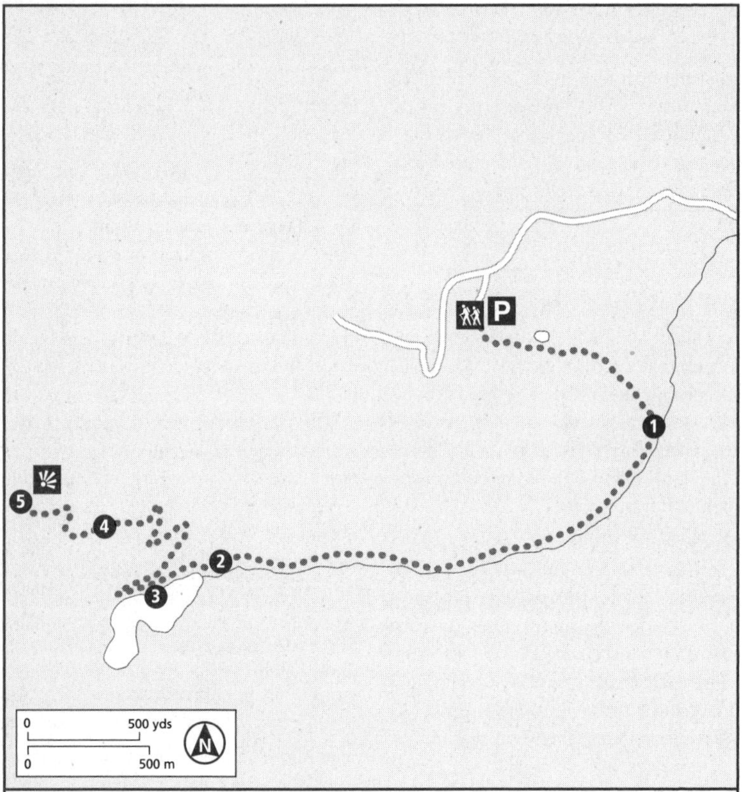

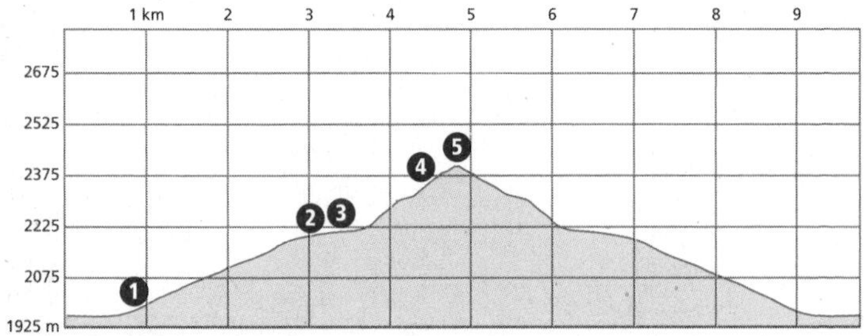

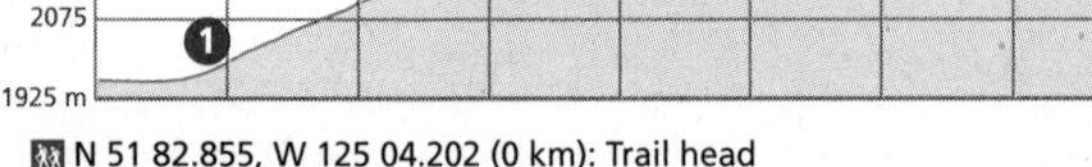

N 51 82.855, W 125 04.202 (0 km): Trail head

1 N 51 82.578, W 125 03.230 (0.8 km): Begin following a glacial creek

2 N 51 82.038, W 125 05.686 (3 km): Catch the first full views of Perkins Peak

3 N 51 81.928, W 125 06.066 (3.3 km): Walk the shore of an alpine lake

4 N 51 82.124, W 125 06.342 (4.4 km): Stop to survey the eastern view

5 N 51 82.238, W 125 06.691 (4.8 km): Reach the viewpoint of the Coast Mountains and Chilcotin

5 BURNT BRIDGE CREEK LOOP ★★ (Kids)

Difficulty rating: Easy to moderate

Distance: 4.8km (3 miles) round trip

Estimated time: 1½ hr.

Elevation gain: 145m (475 ft.)

Costs/permits: None

Best time to go: June–Sept

Website: www.bellacoola.ca/valley/trails.php

Recommended map: Bella Coola Valley Trail Guide (free at the visitor information center)

Trail head GPS: N 52 43.611, W 126 19.220

Trail head directions: The trail head lies at the western boundary of Tweedsmuir Provincial Park. Take Hwy. 20 east 47km (29 miles) from Bella Coola village or 28km (17 miles) from Hagensbourg, then look for the parking lot on your right. Coming west, the trail head is 80km (50 miles) along the highway from Anahim Lake or about 400km (249 miles) from Williams Lake.

This is the short cut to the end of the 420km (261-mile) Alexander Mackenzie Heritage Trail. Venture just a quick distance from the main road and drown your senses in the sounds of the rushing creek, the sights of Stupendous Mountain, and the smells of the well-established forest. A wobbly suspension bridge, a lookout, interesting fungi, and a history lesson will intrigue even the littlest of hikers.

To reach the start of the path from the parking area, cross the highway and walk uphill along the road for about 100m (328 ft.), looking for signs directing you to the Valleyview Loop Trail.

The first portion heads steeply up the highway bank but soon levels off into secluded mossy forest. There are two moderately steady climbs in this hike—the first here at the beginning as you head up a series of switchbacks, and the second after the suspension bridge. But there is also ample easy walking to make the route relaxing, nonetheless.

❶ Fork to Viewpoint After 10 minutes, the trail forks right to the Burnt Bridge Creek Loop, and a dead-end trail turns left to the panoramic lookout. Take either; however, the second leg of the trail will afford you equally fabulous scenes as the viewpoint.

Heading right, the trail plateaus briefly, then zigzags down into thick forest—a mixture of Douglas fir, cottonwood (a type of poplar), cedar, and birch. Watch on either side of the path for the varied yellows and browns of the fungi that love these shady and moist forest glens.

Cross a small plank bridge, and you will soon be greeted by the sound of the rushing waters of the creek.

❷ Creek-Side Pause at the 2km (1¼-mile) mark to watch the clear waters of Burnt Bridge Creek flow past.

From the bank, the trail dips back into the woods and veers slightly right. As you head north, you follow the western boundary of Tweedsmuir Provincial Park: BC's largest park. Tweedsmuir South covers 506,000 hectares (1,954 sq. miles), while Tweedsmuir North encompasses a further 475,000 hectares (1,834 sq. miles). The park, as a whole, is larger than Puerto Rico.

❸ Suspension Bridge Cross the wobbly yet secure suspension bridge at about 2.5km (1½ miles) and hang onto the railings. From the middle of the bridge, look downstream to the perfectly framed 2,682m (8,799-ft.) peak of Stupendous Mountain, part of the magnificent Coast Mountains.

Alexander Mackenzie/Nuxalk–Carrier Grease Trail

Retrace the steps of history on the Nuxalk–Carrier Grease Trail, also known as Alexander Mackenzie Heritage Trail. The 420km (261-mile) route extends inland from southwest of Prince George to Bella Coola in the Dean Channel.

The path follows the one likely taken by Mackenzie in his search for the Northwest Passage. Mackenzie, a surveyor with the North West Company (later merged with the Hudson's Bay Company), sought a trade route to the Pacific Ocean.

From Lake Athabasca in northern Alberta, Mackenzie set out by canoe and on foot to just past Prince George. From there, he trekked west over a network of Grease Carrier trails established by the First Nations communities to transport eulachon (a small fish) grease from the coast to the interior.

Mackenzie completed the first documented transcontinental crossing north of Mexico and reached the Pacific on July 22, 1793, where he inscribed his name and the date on a rock in grease. That inscription, now memorialized in the same stone and accessible only by water, reads: "Alex Mackenzie from Canada by land 22nd July 1793"

Today, the Alexander Mackenzie Heritage Trail (designated in 1987) wends through forestry roads, provincial parks, and networks of paths to reach the western edge of Tweedsmuir Provincial Park.

The full traverse takes experienced hikers about 3 weeks to complete, with the most fantastic portions passing through the colorful and fiery slopes of the Rainbow Range. Logistically, a mid-route food-drop is essential, as are backcountry knowledge and supplies.

The book *In the Steps of Alexander Mackenzie*, by John Woodworth and Hälle Flygare, is regarded as the authority on the trail. Currently in its second edition, the book describes the trail junction by junction. For more details on the trail and hiking preparations, contact the Alexander Mackenzie Voyageur Association at P.O. Box 425, Station A, Kelowna, BC V1Y 7P1; or at www.amvr.org.

TAKE A BREAK On the far side of the suspension bridge some lovely rocks beckon you to sit on a warm day and enjoy the meditative sounds of the creek and downstream mountain views.

From the suspension bridge, veer to the left for the second climb up the second set of switchbacks, which re-immerse you in the woods of the Bella Coola Valley.

This section of the trail is outside the boundaries of the provincial park, and the forest is far younger. With the extra light not stolen by the massive firs and cedars, a few more varieties such as maple have crept in. Continue along the well-maintained path as it descends slightly.

4 Mackenzie Grease Trail Continue straight, but note that a trail joins the path at the 3.5km (2¼-mile) mark. These are the final meters of the historic 420km (261-mile) Alexander Mackenzie/Nuxalk–Carrier Grease Trail.

You are now walking in the same steps as Alexander Mackenzie: the first person to cross North America by land, north of Mexico. Mackenzie likely trod this same path in 1793 as he searched for a water trade route to the Pacific. But this trail long precedes him.

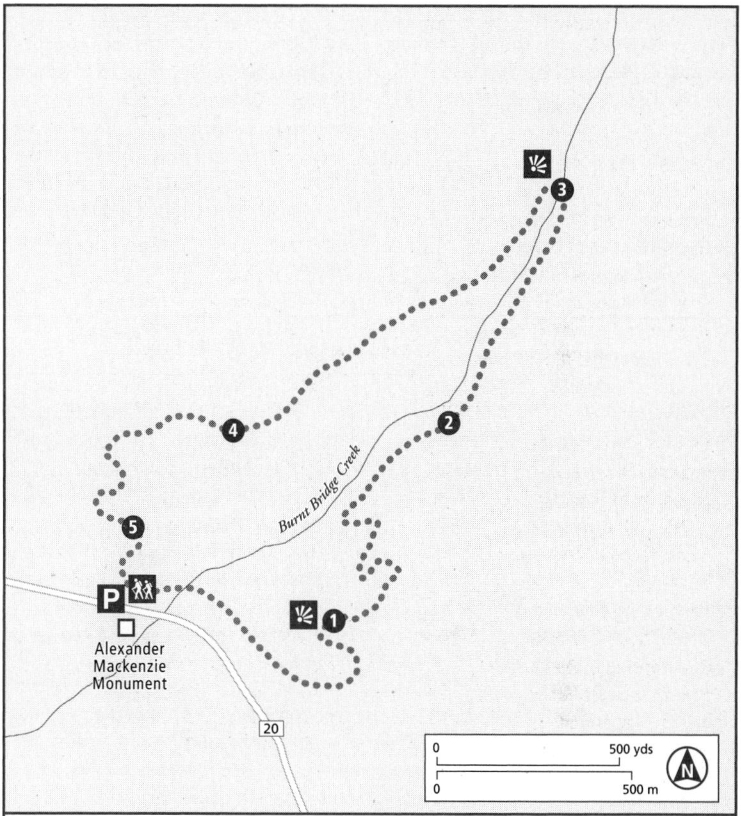

Burnt Bridge Creek
Alexander
Mackenzie
Monument
20
0
500 yds
0
500 m
N

1 km
2
3
4
350
175 m

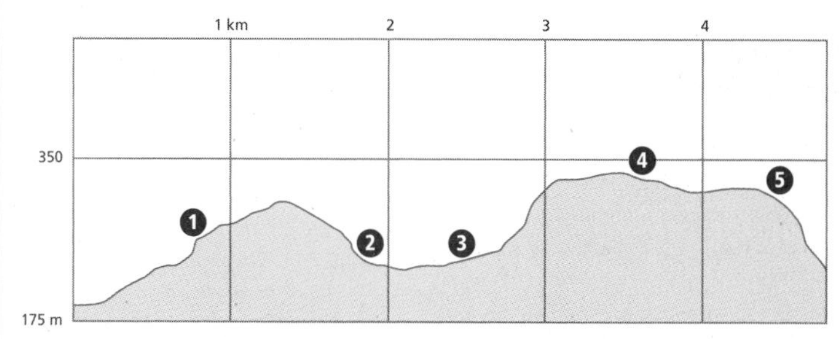

N 52 43.611, W 126 19.220 (0 km): Trail head

❶ N 52 43.530, W 126 18.581 (0.8 km): Turn right to continue the loop trail

❷ N 52 44.000, W 126 18.118 (1.8 km): Arrive at the Burnt Bridge Creek

❸ N 52 44.431, W 126 17.797 (2.4 km): Cross the suspension bridge

❹ N 52 43.959, W 126 18.934 (3.6 km): Follow final steps of the Mackenzie Grease Trail

❺ N 52 43.829, W 126 19.259 (4.5 km): Pause for a final view

The Nuxalk and Carrier people used this route to transport eulachon (a small fish) grease for thousands of years, and Burnt Bridge Creek was the site of a long-established First Nations community that was called the "friendly village" by Mackenzie.

❺ **Final View** Continue along the easy-going path until fantastic views of Stupendous and Table mountains stop you in your tracks. These peaks—part of the Coast Mountains—form the jagged, glacial barrier between the Pacific and the dry plains of the Chilcotin Plateau. The Bella Coola Valley also divides the northern Kitimat and southern Pacific ranges.

Turn your gaze from the views and descend the final portion of the trail towards the highway. A final section through a mossy grove makes a soothing last leg of this beautiful hike. It goes almost without mentioning that this short loop is a far more attainable historical journey than Mackenzie's full route!

6 RAINBOW RANGE ★★★ Finds

Difficulty rating: Strenuous

Distance: 17km (11 miles) round trip

Estimated time: 5 hr.

Elevation gain: 400m (1,312 ft.)

Costs/permits: None

Best time to go: July–Sept

Website: www.env.gov.bc.ca/bcparks/explore/parkpgs/tweeds_s

Recommended map: 93 C/12

Trail head GPS: N 52 53.497, W 125 81.471

Trail head directions: The trail head lies near the eastern boundary of Tweedsmuir Provincial Park close to Heckman Pass. Drive 95km (59 miles) east from Bella Coola and up The Hill, west 41km (25 miles) from Anahim Lake, or 355km (221 miles) from Williams Lake. Turn onto the road marked Rainbow Range Trail Head.

This alpine hike leads to hinted views of the amazing Rainbow Range—the multi-hued volcanic slopes deep within the park. The trail is well marked for the vast portion; however, the final kilometer (½ mile) requires route-finding and orientation skills, as trail markers end and rolling alpine landscape stretches to the mountainous horizons.

Take the marked path that turns left off the roadway and into the forest. This trail head also serves as a gateway to Crystal and Octopus lakes. At the fork 150m (492 ft.) in, make a right to start the first and only significant climb of the hike.

❶ **Tree Line** The switchbacks lead you into a lodgepole pine forest, which thins as you gain elevation and enter alpine terrain. Look back to glimpses of the picturesque Coast Mountains, contrasted with the rugged hardiness of the alpine vegetation ahead.

Some trees are blazed along the trail (and later, cairns mark the alpine route), but there is no consistent marking. Follow the worn path of the route as the first 2km (1¼ miles) winds through marshes and sparse woodland.

❷ **First Lake** The trail curves to the left of an unnamed lake—a popular spot for campers. From here, the trail continues past a series of other small, unnamed lakes forging towards a forested bluff a kilometer (½ mile) or so in the distance.

Soon, you will also see the first volcanically formed mountains, the chillingly named Boneshaker Ridge. These dark humped mountains keep secret the volcanic reds and oranges that blaze the slopes of the Rainbow Range deeper in the park.

❸ **Cairns** At about 5km (3 miles), the trees dwindle and the cairns begin to mark

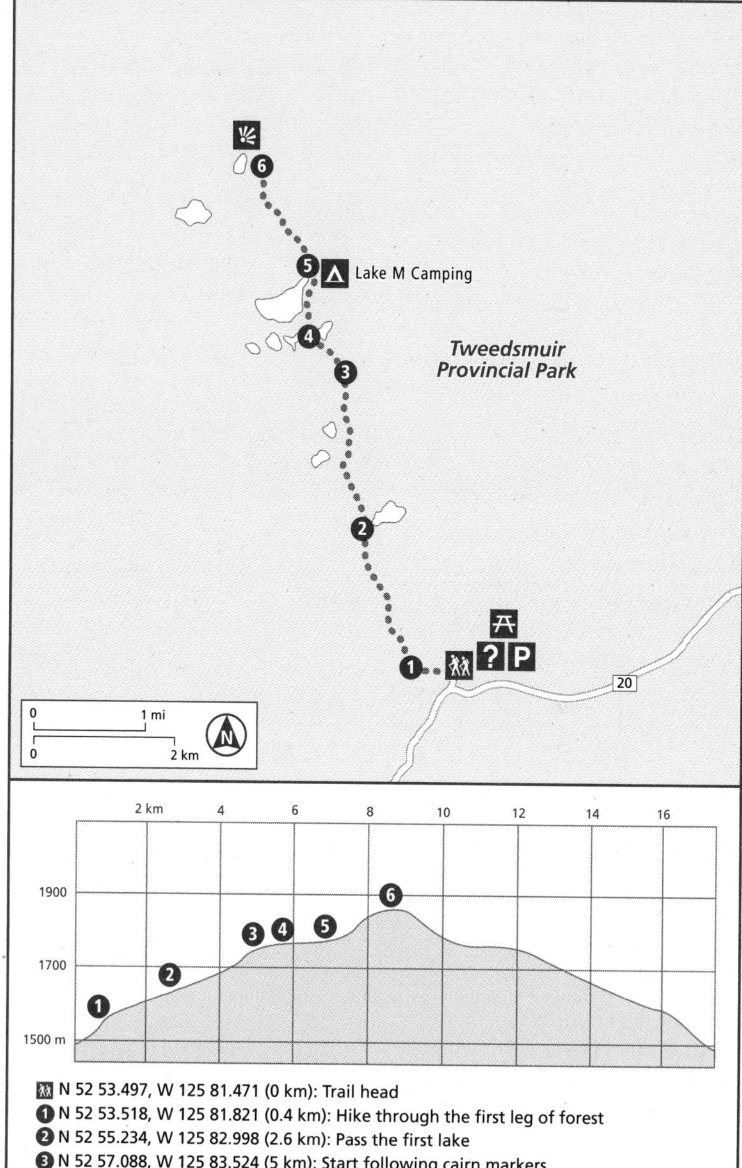

N 52 53.497, W 125 81.471 (0 km): Trail head

1 N 52 53.518, W 125 81.821 (0.4 km): Hike through the first leg of forest

2 N 52 55.234, W 125 82.998 (2.6 km): Pass the first lake

3 N 52 57.088, W 125 83.524 (5 km): Start following cairn markers

4 N 52 57.584, W 125 84.273 (5.9 km): Hike towards the distant Boneshaker Ridge

5 N 52 58.241, W 125 84.158 (6.7 km): Pass Lake M

6 N 52 59.671, W 125 85.372 (8.6 km): Admire hints of rainbow views

the route across the arid alpine landscape. Try to look ahead to be sure your route does not abruptly end and don't venture far if there are no markers in sight. Despite the openness of the terrain, it is easy to get slightly off-course and lose the trail.

4 Boneshaker Ridge Here, the path begins to bear towards Boneshaker Ridge—its slopes streaked with muted colors. The terrain is sprinkled with boulders, clusters of brushy alpine fir, lakes, and rocky ridges.

5 Lake M At one of the few named lakes in this portion of the park (christened for its shape), a campground and bear cache are available for multi-day trekkers. You'll know Lake M by the small island in the northern end.

TAKE A BREAK The wind can whip by quickly and coolly over this wide-open terrain, so pull out your thermos and find a spot blocked from the wind on the shore of this tiny lake. Be sure to pack up any leftovers and garbage from what you pack in.

From the lake, venture northwards towards the rocky bluffs. Look, too, to your right at the misty Chilcotin plateau stretching to the east.

6 Rainbow Views With the Coast Mountains behind you to the west, a small lake and the Chilcotin to your east, and a flare of red on the mountainside to the north, stop here to take in the 360° views.

On top of the rocky outcrop, three poles are lashed to form the frame for an impromptu shelter. Whiteouts do occasionally occur here in summer: so be prepared and check the forecast before heading out.

If you have time, explore a little further, although the truly spectacular fire-hued slopes are still a full day of hiking (or short flight) away. With plenty of light remaining, return along the trail and re-enter the comparatively lush forest with the windswept feeling of having explored the alpine wilds.

7 BARKERVILLE TO SUMMIT ROCK & GROUNDHOG LAKE ★★★ Kids

Difficulty rating: Moderate

Distance: 17km (11 miles) round trip

Estimated time: 4 hr.

Elevation gain: 485m (1,591 ft.)

Costs/permits: None

Best time to go: Aug–Sept

Website: www.barkerville.ca

Recommended map: Available at the Barkerville town gate

Trail head GPS: N 53 06.889, W 121 51.514

Trail head directions: Travel east on Hwy. 26 for 84km (52 miles) from Quesnel, or drive 3km (1¾ miles) from Wells. The trail starts at the town gate (hikers receive admission-free passage through the historic town site). Ask for maps from the gate agent.

Walk through the historic town of Barkerville, then follow the wheel tracks over the famous Cariboo Waggon Road that travels past sites of gold discovery to a pretty lake set in a cirque below Mount Agnes, high above the mining fever.

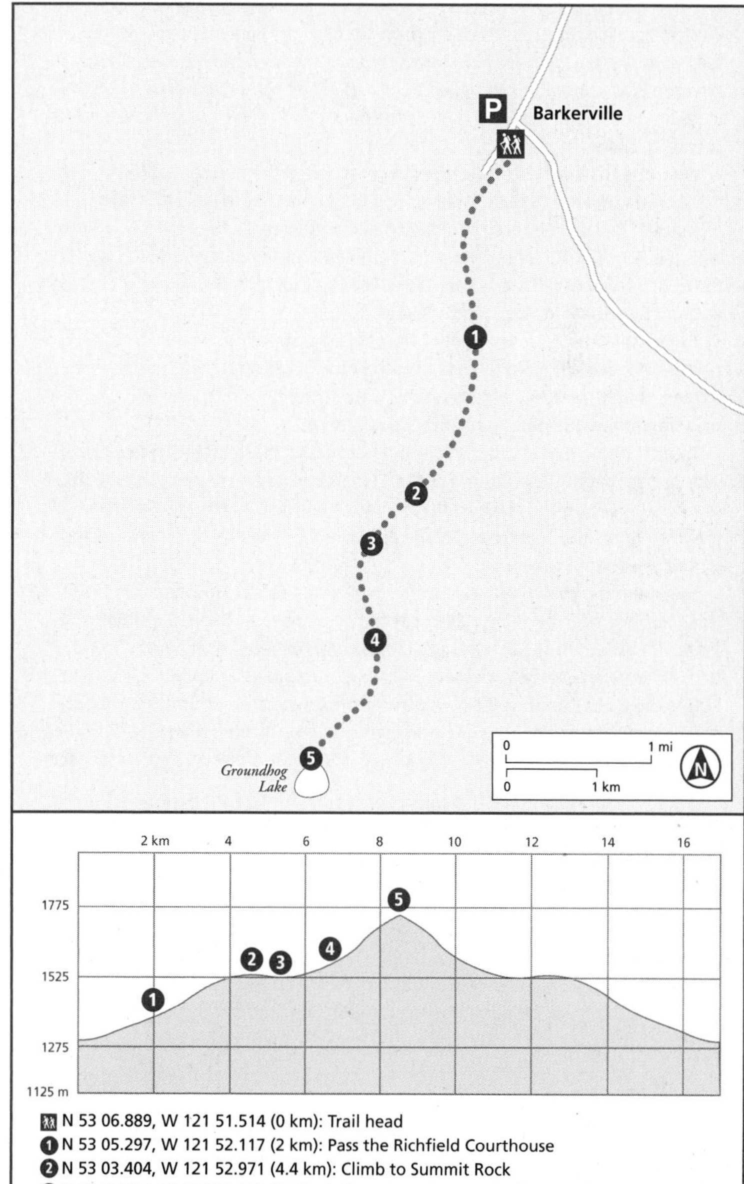

N 53 06.889, W 121 51.514 (0 km): Trail head
❶ N 53 05.297, W 121 52.117 (2 km): Pass the Richfield Courthouse
❷ N 53 03.404, W 121 52.971 (4.4 km): Climb to Summit Rock
❸ N 53 03.060, W 121 53.987 (5.2 km): Pass an emergency shelter
❹ N 53 01.883, W 121 53.850 (6.7 km): Survey the remains of Coopers Cabin
❺ N 53 00.832, W 121 54.900 (8.4 km): Relax at Groundhog Lake

 Barkerville & the Gold Rush

Petticoats rustle through the dusty main street as the Barkerville townspeople, in full 1800s dress, gather to tour visitors through this revived gold rush town. Wooden clapboard and log-walled buildings line the street, advertising all the essential trades and services. There is the dentist, a bakery, a drug store, and (of course) a saloon.

Welcome to New Barkerville, the living version of the Cariboo gold rush town that sprung up around Billy Barker's 1862 gold discovery in Williams Creek.

News of Barker's discovery quickly spread as Barkerville became a boomtown, with the largest population west of Chicago and north of San Francisco. By 1865, the Cariboo Waggon Road wound from Yale through to Barkerville and was soon dubbed the Eighth Wonder of the World.

Today, at 84km (52 miles) east of Quesnel, it's a stretch to believe this quiet backwater once attracted legions of ambitious and adventurous gold seekers. But the more than 125 buildings at this historic site go a long way to recreating that vibrant and full picture of once-upon-a-time.

Tours through Barkerville explore the histories of those buried in the Barkerville cemetery, provide insight into the Chinatown, and recreate lessons in the schoolhouse. From the blacksmith forging horseshoes to comedic theater shows, the town offers the smoky smells, sweet morsels, and interesting sights of a town locked in an 1800s time warp.

Searching for gold remains a local activity with tours or do-it-yourself options available; however, panning is only permitted on private claims. **Gold Safari Tours** (✆ **866/996-4653;** www.cariboojoy.com) operates from nearby Wells. With all tours, the "finders-keepers" rule applies to panned nuggets. Or stop in at **El Dorado Gold Panning & Souvenirs** (at the town gate), where you can purchase a pan of gravel with guaranteed flakes of gold. If, after a few swirls of the gold pan, gold fever has struck, there are many local gold and copper prospects up for grabs.

To complete the authentic experience, book your stay in the **St. George Hotel** (✆ **888/246-7690** or 250/994-0008), where you can relax with a cup of tea in the parlor, or the **Kelly and King Houses** (✆ **250/994-3328**), which are furnished with antiques and feather beds.

To contact Barkerville, call ✆ **866/994-3222** or 250/994-3332, or visit www.barkerville.ca. Admission costs adults (19–64) C$13.50, seniors (65+) C$12.25, youth (13–18) C$8, children (6–12) C$4, children 5 and under free, and family pass C$31. The town is open mid-May through late September from 8am to 8pm.

From the gate of Barkerville, stroll south on the main street past dozens of wooden replica buildings. After 600m (1,969 ft.), the town site ends and Cariboo Waggon Road begins a gentle ascent along Williams Creek—where Billy Barker discovered gold in 1862. Watch for interpretive signs that mark the locations of famous gold claims, tragic deaths, and the site of the first school that was shared by the communities of Barkerville and Richfield.

❶ Richfield Courthouse At 1.4km (3/4 mile), the once-bustling town of Richfield stands today as only the courthouse on your right. Take the left fork of the Cariboo Waggon Road (historically spelled with the double "g") and begin the steep climb tackled by countless wagons that once connected Barkerville, Richfield, and other mining towns to the southern centers.

There is a small trail on the left that leads to Antler Creek and Bald Mountain—more distant destinations in the Mount Agnes Trail Network—but follow signs for Groundhog Lake as the trail advances steadily through forest and banks of blueberry bushes.

❷ Summit Rock The stone, sitting at the 4.5km (2 3/4-mile) mark, marks the end of the tough uphill portion for wagons struggling with heavy loads. Unfortunately for hikers heading to Groundhog Lake, the rock doesn't mark the same end in ascent. Continue straight on the road as a lush meadow opens up on the left. The woods brim with Old Man's Beard year-round, while Indian paintbrush, wild Aster, and other wildflowers bloom in the late summer.

There is an alternate route to Groundhog Lake called the Ditchline trail that wends through the woods to the left; however, the wagon road is equally interesting.

❸ Shelter At the shelter, the wagon road heads right on a lower altitude amble (and turns west and then south towards 100 Mile House and Yale), while the trail to Groundhog Lake continues climbing to the left. Follow this mining road on the left that runs parallel to the Jack of Clubs Creek, and walk towards the tree-covered slopes of Elk Mountain.

❹ Coopers Cabin The flattened silhouette of Coopers Cabin sits unimpressively on the left of the trail at 6.8km (4 1/4 miles). The Waggon Road was rerouted through Devil's Canyon in 1885 to avoid high snowfalls. Bill Brown, one of the road workers, built this cabin here in the late 1890s. Although the cabin was once a popular stopping spot, no one is quite sure who Cooper was. Regardless, this now-dilapidated cabin still bears his moniker.

From the cabin, the trail maintains its incline through open meadows. Pause to look back for beautiful views of the valley and, if you planned your trip in wildflower season, admire the brilliant purples, reds, and yellows of the local flora.

❺ Groundhog Lake After the steep climb, the quiet shores of Groundhog Lake tucked against the slopes of Mount Agnes make a delightful rest spot. The lake was carved by glaciers but was then dammed as a reservoir to supply water to the mining operations downstream. As gold's specific gravity is 19 times heavier than water, it always sinks in a gold pan: helping the panner to separate the riches from the rubble.

TAKE A BREAK A well-maintained recreation cabin is situated to the east. Take some extra time to relax, scan the creek banks for glints of gold, or perch on the shore and watch for wildlife.

If time allows, circumnavigate the lake or explore further on to Mount Agnes and Bald Mountain, part of the larger trail network that serves as a highly popular destination for cross-country skiers and snowmobilers.

From the lakeshore, continue back to town on the same trail. Return in the late afternoon after the town gates have closed, if possible, and delight in the quiet of the abandoned streets. The buildings, once throbbing with re-enactments and costumed actors, are silent. Now, without its performers reviving it, Barkerville truly feels like a 19th-century ghost town.

8 BERGERON CLIFFS & FALLS

Difficulty rating: Moderate
Distance: 12.2km (7.6 miles) round trip
Estimated time: 5 hr.
Elevation gain: 350m (1,148 ft.)
Costs/permits: None
Pet friendly: No
Best time to go: May–Sept
Website: www.pris.bc.ca
Recommended map: 093P02

Trail head GPS: N 55 10.620, W 120 59.580
Trail head directions: Drive north from Tumbler Ridge along Hwy. 29 for 5km (3 miles). Turn right (east) onto the gravel road marked with a hiker sign. Follow this road for 8km (5 miles) to a gravel pit. The town of Tumbler Ridge is 90km (56 miles) southeast of Chetwynd and 115km (71 miles) southwest of Dawson Creek.

The outdoor-loving folks who call the remote town of Tumbler Ridge home have done an admirable job of creating and maintaining an extensive trail system through the surrounding wilderness. One of the most rewarding trails includes two highlights—the sweeping panorama of forest and rivers from Bergeron Cliffs and the photogenic cascade of Bergeron Falls.

Look for the trail head sign at the far corner of the gravel pit. From here, the trail climbs gently up a low ridge to a simple but important junction.

❶ Trail Junction At this first junction, the left fork leads to the cliffs, while the right fork heads off to the falls. If you are planning to include both destinations in your trip, you will be returning down the latter trail in a few hours.

❷ Cutline After a steady ascent through a mixed forest of aspen, spruce, and pine, the trail emerges at a manmade cutline. Upon reaching this point, turn left (the route to the right leads to Bergeron Falls). After around 10 minutes of easy walking, you come to a huge boulder that came to rest here after being dislodged from the upper slopes of Mount Bergeron many thousands of years ago. At this point, head up the hill along an obvious trail.

❸ Bergeron Cliffs After a short, steep stretch, the trail emerges at the Bergeron Cliffs. Here, runoff creates a moist environment where ferns, mosses, and colorful lichens thrive. The views from the first opening are impressive, but don't be tempted to turn around at this point. Continue along the cliff line by following the trail back into the forest for a short distance, where it then re-emerges at a viewpoint with uninterrupted views across the valley.

❹ Valley Views Over the next 600m (1,969 ft.) are four more viewpoints, each more spectacular than the last. Far below, the Murray River's elongated course is easily identified, while to the west (left) is the Wolverine Valley. The town of Tumbler Ridge lies across the Murray River directly to the south, and beyond here is Flatbed Creek, which is renowned for the dinosaur footprints preserved along its banks. The distant mountains are part of the Hart Range, the northernmost extent of the Rocky Mountains. A word of caution: there are no fences or official viewpoints, so keep well away from the edge, and keep children and pets well supervised.

You could return from the cliffs the way you came, but don't. Instead, retrace your route as far as the cutline and continue straight ahead along the cutline for 2km (1¼ miles). This section of trail is not particularly inspiring, with views limited

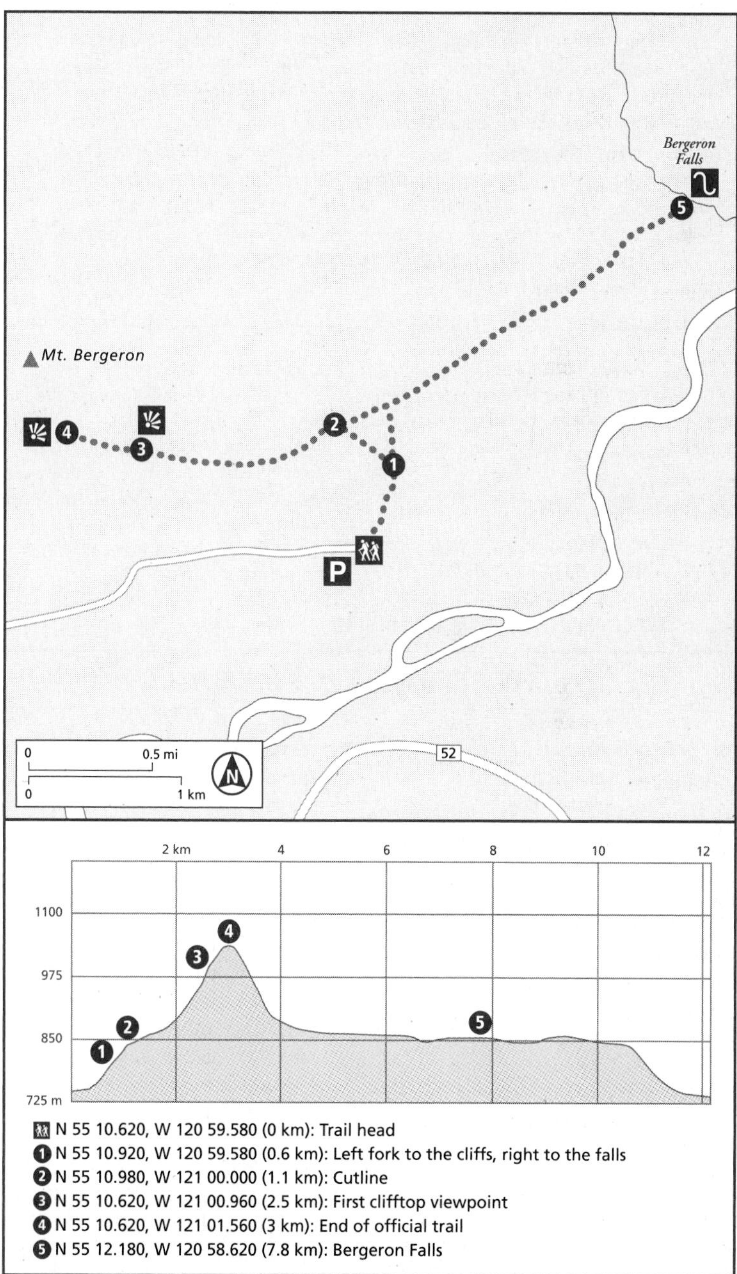
Bergeron Falls
Mt. Bergeron
52
0
0.5 mi
0
1 km
N
2 km
4
6
8
10
12
1100
975
850
725 m
N 55 10.620, W 120 59.580 (0 km): Trail head
1 N 55 10.920, W 120 59.580 (0.6 km): Left fork to the cliffs, right to the falls
2 N 55 10.980, W 121 00.000 (1.1 km): Cutline
3 N 55 10.620, W 121 00.960 (2.5 km): First clifftop viewpoint
4 N 55 10.620, W 121 01.560 (3 km): End of official trail
5 N 55 12.180, W 120 58.620 (7.8 km): Bergeron Falls

Fun Facts Big Feet to Fill

While your footprints will disappear with the next rainfall, there are other footprints in the Tumbler Ridge area that have survived for millions of years. Since the first discovery by two local boys in 2000, dinosaur footprints have been found at various locations around town. One such site is an easy 2km (1¼-mile) walk from Hwy. 29 on the east side of town. The trail ends at Flatbed Creek, where a slab of rock is imbedded with over 200 footprints. Across the creek—and only accessible when water levels are low—is the distinct track way of an ankylosaur. While both these sites can be accessed by the public, plan on joining a guided **Dinosaur Trackway Tour** (✆ **250/242-3123;** www.tumblerridgemuseum.com) for the full effect.

by the surrounding forest and a single creek crossing a little less than 1km (½ mile) from the oversized boulder described above.

5 Bergeron Falls After crossing Bergeron Creek beyond the northeast end of the cutline, the trail loops through the forest before emerging at the top of Bergeron Falls. At 100m (328 ft.) high, it is one of the highest in northern British Columbia. The cascade is most impressive in spring, when runoff is at its peak. Beyond the waterfall, views extend down the steep-sided valley carved by Bergeron Creek to the Murray River Valley.

—Andrew Hempstead

9 HERITAGE RIVER TRAIL

Difficulty rating: Easy

Distance: 9km (5.6 miles) one way

Estimated time: 3 hr.

Elevation gain: None

Costs/permits: None

Best time to go: May–Sept

Website: None

Recommended map: 093G15

Trail head GPS: N 53 55.560, W 122 46.020

Trail head directions: This trail is in Prince George, off of Hwy. 16, 790km (491 miles) north of Vancouver and 540km (336 miles) west of Grande Prairie, Alberta. It is possible to join this loop trail at one of many points, although a popular starting point is the north end of Carney St. Look for the small parking lot at the River Road intersection. An alternative is to park at Fort George Park, at the east end of 20th Ave., catch a taxi to the north end of the trail, and then walk back to your vehicle, a distance of 5.4km (3¼ miles).

Although this trail is entirely within the city limits of northern British Columbia's largest population center, the route traverses a variety of natural habitats, with the Nechako and Fraser rivers rarely out of sight and wildlife such as beaver, fox, and muskrat occasionally spotted. You'll also learn about the region's human history through interpretive boards and two museums along the route.

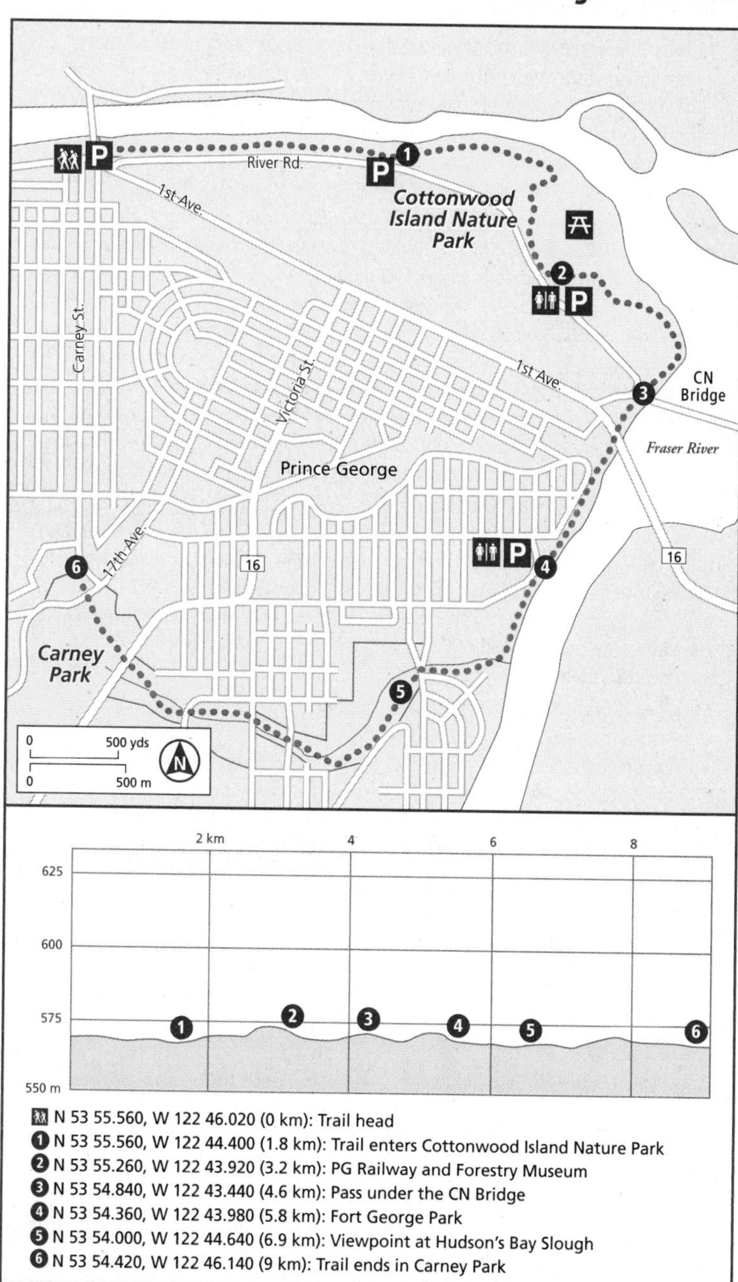
River Rd.
1st Ave.
Cottonwood Island Nature Park
Carney St.
Victoria St.
1st Ave.
CN Bridge
Fraser River
Prince George
17th Ave.
16
16
Carney Park
0
500 yds
0
500 m
N
2 km
4
6
8
625
600
575
550 m
N 53 55.560, W 122 46.020 (0 km): Trail head
1 N 53 55.560, W 122 44.400 (1.8 km): Trail enters Cottonwood Island Nature Park
2 N 53 55.260, W 122 43.920 (3.2 km): PG Railway and Forestry Museum
3 N 53 54.840, W 122 43.440 (4.6 km): Pass under the CN Bridge
4 N 53 54.360, W 122 43.980 (5.8 km): Fort George Park
5 N 53 54.000, W 122 44.640 (6.9 km): Viewpoint at Hudson's Bay Slough
6 N 53 54.420, W 122 46.140 (9 km): Trail ends in Carney Park

Into the Northern Wilderness

Serious wilderness seekers are attracted to northern British Columbia for its remote parks protecting old-growth forests, ancient volcanoes, and untamed rivers. Exploring these parks requires previous backcountry experience, advance planning, and at least a few days in the region. But Northern British Columbia isn't all backpacking and blisters—and we've found room to include details of how to reach one of the most delightful hot springs imaginable:

Mount Edziza Provincial Park Starting 4 million years ago and ending as recently as 10,000 years ago, violent volcanic eruptions have created a moon-like landscape of basalt plateaus and cinder cones now protected by this park. It is possible to reach the core of the park on foot from 100km (62 miles) south of Dease Lake at Kinaskan Lake Provincial Park, or from Telegraph Creek, which lies west of Hwy. 37. Both starting points require a rough 2-day hike just to reach the park boundary, with the latter also entailing a boat ride. Most visitors fly into the park's Buckley Lake, from where day and overnight hikes lead to all the most impressive volcanic features, including the perfectly formed Eve Cone. The 75km (47-mile) trek between Buckley and Mowdade lakes hits all the highlights. It takes around 7 days to complete.

Redfern–Keily Provincial Park Reaching this remote park, a rough 80km (50-mile) drive west of the Alaska Highway from a point 255km (158 miles) west of Fort Nelson, takes longer than completing the main trail—a 2km (1.2-mile) hike each way to and from Fairy Lake. Starting from the eastern end of Redfern Lake, the easy route quickly reaches Fairy Lake, a beautiful turquoise-colored body of water surrounded by old growth forest.

Stone Mountain Provincial Park Located along one of the highest points of the Alaska Highway, 140km (87 miles) northwest of Fort Nelson, the trails in this park reach alpine meadows more easily than elsewhere in the region. The 3km (1.9-mile) Summit Peak Trail rewards hikers with sweeping views across the northern extent of the Rocky Mountains, but the route is very steep. Far less rigorous is the half-day walk to Flower Spring Lake. As the name suggests, this lake is surrounded by colorful wildflowers during the short summer season.

Atlin Provincial Park After a thrilling jet-boat ride from Atlin, in the northwest corner of British Columbia, the Llewellyn Glacier is reached in around 2 hours of moderately strenuous hiking. Most visitors who get to this point will want to continue up onto the ice, but to do so should employ the services of a guide. Recommended is Atlin Quest (www.atlinart.com), the same company that operates the jet-boat.

Liard Hot Springs Provincial Park The most popular trail in all of northern British Columbia leads from the Alaska Highway 305km (190 miles) northwest of Fort Nelson to natural hot springs bubbling up out of a forested wilderness. Reached in less than 10 minutes of easy walking, the Alpha Pool is the hotter of the two, while the Beta Pool is larger and deeper. The trail itself is interesting for surrounding wetlands of lush vegetation that thrives on the warm water flowing from the springs. The hot pools are accessible year-round.

Start the hike from the far corner of the parking lot, where an information board provides an overview of the trail, its route, and its history. Although not open to the public, the first structure passed—a log building—has an interesting use. It was constructed as a fish hatchery by a local non-profit group to help ensure the future of salmon and trout in local waterways.

❶ **Cottonwood Island Nature Park** The Heritage River Trail is well signposted through the heart of this forested park, which is laced with river channels and unpaved walking trails. Take the left fork just beyond the park boundary to follow close to the Nechako River. It is along this stretch of path that the park's namesake black cottonwood trees thrive. Growing to a height of 50m (164 ft.), they are at their blooming best in early summer, when even the lightest of winds fills the air with their cotton-like seeds. This park has experienced extreme springtime flooding in recent years, with up to 1m (3¼ ft.) of water washing over the riverbank. The cause of the flooding is huge chunks of ice that become jammed at the mouth of the Nechako River.

TAKE A BREAK Cottonwood Island Nature Park is a little less than halfway from the trail head to Fort George Park, but for the surrounding trees and watery panorama, it's the best place to stop for a picnic. Some tables offer a complete riverside setting, but those nearest to River Rd. are within a shelter and have adjacent washrooms.

Continue downstream and look for the wooden platform on a side trail. Overlooking a shallow river channel, this is a good spot for spotting the park's abundant birdlife, which includes great horned owls, woodpeckers, and waterthrushes. At dawn or dusk, you may see beavers or muskrats swimming through the shallow water.

❷ **PG Railway and Forestry Museum** Where the trail leaves the park, it passes this museum celebrating the two industries upon which the city has been built. On display are over 70 pieces of rolling stock (including a unique wooden snowplow) and a variety of oversized logging machinery. Dogs are welcome at the museum, making it a friendly stop for those hiking with their pets.

❸ **CN Bridge** Continuing south, the Heritage River Trail passes the confluence of the Nechako and Fraser rivers, then crosses under the CN Bridge. Unique in Canada, this bridge spanning the Fraser river was originally designed for both rail and road traffic, but today is used only by trains.

❹ **Fort George Park** Entering the north end of Fort George Park, forested habitat gives way to open green space with playgrounds, picnic tables, and even a miniature railway. The park is named for a fort established by Simon Fraser in 1807. The fort is long gone, but you can learn about Fraser, local First Nations, and the region's natural history, as well as see full-size dinosaur models, at the park's Exploration Place.

❺ **Hudson's Bay Slough** Fort George Park marks the end of the trail's route along the river. From this point, it jogs west along the south side of an old river channel. After crossing under the Queensway, the trail reaches Hudson's Bay Slough. Following the slough's south bank, you may see birds such as American wigeons, blue-winged teals, and mallard ducks. Noisy red-winged blackbirds are most often heard, rather than seen, as they tend to stay hidden in the cattails surrounding this marshy area.

❻ **Carrie Jane Gray Park** Named for Prince George's only female mayor, this small park marks the official end of the Heritage River Trail. From here, it is a short cab ride back to the trail head, or a 30-minute walk north along Carney Street.

—Andrew Hempstead

10 CAPE FIFE LOOP, HAIDA GWAII ★★

Difficulty rating: Moderate

Distance: 35 km (21.9 miles) round trip (10 km to Cape Fife ranger cabin, 10 km to Rose Spit, 15 km to Tow Hill)

Estimated time: 4½ to 5½ hours to Cape Fife from the trail head, 3½ hours to Rose Spit, 4 hours from Rose Spit to the Tow Hill side of the trailhead. For maximum enjoyment, give yourself three days if you have them, although you can do the hike in two.

Elevation gain: Minimal

Costs/permits: Wilderness camping and ranger cabin are free. If you decide to camp by Tow Hill, the site is run by the Band office in Old Massett: someone will come to your campsite and collect C$20 for the night only in the summer. There's no charge in the off-season.

Pet-friendly: Pets allowed, but should be leashed when others are around.

Best time to go: May to September, although you can hike the trail any time of year. In winter, add time for the Cape Fife portion of the trail to avoid wet portions and plan time well to go with short daylight hours.

Website: www.britishcolumbia.com/parks/?id=200

Recommended map: NTS 103J/4

Trail head GPS: N 54 04.397, W 131 47.581

Trail head directions: The trail begins at the northeast point of Graham Island, Haida Gwaii, 35 km northeast of Massett. From Masset, travel north on Tow Hill Road (also Highway 16) to Tow Hill; it's well signed. Park by the Tow Hill kiosk, where you'll also see a map, and access the trail across the Hiellen bridge and to the right. The trail head is a short walk in, and to the left.

It's not every day you get to travel to the birthplace of humans. This amazing multi-day hike travels through old-growth forest, wetland, and endless beaches of Naikoon Provincial Park in the beautiful islands of Haida Gwaii (Queen Charlotte Islands), starting and ending at the 109m basalt columns of Tow Hill.

From the moment you get to the trailhead, you'll feel like you're headed into a magical world. To your right, the Hiellen River splashes its way to the ocean, and the surrounding forests have a breathing life, lush and mossy with the fresh smell of hemlock and spruce, droplets and badge moss glistening when they are touched by sunlight.

The Cape Fife loop is located in Naikoon Provincial Park (72,640 hectares/179,497 acres) and within the boundaries of the Tow Hill and Rose Spit (170 hectares/420 acres) ecological reserves. You can think of the hike in three separate legs—the forested walk from near the Tow Hill kiosk out to Cape Fife, the East Beach stretch to Rose Spit, and the sunset stretch, from Rose Spit back to Tow Hill, and on to the kiosk. While you can obviously hike the trail in either direction, I'd recommend you start the Cape Fife way—it's the most challenging part of the hike, and it'll be very clear when you reach the Ranger's cabin at the end.

Cape Fife

10km (6.2 miles)

The Cape Fife leg is where, in Haida mythology, Raven coaxed the first humans to life, and most of the islands' ecosystems are represented on this route. It starts in old-growth spruce and hemlock forest and transitions into marvelous cedar and the wetter grounds in which this revered tree loves to grow.

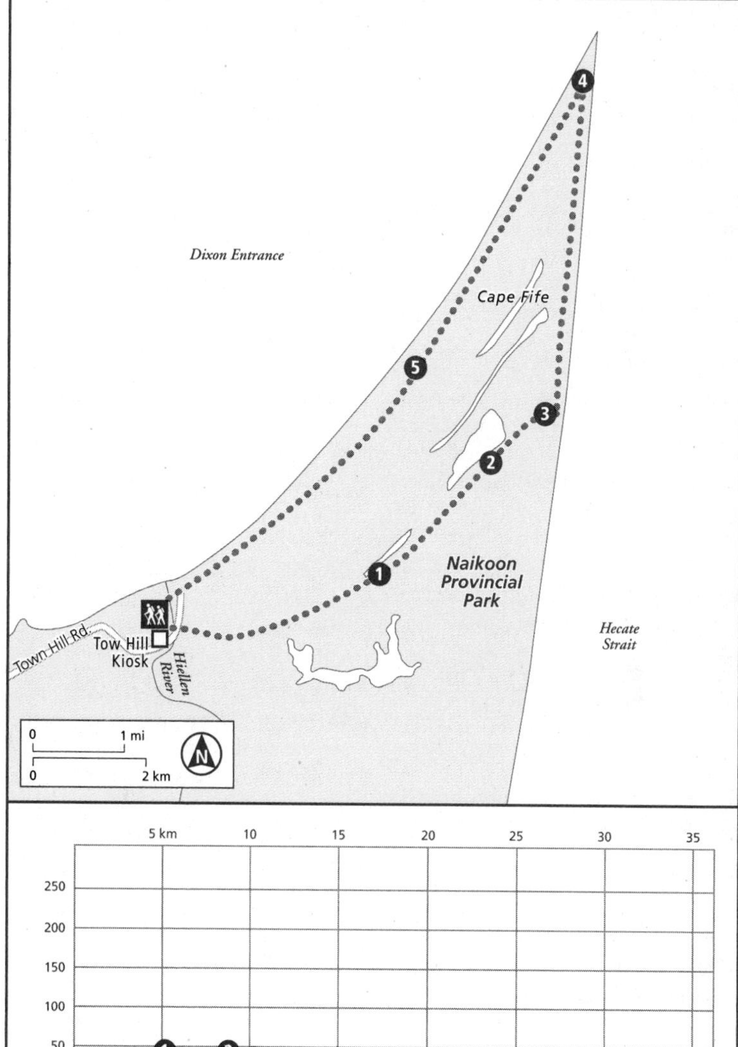

- N 54 04.397, W 131 47.581 (0 km): Trail head
- ❶ N 54 04.742, W 131 43.317 (5.1 km): Sign marks halfway to the ranger cabin
- ❷ N 54 06.023, W 131 41.154 (8.4 km): Cross bridge over stream
- ❸ N 54 06.439, W 131 40.310 (9.7 km): Arrive at Ranger cabin
- ❹ N 54 10.280, W 131 39.331 (19.5 km): Tip of Rose Spit
- ❺ N 54 06.705, W 131 42.946 (26 km): Wreck of old boat sticking out of the sand

Conditions vary on this part of the trail. A lot of it is in boggy area. Bring an extra pair of socks, or gumboots if you have them. Blow downs (fallen trees) are part of the excitement—you'll find yourself at times climbing, crawling, or scrambling over great overturned roots, and over miniature lakes. Sometimes these blow downs or watery areas mean you have to go off the trail to stay dry. Ultimately though, the trail is very defined, and punctuated regularly by boardwalks, with lovely stretches of cedar-padded walks. Don't get fooled by deer trails which are much smaller.

Take time to look around. Once you train your eyes to the color palette around you, the shades of green can be mesmerizing, bright green popping out of the deeper shades, and ferns, salal, fresh hemlock, and cedar roots all boasting their own distinct colors, and textures too. The grasses have harvest shades of reds and oranges and yellow, live impressionist paintings.

❶ Halfway marker The trail is marked at 5km and later at 2 and 1 km. This is handy, as you tend to lose track of time in the forest. Gradually the cedar begins to dominate. The tall rusty red trees here are like people you can get to know; they twist, or grow in twins, their characteristic bark deep and rusty colored, almost cushiony against your hand. If you look carefully you might see signs of cedar bark harvesting, long strips of bark carefully taken from only one side of the tree for weaving.

Look for the distinct patterns of deer hooves, and you may see signs of marten, river otters, raccoons, red squirrels, and muskrats as well. After time spent clambering, your hands will smell like the almost minty scent of hemlock. You might see berries, or the nippy licorice fern, and there are sundews—deceptively delicate looking flowers that eat insects—and single delight, its white-petalled head drooping, intoxicatingly fragrant. Don't pick these though; they, like the orchids you'll see, are protected in the reserve.

❷ Bridge Between the 2 and 1km signposts, there's a delightful—and sturdy—little bridge over the only true stream you'll see along the way. Something about the end of the trail feels like a tale out of a 19th century British children's story—maybe it's the anticipation, or the sense of a wild garden with gnarled trees, but it's a charming finale.

❸ Ranger Cabin The ranger cabin at the end of the trail is a welcome sight, especially if you've been walking through rain, or if there's a storm brewing. It will be very clear where the trail heads towards

Tips When You Go Out in the Woods . . . Be Prepared

On this trail, you want to be what might feel over-prepared. It's a wilderness trail, and not unthinkable that a small slip might mean you twist an ankle or hurt a knee. Bring a first aid kit, with moleskin for blisters. Make sure someone knows where you are and when you plan to come back. Pack the water you need, and more than you think you'll need—there really isn't water along the trail. Cell phones may work, especially on the Tow Hill side of the hike. Check the weather and tides before you go, and do not hike the Cape Fife part of the trail anywhere near dark. Bring a little extra food in case the weather changes and you need to stay, and extra socks and gloves. Get your food in town. Fire starter can be handy in damp weather, and a light tarp and emergency blanket might shorten a long night. Did I mention water?

Getting There & Around

Everything will go more easily if you can be flexible on Haida Gwaii. Flights and ferries are subject to weather conditions and everyone's on "Haida Gwaii" time. Don't be shy to ask questions—locals will be more than happy to give you information.

You can fly directly into Masset from Vancouver with ***Pacific Coastal*** (✆ **800/663-2872;** www.pacificcoastal.com), the plane runs on a regular schedule most days of the week. The flight increases in cost as it fills up, so book early. Prices range from C$280 to C$440. **Air Canada** (✆ **888/247-2262;** www.aircanada.com) flies into Sandspit also from Vancouver every day; the average is about C$250 each way. Make sure to factor in the cost of getting across on the ferry and up to Masset. (See below for some options.)

If you arrive at the south end of the Islands, there are visitor centers at the Sandspit airport and in Queen Charlotte City. The visitor center in Masset is seasonal, open in the summer months, but you can ask at most businesses for a free copy of the *Guide to the Queen Charlotte Islands, Haida Gwaii* that is normally available at the centers. If you want to know what's going on, check bulletin boards or the *Observer*, the local paper, available in most stores.

One highway runs from one end of Graham Island all the way out to Tow Hill. Technically it's Highway 16 and an extension of the Trans-Canada, but after Masset, everyone calls it Tow Hill Road and before that it's just "the highway".

You can rent cars on the island at **Rustic Car Rentals** (✆ **250/559-4641**). **Eagle Transit** (✆ **250/559-4461**) offers a shuttle from the airport in Sandspit to Queen Charlotte City for C$16 (the schedule is coordinated with flight arrivals) and travels between the city and Masset in coordination with the ferry schedule (C$70, call for reservations).

the cabin; you turn right here and down a small incline to a boardwalk and the beginning of the dunes. The structure was erected through a joint effort of the Haida Nation and BC Parks. Recent renovations made it airtight, so you feel cozy inside. Look for the blue homemade slippers. You'll likely find firewood, a hatchet, pots, grills, and a kettle, and maybe even other campers—there's plenty of room.

The cabin is maintained by its users, so consider bringing a little gift—candles, matches, or some cedar kindling if you have any room in your pack—and sweep and tidy before you leave. Campers will often do some little service to the cabin during their stay.

Dump your bags and head out over the dunes to the beach. The driftwood on this beach side of the trail is gorgeous. Some of these logs are massive, and the shapes and curves are worth exploring.

This is a great place to spend the night. If you're lucky the stars will be out and there's much less traffic on this side of the beach. You never know what you'll find—Japanese glass balls used for fishing on the other side of the Pacific are a favorite.

Rose Spit

10km (6.2 miles)

Heading towards Rose Spit on the beach can be tricky, and the beach is always different. A stream parallel to the water cuts the beach in half in front of the cabin, and can sometimes be crossed at low tide. But be aware of a form of quicksand that can be found all along the stretch in front of the cabin. If you're finding it difficult to cross, don't take chances. At high tide there can be a bit of a current and the solidity of the sand underneath can vary.

You'll see a boggy bay that tucks in towards where you turned right to come to the cabin, curving around to a peninsula that you follow to Rose Spit—this is Cape Fife. Following the shore here isn't a good option either—it's a slog through water or floating logs. Instead, walk the opposite way from the bay down the beach until it looks easy to cross.

It's an easy and delightful walk along "East Beach" to Rose Spit. The prevailing wind is behind you, and there are always fascinating shells, myriad colors of rocks, and the semiprecious, almost translucent, yellow and orange agates. This stretch of the hike is when you know you're on holiday—nothing feels rushed and it's all about exploring. The beach goes on and on, and you're not likely to see a soul; you can clamber up sandy rises, as the trees bend to the strong prevailing wind.

❹ **Rose Spit** You can't mistake it when you arrive at Rose Spit— it's long and narrow, the two beaches meet here and you feel a little bit like you're at the end of the world. You can see from one side of the beach to the other, and driftwood lines the shoreline like a wizened backbone. This is where the raven coaxed the first humans out of the clam (or some say cockle) shell. Look for renowned Haida artist Bill Reid's massive rendition of this moment if you're in Vancouver at the Museum of Anthropology.

Make sure you save time to relax at Rose Spit. Even if you didn't know this story, there is a special feeling about the place. There's an old lighthouse here. At low tide you can walk right out on the finger of sand that gives the Spit its name. Sometimes you can see migrating gray whales, or sandhill cranes, and at the right time you may be treated to the tiny sweet wild strawberries that grow in profusion here. You may see signs of bear, but make noise and watch where you're going and you'll be safe. The bears have lots of food to keep them busy and are uninterested in humans.

From the East Beach side you can sometimes see the shape and lights of the mainland, and on a clear day you can see Alaska along the Tow Hill side of the trail. Kayakers have left from here to paddle across, and the Haida used to regularly make crossings to Alaska.

If you are going to camp here, camp well in and remember the tides. But the walk around to the end of the loop, if you got an early start, and if the weather's good in the long days of summer, is very doable.

Tow Hill

15km (9.3 miles)

For most of the way back you can see the distinct shape of Tow Hill in the distance. You'll find Dungeness crab, or scallops after a big storm, and clams after the ebb tide. Check the Tow Hill kiosk when you start out to make sure there is no danger of the "red tide" which can affect shellfish. Also familiarize yourself with the limits on how many crab and clams you can harvest, and with the crab, what size you can take from the beach. Jellyfish wash up an eerie transparent red, or in weird tiny globules of white. Eagles, ravens, and seagulls soar overhead, so the sky and the beach feel limitless.

This side of the beach is much more used, so you might have the entire beach to yourself, or you may encounter other campers. Tides are tricky and cars often get stuck here, so you may find yourself lending a hand.

❺ **Shipwreck** Halfway down the beach you'll see the wreck of an old boat sticking out of the sand. It's a good landmark, and a good preparation to re-enter ordinary reality. Recently, a young whale became

More Local Hiking Options

If you're feeling adventurous, take the time and hike the whole East Beach Trail. Still located in Naikoon Provincial Park, the trail runs 90 km (56 miles) from the Tlell River Bridge (the southern limit of the park) past Cape Fife to Rose Spit, a three-to four-day hike along mostly level terrain, with three shelters along the route. You'll have to decide when you get to the ranger cabin and Cape Fife whether you want to continue on to Rose Spit or take the wooded Cape Fife portion of the trail back to the trailhead by The Hiellen and Tow Hill.

There's another trail that runs 5 km (3.1 miles) one way from the Tlell River Bridge and leads to the Pesuta, an old log barge that was wrecked in 1928. The trail goes along the bluff or along the river at low tide. It's two to three hours each way.

Once at Tow Hill, spend some time in the area. There's so much to do. Two trails start from the base of Tow Hill: the first to the top of Tow Hill, with two viewing platforms, an easy 1km (0.6 mile) climb. The view is lovely. That trail branches off to the Blow Hole, where ocean sprays out at the right tide. Be careful in both places of slippery ground underneath.

Camp by Tow Hill or at the Agate Beach campground back toward town, which has pit toilets, campsites, and water. There's a great intertidal zone along Agate Beach. A little further towards town, you can relax at the **Moon over Naikoon,** which serves soup, fresh baked goods, and tea in the summer, as well as being an informal museum. They have no electricity or phone lines, so you can't call before you go, but they're located about halfway to Tow Hill—you'll see some cabins, a sign for fresh bread and whalebones at the entrance to assure you that you're in the right place. If you're up for more hiking, you can go for day hikes: White Creek is another old settler's trail—look out for the river sign and bridge on the right hand side once you've passed Moon over Naikoon and head on the trail that starts by the bridge on the same non-beach side of the road. Once again you'll see beautiful old cedar stands and then climb up to views of the surrounding areas, including another view of Tow Hill. Be careful as you walk, there can be surprisingly deep holes right by the path. There are a couple of Haida reserves by Yakan Point and Tow Hill, so please respect no-entry signs. Carry a fishing rod and you can fish while you hike, the Sangan, Chown, and Hiellen rivers are all great fishing spots and have wonderful old-growth forests and swimming spots to make wonderful day hikes. The paths to enter are evident when you are by the bridge of each river.

About half way to Masset you can stop at the **Trout House** (✆ **250/626-9330**), a charming stackwall restaurant with organic dishes. It is generally open every day in the summer, or on weekends in the fall and winter.

beached *on this section of the sand*—you can see a video of the rescue efforts on YouTube. The sunsets on this stretch can be glorious, deep pinks and mauves or brilliant glowing orbs on the horizon. Don't get caught too far away from the trail head when the sun goes down though. Darkness here can be very deep; sometimes you can barely see your hand in front of you.

You end your hike at the mouth of the Hiellen, and across from the base of Tow Hill. It's a short walk back along the road to the kiosk, or you can camp in the grounds right by the exit. Permits are available in town.

—Judy McKinley

SLEEPING & EATING

ACCOMMODATIONS

Kids **Barkerville Campgrounds** When gold was discovered here, the Barkerville residents initially slept in the open air. Relive those cool evenings by pitching your tent in one of three campgrounds. Lowhee caters to RVs, Government Hill provides walk-in sites, and Forest Rose is horse-friendly.

Hwy. 26, Barkerville, BC V0K 1B0. ✆ **866/994-3297** or 250/994-3297. www.barkervillecampgrounds.ca. 164 units. C$16–C$19 per campsite. MC, V. **Close to:** Barkerville to Summit Rock and Groundhog Lake.

★★ **Bella Coola's Eagle Lodge** Midway between most outdoor activities in the valley, the ideal location makes this four-star lodge stand out. Once the boys' dormitory for a Seventh Day Adventist Academy, all the rooms have the names of friends dear to owners, Rosemary and Jim. Groups are easily accommodated, and you can find great local tour suggestions available—plus, the Lodge offers camping and RV sites.

1103 Hwy. 20, Bella Coola, BC V0T 1C0. ✆ **866/799-5587** or 250/799-5587. www.eaglelodgebc.com. 9 units. C$99 double; off-season discounts available. AE, MC, V. **Close to:** Burnt Bridge Creek Loop, Rainbow Range.

★ **Cariboo Lodge Resort** Clean and central, the lodge is a great location from which to explore the Marble Range. A lively and bright pub features many trophy mounts of moose, bears, bighorn sheep, and a wolf. Rooms are quiet and tucked behind the main lodge.

1414 Cariboo Hwy., Clinton, BC V0K 1K0. ✆ **877/459-7992** or 250/459-7992. www.bcadventure.com/cariboolodge. 20 units. C$74 double. MC, V. **Close to:** Mount Bowman.

Chilcotin Lodge The innkeepers serve up charming, authentic atmosphere in this quaint and rustic former hunting lodge (which is still frequented by grouse hunters). The lodge sits atop a hill amidst far-reaching ranchlands. Camping and RV sites are also available.

Box 2 (west of Farwell Canyon Rd.), Riske Creek, BC, V0L 1T0. ✆ **888/659-5688** or 250/659-5646. www.chilcotinlodge.com. 10 units. C$148 double. No credit cards. **Close to:** Junction Sheep Range.

★★★ **Echo Valley Ranch & Spa** Guest ranches are common in this neck of the woods, but the 4,047-hectare (10,000-acre) Echo Valley Ranch stands alone in luxury and the details. Horseback riding and hiking evoke a Wild West feel, while spa treatments and architecture offer a unique Thai influence.

50km (31 miles) northwest of Clinton, P.O. Box 16, Jesmond, BC V0K 1K0. ✆ **800/253-8831** or 250/459-2386. www.evranch.com. 21 units. June–Sept C$598 double, 3-day minimum stay; Mar–May and Oct C$440 double. MC, V. Closed Nov–Feb. **Close to:** Mount Bowman.

Four Points by Sheraton Yes, it's a part of a chain, but for its modern rooms and a wide range of facilities, the Sheraton is Prince George's best choice for lodging. Each spacious room has air-conditioning, an LCD TV, free bottled water, and wireless Internet access. Set yourself up for a day of hiking with breakfast at the in-house restaurant and, if you have any energy left at the end of the day, take advantage of the fitness room.

1790 Hwy. 97 S., Prince George, BC V2L 5L3. ✆ **800/368-7764** or 250/564-7100. www.starwoodhotels.com. 74 units. C$135 double; extra person C$15; packages available. AC, MC, V. **Close to:** Heritage River Trail.

★ **Overlander Hotel** Clean, simple, and quiet rooms are full of convenient amenities, including an on-site restaurant. Being located close to the intersection of the main routes coming into town and offering 24-hour reception make this hotel ideal for those arriving late or leaving early.

1118 Lakeview Cres., Williams Lake, BC V2G 1A3. ✆ **800/663-6898** or 250/392-3321. 57 units. C$79–C$111 double. AE, DISC, MC, V. **Close to:** Williams Lake River Valley Trail.

★★★ Finds **Rivers Edge Guest Cottages** Warm, delightful, and relaxing, the two fully equipped log cabins provide that true woodsy feeling without sacrificing any comfort. Brenda McFetridge and Jamie King are ideal hosts for activity-focused folk, offering up great information on local hikes and sites.

19600 Hwy. 20 (30km/19 miles west of Tatla Lake), Kleena Kleene, BC, V0L 1M0. ✆ **250/476-1345.** www.riversedgeguestcottages.com. 2 units. C$95–C$135 cabin; C$115–C$155 cabin with breakfast. AE, DISC, MC, V. **Close to:** Perkins Peak.

Talisman Inn This motel is surrounded by local-award-winning gardens and boasts rooms flexible enough to meet the needs of most travelers. Some rooms have kitchenettes, and others are geared towards those with limited mobility.

753 Front St. (off Hwy. 97), Quesnel, BC V2J 2L2. ✆ **800/663-8090** or 250/992-7247. www.talismaninn.bc.ca. 85 units. C$79–C$95 double; includes breakfast. AE, DC, MC, V. **Close to:** Barkerville to Summit Rock and Groundhog Lake, Williams Lake River Valley Trail.

RESTAURANTS

★★ Finds **Bear's Paw Café** WEST COAST This eclectic café features a large and welcoming patio, delicious coffee, and plenty of homemade treats. Run by Cheryl Macarthy and Dave Jorgenson, the Bear's Paw is also a great source of local trail information.

Hwy. 26, Wells. ✆ **866/994-2345** or 250/994-2345. www.thebearspaw.ca. Main courses C$12–C$22. MC, V. Lunch 11:30am; dinner 5–10pm. **Close to:** Barkerville to Summit Rock and Groundhog Lake.

Bella Coola Valley Restaurant DINER Simple and fresh home-cooking in the heart of Bella Coola village. One of the few eateries in town, you'll see plenty of locals tucking into heaping plates and sipping hot coffee.

Mackenzie St. (near Burke Ave.), Bella Coola. ✆ **250/799-0045.** Main courses C$9–C$18. MC, V. June–Aug, Mon–Thurs and Sat–Sun 7am–8pm, Fri 7am–9pm; Sept–May, Mon–Thurs and Sat 7am–7pm, Fri 7am–8pm, and Sun 7am–2pm. **Close to:** Burnt Bridge Creek Loop, Rainbow Range.

★ Finds **Edelweiss Restaurant** GERMAN/AUSTRIAN This popular local restaurant on the Cariboo Highway serves up a multitude of schnitzel varieties, bratwurst, and spaetzle in a warm, homey dining room.

4016 Cariboo Hwy. 97 S., Lac La Hache. ✆ **250/396-4545.** Reservations recommended. Main courses C$11–C$22. MC, V. Tue–Sun 11:30am–8pm. **Close to:** Mount Bowman, Williams Lake River Valley Trail.

Fort Alexandria Fruit Stand CAFE This truck stop is also a National Historic Site, where a former trading post marks the approximate location where Alexander Mackenzie ended his water journey and began his westward trek to Bella Coola and the Pacific Ocean in 1793. Homemade corn chowder and bacon sandwiches have plenty of lunch appeal. Despite the name, however, there's no fruit available.

9380 Hwy. 97 (south of Quesnel), Quesnel. ✆ **250/747-3998.** Main courses C$7–C$13. MC, V. Mon–Fri 8am–8pm, Sat 8am–6:30pm. **Close to:** Barkerville to Summit Rock and Groundhog Lake, Williams Lake River Valley Trail.

★★ Finds **Gecko Tree** CAFE This funky breakfast and lunch café in downtown Williams Lake makes great coffee to complement the freshly baked goodies. A full breakfast menu and fresh salads will charge you up before you hit the hills or the highway.

54 MacKenzie Ave. N. (at Oliver St.), Williams Lake. ✆ **250/398-8983.** Main courses C$7–C$15. AE, MC, V. Mon–Fri 7:30am–4pm, Sat 9am–4pm. **Close to:** Williams Lake River Valley Trail, Junction Sheep Range.

Value **Oliver Street Bar & Grill** PUB Try the pub's C$3 burger special for a filling and wallet-friendly deal (available most Thurs). Hearty salad portions and friendly service strike the right relaxed atmosphere for you to enjoy an evening planning your next hike or playing pool.

23 Oliver St. (at MacKenzie), Williams Lake. ✆ **250/392-5942.** Main courses C$9–C$21. MC, V. Mon–Tue 11am–9pm, Wed–Thurs 11am–11pm, Fri–Sat 11am–midnight. **Close to:** Williams Lake River Valley Trail, Junction Sheep Range.

Waddling Duck PUB An English-style pub with lots of exposed wood and brickwork, the Waddling Duck provides an enjoyable setting in which to enjoy solid Canadian cooking. The dinner menu is surprisingly creative for the setting, with Canadian-themed fare such as wild salmon baked in a basil and pear emulsion. Be sure to save room for the bananas foster.

1157 5th Ave., Prince George. ✆ **250/561-5550.** www.waddlingduck.ca. Reservations required. Main courses C$10–C$23. MC, V. Lunch & dinner daily. **Close to:** Heritage River Trail.

The Wolf's Cry Pub PUB Located on the Cariboo Highway, this pub serves up the usual hearty selection of burgers, with a few specials like blackened halibut for a unique flair. Friendly service and a light atmosphere make this quick stopping spot a good choice.

1613 Cariboo Hwy. (northern end of the village), Clinton. ✆ **250/459-2610.** Main courses C$8–C$16. MC, V. Wed–Mon noon–2pm and 5–8pm. **Close to:** Mount Bowman.

8

The Okanagan Valley Hikes

by Darlene West

About a half-day's drive from Vancouver, in a rain shadow between the Coast and Monashee mountains, the Okanagan Valley spans about 175 arid kilometers (109 miles) in BC's Southern Interior. With a string of clear lakes and a desert-hot climate, the Okanagan practically screams vacation. Beaches, golf courses, fruit stands, wineries, and ski hills draw visitors to the valley. (Some never leave.) The most urban amenities are found in Kelowna (pop. 106,000), the main center and one of the fastest-growing cities in Canada. From Kelowna, Hwy. 97 runs north along Okanagan Lake to Vernon and south to Osoyoos, next to the Washington border.

The hub of BC's flourishing wine industry, the Okanagan has more than 700 vineyards and 140 wineries (at last count), including one-of-a-kind establishments such as the architecturally imposing Mission Hill, near Kelowna, and North America's first Aboriginal-owned winery, Nk'Mp Cellars, on a sun-bleached setting in Osoyoos. The region celebrates all things wine in a handful of annual fetes, including a 10-day harvest festival in early October. (Visit www.owfs.com for festival dates and schedules.) Although orchards, increasingly, are giving way to vineyards, the Okanagan remains BC's top fruit-growing region. Early summer through fall, fruit stands along Hwy. 97 and on Hwy. 3 in the neighboring Similkameen Valley are the spots to stock up on cherries, peaches, apricots, apples, plums, and pears.

The Okanagan's lakes, desert landscapes, and vineyard-covered slopes add up to scenery that will leave you speechless. Hiking terrain, for the most part, is gentler than what you'll find in some parts of BC, although keep in mind that the valley's sizzling summer temperatures can make hard work of even the easiest trails. This desert-like climate also harbors an amazing diversity of birds, animals, and plants. Hike along a riverbank in the company of osprey, eagles, and great blue herons. Watch for rattlesnakes as you scale rocky bluffs. Tally up wildflowers on hillsides in spring and inhale the scent of sage.

The hikes in this chapter are easy to get to—in many cases, just minutes from a main highway—and close to creature comforts. Although you'll want to devote the better part of a day to some trails, others are hike-able in a few hours—in July and August, get an early morning start and avoid the midday heat. What's more, you'll still have time for a round of golf, a winery lunch, or a trip to the beach.

ESSENTIALS

GETTING THERE

By Plane

Both **Air Canada Jazz** (✆ **888/247-2262;** www.aircanada.ca) and **WestJet** (✆ **888/937-8538;** www.westjet.com) offer daily non-stop flights to Kelowna from Vancouver, Victoria,

Calgary, Edmonton, and Toronto. **Horizon Air** (✆ **800/547-9308;** www.alaskaair.com), a division of Alaska Air, offers daily non-stop service to Kelowna from Seattle. You can fly from Vancouver to Penticton with either Air Canada Jazz or **Pacific Coastal** (✆ **800/663-2872;** www.pacificcoastal.com). Pacific Coastal also offers service between Calgary and Penticton.

By Car

If you're driving to the Okanagan Valley, the most direct route (395km/237 miles) to Kelowna from Vancouver is via Hwy. 5, the **Coquihalla Highway.** It's about a 4-hour trip. The 607km (378-mile) journey to Kelowna from Calgary takes about 8 hours. If you're heading to the southern end of the valley from Vancouver, the quickest (and most scenic) route is via Hwy. 3 through Manning Park and into the hilly **Similkameen Valley,** past orchards, vineyards, and fruit stands. It's a 402km (250-mile) drive to Osoyoos from Vancouver.

By Bus

Greyhound (✆ **800/661-8747;** www.greyhound.ca) runs daily service from Vancouver to Kelowna and Penticton, with service continuing on to Banff and Calgary. A round-trip ticket from Vancouver to Kelowna is C$126. Greyhound also provides service to Oliver and Osoyoos.

VISITOR INFORMATION

The **Kelowna Visitor Centre** is on Hwy. 97 at 544 Harvey Avenue (✆ **800/663-4345** or 250/861-1515; www.tourismkelowna.com). If you're arriving in the south Okanagan, stop at the new **British Columbia Visitor Centre** at Osoyoos, junction of Hwy. 3 and Hwy. 97, for both regional (✆ **800/435-5622;** www.hellobc.com) and **Osoyoos** (✆ **888/676-9667** or 250/495-5070; www.destinationosoyoos.com) visitor information. The center is open 8am to 6pm in summer (July through Sept 4) and 9am to 4pm other months. In Penticton, head for the **Wine Country Visitor Centre** at 553 Railway Street (✆ **800/663-5052** or 250/493-4055; www.tourismpenticton.com), which also houses an excellent wine shop, filled with the best of BC wines, along with cookbooks and gift items.

ORIENTATION The city of Kelowna sprawls along the east side of Okanagan Lake, about half way between Vernon and Penticton. Many points of interest are in a relatively compact area near the city's waterfront. Bernard Street is the main commercial strip. The lovely **City Park,** with a sandy public beach, flanks downtown and links to Waterfront Park, where a boardwalk winds along the lakeshore to the **Grand Hotel.** Adjacent to **Waterfront Park,** on the other side of Water Street, a 6-block **Cultural District** houses art galleries, shops, and museums in a renovated former fruit packing area. The **BC Orchard Industry Museum,** 1304 Ellis Street (✆ **250/764-0433**) is in a former packing house that also contains a wine museum and a wine shop. The **Rotary Centre for the Arts,** 421 Cawston Avenue (✆ **250/717-5304**) is a multi-purpose venue with a 33-seat performing arts theater, plus two art galleries and a number of artist studios.

Hwy. 97, which takes you north to Vernon and south to Penticton, Oliver, and Osoyoos, inches right through the heart of Kelowna. (It's called Harvey Ave. near downtown.) Traffic is heavy, particularly in summer. A new five-lane bridge across Okanagan Lake opened in 2008 and has helped ease the flow of cars, trucks, and motor homes, but

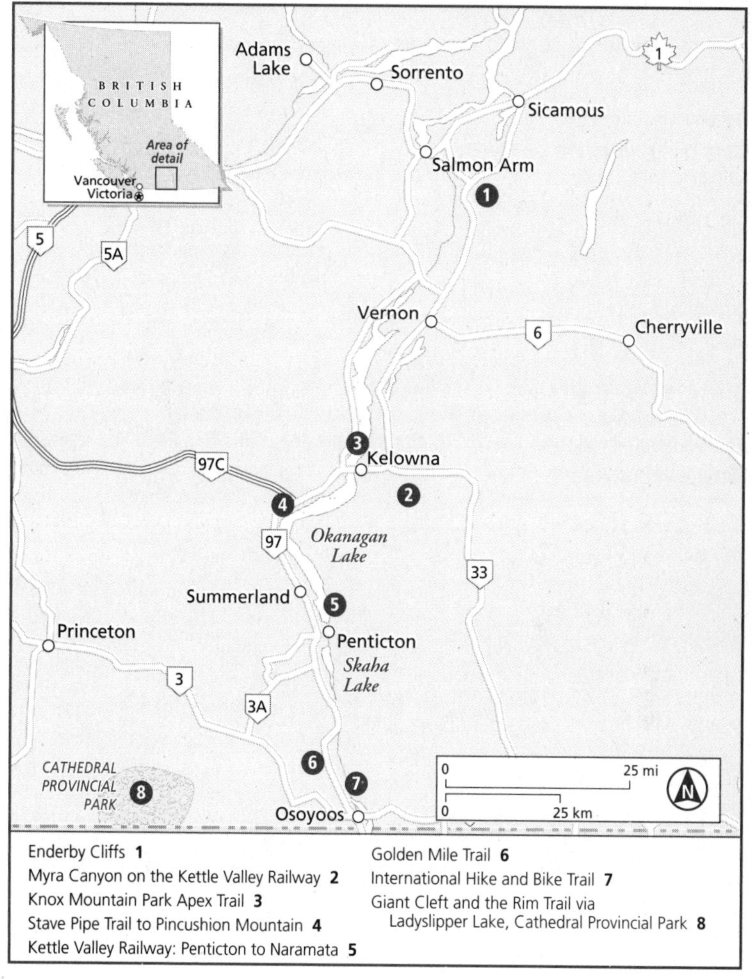

this is still the busiest stretch of highway outside the Lower Mainland, handling 46,000 vehicles a day.

GETTING AROUND

In Kelowna, the local bus service is operated by **Kelowna Regional Transit System** (✆ **250/860-8121**). A one-way fare is C$2. For a taxi, call **Checkmate Cabs** (✆ **250/861-1111**). For bus schedules in Penticton, call **Penticton Transit System** at ✆ **250/492-5602** (one way fare: C$1.75).

1 ENDERBY CLIFFS

Difficulty rating: Strenuous

Distance: 10km (6.2 miles) round trip

Estimated time: 4 hr.

Elevation gain: 660m (2,165 ft.)

Costs/permits: None

Best time to go: A wave of spectacular wild flowers come into bloom from late June–early July.

Website: www.env.gov.bc.ca/bcparks

Recommended map: 82L

Trail head GPS: N 50 34.337, W 119 06.163

Trail head directions: The hike starts near the small city of Enderby, about a half-hour drive north of Vernon. In Enderby, turn right at the traffic light, cross the bridge, and follow Mabel Lake Rd. to Brash-Allen Rd. Turn left on Brash-Allen and drive to the end of the road. Park in the designated hiking lot on your left, not on the lane to your right, which is private property.

With a wooden crucifix blessing the trail head and celestial scenery gracing the summit, this trip feels like a walk through the soul of Enderby. The dramatic Enderby Cliffs really do define this small Okanagan city, both physically (they're hard to miss) and recreationally; thousands of people climb the steep trail to the top each year. Count on exceptional views of the Shuswap River Valley, and in June and July, wildflowers galore.

The trail, part of a 2,246-hectare (5,550-acre) British Columbia provincial park, starts beside a wooden fence at the bottom of a hay field. Follow the field to the edge of the forest and climb straight up, through cedar, alder, and spruce. After about 10 minutes, the path winds to the right. Now and again, clearings in the trees afford glimpses of farms in the river valley.

❶ Carved Crucifix This section of trail crosses lush terrain, scattered with Saskatoon bushes, and intersects with an old logging road where you'll pass a towering carved wooden crucifix and a heavy wooden bench. Hikers and other visitors to the site often leave hand-written prayers and petitions, along with flowers.

❷ Lower Viewpoint A narrow path ascends gradually for about 700m (2,297 ft.) before turning a bend, where views of the bluffs are unveiled. The trail curves around an enormous boulder and climbs to a level area. A rocky outcrop provides a viewpoint from which you can catch your

Fun Facts A Spiritual Setting

The wooden crucifix near the start of the trail to Enderby Cliffs was handcrafted in Oberammergau, Germany, a village renowned for its woodcarving tradition. Enderby resident Hans Walter Hirth, who owned part of the property that now forms the provincial park, brought the monument from his native Germany and installed it beside the trail as a sign of gratitude for the beauty of this area. The project, which involved hauling 3 tons of concrete to the site, follows a custom in the Alps of marking the intersection of two roads with a cross.

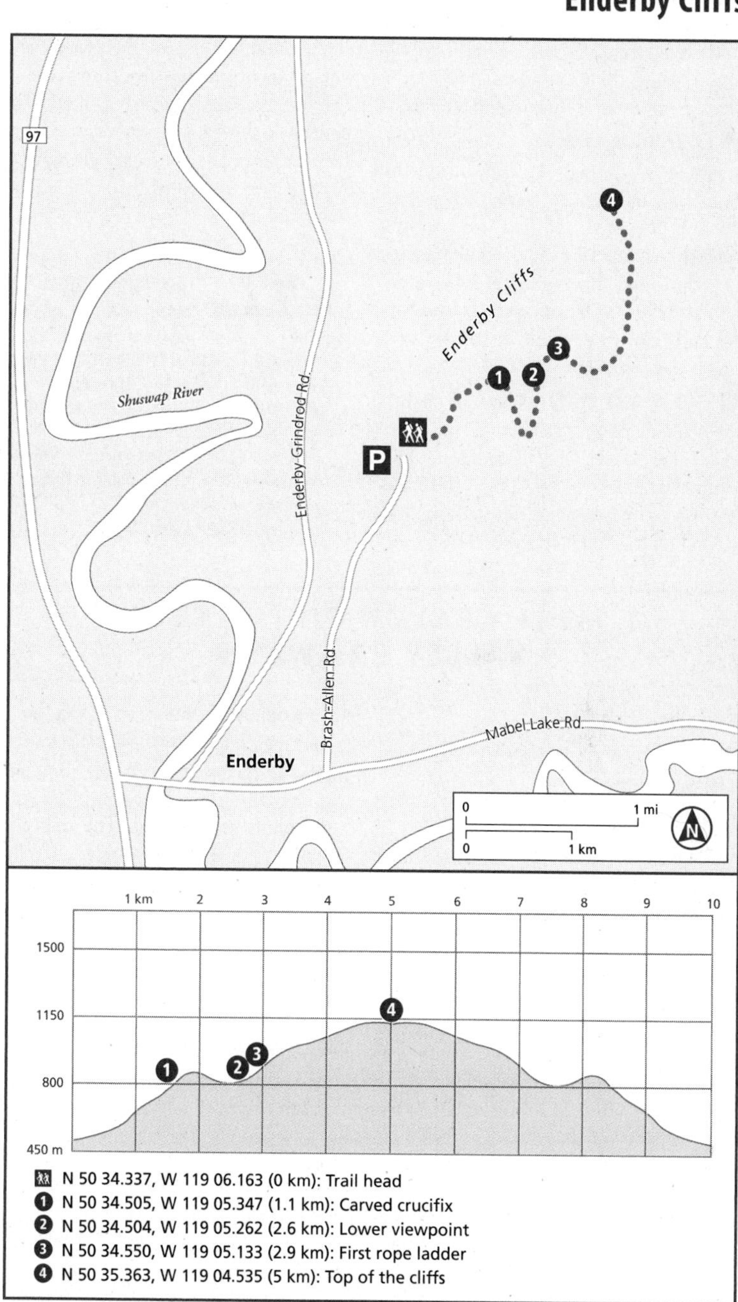

N 50 34.337, W 119 06.163 (0 km): Trail head
❶ N 50 34.505, W 119 05.347 (1.1 km): Carved crucifix
❷ N 50 34.504, W 119 05.262 (2.6 km): Lower viewpoint
❸ N 50 34.550, W 119 05.133 (2.9 km): First rope ladder
❹ N 50 35.363, W 119 04.535 (5 km): Top of the cliffs

breath, peer down on the valley, and perhaps spot a golden eagle. The cliffs you see here were formed 50 million years ago by lava flowing from volcanoes. They were shaped and molded by receding glaciers.

❸ **First Rope Ladder** A well-defined trail climbs through a stand of birch, becoming increasingly steep. When you come to a split in the trail (near a park boundary sign), take the downhill (right) branch, which rolls through a cedar forest and arrives at the base of a vertical stretch. It's fairly easy to scramble up, thanks to a handy rope secured to the trees.

❹ **Top of the Cliffs** The trail pitches up, gaining 300m (984 ft.) in the 2km (1¼-mile) stretch to the summit. The steepest sections of the climb ahead are outfitted with two more rope ladders, the second of which delivers you close to the top of a ridge. From here, it's smooth sailing on a fairly level trail through the trees to the southern end of the escarpment, with views of the sheer rock walls ahead. The trail meanders through a meadow of alpine wild flowers and follows the edge of the escarpment, skirting daringly close to the edge. At the top of the cliffs, a panorama unfolds.

TAKE A BREAK
Stand near the edge (but not *too* near the edge) of the cliffs and take in views of the Shuswap River Valley. The Shuswap, which runs west from Mabel Lake, loops and twists through farmland between Enderby and Grindrod, then flows north to Mara Lake. This is the spot to savor lunch before you head back down the trail.

2 MYRA CANYON ON THE KETTLE VALLEY RAILWAY ★

Difficulty rating: Easy

Distance: 12km (7.5 miles) round trip

Estimated time: 2½ hr.

Elevation gain: None

Costs/permits: None

Best time to go: Get an early start on the day to dodge the crowds.

Website: www.myratrestles.com

Recommended map: Pick up a Myra Canyon map at the visitor center in Kelowna.

Trail head GPS: N 49 48.038, W 119 18.457

Trail head directions: In Kelowna, follow KLO Road to McCulloch Road and past Gallagher's Canyon Golf Course to the Myra Forest Service Road. Drive 8.5km (5¼ miles) on the Myra Service Road to a 200-car parking lot.

In the maximum reward for minimum effort category, this trip scores high: The Kettle Valley Railway trail, on the route of an early 1900s rail line through British Columbia's Southern Interior, is known for scenery, history, and engineering feats. Myra Canyon is without doubt the most well-known stretch of the Kettle Valley Railway. This trip takes you midway into the canyon, across 14 trestles and through two tunnels.

A broad, flat trail leaves the parking lot. When the railway was running, the Myra Station occupied part of this area that's now used for parking. (The stations on either end of the canyon were named for Myra Newman and Ruth McCulluch, who were

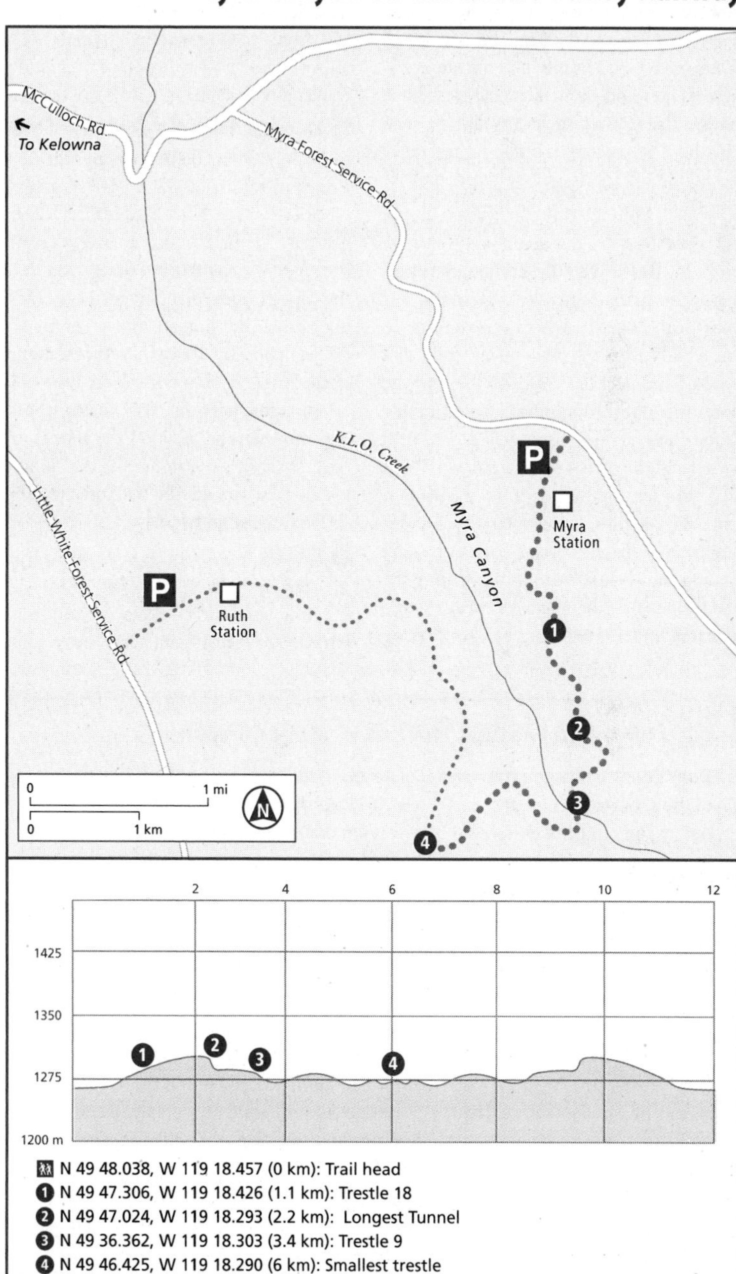
McCulloch Rd.
To Kelowna
Myra Forest Service Rd.
K.L.O. Creek
Myra Canyon
Myra Station
Little White Forest Service Rd.
Ruth Station
P
P
0
1 mi
0
1 km
N
2
4
6
8
10
12
1425
1350
1275
1200 m
N 49 48.038, W 119 18.457 (0 km): Trail head
1 N 49 47.306, W 119 18.426 (1.1 km): Trestle 18
2 N 49 47.024, W 119 18.293 (2.2 km): Longest Tunnel
3 N 49 36.362, W 119 18.303 (3.4 km): Trestle 9
4 N 49 46.425, W 119 18.290 (6 km): Smallest trestle

daughters of railway engineers.) As you follow the sheer rock walls of the canyon, views soon open to the west of Kelowna and Okanagan Lake. Purple blooms are everywhere; firewood, so named because it's one of the first species to re-establish in areas that have been burned, is tall (up to 3m/10 ft. high) and sports globe-shaped pink or purple flowers through the summer.

❶ **Trestle 18** It's about a 15-minute walk to **Trestle 18** (the bridges are numbered from the west, with Trestle 1 just past Ruth Station), which was the first to be rebuilt after a forest fire in 2003 and spans 55m (180 ft.). You can see how the forest fire cut through the canyon, leaving some areas relatively untouched. The next two trestles you'll cross (trestles 17 and 16), in fact, are survivors of the flames. You also see how the burned area is coming back to life with black current bushes, Indian paintbrush, and lupins coloring the landscape. As you make your way along the trail and see towering bridges curving around the canyon's rim, you'll appreciate how this stretch of the KVR gained celebrity from an engineering perspective, as railway builders had to cross remote and challenging terrain.

❷ **Longest Tunnel** A cluster of back-to-back trestles distinguishes this next stretch of the trail, which passes the highest point on the KVR (1,274m/4,180 ft.) just past Trestle 12, also a survivor of the fire. A few steps farther along, you enter the cool darkness of a curved, 114m (375-ft.) tunnel, the longest of two tunnels in the canyon. By designing the elaborate trestle bridges, railway builders were able, for the most part, to avoid major tunneling into the rock. Beyond the tunnel, the trail swings across one of the longest wooden trestles in the canyon and slips through a second tunnel.

❸ **Trestle 9** About 3km (2 miles) from the trail head, Trestle 9, over 100m (328 ft.) in length, curves along the southeastern edge of the canyon. This trestle, along

Fun Facts The Famous Trestles of Myra Canyon

Don't count on having this spectacular setting to yourself. The Myra Canyon leg of the KVR, with its trestles and tunnel bridges, drew 50,000 visitors a year, even before the publicity generated by forest fire damage to the trestles in 2003. Now that the area has been re-opened, trail officials expect visitor numbers to double.

Myra Canyon exemplifies the challenges of routing a railway through mountainous terrain in the early 1900s, and it's been designated a national historic site. The original trestle bridges were constructed with Douglas fir. The two bridges that span the longest gaps in the canyon were eventually replaced with steel structures, but the others, as they deteriorated, were rebuilt with wood.

When the trains stopped running, the Myra Canyon became a popular hiking and cycling trip, although not a particularly safe one, until a group of volunteers (who formed the Myra Canyon Trestle Restoration Society) raised money for repairs and maintenance. The group put decks and guard rails on all 18 trestles and added interpretive signs, transforming this stretch of the KVR into a highlight.

But in 2003, a forest fire roared through the canyon, claiming 12 trestles and the decks of two steel trestles. Again, volunteers rallied, and with a C$17.5 million contribution from federal and provincial governments, the trestles were rebuilt.

Take Me to the Canyon

If you like the notion of letting somebody else handle logistics, consider a Myra Canyon tour. Kelowna-based **Monashee Adventure Tours** (1591 Highland Dr.; ✆ **888/762-9253** or 250/762-9253; www.monasheeadventuretours.com) offers a multitude of hiking and cycling trips on the KVR, ranging in duration from a few hours to a week. The most popular hiking trip to Myra Canyon is the 10km (6¼-mile) round-trip hike from the east end of the canyon. Prices range from about C$60 per person for the guided trip with transportation to C$120 for a trip that includes a pub or winery lunch. The company also runs sunset tours of the canyon. If you're hiking the canyon on your own, Monashee will provide transportation between Ruth Station and Myra Station. The cost is C$150 (minimum) for up to five people and C$30 for each additional person.

with Trestle 6 in the southwest corner, was originally built with wood but eventually replaced with steel. Trestle 6, at 220m (722 ft.), is both the longest and tallest bridge in the canyon. While these two massive steel bridges both survived the flames in 2003, their boardwalks and handrails had to be replaced.

❹ Smallest Trestle The trail sweeps around the southern end of the canyon, towering above KLO Creek, and farther along, crossing Pooley Creek. (If you think views across the canyon are dizzying today, from the vantage point of solid bridges, imagine hiking or cycling here before the railway bed was fitted with guard rails and boardwalks.) Just past the curved steel bridge over Pooley Creek, you'll arrive at the 23m-long (76-ft.) **Trestle 5,** a good vantage point from which to survey the route you've just traveled and a convenient spot to turn back.

The trail continues for about 6km (3¾ miles) to a parking area at Ruth Station, just beyond the first trestle. If you do decide to walk the whole route, keep an eye out for a dome-shaped stone structure to the left of the trail between trestle 1 and Ruth Station. It's a "rock oven" that was used by Italian stonemasons who helped build the railway. See "Take Me to the Canyon," above, for information on arranging transportation from Ruth Station back to Myra Station.

3 KNOX MOUNTAIN PARK APEX TRAIL

Difficulty rating: Moderate

Distance: 5.5km (3.4 miles) round trip

Estimated time: 2 hr.

Elevation gain: 250m (820 ft.)

Costs/permits: None

Best time to go: Wildflowers are spectacular in May and June. (Park is closed to vehicle traffic mid-Nov to mid-Mar.)

Website: www.knoxmountainpark.com

Recommended map: A trail map is posted in the parking area.

Trail head GPS: N 49 54.195, W 119 29.265

Trail head directions: Knox Mountain is just north of downtown Kelowna. Follow Ellis St. to the parking lot at the park entrance.

Knox Mountain Park Apex Trail

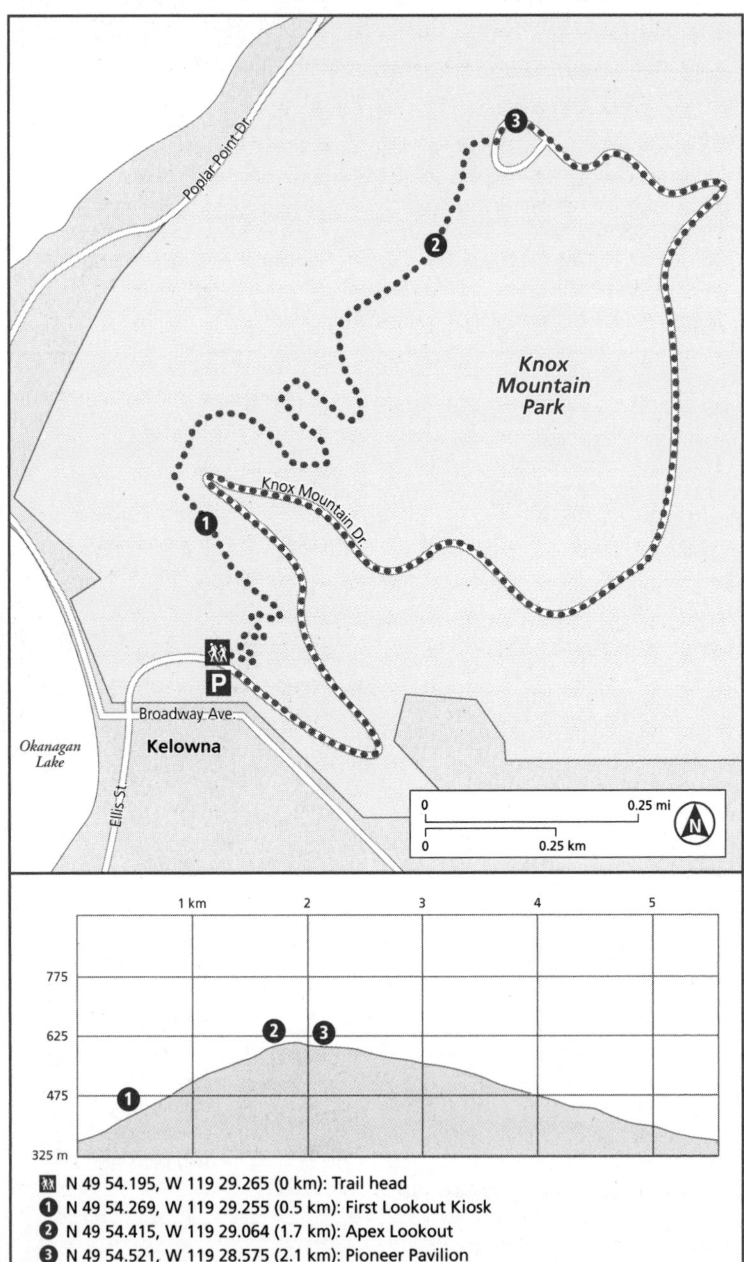

N 49 54.195, W 119 29.265 (0 km): Trail head
1 N 49 54.269, W 119 29.255 (0.5 km): First Lookout Kiosk
2 N 49 54.415, W 119 29.064 (1.7 km): Apex Lookout
3 N 49 54.521, W 119 28.575 (2.1 km): Pioneer Pavilion

Who needs the gym when you have Knox Mountain? Proximity to downtown makes this 250-hectare (618-acre) nature park a favorite with Kelowna runners, cyclists, and other fitness buffs. On the short, steep trail to the summit of Knox Mountain, you get your morning workout and can meditate on the lake views in the span of a couple of hours. (Not that it would be hard to justify a more leisurely stay on the mountain, especially in spring, when Indian paintbrush and arrowleaf balsamroot splash color across the slopes.)

The trail starts just above the main parking lot, where a sandy path kicks off to the left of the paved road and climbs above Okanagan Lake through grasslands dotted with sage and saskatoons.

❶ **First Lookout Kiosk** The path winds through a smattering of Ponderosa Pines and then pitches up to a level spot with a second parking area and the first lookout kiosk. Gaze out across Okanagan Lake and south to downtown Kelowna and the William R. Bennett Bridge, which connects Kelowna and Westbank. The trail continues from the other end of the parking lot. After passing the turnoff to the Paul's Tomb trail, which branches to the left, you'll cross an open slope that's littered with wildflowers in spring. Now and again, the trail slips into a shady patch of pines, and higher up, it winds through Douglas fir. The final stretch to the summit will quicken your heart rate.

❷ **Apex Lookout** On a scorching day, you'll appreciate the cool shade of the second wooden pavilion, the Apex Lookout, located at the summit of Knox Mountain. This is also an impressive vantage point from which to survey the city and its surroundings. Okanagan Lake stretches to the north; Bear Creek is to the west, across the lake; and Mount Boucherie juts up in the south, behind the bridge. Watch for deer as you explore the area around the summit.

❸ **Pioneer Pavilion** Just steps from the lookout, a path winds down to the park warden's residence and the 325-sq.-m (3,500-sq.-ft.) **Pioneer Pavilion,** which houses park interpretive signs. There's a water fountain here, along with a dog water station. When you're ready to turn back, either retrace your steps down to the parking lot or follow the paved road, which is less steep but will take a few minutes longer.

Tips Wildflowers & Wine

Dozens of wildflowers bloom in Knox Mountain Park, from sagebrush buttercup, yellow bell, and lemonweed in April to columbine and wild rose in July. May and June are exceptionally colorful, with purple penstemmon and lupins, white daisies, and yellow brown-eyed Susans. To really get acquainted with the native plants, you may want to consider a guided hike. **Distinctly Kelowna Tours** (✆ **866/979-1211** or 250/979-1211; www.wildflowersandwine.com) offers trips to Knox Mountain (opt for an easy or moderate trail) as part of a hike and winery tour day trip. The 7-hour trip, C$139 per person, includes a morning hike, lunch at a winery restaurant, and an afternoon tour of Kelowna-area wineries. The company picks you up at your hotel and provides water, an energy bar, and hiking poles.

4 STAVE PIPE TRAIL TO PINCUSHION MOUNTAIN

Difficulty rating: Moderate

Distance: 8.4km (5.2 miles) round trip

Estimated time: 4 hr.

Elevation gain: 442m (1,450 ft.)

Costs/permits: None

Best time to go: June or Sept to avoid midsummer heat.

Website: None

Recommended map: Pick up a trail map from the visitor center on the Peachland waterfront (5812 Beach Ave.).

Trail head GPS: N 49 47.096, W 119 43.055

Trail head directions: In Peachland, turn west off Hwy. 97 onto Clements Crescent (beside the Peachland Centre Mall). Follow Clements Crescent to the Peachland Elementary School. The trail starts near the southeast corner of the schoolyard. Look for an orange, peach-shaped marker on a tree, just outside (to the left of) the schoolyard fence.

Just a short drive from Peachland's waterfront (which is worth a stroll in itself), this user-friendly trail disappears into a forest, crawls above a canyon, and emerges on the summit of Pincushion Mountain. Along the way, step into the shade of Ponderosa Pines, drop by a waterfall, and nose around on neighboring trails. Choose a clear day; dramatic lake views await you at the top.

The hike starts on the Stave Pipe Trail, which follows a fence along the southern edge of the schoolyard and moseys into a coniferous forest above Trepanier Creek. (In the early 1900s, water from Trepanier Creek was delivered to Peachland in "stave pipes," made from thin strips of wood bound together by wire.) This trail and two connecting routes are maintained by members of the local Volkssport Club, who also installed the trail-markers. The routes are numbered, color-coded (orange #1 markers on the Stave Pipe Trail), and a cinch to follow.

❶ Settling Reservoir A narrow, sand and gravel path climbs through pine and fir trees for about 5 minutes before leveling out near a concrete tank that was once used as a settling reservoir for drinking water from Trepanier Creek.

❷ Waterfall Viewing Spot Beyond the reservoir, a level trail runs high above the Trepanier Creek canyon, offering glimpses of Okanagan Lake and Okanagan Mountain Park to the east. About 100m (328 ft.) past the reservoir, the trail meanders over to a viewing spot near the edge of the canyon where you can watch

Fun Facts **Trepanation on the Trepanier**

Trepanier Creek reportedly takes its name from a primitive surgical procedure (a trepanation) that involved cutting a hole in the skull with a cylindrical saw (a trepan). A fur-trader performed the surgery here in 1817, historical records indicate. The patient was a Shuswap chief named Short Legs who had been wounded in the head by a bear and required relief from swelling of the brain.

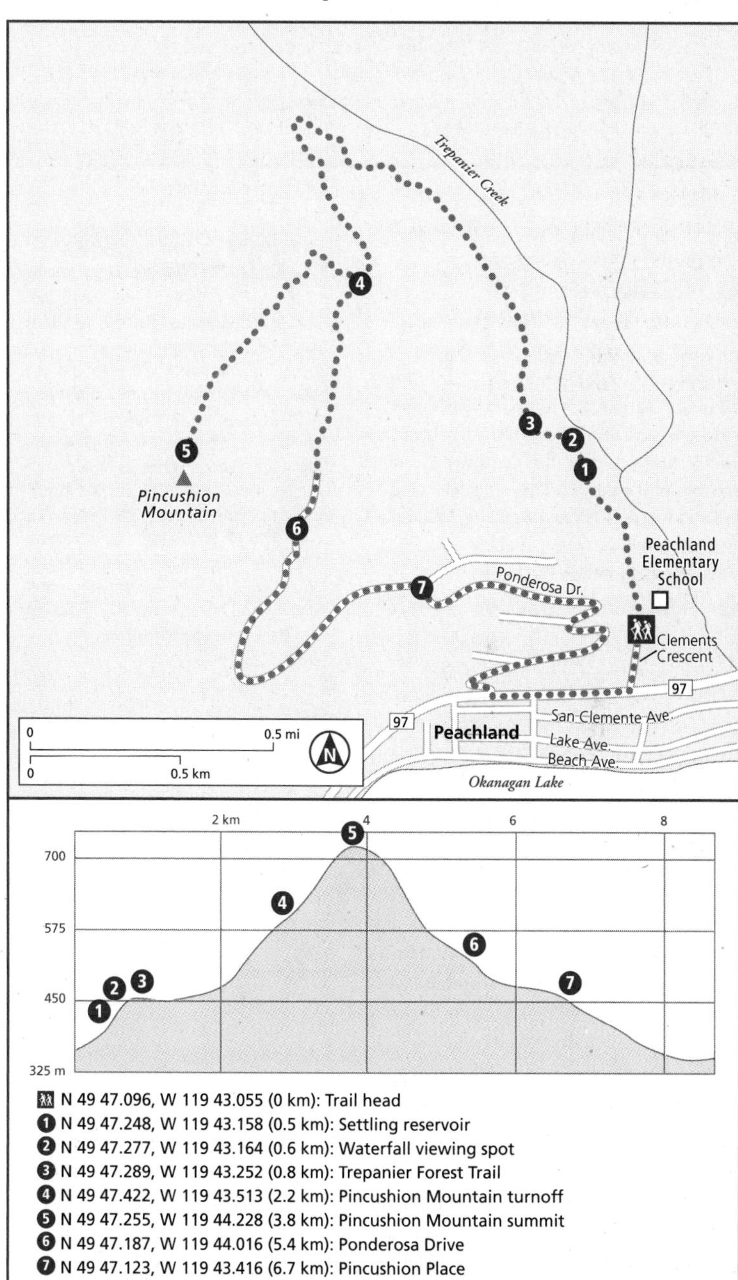
Trepanier Creek
Pincushion Mountain
Peachland Elementary School
Ponderosa Dr.
Clements Crescent
97
San Clemente Ave.
Peachland
Lake Ave.
Beach Ave.
Okanagan Lake
0 0.5 mi
0 0.5 km
N
2 km
4
6
8
700
575
450
325 m
N 49 47.096, W 119 43.055 (0 km): Trail head
1 N 49 47.248, W 119 43.158 (0.5 km): Settling reservoir
2 N 49 47.277, W 119 43.164 (0.6 km): Waterfall viewing spot
3 N 49 47.289, W 119 43.252 (0.8 km): Trepanier Forest Trail
4 N 49 47.422, W 119 43.513 (2.2 km): Pincushion Mountain turnoff
5 N 49 47.255, W 119 44.228 (3.8 km): Pincushion Mountain summit
6 N 49 47.187, W 119 44.016 (5.4 km): Ponderosa Drive
7 N 49 47.123, W 119 43.416 (6.7 km): Pincushion Place

Fun Facts Lights Out, Everyone

In 1909, a dam was built on Trepanier Creek to supply hydroelectric power to Peachland. The power plant operated for several decades, although water flow from the creek proved scanty; it's said that power users had to turn the lights out at midnight while the dam refilled.

the creek cascading over a wall of rock. (You'll hear it before you see it.)

3 Trepanier Forest Trail Continue uphill on the Stave Pipe Trail, which ascends through the pine trees. Notice the rock piles on the slopes to your left—possibly the remnants of a glacier that moved through the valley. Just ahead, you'll come to an intersection, called Hermit's Crossing on trail maps (there's a little lean-to beside the trail). Take a right at the intersection, onto the Trepanier Forest Trail, and follow the yellow #2 markers.

4 Pincushion Mountain Turnoff The first 1.5km (1-mile) stretch of the Trepanier Forest Trail loops through the woods along the edge of a gully and dips down to a junction with a forestry road. Turn left at the forestry road, head uphill, and follow the boulder-strewn path. You'll climb for about 15 minutes and gain around 100m (328 ft.) to reach the turnoff to the Pincushion Mountain Trail (red #3 markers). Take a water break while you take in the lake views.

5 Pincushion Mountain Summit It's just over a kilometer (a little more than 1/2 mile) to the summit of Pincushion Mountain. This is the only leg of the hike where you really have to work; the climb gets considerably steeper. A rocky path, scattered with scraggly, crawling junipers, wriggles between boulders and skirts across flat slabs of rock. Lake views catch your attention as you ascend. And, just when you're convinced the summit is around the bend . . . well, keep on walking.

TAKE A BREAK
Sheltered areas among the pine trees and rocks at the summit of Pincushion Mountain provide ideal spots for lunch, high above the Peachland waterfront. If you believe in lake monsters, this might be a good perspective from which to scan Okanagan Lake for a sign of Ogopogo. While the famous serpent-shaped creature has reportedly been sighted in various parts of the lake, its home base is said to be around Rattlesnake Island, directly across from Peachland. At any rate, the big-screen lake view, northeast toward Kelowna and southeast to Naramata and Penticton, is compelling on its own.

From the summit, a short trail to your right winds down to another viewpoint. Although the flag was missing when we hiked this trail, the pole at the viewpoint usually bears the Canadian flag. You can see it from the golf course below.

6 Ponderosa Drive From the summit, head back to the Pincushion Trail turnoff and take the trail to your right. This short section (about .5km/1/4 mile) is part of both the Pincushion and Trepanier Forest trail systems, so you'll spot both red and yellow markers on the trees. The trail, along a logging road, rolls across a grassy area through patches of tall pines. You'll pass a fork in the road, but continue straight ahead to a gate at the edge of a subdivision and out to Ponderosa Drive.

❼ **Pincushion Place** This route back to the trail head, through a residential area, loops around the Ponderosa Golf Course. When you reach Pincushion Place, at the corner of Ponderosa Drive and 6th Avenue, you have an option to detour back into the wooded area and follow the Stave Pipe Trail to Hermit's Crossing and down to the trail head. It's about a 2km (1¼-mile) walk. Otherwise, Ponderosa Drive winds down to Hwy. 97. It's a noisy (but very short) walk along the busy highway back to the Peachland Shopping Center, just a half-kilometer (¼ mile) to the north.

5 KETTLE VALLEY RAILWAY: PENTICTON TO NARAMATA

Difficulty rating: Easy

Distance: 10km (6.2 miles) round trip

Estimated time: 2 hr.

Elevation gain: 60m (197 ft.)

Costs/permits: None

Best time to go: In June or Sept, enjoy a patio lunch (without the sizzling heat of mid-summer).

Website: None

Recommended map: Maps of downtown Penticton and the KVR trail are available from the visitor center in Penticton.

Trail head GPS: N 49 30.114, W 119 34.572

Trail head directions: From the north end of Main St. in Penticton, follow Front St. to the parking lot next to Okanagan Lake. The trail head is about a 5-minute walk up Vancouver Ave., past the Penticton Community Gardens. Turn left at Vancouver Place.

Part urban stroll, part wine-county ramble, this gentle stretch of the KVR slips out of Penticton and crawls into the hills above Naramata. Views of Okanagan Lake are magnificent from many points on the trail, which crosses a historic trestle bridge, runs through vineyards and orchards, and leads practically to the front door of a winery restaurant.

The hike starts in a quiet neighborhood and quickly winds into an open area along the edge of the bluffs overlooking the lake. It's easy to tell you're in one of Canada's hot spots; sage, rabbit brush, and other desert-loving shrubs line the path. Notice the bluebird houses by the side of the trail, compliments of the Southern Interior Bluebird Society.

❶ **Lakeview Cemetery** A broad, flat trail, popular with runners and cyclists,

Tips Onward Bound

Beyond Hillside Estates, this scenic stretch of the KVR runs above the Naramata Bench for nearly 12km (7½ miles) to Little Tunnel, the first of two tunnels cut through the rock, just above the village of Naramata. From here, the trail climbs to Chute Lake and heads north to the Myra Canyon near Kelowna. See p. 196 for a description of the Myra Canyon hike.

Kettle Valley Railway: Penticton to Naramata

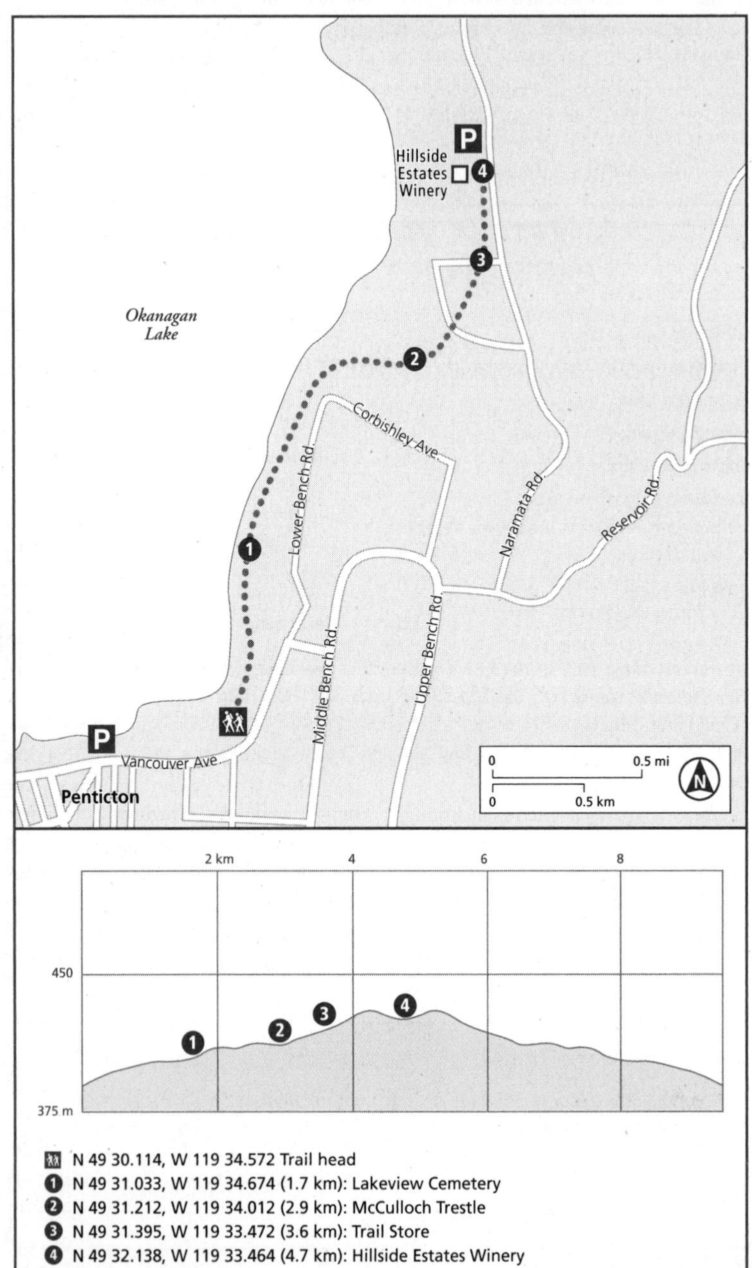

N 49 30.114, W 119 34.572 Trail head

❶ N 49 31.033, W 119 34.674 (1.7 km): Lakeview Cemetery

❷ N 49 31.212, W 119 34.012 (2.9 km): McCulloch Trestle

❸ N 49 31.395, W 119 33.472 (3.6 km): Trail Store

❹ N 49 32.138, W 119 33.464 (4.7 km): Hillside Estates Winery

Fun Facts KVR: A Wonder of Trestles & Tunnels

The Kettle Valley Railway, built in the early 1900s to connect mining centers in the Kootenay region of southeastern BC with the West Coast, climbed, dipped, and curved through a mountainous, 500km (311-mile) stretch of the province's Southern Interior. To cross this rugged terrain, railway builders devised elaborate bridges, trestles, and tunnels. The KVR was considered an engineering marvel and referred to as "McCulloch's Wonder," after Andrew McCulloch, the chief engineer.

Beginning in the 1960s, with competition from new highways, the Canadian Pacific Railway phased out service on the KVR line and removed most of the rails. The corridor was converted to a recreational trail.

Today, the former railway route is part of both the TransCanada Trail and BC's Spirit of 2010 network of trails on abandoned rail lines. The KVR is a classic multiday cycling trip. Some sections—such as the route through Naramata wine country and the stretch through the Myra Canyon near Kelowna—also make for easy walks through spectacular settings.

runs for about 1km (1/2 mile) to the **Lakeview Cemetery,** which dates to the early 1900s and is the burial place of Andrew McCulloch, chief engineer on the Kettle Valley Railway, who died in 1945. As you approach the cemetery, Munson Mountain is visible to the east. (Look for the word "Penticton" in big concrete letters.)

2 McCulloch Trestle Beyond the cemetery, the trail rolls along between two blocks of grapevines, offering increasingly impressive views of the lake and area vineyards. The silver-roofed, tan-and-gold building in the background (at the base of a hill) as you approach the **McCulloch Trestle** is Red Rooster winery. The trestle bridge, which spans an 86m (282-ft.) gully, was built in 2002 in a style similar to that of the original trestles on the KVR.

3 Trail Store Beyond the bridge, the trail skirts past vineyards and orchards for about half a kilometer (1/4 mile) to the tiny **Trail, Fruit and More Store.** Owned by a local orchardist, the store sells fresh, in-season fruit (cherries, peaches, plums, and apples). You can buy ice-cream and cold drinks in hot weather and, later in the season, apple pie, muffins, and coffee. The Trail Store is usually open from about 11am to 5pm, May through October. This section of the path parallels Naramata Road, which links Penticton with the village of Naramata. You'll cross three side roads and reach a parking lot on Poplar Grove Road.

4 Hillside Estates Winery From the parking lot, the trail continues on the opposite side of the highway, climbing a short slope to **Hillside Estate Winery,** where you can savor the scenery while you sample the wine. The winery bistro, with patios on two levels, offers commanding views of Okanagan Lake and the Naramata Bench. It's open daily for both lunch (11:30am–3pm) and dinner (6–9pm), and serves wraps (try the Mediterranean, with grilled vegetables and Okanagan goat cheese) and other casual items, along with fancier fare. The Hillside Estate wine tasting room is open daily, 10am to 6pm. After your winery visit, retrace your steps along the trail to Penticton to complete the 10m (6 1/4-mile) hike.

Tips **Hiking in the Heat?**

The park benches under the oak trees at the edge of the Lakeview Cemetery, overlooking the lake, are about the only spots on this hike to find shade.

6 GOLDEN MILE TRAIL

Difficulty rating: Easy

Distance: 8.5km (5.3 miles) round trip

Estimated time: 3 hr.

Elevation gain: 180m (591 ft.)

Costs/permits: None

Best time to go: In early Oct, catch local and regional grape harvest and wine festival events.

Website: www.hellobc.com/en-CA/SightsActivitiesEvents/Oliver.htm

Recommended map: Trail maps are available from the Oliver Visitor Centre (36205 93rd St.)

Trail head GPS: N 49 09.043, W 119 35.336

Trail head directions: From Hwy. 97 south of Oliver, turn right on Rd 7 and follow Tinhorn Creek Rd. to the Tinhorn Creek Winery. Park by the winery and follow signs to the Golden Mile trail.

Climb into the hills above the west bench of the Okanagan River Valley and wander through a sagebrush meadow while you gaze down on wine country. Many points on this trail offer exceptional views of the south Okanagan, from the town of Oliver to Osoyoos Lake. What's more, the trip starts (and ends) at a winery: Tinhorn Creek.

A well-marked route begins in the vineyard, following a gravel lane past rows of Pinot Gris, Kerner, and Merlot. In about 10 minutes, you'll reach a native plant restoration area and a low, mesh fence, installed to keep snakes out of the vineyard. Just ahead, a gate in a deer fence (be sure to close the gate behind you) leads to an open area beside a dry creek bed (Tinhorn Creek).

❶ Top of the Ridge A short, moderately steep path winds to the **top of a ridge,** from which you can look out over the vineyards of Tinhorn Creek and its winery neighbors, Hester Creek and Gehringer Brothers. This is the top of the Golden Mile stretch of prime grape-growing land in the Okanagan. The Oliver area, which also includes the Black Sage Bench across the valley, produces nearly 40 percent of the province's wine grapes. In particular, you'll see many plantings of Merlot, Chardonnay, Pinot Gris, Cabernet Sauvignon, and Sauvignon Blanc.

❷ Stamp Mill After you catch your breath, turn off the Golden Mile trail to your left and follow the sign to the **Stamp Mill,** a half-kilometer (¼ mile) wander down the path. In the early 1800s, this part of the valley gained brief celebrity as a gold mining center. Prospectors staked numerous claims (Stemwinder, Morning Star, and Rattler, to name a few) in the hills above Oliver. The trail winds down to a crumbling stone wall, which is all that remains of a century-old stamp mill where gold-bearing ore was pulverized before being sent to smelters. From here, retrace your steps back to the Golden Mile trail.

❸ Viewpoint An easy-to-follow path dips through a cluster of pine trees, rolls

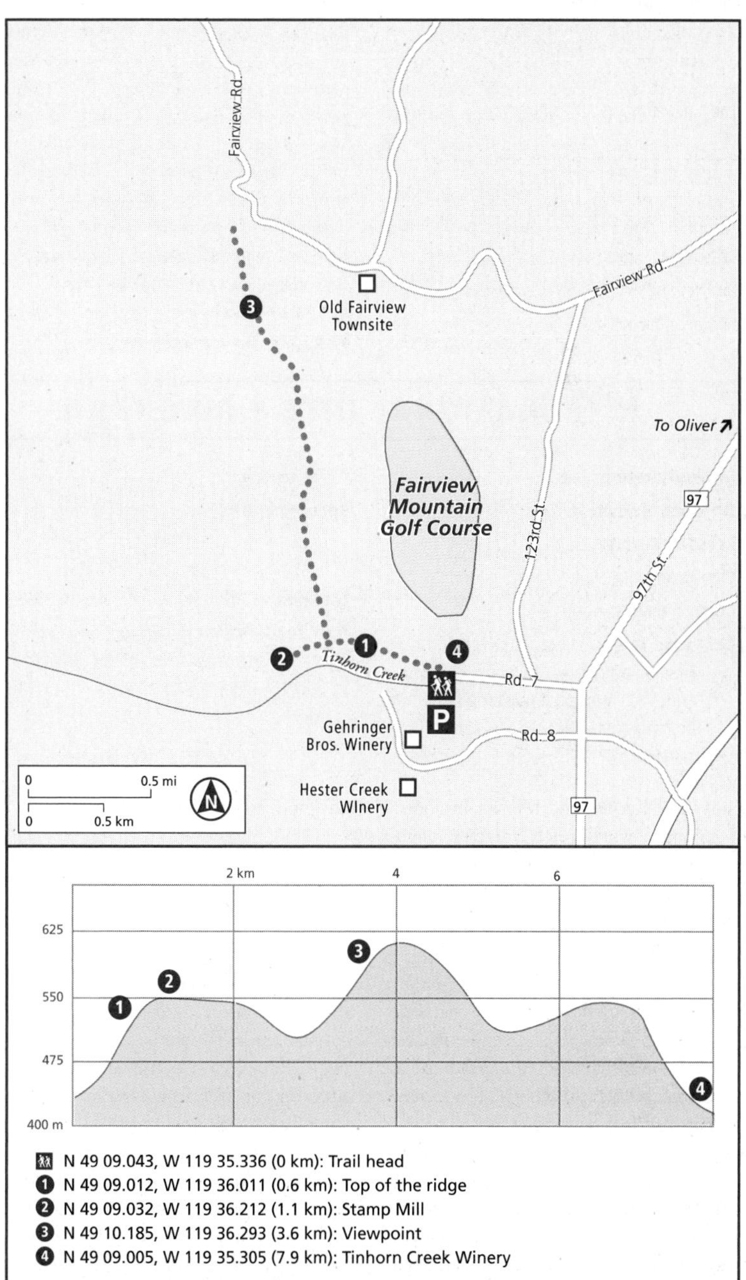

N 49 09.043, W 119 35.336 (0 km): Trail head

❶ N 49 09.012, W 119 36.011 (0.6 km): Top of the ridge

❷ N 49 09.032, W 119 36.212 (1.1 km): Stamp Mill

❸ N 49 10.185, W 119 36.293 (3.6 km): Viewpoint

❹ N 49 09.005, W 119 35.305 (7.9 km): Tinhorn Creek Winery

across a wide meadow where cattle graze, and after about 2.5km (1½ miles), reaches a vantage point with a commanding view. You can see the outskirts of Oliver to the north, Mount Baldy to the west, and Osoyoos Lake in the south. The greens of the Fairview Mountain Golf Course sweep across the lower slopes, near the historic site of Fairview, an early-1900s gold-mining town that predates the town of Oliver. In spring, balsam root and sagebrush buttercups cover the slopes with patches of yellow.

4 Tinhorn Creek Winery Turn around at the gate in the fence and follow the trail back down to **Tinhorn Creek.** You can check out the winery and vineyards on a self-guided tour. The tasting room is open daily from 10am to 6pm, and you can buy wine and picnic items for a patio lunch. At press time, Tinhorn had also announced plans to open an onsite restaurant. A partnership with Manuel Ferreira, owner of Le Gavroche Restaurant in Vancouver, the new eatery will be located above Tinhorn's existing barrel cellar and is slated to open summer 2009.

7 INTERNATIONAL HIKE & BIKE TRAIL

Difficulty rating: Easy

Distance: 11km (6.8 miles) round trip

Estimated time: 2½ hr.

Elevation gain: None

Costs/permits: None

Best time to go: The Meadowlark Festival (www.meadowlarkfestival.bc.ca), held annually in May, hosts dozens of birding and naturalist events in the South Okanagan.

Website: None

Recommended map: There's a map on a sign near the trail head—it's nearly impossible to get lost on this route.

Trail head GPS: N 49 05.192, W 119 32.081

Trail head directions: From Hwy. 97 south of Oliver, turn east on Rd. 22, drive 1km (½ mile), and park in the lot on the right.

You needn't break a sweat on this hike; exertion isn't the point. This tranquil stretch of the south Okanagan is a place to meditate and unwind. A level trail along the Okanagan River canal, past small farms and orchards, offers views of vineyards and opportunities to spot wildlife, plus a meander through one of the best birding spots in the valley.

Interpretive signs in a kiosk at the edge of the parking lot describe the desert-like environment in this corner of the South Okanagan. From the parking lot, walk toward the bridge and turn left onto the hike and bike path. The trail, a maintenance road for the canal (on both sides of the river) is more akin to a country lane than a backcountry trail. It's closed to general traffic, although you may pass the occasional farm truck delivering a load of hay. As you make your way along the trail, highway sounds soon fade against a melody of bird calls.

1 Road 18 The region between Oliver and Osoyoos is prime grape-growing country, home to 20 wineries (at last count), with vineyards clustered along Hwy. 97, in an area called the Golden Mile on the west side of the river and along Black Sage Road on the east side.

As you head north, views open of wineries and vineyards on the higher benches. The prominent, golden-hued winery beaming down on the valley from a 57-hectare (140-acre) vineyard on the west bench is Burrowing Owl Estate Winery. Just to the north is Desert Hills Estate

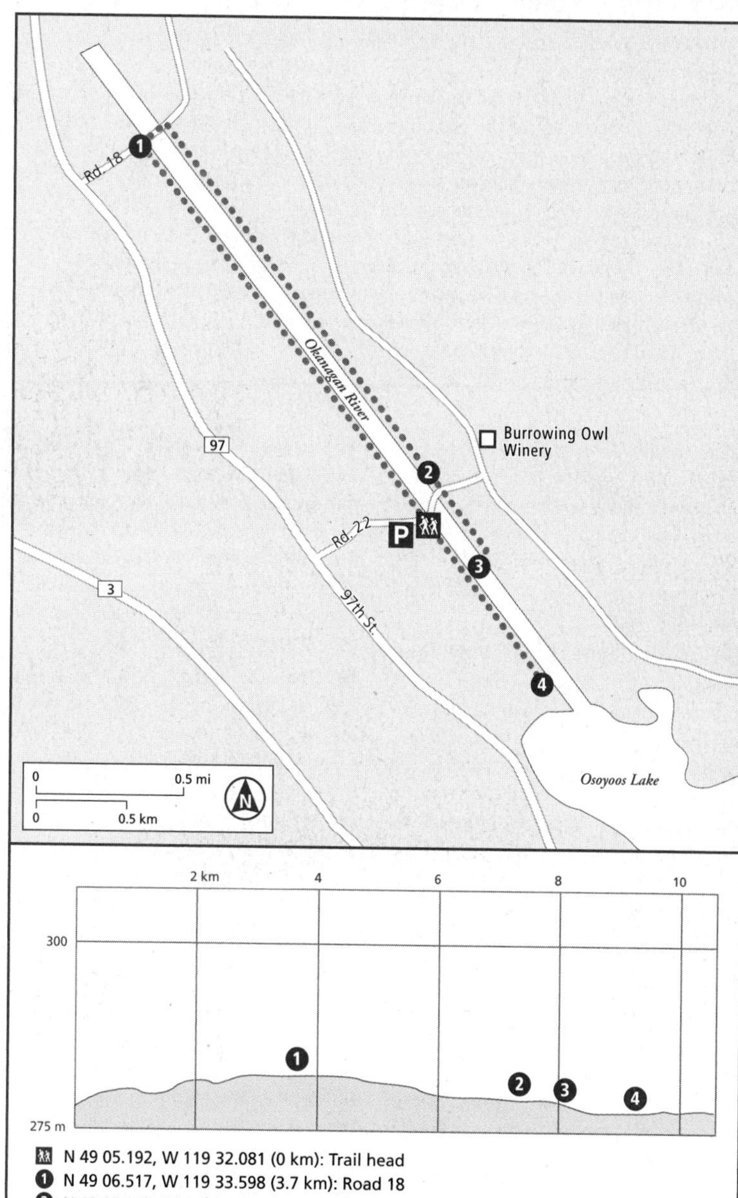

🚶 N 49 05.192, W 119 32.081 (0 km): Trail head
❶ N 49 06.517, W 119 33.598 (3.7 km): Road 18
❷ N 49 05.243, W 119 32.087 (7.5 km): Historic Haynes Ranch Viewpoint
❸ N 49 05.092, W 119 31.491 (8.1 km): Pedestrian Bridge
❹ N 49 04.426, W 119 31.178 (9.2 km): Osoyoos Lake

Fun Facts Restoring the Run of the River

The Osoyoos oxbows around the southern end of the Okanagan River support an enormous variety of bird species and provide spawning grounds for sockeye salmon. Considerable natural wetland habitat in this area, however, was destroyed when the river was straightened and diked for flood control in the 1950s. At press time, work was underway to restore a 1km (1/2-mile) section of the river north of the town of Oliver to its natural course. The project, a joint effort between the provincial government and conservation groups, involves moving back dikes so the river can meander, and planting wetland trees such as cottonwoods and willows. The goal is to provide habitat for salmon and trout along with plants, animals, and birds, many of which are rare or endangered. The hike and bike trail through this 1km (1/2-mile) area, to be closed during construction, was slated to re-open early in 2009.

Winery (tan-colored with a red roof), and farther along, past the pedestrian bridge, you'll see a modern, flat-roofed concrete winery, built recently by Black Hills Estate Winery. When you arrive at **Road 18,** cross the bridge and loop back on the east side of the river.

2 Historic Haynes Ranch Viewpoint Spring through fall, when vineyards are in leaf, lush green hillsides dominate the scenery. But besides looking up, be sure to look around. You're bound to spot wildlife on this trail, especially if you get an early start. In our morning rambles along the riverbank, we've watched deer bounce through the fields, painted turtles saunter across the path, and great blue herons leap off the side of the bridge. We've seen coyotes, bull snakes, beavers, and yellow-bellied marmots. In the fall, you'll also see spawning salmon. Just before you approach Road 22, you'll notice, to the left, a couple of poetically dilapidated, long-abandoned farm buildings. That's the site of Haynes Ranch, one of the original ranches in this area (and one of the most frequently photographed settings in rural Oliver). It's been uninhabited since the 1960s (unless you count the current residents: long-eared bats). The land around the historic ranch is a protected area and ecological reserve.

3 Pedestrian Bridge Cross Road 22 and keep heading south. Here, the path runs past clusters of wild rose and sumac. When you reach the pedestrian bridge, cross to the west side of the river. In October, you're apt to see salmon—primarily sockeye—returning from the Pacific Ocean to their spawning grounds in the Okanagan River.

4 Osoyoos Lake Before you head back to the parking lot, detour down to the head of Osoyoos Lake (half-hour, round trip). The oxbows and wetlands in this area support about 200 different species of birds, some of which are endangered. Birders come here from around the world. Not that you need to know a blackbird from a bobolink to appreciate the beauty of this place; stop anywhere and listen to the whistles, twitters, and twills. Among the more colorful birds to watch for: Bullock's oriole (orange and black) and the flashy yellow American goldfinch. The Northern shrike, known for its habit of impaling other birds on barbed wire or sharp weeds, winters here, and the Downy woodpecker (Canada's smallest woodpecker) is in the area all year. And the nearby meadows are considered the best nesting ground in Canada for the bobolink, a migratory bird named for its distinctive bubbly song.

8 GIANT CLEFT & THE RIM TRAIL VIA LADYSLIPPER LAKE, CATHEDRAL PROVINCIAL PARK ★★★

Difficulty rating: Strenuous

Distance: 12km (7.5 miles) round trip

Estimated time: 8 hr.

Elevation gain: 490m (1,608 ft.)

Costs/permits: Transportation to the lodge and main hiking area from Cathedral Park base camp: July 1 to Sept 4, C$120 per person, round-trip; other months, C$90 per person, round-trip. No charge to hike to the lodge. Camping fee: C$5 per person per night. Lodge accommodation for 2 nights in high season: C$490 per person, including meals and transportation.

Pet friendly: No

Best time to go: Weather is nicest and wildflowers are showiest in July and Aug.

Website: www.env.gov.bc.ca/bcparks/explore/parkpgs/cathedral; www.cathedral-lakes-lodge.com

Recommended map: 92H1

Trail head GPS: N 49 03.519, W 120 11.469

Trail head directions: Follow Hwy. 3 through the Similkameen Valley to the town of Keremeos, drive west for 3km (1¾ miles), turn left at the Cathedral Lakes sign, and cross the red bridge. It's about a 20-minute drive (21km/13 miles) through the Ashnola Valley to the Cathedral Provincial Park base camp, where jeeps depart for the lodge and trail heads.

Believe the rave reviews: This trip is a blast (even before you get to the trail head). Hop in a jeep and rattle up a rough road to a lakeshore in the wilderness. Hit the trail and hike to a lofty ridge. Wind your way through a lunar-like landscape of bizarre rock formations ringed by summits topped with snow. And there's more: abundant wildflowers in summer, golden larches in fall, and photo-friendly mountain goats any time.

❶ Cathedral Lakes Lodge Cathedral Provincial Park protects a chain of seven lakes in a 32,376-hectare (80,000-acre) wilderness area between the Okanagan and the North Cascade mountains. Within the provincial park, a guest lodge and five cabins are privately operated. The comfortably rustic white stucco lodge houses six guestrooms on the second level and a dining area and lounge with a stone fireplace on the main floor. If you're on a day trip, you can stop at the lodge before your hike to pick up lunch ingredients, or if you prefer, return for a lodge lunch.

❷ Pyramid Lake In front of the lodge, near the east end of Quiniscoe Lake, follow the path past the ranger station and watch for a sign to Pyramid Lake. In a dramatic change from the desert-like climate on the valley floor, this trail leads you through a cool, lush setting. A boulder-strewn path winds through the trees and past patches of lupines for about 30 minutes before dipping gently and then climbing to the shores of Pyramid Lake.

❸ Ladyslipper Lake The trail continues past the lake, ascending through a spruce and larch forest on a needle-covered path. Potentilla flowers add splashes of bright yellow to the rocky terrain. On our trip, we came eyeball-to-eyeball with a kid goat and its mother on this stretch of the trail. They eyed us curiously, posed for photos, and ambled down a rocky slope. The trail climbs above the trees where cairns mark the route across the top of a

Tips: Follow Your Inner Girl Scout

It may be 40°C (104°F) outside your hotel in the south Okanagan, but count on chilly weather on the trails above Cathedral Lakes Lodge. When you pack, bear in mind that you'll likely be peeling off your fleece on the first leg of the hike and reaching for a windbreaker on the high ridges. Gloves may come in handy, too.

slope to the edge of a meadow. You'll have ample opportunity to gaze down on Ladyslipper Lake before the trail drops to the shoreline of the emerald green beauty, which is considered the top spot in the area to fish for rainbow trout.

❹ Top of the Ridge Beyond the lake, the trail descends and then climbs again through a stony landscape, where hostas and wildflowers brighten moss-covered slopes. A trail of fine sand winds between larch trees and giant slabs of smooth rock. The going gets tougher here as you climb 370m (1,214 ft.) above the lake and catch your first sight of the rock formations on the ridge. You also get a hint of the scenery to come: Boulders litter the path, like pebbles tossed from a giant's hand. Above the tree line, the path levels and then climbs steadily again. Stellar views of Ladyslipper Lake deliver inspiration as you scramble up the final steep leg, over loose rock, to the Rim Trail and Stone City, a cluster of sculpted, wind-eroded rocks. The Rim Trail runs along the top of the ridge.

SPECTACULAR LOOKOUT
On a clear day, the top-of-the-world view from the top of the ridge will leave you breathless. What's more, you get to enjoy it from various vantage points as you travel this 2,500m-high (8,202-ft.) trail. You're ringed by mountains: Mount Baker and the North Cascades to the south and west, the Coast Range to the north-west, and the Monashees in the east.

❺ Smokey the Bear Before looping back to the lodge along the lofty Rim Trail, you'll want a couple of hours (round trip) to detour to two of the unique geological formations for which this park is renowned. A sign to your left points the way to Smokey the Bear, a mammoth rock that resembles—from some angles—the famous protector of American forests. The drop from the ridge is dizzyingly straight. Flat rocks and sheltered areas near Smokey make ideal spots for your lunch break.

❻ Giant Cleft On the next stretch of the trail, you waltz across an unworldly landscape of boulders, black with lichen, ringed by snow-capped peaks for about 300m (984 ft.), then scramble down through the rocks for an up-close view of a skyscraping split in the mountain, formed by erosion, and known as the Giant Cleft. After you pose for photos, turn around and wind your way back to the junction of the Lady Slipper Trail and the ridge.

❼ Devil's Wood Pile Cairns mark a path that swings to the left away from the ridge and through Stone City. From here, you climb about 700m (2,297 ft.) to the Devil's Wood Pile (so-called because it's been described as the ingredients for Satan's furnace), broken rock that looks as though it's been whipped into towers. An easy-going stretch of trail winds along the ridge, dropping through rock piles and rolling across slopes.

❽ Glacier Lake Trail Turnoff About an hour's walk (from the intersection with

Giant Cleft & the Rim Trail via Ladyslipper Lake, Cathedral Provincial Park

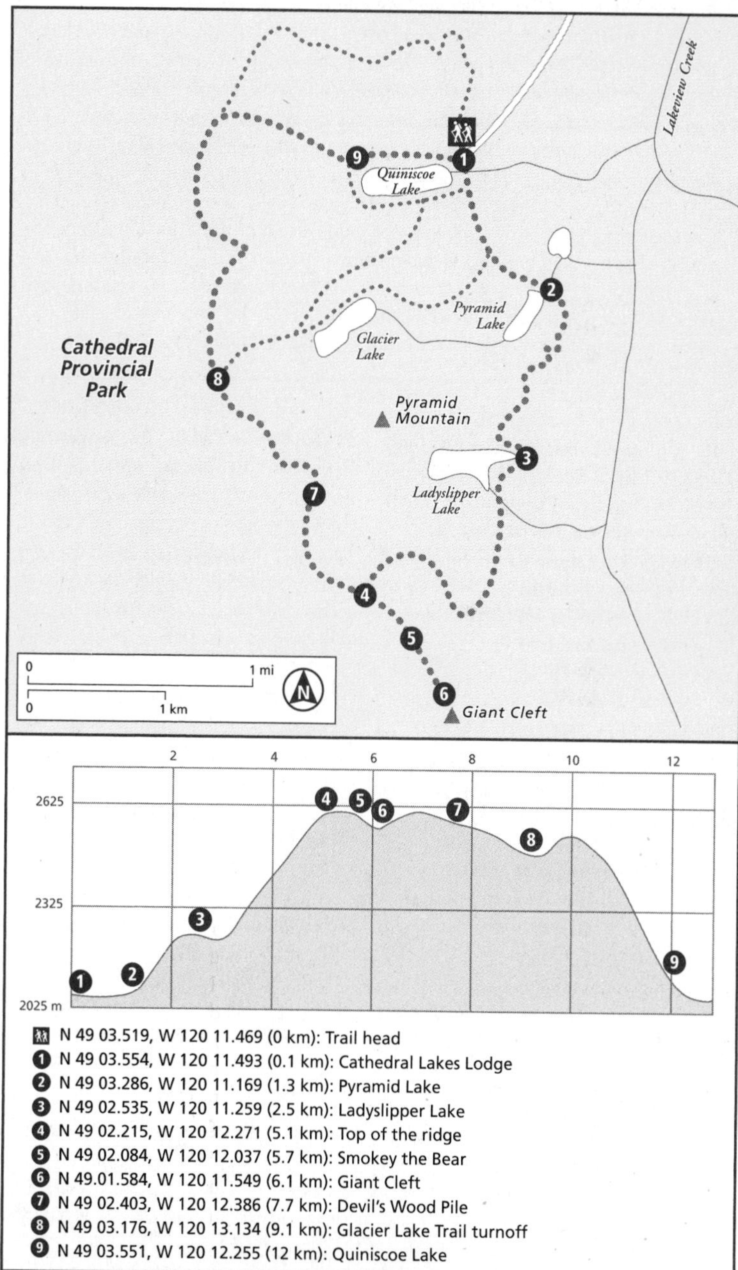

N 49 03.519, W 120 11.469 (0 km): Trail head

1. N 49 03.554, W 120 11.493 (0.1 km): Cathedral Lakes Lodge
2. N 49 03.286, W 120 11.169 (1.3 km): Pyramid Lake
3. N 49 02.535, W 120 11.259 (2.5 km): Ladyslipper Lake
4. N 49 02.215, W 120 12.271 (5.1 km): Top of the ridge
5. N 49 02.084, W 120 12.037 (5.7 km): Smokey the Bear
6. N 49.01.584, W 120 11.549 (6.1 km): Giant Cleft
7. N 49 02.403, W 120 12.386 (7.7 km): Devil's Wood Pile
8. N 49 03.176, W 120 13.134 (9.1 km): Glacier Lake Trail turnoff
9. N 49 03.551, W 120 12.255 (12 km): Quiniscoe Lake

Getting There Is Half the Fun

You could happily spend a few days exploring the high ridges and curious geology of Cathedral Provincial Park. Some 60km (37 miles) of well-marked trails link alpine meadows, lakes, and peaks. The 16km (10-mile) road to the park is closed to public traffic, so your options are to hike in (the shortest route takes about 8 hr.) or to book a ride with Cathedral Lakes Lodge, which runs a transportation service for both lodge guests and campers. A unimog (open-sided jeep) bounces and shakes as it clambers up switchbacks, climbing 1,500m (4,921 ft.) above the river valley to a lodge near the shores of Quiniscoe Lake. The trip takes 1 hour. Three times a week (Fri, Sat, and Sun) the lodge also runs day trips to the park (C$140 per person, round trip, including lunch). Book online (www.cathedral-lakes-lodge.com) or call © **888/255-4453.** The 8am departure gives you time for a full day hike on the Rim Trail before catching the 5:30pm jeep back to base camp. You should reserve well in advance. Day trips are limited to 15 people.

Ladyslipper Trail) along the Rim Trail, you'll arrive at a turnoff on the right to the Glacier Lake Trail. This trail is the easiest and most direct route back to the lodge. We continued along the Rim Trail for nearly 1km (1/2 mile), winding our way up to Quiniscoe Mountain to take in the views of the lodge and surrounding lakes, and descended along the steeper and less well-defined Quiniscoe Lake route, the upper section of which was covered in snow.

9 Quiniscoe Lake At the base of the slope, the Quiniscoe route crosses a meadow of tall grass and winds through the trees to the western end of Quiniscoe Lake, a short stroll from the lodge. Keep an eye out for the resident marmots and pikas. If you're on a day trip, you'll probably have time to catch some sun on the wooden benches beside the lodge while you wait for the jeep.

SLEEPING & EATING

ACCOMMODATIONS

Value Abbott Villa Travelodge Kelowna For the money, this is one of the best places to stay in Kelowna, as it has one of the best locations downtown—right across from the City Park beaches. You'll be able to walk to the lakefront and to your favorite restaurants. The standard-issue motel units are clean and well-maintained.

1627 Abbott St., Kelowna, BC V1Y 1A9. © **800/578-7878** or 250/763-7771. www.travelodge.com. 52 units. C$134–C$167 double. AE, MC, V. **Close to:** Knox Mountain Apex Trail, Myra Canyon on the Kettle Valley Railway.

Bear Creek Provincial Park This lovely park offers camping in shady sites on the shores of Okanagan Lake. The campground also has 5km (3 miles) of (mostly easy) hiking trails.

9km off Hwy. 97 on Westside Rd., BC V4V 1Z8. © **800/689-9025** or 604/689-9025. www.discovercamping.ca. 122 campsites. C$24 for campsite. Reservations accepted (and highly recommended). **Close to:** Knox Mountain Apex Trail, Myra Canyon on the Kettle Valley Railway, Stave Pipe Trail to Pincushion Mountain.

Coast Capri Hotel You'll need to drive to the beaches from here, and the surrounding blocks are filled with strip malls, but if you can't get into one of the beachfront hotels, yet still want high-quality lodgings, this is your next-best choice.

1171 Harvey Ave., Kelowna, BC V1Y 6E8. ✆ **800/716-6199** or 250/860-6060. www.coasthotels.com. 185 units. C$158–C$196 double. AE, MC, V. **Close to:** Knox Mountain Apex Trail, Myra Canyon on the Kettle Valley Railway.

★★ **Hotel Eldorado** This is one of the most charming places to stay in Kelowna if you like historic inns. The Eldorado has been fully restored and is now decorated with a unique mix of antiques.

500 Cook Rd. (at Lakeshore Rd.), Kelowna, BC V1W 3G9. ✆ **866/608-7500** or 250/763-7500. www.eldoradokelowna.com. 55 units. C$179–C$269 double; lakeview rooms and luxury suites from C$429. AE, DC, MC, V. From downtown, follow Pandosy Rd. south 1.5km (1 mile). Turn right on Cook Rd. **Close to:** Knox Mountain Apex Trail, Myra Canyon on the Kettle Valley Railway.

Naramata Heritage Inn & Spa Built in 1908, the Naramata Inn has undergone extensive and loving renovation. If you're coming to the Okanagan for a romantic getaway, or simply have an aversion to mom-and-pop motels and corporate hotels, then look no further. Rooms are charming (although some are small) with period finery and modern luxury.

3625 First St., Naramata, BC V0H 1N0 (19km/12 miles north of Penticton on the east side of Okanagan Lake). ✆ **866/617-1188** or 250/497-6808. www.naramatainn.com. 12 units. C$187–C$289 double; C$470–C$520 suites. AE, MC, V. **Close to:** Kettle Valley Railway: Penticton to Naramata.

★ **Ramada Inn & Suites** The newest hotel in the Penticton area, the Ramada isn't particularly near the lakefront, but it's a nice choice if you have no patience for older lodgings. Rooms are large, nicely furnished, and in a resort-like setting.

1050 Eckhardt Ave. W., Penticton, BC V2A 2C3. ✆ **800/665-4966** or 250/492-8926. www.pentictonramada.com. 125 units. C$159–C$219 double; suites from C$259. AE, DC, MC, V. **Close to:** Kettle Valley Railway: Penticton to Naramata.

★★ **Spirit Ridge Vineyard Resort & Spa** This luxury-level lodging overlooks Lake Osoyoos, the steep-sloped Okanagan Valley, and miles of vineyards. Opened in 2007, Spirit Ridge brings a Santa Fe look to the desert landscape. Lodgings are in one-bedroom suites, or one- or two-bedroom villas, each with full kitchen, dining, and living room.

1200 Rancher Creek Rd., Osoyoos, BC V0H 1T0. ✆ **877/313-9463** or 250/495-5445. www.spiritridge.ca. 94 units. C$289–C$309 1-bedroom suite; C$349 1-bedroom villa; C$429 2-bedroom villa. Mid-season and low-season rates also available. AE, MC, V. **Close to:** International Hike and Bike Trail, Golden Mile Trail.

RESTAURANTS

★ **Bouchons Bistro** FRENCH This Gallic transplant offers classic French bistro fare just a few blocks from the Okanagan lakefront. The dining room, with ocher walls, stained-glass panels, and handwritten menus, actually feels Parisian. The menu doesn't stray far from classic French (prepared with the best of local products). The wine list is half French, half Okanagan.

105–1180 Sunset Dr., Kelowna. ✆ **250/763-6595.** www.bouchonsbistro.com. Reservations suggested. Main courses C$20–C$35. MC, V. Daily 5:30–10:30pm. Closed mid-Feb to mid-Mar. **Close to:** Knox Mountain Apex Trail, Myra Canyon on the Kettle Valley Railway.

★★★ **Fresco** NEW CANADIAN This upbeat eatery in a historic brick building in downtown Kelowna has earned rave reviews since it opened in 2001. Chef/owner Rod Butters built his reputation on a commitment to local and regional producers. The food is scrumptious (try Butters' signature oat-crusted Arctic char), service is top notch, and the wine list celebrates the Okanagan.

1560 Water St., Kelowna. ✆ **250/868-8805.** www.frescorestaurant.net. Reservations recommended. Main courses C$24–C$38. AE, MC, V. Tues–Sat 5:30–10pm. **Close to:** Knox Mountain Apex Trail, Myra Canyon on the Kettle Valley Railway.

★ **Mon Thong Thai Restaurant** THAI Mon Thong has an encyclopedic menu of house specialties, making it the best Thai restaurant in the Okanagan. Almost all dishes can be made vegetarian. Choose from red, green, or yellow curries, or from signature dishes like *goong pad num prick pao,* stir-fried shrimp with fresh vegetables in fiery Thai sauce.

1530 Water St., Kelowna. ✆ **250/763-8600.** Reservations not needed. Main courses C$9–C$15. MC, V. Mon–Fri 11:30am–2:30pm and 5:30–9:30pm; Sat–Sun 5:30–9:30pm. **Close to:** Knox Mountain Apex Trail, Myra Canyon on the Kettle Valley Railway.

★ **Passatempo** NEW CANADIAN Opt for a seat in the sleek dining room or the sprawling patio. Either way, the creative menu lives up to the lake views. For a light lunch, try quinoa and spinach salad with fried chickpeas, feta cheese, and grilled prawns. The tapas selections are great for wine pairing.

1200 Rancher Creek Rd., Osoyoos. ✆ **250/495-8007.** http://osoyoos.manduco.biz. Reservations recommended. Main courses C$24–C$32. AE, MC, V. July–Aug daily 7am–11pm; Sept to mid-Oct daily 9am–10pm; other months daily 9am–9pm. **Close to:** International Hike and Bike Trail, Golden Mile Trail.

(Value) **Theo's Greek Restaurant** GREEK Don't be surprised when previous visitors to Penticton immediately offer testimonials about Theo's. It's a popular spot with flavorful food. The menu features delectable calamari, succulent marinated lamb, and specialties like seared chicken livers and a standout moussaka.

687 Main St., Penticton. ✆ **250/492-4019.** www.eatsquid.com. Reservations recommended. Main courses C$14–C$29. AE, DC, MC, V. Mon–Thurs 11am–10pm; Fri–Sat 11am–11pm; Sun 4–10pm. **Close to:** Kettle Valley Railway: Penticton to Naramata.

★ **Villa Rosa Ristorante** ITALIAN Villa Rosa is one of the top Penticton options for traditional Italian cuisine. It has an especially attractive patio shaded by grapevines—just the spot on a warm evening. The menu is varied, with classic dishes such as *osso buco,* chicken Marsala, and pasta joining Canadian specialties such as steaks and salmon.

795 W. Westminster Ave., Penticton. ✆ **250/490-9595.** www.thevillarosa.com. Reservations suggested. Main courses C$16–C$37. AE, MC, V. Daily 5–9:30pm. **Close to:** Kettle Valley Railway: Penticton to Naramata.

The Canadian Rockies & the Kootenays Hikes

by Christie Pashby

With giant peaks, towering rock walls, spectacular waterfalls, pristine emerald lakes, glaciers, and grizzlies, the mountains of eastern British Columbia (the Canadian Rockies and the Kootenays) offer some of the most outstanding, rewarding, and varied hiking in the entire world.

Nestled along the western slope of the Continental Divide that splits the watersheds of North America, the Canadian Rockies of British Columbia make up part of a UNESCO World Heritage Site and are a true treasure trove of mountain memories.

The two national parks in the area, Kootenay National Park and Yoho National Park, are often overlooked by the spotlight that shines on their Alberta neighbors, Jasper and Banff national parks. However, we've long felt that Kootenay and Yoho offer equal if not better hiking opportunities—not to mention fewer people and some absolutely delightful lodging options. Hiking trails in these parks—along with Glacier National Park at Rogers Pass—are meticulously maintained and are the pride of the nation.

Further to the west, there are hundreds of kilometers of mountain ranges offering equally diverse and spectacular mountain scenery, including the Columbia Valley, the Purcell Mountains, the Columbia Mountains at Glacier National Park, and the Selkirks in the Kootenays area of south-central British Columbia.

In the wide range of alpine peaks that stretch from the Alberta border over towards the Okanagan and Caribou regions of central British Columbia, there are hundreds of little-known hiking trails that have kept many local mountain lovers busy for a lifetime. The list is endless! This chapter highlights three of the area's most alluring provincial parks, Mt Robson, Bugaboo Spires, and Kokanee Glacier.

The area is large and the distances are vast. These hikes can be put together to form a 2-week or 10-day hiking trip, but you'll have a few driving days as you attempt to connect the dots. In between, find comfort in charming mountain towns like Revelstoke, Nelson, Radium Hot Springs, and tiny Field.

This selection includes the absolutely best hikes across the wide region; it was not easy to narrow them down to just ten. From a simple family stroll around a jewel-colored lake to an epic full day in the high mountains, there is something for everyone.

ESSENTIALS

GETTING THERE

By Air

With the expansion of the international airport at Cranbrook, BC, it's easy to reach the Kootenays and the southern BC Rockies thanks to direct flights from Vancouver,

 Calgary, and the U.S. The closest airport to Mt Robson Provincial Park is in Prince George, 3½ hours away.

By Car

From Calgary, drive 2 hours west on the Trans-Canada Hwy. 1 through Banff National Park. Turn west at Castle Junction on Hwy. 93 to reach Kootenay National Park. Continue further on the TCH past Lake Louise to reach Yoho National Park. The Columbia Valley can be reached by either of these routes, connecting the BC towns of Golden and Radium Hot Springs. Continue on the TCH Hwy. 1 to Rogers Pass and Glacier National Park. To reach the area from the south, take Hwy. 93 north from Cranbrook to Radium.

To reach the Kootenays, take Hwy. 3 east from Vancouver through Osoyoos, or Hwy. 3 west from Cranbrook.

To reach Mt. Robson, take Hwy. 16, the Yellowhead Highway, east from Prince George or west from Jasper, Alberta.

By Bus

Greyhound Bus Lines (✆ **800/661-8747;** www.greyhound.ca) operates buses to all of these areas.

VISITOR INFORMATION

The following websites will help with planning your trip to the BC Rockies and the Kootenays: www.travel.bc.ca; www.radiumhotsprings.com; www.kootenayrockies.com.

Trail reports in the national parks are updated frequently (often daily). In provincial parks and forest service areas, trail reports are less reliable, but definitely important to check.

Yoho National Park: www.pc.gc.ca/apps/tcond/cond_e.asp?oPark=100438
Kootenay National Park: www.pc.gc.ca/apps/tcond/cond_e.asp?oPark=100253
Glacier National Park: www.pc.gc.ca/apps/tcond/cond_e.asp?oPark=100205
For BC Provincial Parks, start at www.env.gov.bc.ca/bcparks and follow the links to individual parks, including Bugaboo Spires Provincial Park, Kokanee Glacier Provincial Park, and Mt. Robson Provincial Park.

ORIENTATION

The BC Rockies border the province of Alberta to the east, the U.S. states of Washington, Idaho, and Montana to the south, and the BC Thompson-Okanagan region to the west and north. The main mountain ranges are the Canadian Rockies, the Selkirk Mountains, and the Purcell Mountains.

GETTING AROUND

The easiest way to get around, and to get to remote trail heads, is in your own vehicle. Commercial buses will help you link towns, but will not drop you at remote spots.

How to Organize Your Time

The best hiking, in our opinion, is to be had in Yoho National Park. The mixture of human history, high alpine lakes, cascading waterfalls at every turn, and great food and lodging make it practically unbeatable. Basing yourself out of one of the cozy mountain

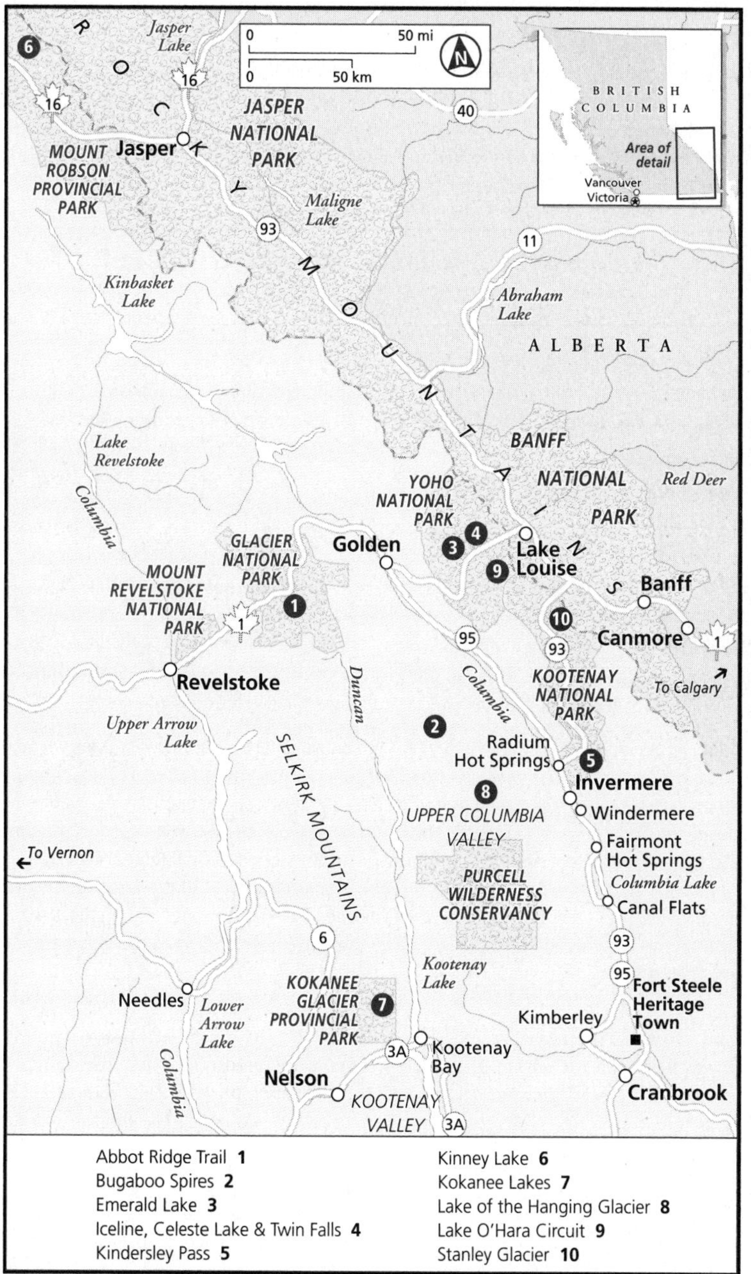
0 50 mi
0 50 km
BRITISH COLUMBIA
Area of detail
Vancouver
Victoria
ROCKY MOUNTAINS
Jasper Lake
JASPER NATIONAL PARK
MOUNT ROBSON PROVINCIAL PARK
Jasper
Maligne Lake
Kinbasket Lake
Abraham Lake
ALBERTA
BANFF NATIONAL PARK
Red Deer
Lake Revelstoke
Columbia
YOHO NATIONAL PARK
GLACIER NATIONAL PARK
Golden
Lake Louise
Banff
MOUNT REVELSTOKE NATIONAL PARK
Canmore
Revelstoke
Duncan
Columbia
KOOTENAY NATIONAL PARK
To Calgary
Upper Arrow Lake
SELKIRK MOUNTAINS
Radium Hot Springs
Invermere
Windermere
UPPER COLUMBIA VALLEY
Fairmont Hot Springs
To Vernon
PURCELL WILDERNESS CONSERVANCY
Columbia Lake
Canal Flats
Kootenay Lake
Fort Steele Heritage Town
Needles
Lower Arrow Lake
KOKANEE GLACIER PROVINCIAL PARK
Kimberley
Kootenay Bay
Columbia
Nelson
KOOTENAY VALLEY
Cranbrook
Abbot Ridge Trail 1
Bugaboo Spires 2
Emerald Lake 3
Iceline, Celeste Lake & Twin Falls 4
Kindersley Pass 5
Kinney Lake 6
Kokanee Lakes 7
Lake of the Hanging Glacier 8
Lake O'Hara Circuit 9
Stanley Glacier 10

lodges of Yoho for at least 3 nights ought to give you a chance to sample the best. In 3 days, you can spend a day warming up at Emerald Lake, a day at Lake O'Hara, and a third day in the Little Yoho Valley.

Alternately, if a road trip is more in your mind, you can fit some of these hikes into half days. Starting at the border in Kootenay National Park, head to the Stanley Glacier, and then drive on to Radium that night. Hike to the Lake of the Hanging Glacier the next day, and spend that night near Golden, BC. The following day, you can be at the trail head in Rogers Pass before noon, plenty of time to explore Glacier National Park, where camping is the best option, in the afternoon.

1 ABBOTT RIDGE TRAIL, GLACIER NATIONAL PARK ★

Difficulty rating: Strenuous

Distance: 10km (6.2 miles) round trip

Estimated time: 5 hr.

Elevation gain: 1,040m (3,412 ft.)

Costs/permits: National Park pass required for vehicles, C$9.80 per adult or C$19.60 per family

Pet friendly: No

Best time to go: July–Sept

Website: www.parkscanada.gc.ca/glacier

Recommended map: 82N/4 and 82 N/5

Trail head GPS: N 51 15.503, W 117 29.294

Trail head directions: Leave your car at the parking lot outside the Illecillewaet Campground, 2.6km (1½ miles) west of the Rogers Pass Discovery Centre on Hwy. 1, the Trans-Canada. This is 81km (50 miles) west from Golden and 73km (45 miles) east from Revelstoke. From here, head right across the Illecillewaet River and through the Interpretive Trail at the Glacier House ruins 100m (328 ft.) later. The Abbott Ridge trail heads right/west from the middle of the ruins.

Climbing an intimidating 1,040m (3,412 ft.) in only 5km (3 miles), this is a short yet very steep hike in Glacier National Park, the heart of BC's striking Selkirk Mountains. And it's an unbeatable outing for strong hikers. All your hard work on the uphill is undeniably and deeply rewarding. From the top of Abbott Ridge, you can see five jaw-dropping glaciers, like the world laid out before you. All the hikes in Glacier National Park are steep; you can't avoid the climb. But this one is the best since you get out of the forest quickly for great views. Don't be disheartened when your heart starts pumping hard on the way up. Just take your time, and bring hiking poles to help you out. This is incredible bang for your hiking buck.

The Abbott Ridge trail technically begins at the Illecillewaet Trail Head, so this is where you begin counting distance and elevation. Heading past the historic Glacier House ruins and interpretive trail—once the site of a raging mountain resort and the launching pad for ground-breaking mountaineering feats well over a century ago—turn left just before the stone monument, following the main trail for 100m (328 ft.). The Marion Lake–Abbott Ridge trail is the first one on the right.

❶ **Glacier House** You'll have time to browse the ruins later. Now, go hiking. Right away, the uphill begins through a

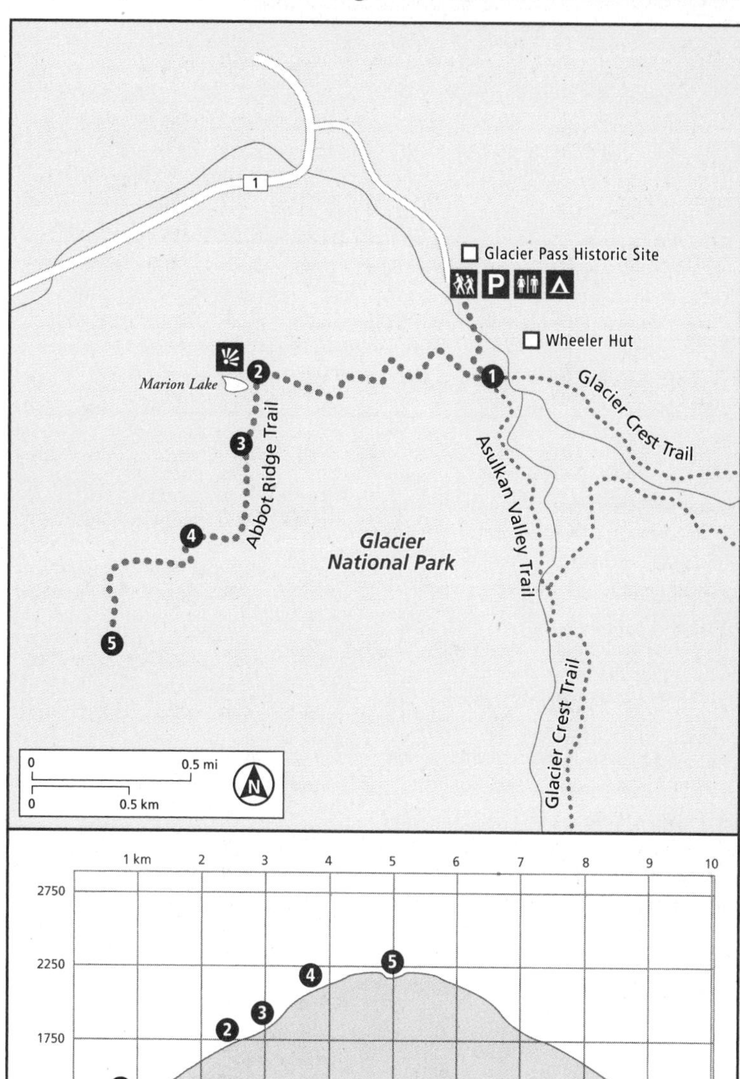

N 51 15.503, W 117 29.294 (0 km): Trail head
❶ N 51 15.428, W 117 29.337 (0.8 km): Join Marion Lake-Abbot ridge trail past ruins
❷ N 51 15.363, W 117 30.273 (2.4 km): Arrive at Marion Lake
❸ N 51 12.287, W 117 30.157 (3 km): Stay right, follow trail marked "short-cut"
❹ N 51 12.060, W 117 30.260 (3.8 km): Abbott Ridge weather station on your right
❺ N 51 14.541, W 117 30.503 (5 km): Trail switchbacks along an open ledge

Fun Facts Rogers Pass: Avalanche Zone!

Famed mountaineer Edward Whymper called it "Fifty Switzerlands in one." Glacier National Park (est. 1886) and the CPR Railway are here thanks to Major A.B. Rogers, a railway surveyor who, in 1881, discovered a narrow valley surrounded by phenomenally steep mountains that forms a short cut around the "Big Bend" of the Columbia River. Today, Rogers Pass, at 1,330m (4,364 ft.), is a National Historic Site of Canada, recognized for its nation-building importance in constructing the trans-continental railway. Opening up the pass may have made the trip shorter, but it sure posed challenges—mainly from the endless threat of avalanches, which continue to this day. There are 31 snow sheds, earth dams, and a 15km (9¼-mile) tunnel through the pass, a massive effort to deal with precariously vertical slopes and the more than 10m (33 ft.) of annual snow fall in the area. With constant avalanche monitoring and controlling, Rogers Pass is home to the largest mobile avalanche forecasting and control system in the world.

thick forest of cedars. It seems like a never-ending trail that goes up and up and up, but there are a few benches for resting, and quite quickly, the first views open to the east, taking in the Trans-Canada Highway below and the gorgeous Sir Donald Range across to the east. Take a breather and enjoy! You will also get your first views of the Illecillewaet Glacier to the south. But frankly, this is a time to put your head down and hike up. Don't fret; the pay-off is major!

❷ Marion Lake After an hour-long slog, you reach Marion Lake, 2.2km (1¼ miles) from the trail head. At this point, at 1,707m (5,600 ft.), you've got 425m (1,394 ft.)—nearly half!—of the climbing behind you. Marion Lake is nestled in a basin gouged by glaciers in the last Ice Age. In such a harsh climate, it's a stagnant, nutrient-poor lake, barely even worth a photo. Yet, if you continue around the front of the lake another 200m (656 ft.) to a lookout, you'll be snap-happy and proud as you gaze across at Rogers Pass.

SPECTACULAR LOOKOUT You'll be overwhelmed with pride and a sense of accomplishment as you take in the brilliant views from the lookout just to the north of Marian Lake—they are promises of what is to come as you reach the ridge above. This ledge does make a great rest stop. There are giant boulders that provide a place to drop your pack and stretch, and let you dig out your camera. In front of you, you've got the Ursus Major and Minor peaks; to the northeast, you can't miss the Hermit Glacier; and way down below, you can spot the winding Trans-Canada Highway, the marvels of the CPR avalanche tunnels, and the turquoise roof of the Rogers Pass Discovery Centre and Glacier House hotel.

❸ From Boulders to Alpine Meadow Continuing past Marion Lake, the trail gets narrower and the foliage starts thinning. Stay right, following the trail marked "shortcut" up a boulder-strewn gulley. As the boulders get bigger, the trees get tinier, finally tossing you out onto an alpine meadow for a short but sweet flat stretch.

In late July and early August, the meadow is a joyful kaleidoscope of wildflowers.

❹ **Weather Station** The Abbott Ridge weather station, to the right on the edge of a cliff, monitors the snow pack and weather conditions of the complex Rogers Pass area through the year, providing key data to avalanche forecasters. It is not open to visitors. At this point, you'll be encouraged by the hikers heading down, who remind you of the treasure awaiting you atop the ridge!

❺ **Abbott Ridge** Above the weather station, the trail switchbacks across an open ledge. Here, you are reaching into classic alpine tundra, the land above the tree line. The trail winds around the northwest slope of Mount Abbott, opening up new views of the western reaches of Glacier National Park and the majestic Bonney Glacier. A final push upward leads to an astonishing panoramic view. The trail marker on the tip of a narrow ridge identifies the ultimate trail ending, although some strong hikers continue on for a technical scramble to the next ledge. There are massive sheets of ice all around you, including the Asulkan, Vaux, Bonney, Hermit, and Illecillewaet glaciers.

It's going to take you about an hour to get back down, so spend as much time up here as you can—as long as there is no storm on the horizon! The hike down is straight-forward but can be tough on the knees.

2 BUGABOO SPIRES ★

Difficulty rating: Moderate

Distance: 10km (6.2 miles) round trip

Estimated time: 5 hr.

Elevation gain: 660m (2,165 ft.)

Costs/permits: None

Pet friendly: No

Best time to go: July–Sept

Website: www.env.gov.bc.ca/bcparks/explore/parkpgs/bugaboo

Recommended map: 82 K/10

Trail head GPS: N 50 44.440, W116 43.360

Trail head directions: The road to the trail head is a series of logging and mining roads, half-way between Golden and Radium Hot Springs. Four-wheel drive is recommended but not essential. It will take approximately 45 minutes from Hwy. 93. Turn west off Hwy. 93 28km (17 miles) north of Radium Hot Springs at the village of Brisco and follow the sign for Bugaboo Glacier Provincial Park. Head downhill past a lumber mill. Set your odometer to 0 here. Turn left after 4.9km (3 miles) onto Mine Hill Rd, just after the bridge. Follow signs to Cartwright Lake, CMH Bugaboos. Go straight through an intersection when the odometer hits 7.1km (4½ miles). Keep right at the Cartwright Lake Rd. intersection at 19km (12 miles). At 40km (25 miles), you'll see Bugaboo Falls. At 42km (26 miles), you enter Bugaboo Provincial Park. At 43km (27 miles), turn right to the parking lot and trail head, another 2.9km (1¾ miles) down a dirt road past the private CMH Bugaboo Lodge to 46km (29 miles). At the parking lot, you'll see a pile of chicken wire, which many people use to protect their cars from porcupines by building a fence around their vehicles. Help yourself and follow the example of other cars.

Remote, rugged, and sublimely structural, the incredible Bugaboo Spires reach over 3,000m (9,843 ft.) high and have been the stuff of mountaineering dreams for generations. This is one of the most famous alpine climbing areas in the world, and the Conrad Kain Hut—your destination on this day hike—is a base camp for the best in the business. The giant granite towers dramatically burst out of the Purcell Mountains in eastern British Columbia with panache and presence. Non-climbers can taste alpine glory on this lovely day hike. This trail has a few technical sections and some gnarly exposure; it is recommended for experienced hikers only. This is an isolated mountain wilderness with basically no services, so plan ahead.

From the parking lot, you can just make out your destination—the Conrad Kain Hut sitting atop a bluff looking south over the Bugaboo Glacier. It's a steep and challenging 2½-hour trip up to the hut, on a trail that includes aluminum ladders and cables. Kind of like an extreme workout on a Stairmaster; have a good breakfast and go early so you have time to enjoy the views and linger in alpine la-la land.

❶ **Forest** From the parking lot, the trail goes through a lush forest, with a heavy undergrowth rich with blueberries, huckleberries, gooseberries, and willows, and then across a series of boardwalks which protect the marshy environment. It moves across a boulder field, then back into the forest and through a tunnel of alder trees. There is a junction at 2km (1¼ miles). Head right and up the trail, following the north side of the valley across lateral moraines towards the Conrad Kain Hut.

❷ **The Aluminum Ladder** Soon, the trail leaves the forest completely and goes steeply through an avalanche path, towards the technical section of the hike. Placed by focused climbers loaded with heavy packs to sustain a weeks-long expedition, this is the tricky section of this trail. The cables are there for your use, just keep one hand on them at all times as you inch your way upwards and focus. Carved rock stairs also ease the climb. At 3.5km (2¼ miles), there's a simple ladder attached by a sturdy system of ropes and hooks to the side of a cliff. Helpful and nerve-racking at the same time, the exposure here is high (in other words, it's a long way down!), but intermediate hikers should have no problem. Just stay focused!

❸ **Rock Bluffs** The trail then goes up through rock bluffs, the most demanding section of the hike. In some areas, the trail has been chiseled or blasted through the rocks. You can see the hut in the distance.

❹ **Trail Widening** The trail opens into a basin beneath the Eastpost Spire and the Applebee Dome. Then, the trail crosses a creek and takes you on the final push to the hut. Just above you, Hound's Tooth, Marmolata, Bugaboo, and Snowpatch spires stand elegantly at attention above the vast glacier that encompasses them all. What a sight!

❺ **Conrad Kain Hut** Named for an alpinist who worked as a guide here from 1916 to the 1930s and carved out routes which continue to baffle high-level climbers, the tin-roofed, gothic-arched hut is run by the Alpine Club of Canada and was erected in 1972. It has provided shelter to some of the most famous climbers in the world. You must have a reservation to stay here (see "Staying in the Backcountry," later in this chapter). This is a wonderful lookout to witness mere mortals tackle the massive granite monoliths. Don't forget your binoculars! Give yourself some time for lunch and to roam the high meadow, which can be dotted with wildflowers in late July and August. Look for glacier lilies, heathers, and saxifrages.

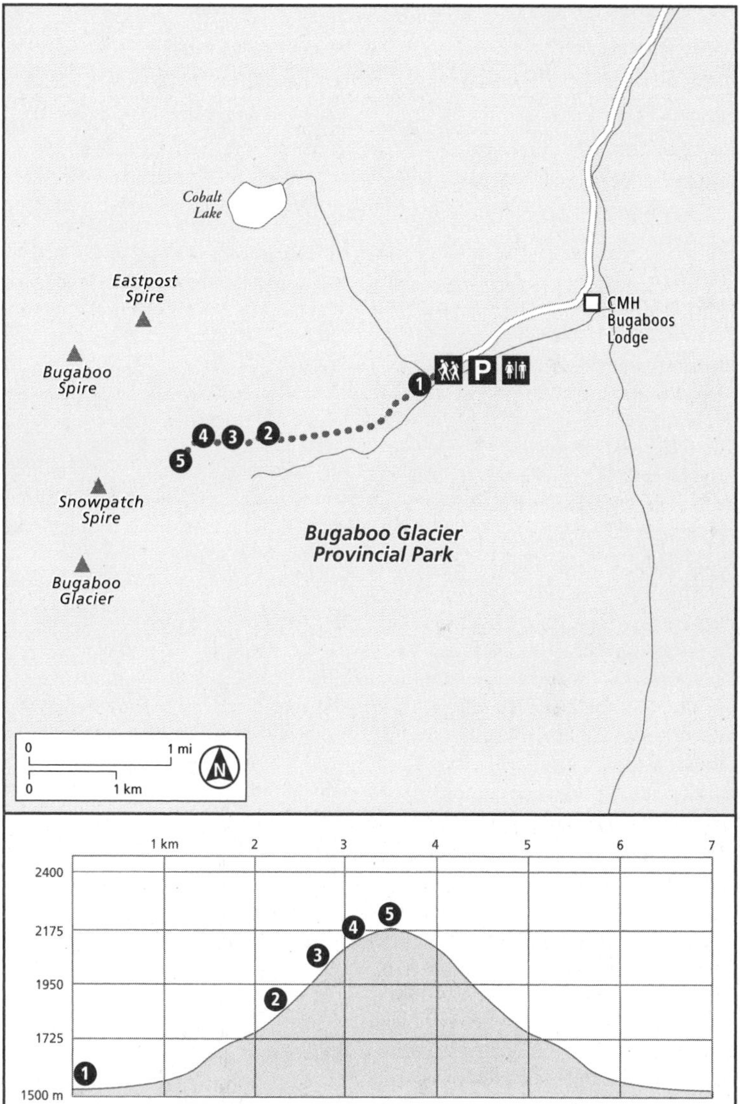

Cobalt Lake
Eastpost Spire
Bugaboo Spire
Snowpatch Spire
Bugaboo Glacier
CMH Bugaboos Lodge
Bugaboo Glacier Provincial Park
0 1 mi
0 1 km

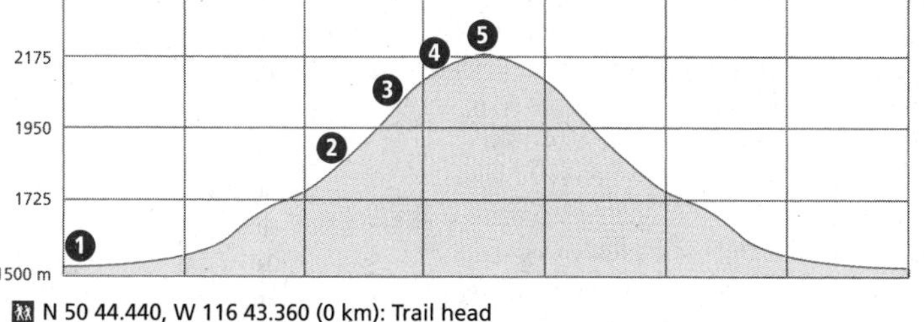

N 50 44.440, W 116 43.360 (0 km): Trail head

❶ N 50 44.735, W 116 43.715 (0.1 km): Follow trail through lush forest

❷ N 50 44.210, W 116 45.270 (2.2 km): Trail leaves forest, goes up steep path

❸ N 50 44.240, W 116 44.310 (2.7 km): Trail goes up through rock bluffs

❹ N 50 44.310, W 116 46.050 (3.1 km): Trail opens into basin, crosses creek

❺ N 50 44.180, W 116 45.480 (3.5 km): Arrive at Conrad Kain Hut

3 EMERALD LAKE ★

Difficulty rating: Easy

Distance: 5.2km (3.2 miles) round trip

Estimated time: 2 hr.

Elevation gain: 89m (292 ft.)

Costs/permits: National Park pass required for vehicles, C$9.80 per adult or C$19.60 per family

Pet friendly: No

Best time to go: June–Sept, late afternoon (after 4pm) to avoid crowds

Website: www.parkscanada.gc.ca/yoho and www.friendsofyoho.ca

Recommended map: 31 L/4, Edition 5 MCE

Trail head GPS: N 51 26.20, W 116 32.261

Trail head directions: One km (1/2 mile) south of Field, turn onto the Emerald Lake Rd. off Hwy. 1, the Trans-Canada Highway. Follow the road for 6km (3 3/4 miles) to Emerald Lake parking lot. This is a busy parking lot; be sure to lock your vehicle! The trail heads to the west or left side of the boathouse.

With just a little bit of up and down, this wide trail that circles the pristine Emerald Lake is rich and delightful, almost easy enough to be considered a stroll. Legendary local guide Tom Wilson is credited for having "discovered" this natural marvel in 1882 as part of route-scouting for the Canadian Pacific Railroad. This is a great family outing or leg-stretcher; it showcases a gem of a lake, and the interpretive signs are informative.

Once you get past the crowded parking lot, often jammed with RVs and tour buses, you'll rejoice in the high return for low input on this trail. It'll take you an hour or two, and offers plenty of time for leisurely photography.

❶ Trail Head We suggest you head clockwise from the trail head, to your left behind the boathouse, allowing a stop at Emerald Lake Lodge's lakeside restaurant as a reward at the end of your outing. So, move away from the hustle and bustle, and take a few moments to look over the map posted at the trail head. The trail then passes a handful of interpretive signs outlining natural history, including one that tells the story of the nearby fossil wonderland that is the Burgess Shale. The trail passes through a classic avalanche path, ideal grizzly bear terrain, although there is enough traffic to keep bears away most of the time. Across and above the lake, you'll see Mount Burgess. Within 10 minutes, you are away from the crowds.

❷ Junction with Emerald Basin At the far northwest end of the lake, a trail splits off to Emerald Basin, 20 minutes into your hike. This is a great alternative for those with extra energy in their legs, as it takes you quickly to a high, natural amphitheater of hanging glaciers and avalanche paths. It will add another 2.9km (1 3/4 miles) and two hours to your hike.

TAKE A BREAK
Just before the bridge, there is a series of lovely wooden benches, each facing a different direction, which make a great pit stop. In late spring, you'll catch avalanches above the lake, as well—bring binoculars.

❸ The Bridge A mighty bridge takes you over the raging creek that drains into Emerald Lake from Yoho Pass to the left. Then, you head back into the trees into what is a very different environment. A boardwalk leads through a thick bog with

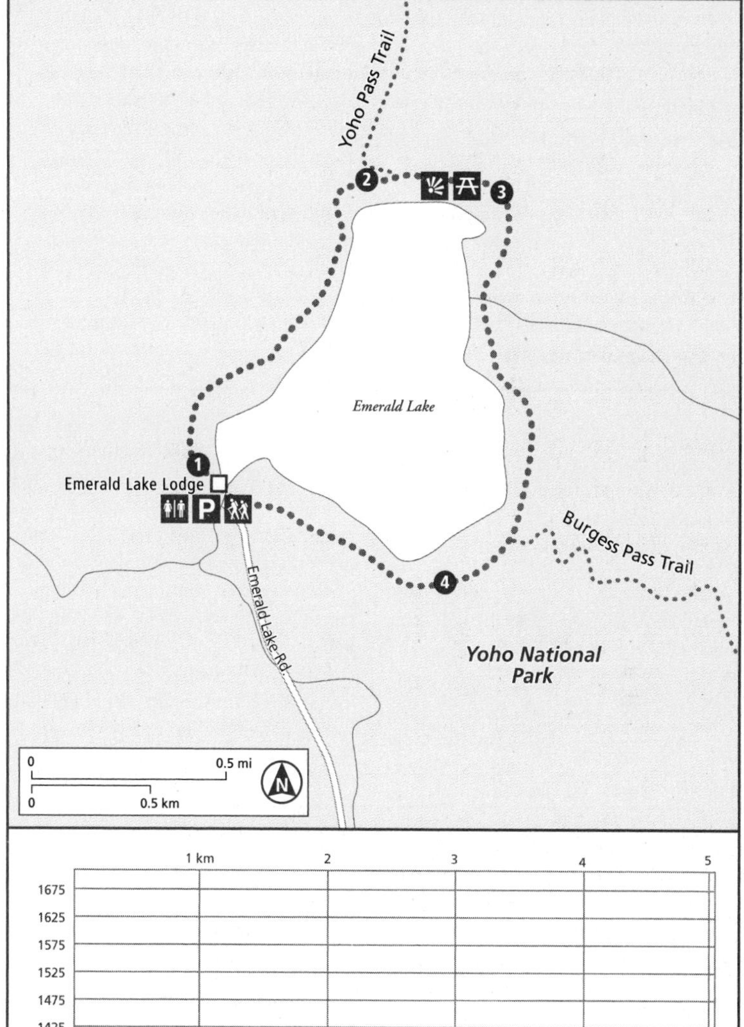

- N 51 26.200, W 116 32.261 (0 km): Trail head
- ❶ N 51 26.200, W 116 32.261 (0 km): Follow trail left behind the boathouse
- ❷ N 51 26.270, W 116 31.534 (1.6 km): Trail junction with Emerald Basin
- ❸ N 51 27.035, W 116 31.239 (2.1 km): Cross bridge over creek
- ❹ N 51 26.204, W 116 31.682 (3.8 km): Take right at fork for Emerald Lake Lodge

Fun Facts The Burgess Shale

The Canadian Rockies' greatest contribution to archaeology is the 515-million-year-old Burgess Shale, a fossil bed discovered at the base of Mount Stephen just above Emerald Lake. This discovery transformed our understanding of the evolution of life on Earth and gave real examples of the amazing biodiversity of the mass extinction of species—half of the animal groups seen in the shale have since disappeared from Earth. You can get there to see them only on a 6-hour, 6km (3¾-mile) guided hike organized by the Yoho Burgess Shale Foundation. This is a must for archaeology buffs, but only those with the dedication and fitness to trek into the site. You cannot drive to the Burgess Shale or visit it on your own; you must hike in to the site on an official tour with a registered guide. You will not enjoy this trip unless you are quite fit. Kids will enjoy the shorter hike to the Mount Stephen Fossil Beds. Reserve ahead of time at the Shale's website: www.burgess-shale.bc.ca.

giant Western red cedar, yew, and spruce trees. This is in stark contrast to the dry open alpine. Out of the wind, it's a fun section that soon opens at a bay to views across Emerald Basin. The trail is thick with beargrass and foliage. It winds around towards a fork. Take the right trail for a quick visit to Emerald Lake Lodge.

❹ Emerald Lake Lodge After climbing the moraine that dams Emerald Lake, the turquoise roofs of this historic lodge come into view. The original guest house at this site was built by the Canadian Pacific Railway in 1902; guests were brought in by rail or horse-drawn carriages. The government forbid any expansion or additional development at the site, so the hotel has been meticulously maintained and restored. The main building houses a formal dining area. For a great post-hike refreshment, hit the patio at Cilantro's on the lake for a beer and gourmet pizza (see "Where to Eat," later in this chapter).

4 ICELINE, CELESTE LAKE & TWIN FALLS ★★

Difficulty rating: Strenuous

Distance: 24km (15 miles) round trip

Estimated time: 7–9 hr.

Elevation gain: 700m (2,297 ft.)

Costs/permits: National Park pass required for vehicles, C$9.80 per adult or C$19.60 per family

Pet friendly: No

Best time to go: late June–Sept. Check with the visitor center in Field for updated trail conditions.

Website: www.pc.gc.ca/yoho

Recommended map: Yoho National Park Backcountry Guide map

Trail head GPS: N 51 29.558, W 116 29.045

Trail head directions: Turn north on the Trans-Canada Hwy. 1 60km (37 miles) east of Golden and 3.6km (2¼ miles) east of Field. Drive 13km (8 miles) north on the Takakkaw Falls—Yoho Valley Rd. Park at the far north end the Takakkaw Falls parking lot. Then, walk back through the parking lot, down the road 500m (1,640 ft.) to the Whiskey Jack Hostel. The trail begins behind the hostel.

If you love waterfalls, high glaciers, cozy history, tremendous views, and rambling trails, you are going to love this hike! Combining a handful of trails into one full-day hike, this outing shows off why Yoho National Park got its name—*yoho* is an expression that means wonder and astonishment in the native Cree language. Surely, you'll be thrilled.

There are many, many different variations on this hike, ranging from the 16km (10-mile) Twin Falls trail to the extended Iceline version that takes in an intimidating 28km (17 miles) via the Whaleback trail and requires you spend one night in the backcountry at either a campground, the Alpine Club of Canada's Stanley Mitchell Hut, or at the Twin Falls Chalet. Take a good look at the options before you head out; and if you find you're tired or it's getting late, follow the signs straight back to your car in the parking lot.

Park in the Takakkaw Falls parking lot and head back down Yoho Valley Road the way you came (south) 500m (1,640 ft.) to the trail head behind the Whiskey Jack Hostel.

❶ Glacier Lookout Get the main elevation gain out of the way at the start of the hike, heading up the hill behind the Hostel at the trail sign. This is the trail to Yoho Pass. Stay right—you do not want to go to the Yoho Lake campground or to Hidden Lake.

For about 30 minutes, steep switchbacks climb through a forest lush with dense old growth spruce trees. Turn to your right and gaze across the valley at the dramatic Takakkaw Falls, with the Daly Glacier behind it branching out of the Waputik Icefield. The falls' highest point is 384m (1,260 ft.), but its "freefall" is 254m (833 ft.), making it the second-highest waterfall in Canada (after Della Falls on Vancouver Island). *Takakkaw* is a native Cree word for magnificent. From here, you can also spot the majestic Cathedral Mountain, Mount Ogden, and Mount Stephen to the southeast, Wapta Mountain due south, and the President and Vice-President Peaks around the northwest.

❷ Emerald Glacier The trail emerges onto rocky slabs, continuing into its most stunning section, climbing up to and then crossing the rubble left behind as the Emerald Glacier retreated. Likely, this trail was covered by the glacier only 100 years ago—practically yesterday in geological terms! You'll first see the Emerald Glacier at approximately 3.7km (2¼ miles) into the hike. From here, it's a 45-minute ramble across a high mountain dreamland with incredible panoramic views. Desolate talus surrounds you. At four separate points, the trail comes very close to the glacier. The trail meanders along beneath the glacier over smooth limestone slabs. Stone cairns mark the path through barren rock dampened by glacier runoff. This area can be covered in snow into mid-July.

❸ Celeste Lake Connector The trail passes a gray-green glacial pond, making its way around towards the Little Yoho Valley. The Iceline technically continues further to the top of the Little Yoho River and the Alpine Club of Canada's Stanley Mitchell Hut (turning it into one extremely long day or a 2-day backpacking trip), but you are turning right through a meadow on to the barren talus beneath the Emerald Glacier. Say goodbye to the high alpine; this is approximately 6km (3¾ miles) into the trail, just beyond the outlet of the second glacier pond. The meadow is often ablaze with colorful Indian paintbrush and columbine, as well as wild heather, mosses, and phlox. After dropping into a forest predominated by Douglas fir, you will

Wear Sunscreen and Cover Up!

Here, well above tree line, the sun can be incredibly strong and yet the cool breezes coming off the glacier may make you forget its power. On a hot sunny summer day, it's very important to do what you can to prevent sunstroke; wear a sunhat, lather on the sunscreen, and drink plenty of water.

reach the gentle glacial-fed aquamarine Celeste Lake. Continue past the lake until you reach the junction with the Little Yoho trail.

❹ **Marpole Lake** Follow the trail down to the right for less than 1km (1/2 mile) and hang a left on the Marpole Lake trail. If you've come this far and it's later than 4 or 5pm in summer, you can consider hiking right down the Little Yoho Valley trail back to the trail head. But if you have another 2 hours, you will not regret visiting the Twin Falls area. Once you've branched off, you're quickly cruising across a stunning rock field, the debris from massive avalanches. The historic trail sneaks through giant boulders. Marpole Lake is cool and clear, and full of deadhead logs, more avalanche debris.

❺ **Twin Falls** Soon the trail crosses a giant iron bridge that offers a wonderful lookout over the plummeting Twin Falls. A massive block split the Twin Falls Creek in two branches, which then drop 80m (262 ft.) over a limestone cliff in neighboring channels. Some say these are the loveliest falls in the Rockies—and the competition is fierce! The falls then drop through a massive canyon and eventually braid together into one river, making its way to the Yoho River below.

TAKE A BREAK
Twin Falls is a great break point. If it's nice outside, sit on one of the benches beneath the falls. If it's nasty out, you can sneak inside the chalet for a warm (but quite expensive) cup of tea. You can't eat your lunch inside the chalet, but you can purchase a snack and a warm mug.

❻ **Yoho River** Leaving the roar of Twin Falls behind, you'll head past the Twin Falls Campground and make your way down the gentle forested slope to the Yoho River. A trail heads to the left that takes you closer to the **Yoho Glacier.** It's a hard-to-follow trail that offers only limited views. Best to keep heading down the Yoho River.

❼ **Laughing Falls** Another 4km (2 1/2 miles) down the river, Laughing Falls squirts itself out of a 5m (16-ft.) gorge in the Little Yoho River. It's a thunderous spot. There's another campground here. After crossing the bridge, the trail levels out significantly. Two more short side trips off the main trail take you to quiet, shallow Duchesnay Lake and a viewpoint of the laced-slope of **Angel Staircase Falls.**

The trail then opens into a wide two-lane trail. It's a fast, humdrum, and almost relaxing final few kilometers back to your vehicle waiting in the Takakkaw Falls parking lot.

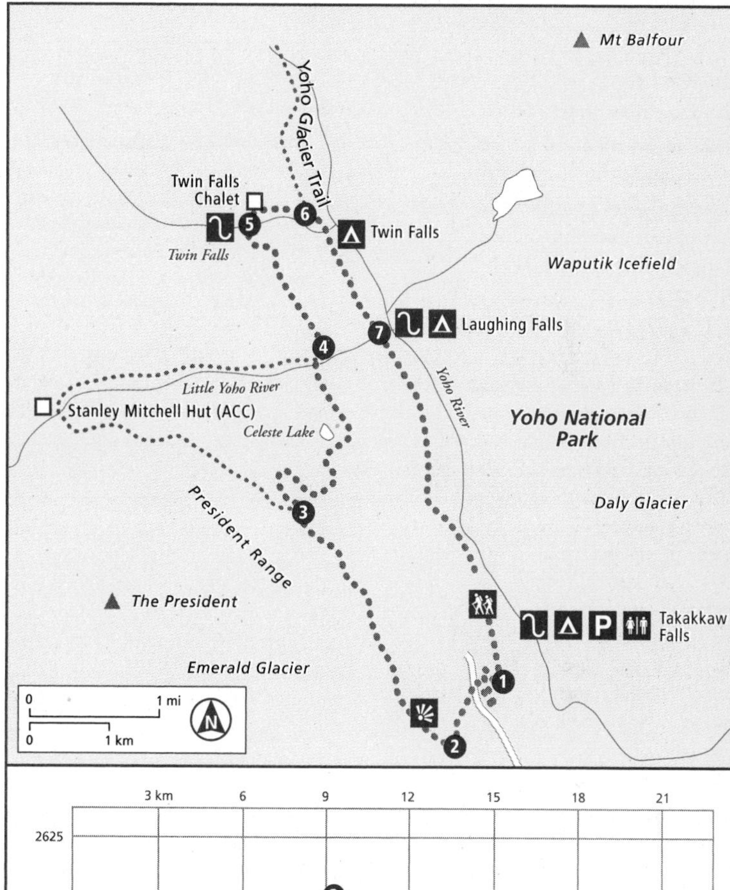

	3 km	6	9	12	15	18	21
2625							
2250							
1875							
1500 m							

N 51 29.558, W 116 29.045 (0 km): Trail head

1. N 51 30.000, W 116 31.000 (1.4 km): Head up the hill behind the hostel at trail sign
2. N 51.28.722, W 116.29.410 (5.1 km): Trail emerges onto rocky slabs
3. N 51 32.382, W 116 31.515 (9.3 km): Trail passes glacial pond
4. N 51 31.440, W 116 30.550 (14 km): Go left on Marpole Lake Trail
5. N 51 32.382, W 116 31.515 (16.4 km): Trail crosses iron bridge with view of Twin Falls
6. N 51 32.420, W 116 31.110 (17.5 km): Pass junction with Yoho Glacier Trail
7. N 51 31.530, W 116 30.240 (19.2 km): Cross bridge past Laughing Falls

5 KINDERSLEY PASS ★

Difficulty rating: Strenuous

Distance: 13km (8 miles) round trip

Estimated time: 6 hr.

Elevation gain: 1,135m (3,724 ft.)

Costs/permits: National Park pass required for vehicles, C$9.80 per adult or C$19.60 per family

Pet friendly: No

Best time to go: June–Sept

Website: www.pc.gc.ca/kootenay

Recommended map: Kootenay National Park Backcountry Guide map

Trail head GPS: N 50 39.555, W 115 57.203

Trail head directions: Park in a small lot on the south side of Hwy. 93, 9.1km (5¾ miles) east of the Kootenay National Park gate at Radium Hot Springs and 84km (52 miles) west of the Kootenay National Park/Banff National Park Border. Cross the highway to the trail marker.

One of the least-known but most enchanting full-day hikes in Kootenay National Park, the loop that heads up to Kindersley Pass and down Sinclair Creek takes you atop a beautiful alpine ridge. Since there are usually so few people hiking here, it's a quiet and intimate exploration of sublime mountain scenery and a good place for wildlife-watching.

Crossing Hwy. 93 in mid-summer tourist traffic may be one of the most challenging moments of this hike. Be careful and look both ways! Once you've made it to the north side of the highway, you'll find a small trail marker pointing you to Kindersley Pass. The trail then heads into a thick forest and begins to climb up a series of switchbacks that are tapered by level sections.

❶ Avalanche Path Around 40 minutes and 3.5km (2¼ miles) into the hike, the trail crosses a giant avalanche path. This is a good spot to see bears (read the sidebar "Bear Safety!" below, if you'd rather not see any). The trail veers to the right, following the slope and gradually climbing up the avalanche path. Besides being home to grizzly and black bears, this is prime wildflower territory. In July, you'll likely be awed by the presence of yellow glacier lilies and columbine, pink wild roses, Indian paintbrush, fireweed, and blue clematis.

❷ Lookout Point Switchbacks continue as you pass over a dry creek bed, quickly turning to the right, back into the forest, and out into another avalanche path. Views of Mount Sinclair open to the south, your left. This is some serious elevation gain, but it's pleasantly in and out of the trees. The trail soon crests on the top of Lookout Point, taking you into the north-facing slopes. Above and on the next slope to the right is your destination—Kindersley Summit.

A handful of footbridges take you over fast-running creeks, some precarious in late June and early July with the heavy runoffs. Having a hiking pole will help with any hopping or jumping.

❸ Kindersley Pass Crossing beneath a waterfall, the trail meets up with a hefty bridge that takes you over the main drainage. Heading up the opposite side of the valley now, the views open up as you travel through wide meadows. Turn around to take in a view of where you've come from.

Then, you'll arrive at Kindersley Pass, which is also the border of Kootenay National Park. The air is clear here, and a

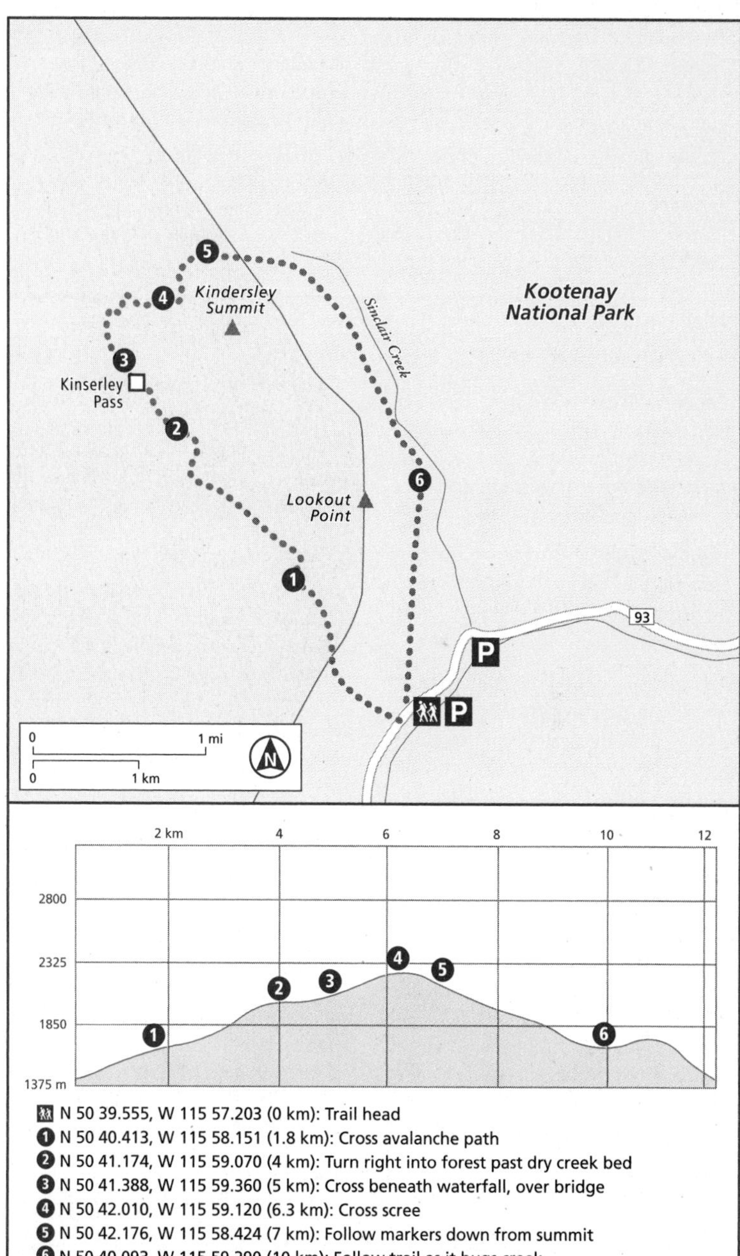

N 50 39.555, W 115 57.203 (0 km): Trail head

❶ N 50 40.413, W 115 58.151 (1.8 km): Cross avalanche path

❷ N 50 41.174, W 115 59.070 (4 km): Turn right into forest past dry creek bed

❸ N 50 41.388, W 115 59.360 (5 km): Cross beneath waterfall, over bridge

❹ N 50 42.010, W 115 59.120 (6.3 km): Cross scree

❺ N 50 42.176, W 115 58.424 (7 km): Follow markers down from summit

❻ N 50 40.093, W 115 59.290 (10 km): Follow trail as it hugs creek

Fun Facts **Bear Safety!**

Although there are many products on the market to help you stay safe in bear territory, perhaps the best tool is your own voice. Use it as much and in any way you can while hiking in black and grizzly bear territory like this. Sing, laugh, recite poetry, holler, yodel, chat with your friends—just try to make your presence known and thus keep from surprising a bear. Bear bells will help with this no-surprise factor. And bear spray, when used properly, should effectively turn back a bear that is at close range (make sure you thoroughly read the instructions before hitting the trail!). But it's best to never get close enough to actually need bear spray.

view to the northwest takes in the Brisco Range on the opposite side of the Columbia Valley.

TAKE A BREAK
This is a great place to stop for a snack and to fuel up before the final push on to the summit. It's also more protected from the wind and weather of the summit.

4 Kindersley Summit You've already come a long way down a varied and interesting trail, yet the most interesting part of the hike lies ahead of you. As you make your way out of the trees and into the alpine, a section of scree and slab is the sign that you are on the final push to the saddle between the two peaks. Richardson ground squirrels, pikas, and marmots make themselves at home here.

Follow rock cairns to a trail sign marking Kindersley Summit. You can still hear the waterfall down behind you. Many animal tracks look like trails. However, there are only two short trails leading to the opposite peaks, both of which make excellent side trips if you have time. Views from both are incredible—you can make out the Matterhorn-like Mount Assiniboine due east on a clear day. The southeast peak is slightly lower.

5 Sinclair Creek This section is often covered in snow into July. Follow the markers as you head down the easterly slope from the summit. You are following the runoff that eventually turns into Sinclair Creek. En route, pass through a beautiful meadow (look for calypso orchids) and what can be a very damp avalanche runoff, especially mucky in early summer. Again, this is bear territory, so make lots of noise as you hike. The trail heads into a thicker forest with Douglas fir trees.

6 Hwy. 93 The Sinclair Creek heads into a narrower canyon here, and the trail hugs first the left and then the right side of the creek. There are a handful of avalanche paths and a quite rapid elevation descent here. The final bridge, 1.2km (3/4 mile) from the end of the trail, leads to a drier and wider trail. From here, it's straight down to the concrete at Hwy. 93.

The trail ends 1.2km (3/4 mile) east of the trail head for Kindersley Pass. You'll need to hike down the side of the highway for five minutes to get back to your car.

6 MOUNT ROBSON PROVINCIAL PARK & KINNEY LAKE

Difficulty rating: Easy

Distance: 6.5km (4.1 miles) one way

Estimated time: 3 hr.

Elevation gain: 130m (427 ft.)

Costs/permits: None

Pet friendly: Pets must be leashed

Best time to go: May–Oct

Website: www.env.gov.bc.ca/bcparks/explore/parkpgs/mt_robson

Recommended Map: NTS 83E/03

Trail head GPS: N 53 03.06, W 119 12.36

Trail head directions: 82km (51 miles) west of the Town of Jasper, on the Yellowhead Highway, and 25km (16 miles) west of the Alberta/British Columbia border. Turn into the parking lot behind the visitors center. Continue 2km (1¼ miles) to the parking lot.

Wide, well-marked, and a wonderful introduction to hiking, this is one of the most-popular trails in western Canada, the kind of place families return to year after year and generation after generation. You'll be hiking in the shadow of Mount Robson, the tallest peak in the Canadian Rockies. Part of a massive track of protected wilderness that includes four national parks nearby, Mt Robson Provincial Park is a UNESCO World Heritage Site. This is an accessible and family-friendly hike with plenty of learning opportunities and rewards.

First, drop by the Mount Robson Provincial Park Visitors Centre for updated trail reports and to register your party with park staff. You can pick up supplies at the convenience store nearby. Then drive 2km (1¼ miles) to the parking lot behind the Visitors Centre to the trail head, getting a good look at Mount Robson down the road ahead of you.

❶ Knowlton Falls The trail starts by crossing a large footbridge over the milky Robson River, which drains the Berg, Mist, and Robson glaciers. Check out that huge snow-capped peak up the river; that's Mount Robson! Shortly, you'll pass Knowlton Falls on the Robson River. To the side of the trail, there are boardwalks over moist bog areas and interpretive signs explaining the ecosystem. Bicycling and horseback riding are also permitted on the trail, although pedestrians have a right of way.

The trail then winds up the west side of the same rushing river through a lush old-growth forest with giant cedar and hemlock trees. This is an interior temperate rainforest.

❷ Avalanche Paths The trail takes a modest uphill, and soon the air dries, leaving giant thimbleberry leaves, cedars, and hemlocks behind. Aspen, birch, lodgepole pine, and Douglas fir trees now take over. The trail crosses a large avalanche path rich in blueberries, which make this prime bear habitat in summertime.

❸ South End of Kinney Lake A bridge takes you across the outlet of Kinney Lake, your first chance to gaze at this incredibly reflective masterpiece. There is a picnic spot and great lookout here across the lake at Whitehorn Mountain. The ridge to the far back right of you is part of Mount Robson. We suggest you continue around on to the north side of the lake and spread out on the lakeshore near the Kinney Lake campground for lunch.

❹ Lakeshore Lookout As you make your way around the lake, the trail crosses more runoffs and creek beds, all rushing down the southwest slope of Mount Robson. One kilometer (½ mile) around the lake, you'll arrive at the Kinney Lake

Kinney Lake

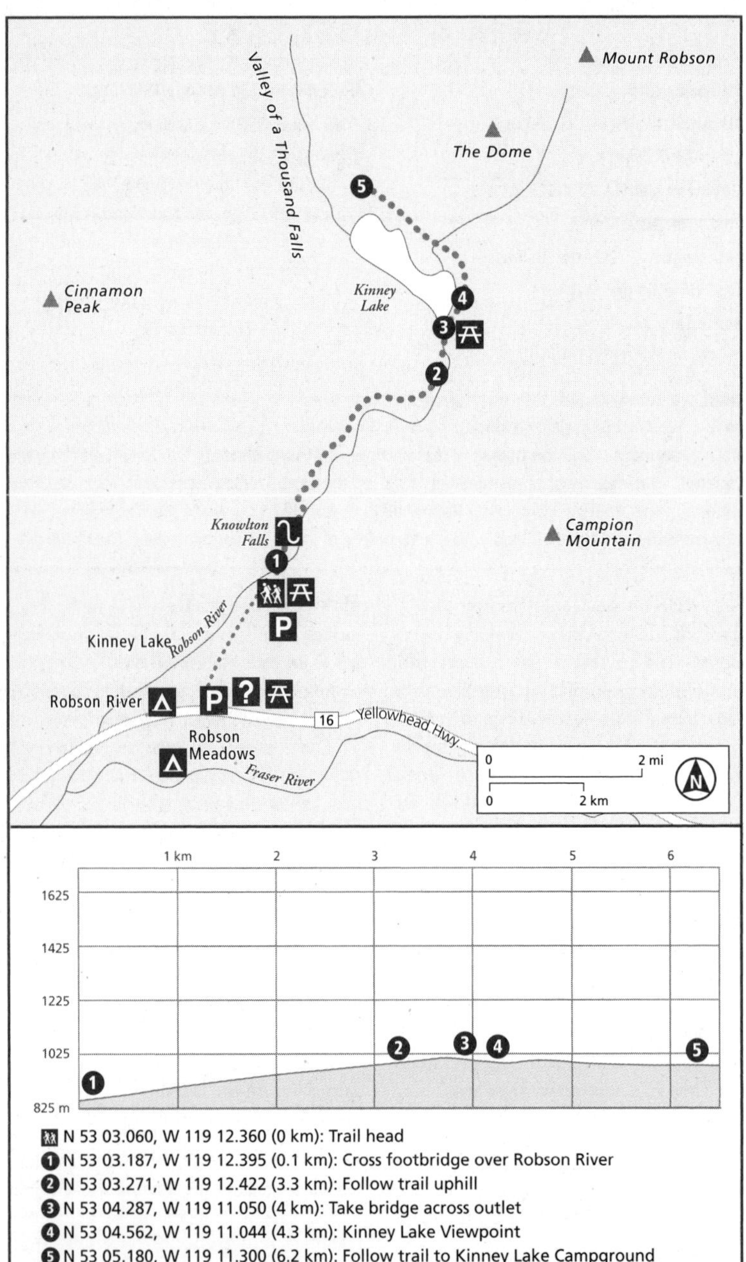

N 53 03.060, W 119 12.360 (0 km): Trail head

1 N 53 03.187, W 119 12.395 (0.1 km): Cross footbridge over Robson River

2 N 53 03.271, W 119 12.422 (3.3 km): Follow trail uphill

3 N 53 04.287, W 119 11.050 (4 km): Take bridge across outlet

4 N 53 04.562, W 119 11.044 (4.3 km): Kinney Lake Viewpoint

5 N 53 05.180, W 119 11.300 (6.2 km): Follow trail to Kinney Lake Campground

Fun Facts **A Rainforest in the Rockies**

Within the Rocky Mountains, it's highly unusual to see such towering, ancient trees. The massive peak of Mount Robson, however, has drastically shaped the climate here. Prevailing Pacific air masses are lifted over Mount Robson on their way east to the prairies, dropping condensation and rain into this valley and making it feel remarkably similar to a coastal climate. Robson itself is covered in cloud 4 days out of 5. And so trees that require lots of moisture thrive here.

viewpoint. Shortly after that, there is a wide pebbly beach, which is a good spot to dip your fingers in the ice-cold lake.

❺ **Kinney Lake Campground** The trail climbs a short section then drops back down and leads directly to the Kinney Lake campsite, which has seven tent sites available (reservations required). There is a shelter here where you can escape bad weather. This is the high point of the trail if you're only going to Kinney Lake. You can say goodbye to backpackers with heavy loads of gear who will continue on into the Valley of a Thousand Falls and to Berg Lake. Enjoy the view for as long as you'd like; it'll take you an hour to get back down to your car.

7 KOKANEE LAKES ★★

Difficulty rating: Moderate

Distance: 17km (11 miles) round trip

Estimated time: 6 hr.

Elevation gain: 490m (1,608 ft.)

Costs/permits: None

Pet friendly: No dogs permitted in park

Best time to go: July–Sept. Larches are stunning in Sept.

Website: www.env.gov.bc.ca/bcparks/explore/parkpgs/kokanee_gl

Recommended map: 82 F/11 and F/14

Trail head GPS: N 49 43.36, W 118 09.18

Trail head directions: Follow Hwy. 3A east from Nelson 19km (12 miles) to the Kokanee Creek Rd., turning left 400m (1,312 ft.) past the Kokanee Creek Provincial Park, which is on your right on the lakeshore. Turn left quickly again onto Gibson Lake Rd., follow it for 16km (10 miles) or approx. 25 min. to trail head. 4WD is suggested but not crucial. Grab some of the chicken wire at the trail head and wrap a stiff fence around your car to keep porcupines and other critters from gnawing at your tires.

Located north of the town of Nelson, Kokanee Glacier Provincial Park offers a wealth of varied trails and outstanding alpine terrain for hikers. Leading you into a high plateau known as the Nelson Batholith, which straddles the ridges and valleys between Kootenay and Slocan lakes, this is the premiere hike in the West Kootenay area of the Selkirk Mountains. Taking in the main highlights of the provincial park, including a handful of stunning alpine lakes, this hike is deeply pleasing.

Kokanee Glacier Cabin

Tucked on the north shore of Kaslo Lake, this stunning three-story timber-frame lodge was rebuilt in 2002 in an effort led by two of the sons and the ex-wife of former Canadian Prime Minister Pierre Trudeau, whose youngest son Michel Trudeau was killed in an avalanche near Kokanee Lake in 1998. Inside, the cabin has plenty of information on avalanche safety and humbly honors the adventurers who have lost their lives in the nearby peaks. Accommodating up to 20 hikers, this makes a superb base camp for a few days exploring the high alpine area of Kokanee Glacier Provincial Park and is run by the Alpine Club of Canada. Reservations are required; book by calling ✆ **403/678-3200 ext. 1** or e-mailing info@alpineclubofcanada.ca.

You are going to follow the well-maintained trail up and down the same route. After securing your vehicle from nasty porcupines (who like to nibble at tires and brake lines) with chicken wire, take a good look at the trail information sign for any updates and to orient yourself. Then, head up an old road into a thick forest, turning a sharp left at a waterfall.

❶ **Second Arrow** After about .5km (1/4 mile), a real uphill begins. A second arrow points you in the right direction, another 2.5km (1 1/2 miles) to Kokanee Lake. There are a series of switchbacks, finally ending on a large avalanche path. Here, the grunt softens. Make your way across a boulder field and past a dried rocky basin.

❷ **Kokanee Lake** Head over the hump and then drop down a gentle slope dotted with wildflowers to the gorgeous sapphire Kokanee Lake. Nestled in a narrow basin, it is ice cold, just like the beer named for it. A great destination in its own right, there are icebergs floating in the lake in early summer. Most of the elevation gain is behind you at this point. There is an outhouse at the south end of the lake. The trail skirts the lake over an entertaining series of boulder hops across talus slopes on the lake's west side.

❸ **Kokanee Pass** Leaving Kokanee Lake behind, the trail meanders across a lush small meadow with beautiful wildflowers, including Indian paintbrush and daisies. This meadow is also home to a handful of very friendly marmots—don't feed them! A bridge takes you over the creek and then up the gentle slope, into the trees to Kokanee Pass.

❹ **Kokanee Glacier Cabin** On the other side of the pass, heading generally northwest, you'll hike past two more small treasures, Keen and Garland lakes. Both are slightly off the trail and not easy to photograph. The area becomes very wet and boggy, but the trail keeps above the muck. Then, a trail marker points the way to the Kokanee Glacier Cabin, on the shores of Kaslo Lake, run by the Alpine Club of Canada.

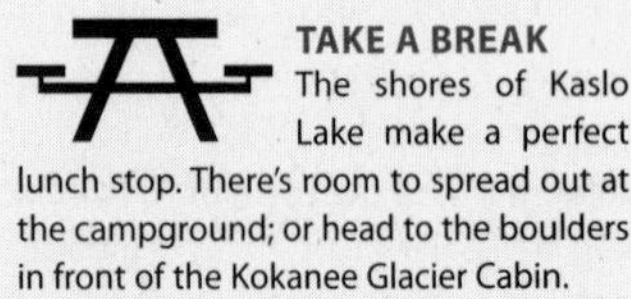

TAKE A BREAK The shores of Kaslo Lake make a perfect lunch stop. There's room to spread out at the campground; or head to the boulders in front of the Kokanee Glacier Cabin.

❺ **Slocan Chief Cabin** Head back to the trail marker you passed just before turning to the Kokanee Glacier Cabin.

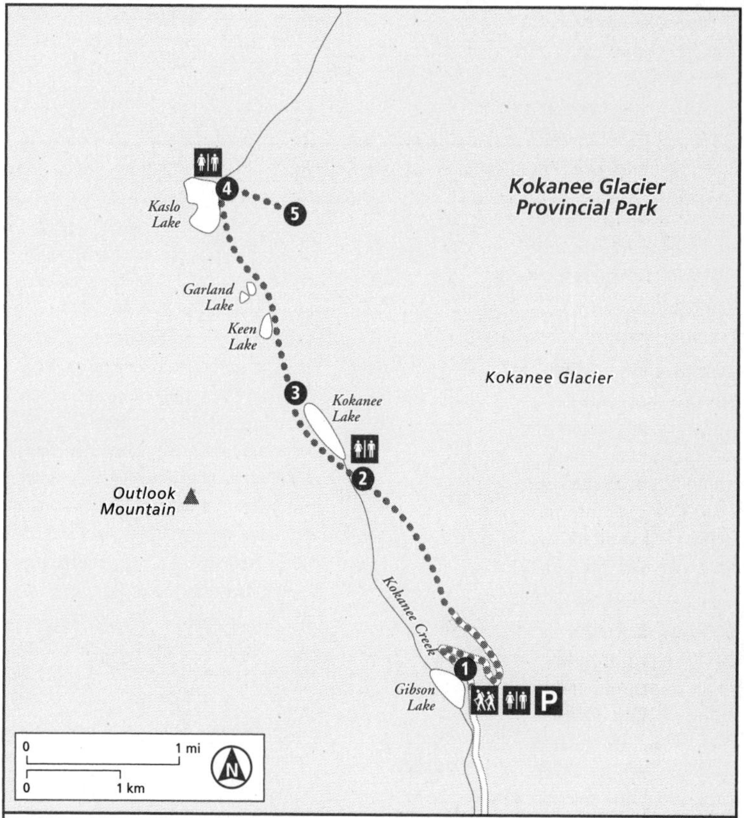

Kokanee Glacier
Provincial Park
Kaslo
Lake
Garland
Lake
Keen
Lake
Kokanee
Lake
Kokanee Glacier
Outlook
Mountain
Kokanee Creek
Gibson
Lake
P
0
1 mi
0
1 km
N

3 km
6
9
12
15
2600
2075
1550 m

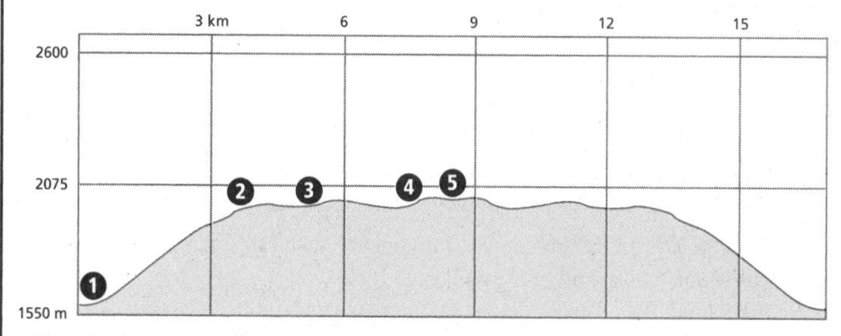

N 49 43.360, W 118 09.180 (0 km): Trail head
❶ N 49 43.486, W 117 09.095 (0.3 km): Follow arrow to Kokanee Lake
❷ N 49 44.367, W 117 10.074 (3.8 km): Head over hump, down gentle slope
❸ N 49 45.254, W 117 10.542 (5.2 km): Cross bridge, climb to Kokanee Pass
❹ N 49 46.137, W 117 11.344 (7.5 km): Follow trail markers to Kokanee Glacier Cabin
❺ N 49 46.055, W 117 10.397 (8.5 km): Cross valley to Slocan Chief Cabin

From here, head straight up a hill and over to the next valley. On a bedrock bluff just above Kalmia Lake is the historic Slocan Chief Cabin. Built originally in 1896 to house miners working nearby, the cabin became a hub for mountaineering activities. Two major restorations, in 1962 and 2004, have kept it standing. Today, there is a charming interpretive center inside. From here, turn around and head back the way you came in.

8 LAKE OF THE HANGING GLACIER ★★

Difficulty rating: Strenuous

Distance: 16km (10 miles) round trip

Estimated time: 6–7 hr.

Elevation gain: 720m (2,362 ft.)

Costs/permits: None

Pet friendly: No

Best time to go: Mid-July to Sept only. Bridges are removed and make hiking here impossible during the rest of the year. The trail is driest in Sept.

Website: www.for.gov.bc.ca/drm/Recreation/RecreationTrails/SteamboatInvermre/LakeHangingGlacier.htm

Recommended Map: Duncan Lake 82 K/7

Trail head GPS: N 50 29.12, W 116 35.06

Trail head directions: Just over 45 min. from Radium along a logging road that can be busy with raging logging trucks—stay to the right and be cautious. There are water bars and washouts that change season to season—check with the Ministry of Forests for updated road reports (call ✆ 250/426-1700). From the junction of Hwy. 93 and Hwy. 95 in Radium Hot Springs, drive west to Forsters Landing Rd., next to the Prestige Inn. You'll pass a mill and then continue west on the Horsethief Creek Forest Service Rd. Stay left at a crossroad at 4.3km (2¾ miles) and drive straight on the main road that meets with the Westside Rd. Set your odometer at 0 here. Stay right at 27km (17 miles). There is a campground at 30km (19 miles). Be alert for deep water bars! You cross a narrow wooden bridge at 33km (21 miles). Turn right at 38km (24 miles) over the Horsethief Creek, just past the turnoff for the Farnham Creek trail. The final 2.6km (1½ miles) include a number of wash-outs that are passable by 4WD vehicles only. Park on the river side of the road just before a massive landslide. Hike around the landslide to the official trail head.

There are so many dazzling alpine lakes in the mountains of Western Canada. In our opinion, however, none measure up to the stark and dramatic beauty of this remote lake in the Central Purcell Mountains. The hike to get there is isolated, and just getting to the trail head is a task in itself. But once you're on the trail, you'll be busy enough getting deeper and deeper into the mountains. And once you see this incredible rock-and-ice-encircled lake, you'll forget all your troubles.

The trail to the Lake of the Hanging Glacier is varied and pleasant, crossing creeks and circling through lush forests. There's only one really steep section. With gushing waterfalls, perfect little foot bridges, an alpine meadow, and the giant reward at the top, this is very pleasurable hiking. It's well off the beaten path, though, with few services. You should be comfortable in a very remote setting to hike here. At the start of the hike, keep an eye out for moose along the riverbed.

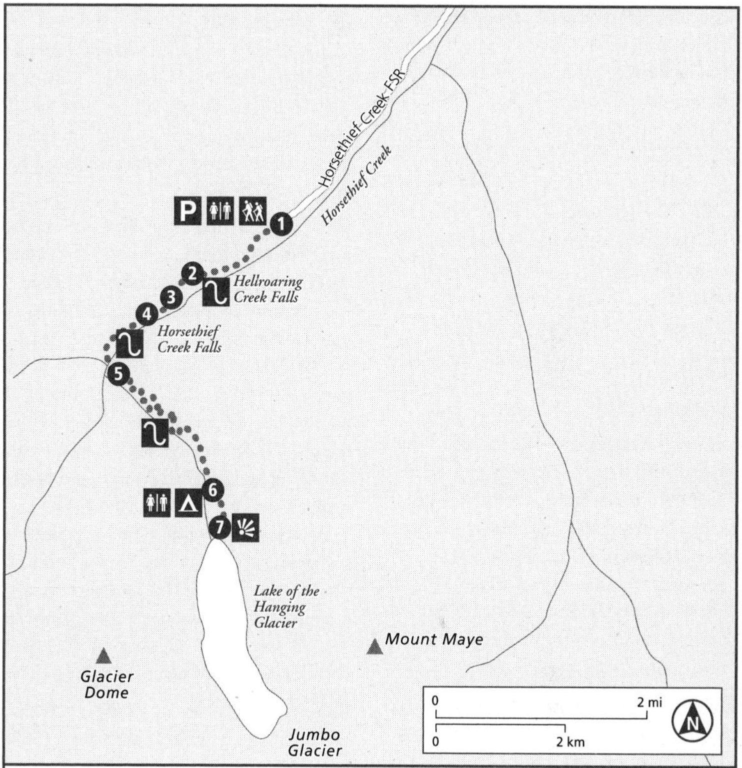

Horsethief-Creek-FSR
Horsethief Creek
Hellroaring Creek Falls
Horsethief Creek Falls
Lake of the Hanging Glacier
Mount Maye
Glacier Dome
Jumbo Glacier
0 2 mi
0 2 km

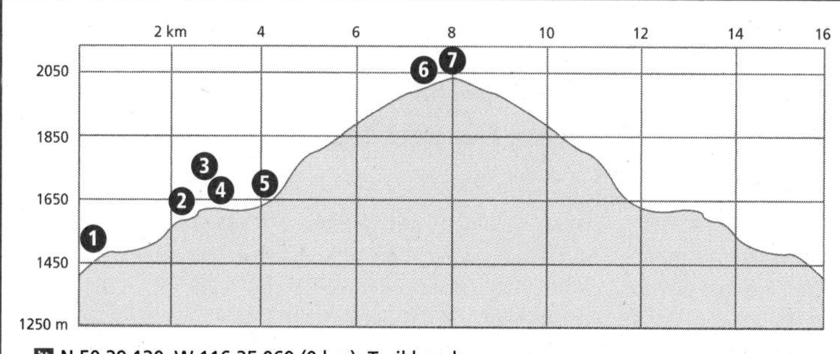

- N 50 29.120, W 116 35.060 (0 km): Trail head
- ❶ N 50 29.411, W 116 35.376 (0.2 km): Follow forest trail to logging road
- ❷ N 50 29.019, W 116 36.429 (2.2 km): Cross steel bridge
- ❸ N 50 29.038, W 116 36.417 (2.9 km): Turn right at fork
- ❹ N 50 28.502, W 116 36.456 (3 km): Cross bridge above Horsethief Falls
- ❺ N 50 28.180, W 116 36.540 (4.1 km): Switchbacks begin
- ❻ N 50 27.081, W 116 35.576 (7.6 km): Pass campsite at right
- ❼ N 50 27.068, W 116 35.524 (8 km): Arrive at Lake of the Hanging Glacier

❶ Through the Forest Once you've found the proper place to park your car, you must cross a washed-out stretch of road to the true trail head, where there is a trail book inside a tin box and marker. The trail starts to the right of the marker.

Here, you begin winding up the headwaters of Horsethief Creek through a cool, lush forest, and then on to an old logging road. There are expansive views of the falls and glaciers both ahead and behind. You are getting further and further into the wilderness.

❷ Hell Roaring Creek Bridge You can barely hear yourself think as you cross this creek! At the 2.4km (1½-mile) mark, drop down to the steel bridge, making your safe passage across this violent creek. Placed by trail maintenance crews in mid-July, it's taken out in September. During the rest of the year, this trail is definitely off limits since it's essentially impossible to cross the appropriately named creek. Take the foot path to the left, heading into a lovely forest with tall trees, ferns, horsetails, and a wide (albeit, sometimes muddy) trail.

❸ Intersection with Horse Path Just a short distance later, the trail meets a fork, with the right arm a horse trail (although it's not clear where it leads). Take the footpath down to the left, 100m (328 ft.) to the next bridge.

❹ Horsethief Creek Bridge At 3.1km (2 miles), you'll cross an impressive bridge just above Horsethief Falls. The trail continues along the left side of the creek on a curvy, level stretch. Up the valley, you'll see your first views of the glaciers on Mount Monica.

❺ Uphill Begins Back into yet another lush, beautiful forest, at 4.5km (2¾ miles), the climbing begins. Welcome to a demanding series of 13 switchbacks alongside the loud crashing of the creek draining the Lake of the Hanging Glacier! You will climb nearly 400m (1,312 ft.) in 2.3km (1½ miles). The falls are very loud here, but there are a few viewpoints to take in the pounding and gorging cascade, and to give yourself a chance to catch your breath.

As you climb higher into a more level meadow, some sections of the trail are washed out. The trail crisscrosses past large avalanche slopes and over two short log bridges, eventually heading onto a wide, boulder- and wildflower-dotted meadow.

❻ Campground The forest thins at an avalanche path, and larch trees appear (they turn a gorgeous golden color in autumn). The gradient eases into a subalpine meadow.

The View from Up Here: The Backdrop to Lake of the Hanging Glaciers

Besides often having floating icebergs, this silt-green lake has got one of the most picturesque backdrops of any lake in British Columbia. The names of the glaciers are often whispered amongst mountain lovers; however, few actually make the journey to see them with their own eyes.

From your jaw-dropping viewpoint at the north end of the lake, here's what you've got in front of you:

- Commander Mountain, the tall peak at the far back of the lake on the left
- The tongue of the Jumbo Neve Glacier to the left
- Glacier Dome to the right (southwest)
- The rock wall of the Lieutenants in the middle
- Granite Peak to the east/northeast

Take a lot of pictures!

To the right, there's a campsite and outhouse at 7.4km (4½ miles). This is a nice place to spend the night in utter alpine glee atop mop tops and amidst the paintbrushes. Pikas and marmots may peak their heads out for a quick hello!

7 Lake of the Hanging Glacier Another quick 600m (1,969 ft.) brings you up past a vast cascade and onto a wide plain of rocks at the north end of the Lake of the Hanging Glacier. Pick a comfy spot and relax.

In front of you, 2.5km (1½ miles) across the lake, map out the glaciers (see the sidebar "The View from Up Here: The Backdrop to Lake of the Hanging Glaciers," above). This is a classic rock and ice cirque. With clouds rushing above and icebergs floating in front, there is plenty to keep your thoughts adrift.

When it's time to head back to civilization, just turn around and float back down the trail—you'll be forever marked by this chillingly beautiful spot. The views on the way down are equally lovely.

9 LAKE O'HARA CIRCUIT ★★★

Difficulty rating: Strenuous

Distance: 10.1km (6.3 miles) round trip

Estimated time: 6–7 hr.

Elevation gain: 315m (1,033 ft.)

Costs/permits: National Park permit required for your vehicle (C$9.80 per adult or C$19.60 per family); reservations and fee required for bus access (C$14.70 adults, C$7.30 youth)

Pet friendly: No

Best time to go: Mid-June to early Oct. Fall is particularly lovely.

Website: www.parkscanada.gc.ca/yoho

Recommended map: Lake O'Hara Backcountry Map from Yoho National Park

Trail head GPS: N 51 21.24, W 116 20.18

Trail head directions: Access to Lake O'Hara is limited to regularly scheduled school bus departures from a parking lot 15km (9¼ miles) east from Field and 11km (6¾ miles) west from Lake Louise, Alberta on Hwy. 1, the Trans-Canada Highway.

Just the mention of Lake O'Hara makes die-hard hikers get misty in the eyes. Few places in the world can rival the stunning scenery, historic trail system, varied landscape, and special charm of this tiny area tucked beneath the Continental Divide. This hike, a true Rocky Mountain classic, takes in the highlights and is easily doable in a well-organized day. Just remember, you need to book a bus well ahead of time, and you must get on the first bus in and the last bus out!

Only 42 hikers are allowed into Lake O'Hara each day (plus those staying at the small Lake O'Hara Lodge, two Alpine Club of Canada huts, and the nearby Parks Canada campground). Reservations are required for spots on the bus that takes you to the lake from the parking lot—and can be made by telephone only, and only three months ahead of your planned visit. Call ✆ **250/343-6433.** The bus drops you off in front of the Le Relais Day Shelter, steps from the shore of the lake. Head down to the water and turn to your right, following the trail around the turquoise lake in front of the historic Lake O'Hara Lodge.

1 Turn to Mary Lake In operation since 1926, Lake O'Hara Lodge is one of Canada's most beloved and famous backcountry lodges. The lodge is not open to the public; walk right through the property and around the southwest end of the lake.

Tips In Case of Rain, or In Case You're Late . . .

If you happen to be at Lake O'Hara on a rainy day, stick to the East Opabin Trail and head right back to Lake O'Hara—the Yukness Ledges can be very, very slippery and dangerous in wet weather! Similarly, if you have arrived at this point any time after 2pm, then you need to think about heading back to the bus stop. The rest of the hike will take you another 2 or 3 hours. Remember: The last bus goes down at 6:30pm. Ask at the Relais center for updated trail reports.

Take a right at the fork 300m (984 ft.) past the lodge towards Mary Lake and the West Opabin Trail, heading uphill quickly and staying left at the next sign. Stagnant Mary Lake is the first in a series of lakes tucked into the slopes that drain the Opabin Plateau.

2 The Opabin Prospect Following the shore of Mary Lake, the trail then climbs in earnest, steeply ascending a talus slope. The climb is exposed and requires your full attention. You'll climb 120m (394 ft.), leveling off at a grassy cleft. Welcome to the Opabin Plateau! Continue past the turnoff to the All Soul's Prospect Alpine Route.

Take a quick left on a small path east to the head of a cliff overlooking Lake O'Hara. This is the scene of a famous painting by Canadian artist Lawren Harris. In fact, the entire Opabin area has long been an artist's Mecca. Larches in the fall make this lookout particularly spectacular.

3 Lake Opabin The Opabin Plateau Circuit continues southeast. There is a labyrinth of trails here; stick to the right (west) side of the valley, crossing a bridge over the Opabin Creek and travelling upstream. You'll pass Hungabee Lake on your left, climb up over a knoll, and then, about an hour and a half into the hike, you'll get your first look at Opabin Lake. Behind the lake and slightly to the left is Mount Hungabee. To the right are the slopes of Mount Shäffer and Mount Biddle. In between is a glacier about 800m (2,625 ft.) long. Follow the trail down to the lakeshore.

TAKE A BREAK
This is a great place to stop for a snack. Put your pack down on one of the boulders and enjoy the view. You can put your fingers in the ice-cold lake at the creek's outlet on the far north shore. Just remember to stay on the trail—this is a very fragile area, and trail maintenance crews take special care to keep impact to a minimum.

4 Yukness Ledges From here, you will connect with the East Opabin Trail and head back along the plateau, following the slope of Yukness Mountain.

Just opposite the southeast corner of Hungabee Lake, follow trail markers up the slope to the Yukness Ledges. Here, the trail-finding can be tricky; follow a series of navy blue triangles with yellow dashes painted onto large, sharp boulders that lead you up and to the left. You can't lose your way once you get to the correct height, about 100m (328 ft.) up, to where the trail becomes obvious clinging to the ridge.

A rugged traverse across large boulders around the ledge begins. Watch your footing! Ledges are narrow and can be slippery, and well, it's a long way down. But the views are exceptional. Follow the paint markers around the curve.

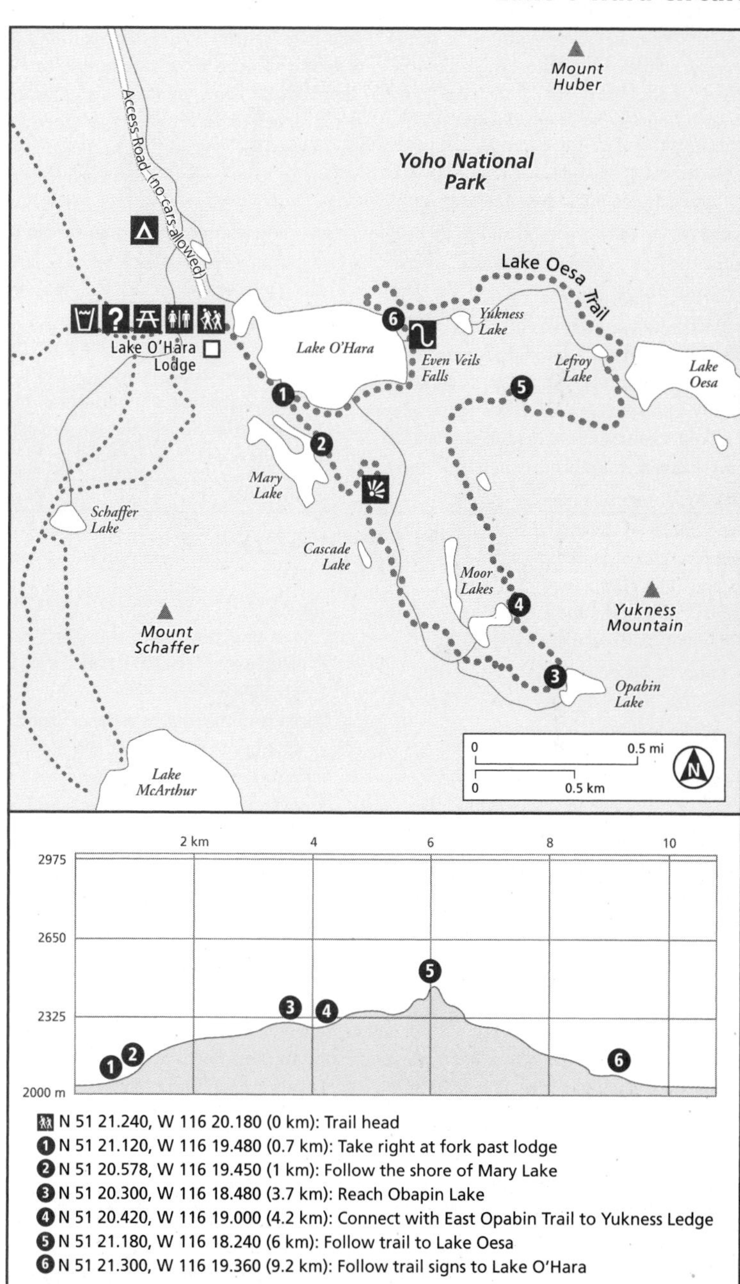
Mount Huber
Access Road (no cars allowed)
Yoho National Park
Lake Oesa Trail
Yukness Lake
Lake O'Hara
Lake O'Hara Lodge
Even Veils Falls
Lefroy Lake
Lake Oesa
Mary Lake
Schaffer Lake
Cascade Lake
Moor Lakes
Yukness Mountain
Mount Schaffer
Opabin Lake
Lake McArthur
0 0.5 mi
0 0.5 km
N
2 km 4 6 8 10
2975
2650
2325
2000 m
N 51 21.240, W 116 20.180 (0 km): Trail head
1 N 51 21.120, W 116 19.480 (0.7 km): Take right at fork past lodge
2 N 51 20.578, W 116 19.450 (1 km): Follow the shore of Mary Lake
3 N 51 20.300, W 116 18.480 (3.7 km): Reach Obapin Lake
4 N 51 20.420, W 116 19.000 (4.2 km): Connect with East Opabin Trail to Yukness Ledge
5 N 51 21.180, W 116 18.240 (6 km): Follow trail to Lake Oesa
6 N 51 21.300, W 116 19.360 (9.2 km): Follow trail signs to Lake O'Hara

5 Lake Oesa The trail clings to the edge of the ledge's steep rim here. Stay high; you'll eventually drop down to a gentle plateau which culminates at Lake Oesa. Oesa, which means "ice" in the local native Stoney language, is a deep-blue-tinged lake (versus the creamy green of Opabin).

This is your second break point, another lakeshore picnic spot. Peer high up to the ridge of Mt Lefroy, behind and to the left, and you'll see the Continental Divide. Directly on the opposite side of the peak are Lake Louise and the Victoria Glacier.

6 Lake O'Hara Head back down the rock slabs that nestle Lake Oesa, following trail signs to Lake O'Hara. This short (3.2km/2 miles) section may be our favorite of the entire hike. The trail was lovingly constructed by famed trail-maker Lawrence Grassi, a former coal miner, mountain guide, and park warden here in the late 1950s. It descends through a bedrock trough, over a short, grassy slope, and past a thundering waterfall before reaching a delicate meadow surrounded by quartzite cliffs. Rocks here appear in every color of the rainbow, from plum to ginger. Stone steps carved by Grassi usher you down through a stunted forest to a cliff that provides your last lookout of Lake O'Hara. From here, switchbacks drop down to the lakeshore.

You can head right and back to the Relais via Cataract Brook; it's the shortest route. If you have another hour before your bus departs, take the left and longer route that takes you over Seven Veils Falls.

10 STANLEY GLACIER ★

Difficulty rating: Moderate

Distance: 9km (5.6 miles) round trip

Estimated time: 3 hr.

Elevation gain: 395m (1,296 ft.)

Costs/permits: National Park permit required on display in your vehicle

Pet friendly: Allowed on a leash

Best time to go: Late June to Oct. Before 9am or after 3pm to avoid crowds.

Website: www.parkscanada.gc.ca/kootenay

Recommended map: Kootenay National Park Backcountry Guide map

Trail head GPS: N 51 12.190, W 116 04.530

Trail head directions: On Hwy. 93, 3.2km (2 miles) west of the Banff National Park and Kootenay National Park borders (also the border between the provinces of Alberta and British Columbia). Parking lot is on the south side of the highway. From Banff, drive the Trans-Canada Highway to Castle Junction and take Hwy. 93 south. From Radium Hot Springs, take Hwy. 93 north 93km (58 miles) towards Banff.

Taking you from fire to ice in only 2.5km (1½ miles), this is a relatively short and only moderately steep half-day hike on the crest of the Continental Divide. The trail takes you up to a hanging valley with a giant glacier clinging to the limestone cliffs at the back. There are great views throughout the entire hike. Family friendly and particularly good in the shoulder seasons (late spring or early fall), this is classic Rocky Mountain hiking!

With relatively little elevation gain (most of which you knock off at the very beginning) and yet access to breathtaking views, this trail is a great way to get up into the alpine zone quickly. Since it's so close to Banff (35 minutes from the Town of Banff), it's also very popular. Once up amidst the meadows, though, you'll want to linger; so come either early in the morning (around 9am) or in the mid-afternoon to avoid the crowds and give yourself time.

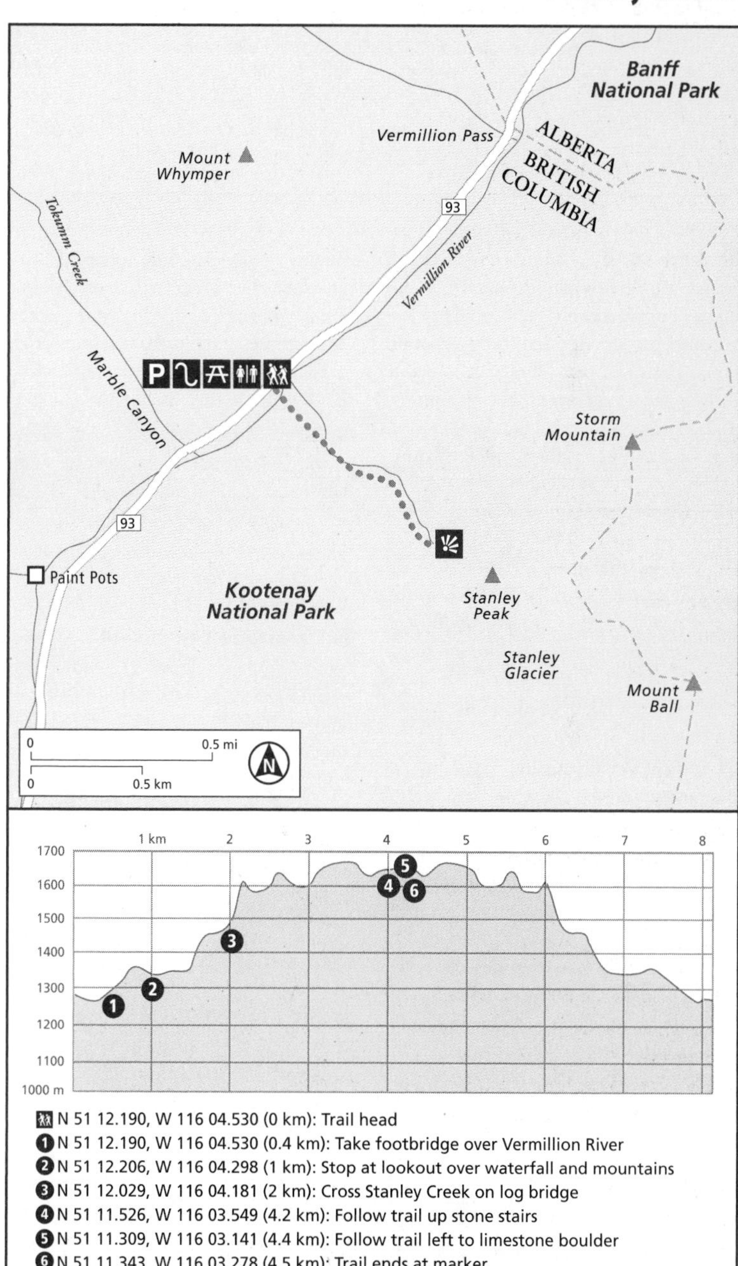

N 51 12.190, W 116 04.530 (0 km): Trail head

❶ N 51 12.190, W 116 04.530 (0.4 km): Take footbridge over Vermillion River

❷ N 51 12.206, W 116 04.298 (1 km): Stop at lookout over waterfall and mountains

❸ N 51 12.029, W 116 04.181 (2 km): Cross Stanley Creek on log bridge

❹ N 51 11.526, W 116 03.549 (4.2 km): Follow trail up stone stairs

❺ N 51 11.309, W 116 03.141 (4.4 km): Follow trail left to limestone boulder

❻ N 51 11.343, W 116 03.278 (4.5 km): Trail ends at marker

Fun Facts Fire!

To learn more about the role of fire in forest management, visit the Fireweed Interpretive Trail just 3km (1¾ miles) east of the Stanley Glacier trail head. Along a family-friendly 15-minute trail, there are signs explaining the healing power of fire. It's also the Continental Divide, where rivers split between those flowing east to the Atlantic Ocean and west to the Pacific Ocean.

❶ Burn Land A footbridge over the Vermillion River marks the start of this hike. The trail switchbacks through a forest that burned after a **lightning strike** hit the slopes of Mount Whymper in 1968. Driven by strong winds, the fire moved quickly across the Vermillion Pass, eventually burning more than 2,950 hectares (7,290 acres) of subalpine forest. One of the most studied burns in Canada, this is a place to marvel at nature's own way of cleaning up after itself. Far from a darkened burn, this area is richly colorful, where new lodgepole pine and wildflowers bloom industriously in the freshly fertilized, recycled, and renewed soil.

It's like getting a glimpse into ancient times.

❷ Mountain Lookout The thinned forest also offers lovely views that would otherwise be blocked by trees. Five minutes up the trail, Stanley Creek drains in a dramatic, wide waterfall tapering down the slope. There's a lookout that is a great spot to admire big Rocky Mountains like Castle Mountain (just over the ridge to the east in Alberta), Storm Mountain, Mount Whymper, and Boom Mountain. You're also looking at the Continental Divide and the Vermillion Pass.

❸ Stanley Creek Bridge Thirty minutes and 2km (1¼ miles) into the hike, the trail levels out, crossing Stanley Creek on a log bridge. Welcome to the hanging valley!

This is your first chance to snap a photo of Stanley Glacier, which you'll spot in the distance to the southwest clinging to a limestone cliff. From here, the creek goes mostly underground. Continue another 1km (½ mile) along the east side of the creek bed to the head of the basin and to the edge of the tree line.

❹ Scree Stairs After crossing an avalanche path, the hike becomes a true mountain trail. The forest thins and the trail leads up haphazard stones serving as stairs through an open talus slope. This is prime pika territory—watch for the little hamster-like critters hiding behind boulders!

❺ Limestone Lunch Spot The trail continues to the left up and through the trees to a clearing with a white limestone boulder.

TAKE A BREAK
This is a great place to stop for lunch, with the large white limestone boulder allowing you to spread out a small picnic. Take out your camera and soak up the amazing views of Stanley Glacier!

❻ End Atop an Old Moraine About 200m (656 ft.) past the boulder, the trail ends with a marker. Scramble routes can be seen branching off in various directions. Stanley Glacier is to the southwest on the north face of Stanley Peak. Flowing in two directions, the toe visible from the trail is the easternmost flow. The main section of the glacier is above and to the right, out of site.

Fun Facts **Go Stanley!**

Hockey fans will be interested to know that mountaineer Edward Whymper named the Stanley Peak—and the Stanley Glacier—after Frederick Stanley, the sixth Governor-General of Canada, and the same man who had a large park in downtown Vancouver and a certain hockey trophy named after him.

From here, experienced hikers can explore further, making a loop heading left from the trail marker. The trail heads up a steep scree slope, eventually passing caves tucked into the limestone cliffs on the left, and getting quite close to the tip of Stanley Glacier.

SLEEPING & EATING

ACCOMMODATIONS

Cathedral Mountain Lodge A cozy gathering of wooden chalets tucked along the Kicking Horse River, this is a superb location for exploring the trails of Yoho National Park. Although the setting is a little squished, it's great for families with active, older kids, and yet it still has an element of romanticism. Cabins are close together but very comfortable.

Mailing address: P.O. Box 40, Field, BC V0A 1G0. ✆ **866/619-6442** or 250/343-6442. www.cathedralmountain.com. 31 units. C$195–C$390 double; rates include breakfast. AE, MC, V. No children under 8 allowed. **Close to:** Iceline Trail, Lake O'Hara Circuit, Emerald Lake.

Illecillewaet Campground Pitch your tent directly at the trail head for the Abbott Pass and other awesome hikes in Glacier National Park. The nearby Best Western hotel is in a bad state, and hotels in Revelstoke are another 30 to 45 minutes away. Right beside the Illecillewaet River, this is a cozy spot for hearty hikers. Sites are on a first-come, first-served basis; no reservations are accepted. The best time to arrive and find a site is before 10am.

3km (1¾ miles) west of summit of Rogers Pass on the Trans-Canada Hwy. 1, Glacier National Park. ✆ **250/837-7500.** www.pc.gc.ca/glacier. 60 campsites. C$21.50 for campsite. Open late June–early Sept. No reservations. **Close to:** Abbott Ridge.

Mount Robson Ranch A heritage ranch that's been operating since 1921 on the south side of the Fraser River, the cozy log cabins and campsites here have fantastic views of the namesake peak. It's peaceful in the evenings. Log cabins sleep up to six, and there are also 14 campsites. All have incredible views of the famous peak.

Mailing address: P.O. Box 548, 8925 Haregreaves Rd., Valemount, BC V0E 2Z0. ✆ **877/566-4654** or 250/566-4654. www.mountrobsonranch.com. 7 cabins and 14 campsites. C$100 for cabin; C$25 for campsite with shower and electrical hookup. V, MC. 85km (53 miles) from Jasper on Hwy. 16. Turn left at Mount Robson Visitors Centre and follow for 2.5km (1½ miles). **Close to:** Kinney Lake.

Mountain Hound Inn A budget-friendly option in downtown Nelson, this hotel makes a great base for those intent on spending their days in the mountains. Slightly

Staying in the Backcountry

The **Alpine Club of Canada** runs a handful of backcountry huts located near or directly on some of these trails, including the Elizabeth Parker Hut at Lake O'Hara, the Stanley Mitchell Hut in the Little Yoho Valley, the A.O. Wheeler Hut in Glacier National Park, the Conrad Kain Hut in Bugaboo Provincial Park, and the Kokanee Glacier Cabin on Kaslo Lake in the Kootenays. These are generally very rustic huts with little or no services. Rates are C$35 per night for non-members. Reservations are required for all huts and can be made via the ACC's office in Canmore, Alberta, ✆ **403/678-3200** or info@alpineclubofcanada.ca.

Canadian Mountain Holidays (✆ **800/661-0252** or 403/762-7100; www.cmhhike.com) offers true backcountry luxury at their six outstanding helicopter-accessed wilderness lodges dotted throughout the mountains of eastern British Columbia. Helicopters whisk you each morning into the high alpine and, after you spend a day exploring the high peaks, take you back to the lodge for a gourmet meal, massage, and a fluffy duvet. Three-day heli-hiking trips start at C$2,490 per person.

dormitory-style, there's a complimentary breakfast and very attentive staff. Rooms have air conditioning and flat-screen TVs. Rooms 121 and 122 are the only ones with views.

621 Baker St., Nelson, BC V1L4J3. ✆ **866/452-6490** or 250/352-6490. www.mountainhound.com. 19 units. C$89–C$105 double; rates include continental breakfast. AE, MC, V. **Close to:** Kootenay Lakes.

Redstreak Campground With a whopping 242 sites, this is the largest campground in Kootenay National Park and is very close to the village of Radium Hot Springs. There are regular interpretive events, a playground for kids, and a great trail system heading right from your front flap.

Redstreak Rd., Radium Hot Springs, BC V0A1M0. ✆ **877/737-3783.** www.pccamping.ca. 242 sites. C$38.20 full hookup; C$32.50 electrical hookup; C$27.40 non-serviced site. Open May 9–Oct 8. Drive south at the end of Main St. in Radium Hot Springs for 2.5km (1½ miles) on Redstreak Rd. Reservations required. **Close to:** Kindersley Pass, Lake of the Hanging Glacier, Bugaboo Spires.

RESTAURANTS

★ **Cedar House Restaurant** CANADIAN The setting is splendid, and the food is fresh and inspired. Located in a 4-hectare (10-acre) forest 5 minutes south of Golden, the Cedar House is a warm and friendly spot that oozes atmosphere. The passionate chefs offer simple and local ingredients, creating entrees like roasted free range chicken supreme, slow-braised lamb shank, and a spectacular pan-seared peppered duck breast. Meats are all natural, and the fish is wild. For dessert, there are homemade sorbets.

735 Hefti Rd., Golden. ✆ **250/344-4679.** www.cedarhousecafe.com. Reservations recommended. Main courses C$17–C$38. MC, V. Daily from 5pm. **Close to:** Abbott Ridge, Emerald Lake, Bugaboo Spires.

Chercher La Vache Café DELI Drop by this cozy deli any time of day: pre-hike for a breakfast sandwich or to get a "designer" sandwich to go (great trail lunch!). Or come by post-hike for a date square, brownie, and cup of tea. It's even open for dinner, with salads, pastas, and a great veggie chili.

318 Stephen Ave., at the corner of Kicking Horse Ave, Field. ✆ **250/343-6336.** www.chercherlavachecafe.com. Lunch C$7–C$14; dinner main courses C$14–C$32. MC, V. Daily 8am–8pm. **Close to:** Emerald Lake, Iceline Trail, Lake O'Hara Circuit.

★ **Cilantro on the Lake** CASUAL CALIFORNIAN Open during the summertime only, Cilantro's is a dreamy mountain bistro offering wood-fired flatbread pizzas, gourmet burgers, and micro-brewed beer in a sublimely beautiful setting. Sit on the lovely, sunny patio overlooking Emerald Lake or inside the spectacular timber-frame lodge.

On Emerald Lake Rd., 8km (5 miles) off Trans-Canada Hwy., at a turnoff 2km (1¼ miles) south of Field. ✆ **250/343-6321.** Main courses C$15–C$28. AE, MC, V. Daily 11am–9pm June to mid-Aug; daily 11am–5pm mid-Aug to end of Aug. Closed end of Aug–June. **Close to:** Emerald Lake, Iceline Trail, Lake O'Hara Circuit.

★ Finds **El Taco** MEXICAN When you are very, very hungry from a long day in the mountains, stop by this funky little Mexican joint in downtown Nelson. Entrees, like a stuffed 1-pound loaded veggie burrito or a fish taco with guacamole, are huge and healthy. This is superb value that goes great with a post-hike margarita!

306 Victoria St., Nelson. ✆ **250/352-2060.** Main courses C$6.50–C$9. Mon–Sat 11am–8pm. **Close to:** Kokanee Lakes.

Horsethief Creek Pub PUB The menu here is almost as expansive as the views across the Columbia Valley. The famous ½-pound burger comes with mushrooms, bacon, and melted cheese. It's also a nice spot for a post-hike beer and nibbles. They've got microbrews on tap and a good list of fun summer cocktails.

7538 Main St., Radium Hot Springs. ✆ **250/347-6400.** Main courses C$9–C$22. MC, V. Sun–Thurs 11am–10pm; Sat–Sun 11am–11pm; bar open weekends until midnight. **Close to:** Kindersley Pass, Lake of the Hanging Glacier, Bugaboo Spires.

Oso Negro Café CAFE With laid-back Nelson locals hanging out on the Zen patio, get fueled up here pre-hike with a steaming organic, fair-trade coffee. Pair an Americano with a breakfast spelt bun (eggs, sprouts, their famous dip, and optional bacon), or grab a grilled artichoke pesto panini to take on the trail.

604 Ward St., Nelson. ✆ **250-352-7661.** www.osonegrocoffee.com. Breakfasts C$7–C$13; lunch C$12–C$18. Mon–Sat 7am–6pm; Sun 8am–4pm. **Close to:** Kokanee Lakes.

Appendix: Fast Facts, Toll-Free Numbers & Websites

FAST FACTS: BRITISH COLUMBIA

AREA CODES Numbers are made up of the 3-digit area code and the 7-digit local number. For the lower mainland area of urban Vancouver, as well as Squamish and Whistler, the area code is 604. For the rest of British Columbia, the area code is 250.

ATM NETWORKS/CASH POINTS In Canada, ATMs offer the best exchange rate. The **Cirrus** (✆ **800/424-7787;** www.mastercard.com) and **PLUS** (✆ **800/843-7587;** www.visa.com) networks can be found throughout BC. Many banks impose a fee every time you use a card at another bank's ATM, and that fee can be higher for international transactions (up to C$5 or more) than for domestic ones (where they are rarely more than C$2). In addition, the bank from which you withdraw cash may charge its own fee. For international withdrawal fees, ask your bank.

AUTOMOBILE ORGANIZATIONS Motor clubs will supply maps, suggested routes, guidebooks, accident and bail-bond insurance, and emergency road service. The **Canadian Automobile Association (CAA)** is the major auto club in Canada and works closely with the American Automobile Association in the United States. If you belong to a motor club in your home country, inquire about CAA reciprocity before you leave. You may be able to join CAA, even if you're not a member of a reciprocal club; to inquire, call CAA (✆ **877/325-8888;** www.caa.ca). CAA is actually an organization of provincial motor clubs, so look under "CAA Automobile Club" in the White Pages of the telephone directory. In British Columbia, the reciprocal organization is the BCAA (✆ **604/293-2222**).

CAR RENTALS British Columbia has scores of rental-car companies: See the list in the "Toll-Free Numbers & Websites" section, later in this appendix. Four-wheel drive vehicles are recommended for some of the more remote trail heads.

CELLPHONES The good news for most U.S. citizens traveling in British Columbia—your cellphone will likely work just fine here. Call your service provider to make certain, though.

Cellular phone reception is good in most towns and cities, but very spotty in remote wilderness areas. You cannot rely on your cellphone to work should you need to make an emergency call.

Your home network from anywhere in the U.S. should allow you roaming privileges in British Columbia. But calls on a U.S. phone using a Canadian network can be expensive.

For cellphone users from Asia, Australia, and Europe, the situation is more complicated. In Canada, GSM networks are much less common than in these regions.

One option is to purchase a local SIM card and use a pay-as-you-go service. This is only going to be helpful if you are making many local calls. The main local carriers are **Rogers** (www.rogers.com) and **Telus** (www.telus.com). Both use GSM networks. You can also use their websites to compare coverage maps.

Renting a phone is another option. There are scores of companies offering this service, including **CellularAbroad** (✆ **800/287-5072;** www.cellularabroad.com) and **Planet Omni** (✆ **877/37-5076;** www.planetomni.com).

CREDIT CARDS Canadian businesses honor the same credit cards as in the U.S. and the U.K. Visa and MasterCard are the most common, although American Express is also normally accepted in hotels and restaurants catering to tourists. Discover and Diners Club cards are somewhat less frequently accepted.

Note that many banks now asses a 1% to 3% "transaction fee" on all charges you incur abroad.

CURRENCY Canadian currency is counted in dollars and cents, just like the currency system in the U.S. However, in addition to pennies, nickels, dimes, and quarters, there are one- and two-dollar coins (there are no dollar or two-dollar bills). Canadian dollar coins are bronze-plated coins and bear the picture of a loon—hence their nickname, "loonies." There's also a two-toned C$2 coin often called a "toonie." Paper currency begins with C$5 bills.

Exchanging currency is pretty straightforward, particularly if you are changing U.S. dollars into Canadian. The easiest way to procure Canadian currency is to simply withdraw money from an ATM.

Often, Canadian businesses will accept U.S. dollars in payment, making the currency value exchange at the till.

DRINKING LAWS The legal age for purchase and consumption of alcoholic beverages in British Columbia is 19; proof of age is required and often requested at bars, nightclubs, and restaurants, so it's always a good idea to bring ID when you go out. Liquor is sold only in government-run liquor stores, although in larger communities such as Victoria, Vancouver, Nanaimo, Prince George, and Kamloops, you'll find beer and wine sold from independent, government-licensed specialty shops.

Do not carry open containers of alcohol in your car or any public area that isn't zoned for alcohol consumption. The police can fine you on the spot. And nothing will ruin your trip faster than getting a citation for DUI ("driving under the influence"), so don't even think about driving while intoxicated.

ELECTRICITY Like the U.S., Canada uses 110 to 120 volts AC (60 cycles), compared to 220 to 240 volts AC (50 cycles) in most of Europe, Australia, and New Zealand. Downward converters that change 220 to 240 volts into 110 to 120 volts are difficult to find in Canada, so bring one with you.

EMBASSIES & CONSULATES All embassies are located in the nation's capital, Ottawa, Ontario. Some consulates are located in Vancouver, including those listed below.

The consulate of **Australia** is at 1225-888 Dunsmuir St, Vancouver, BC V6C 3K4 (✆ **604/684-1177**).

The local consulate for **Ireland** is at 100 West Pender St., 10th Floor, Vancouver, BC V6B 1R8 (✆ **604/683-9233**).

The Consulate General of **New Zealand** is at 1200-888 Dunsmuir St., Vancouver, BC V6C 3K4 (✆ **604/684-7388**).

The Consulate General of the **United Kingdom** is at 800-1111 Melville St., Vancouver, BC V6E 3V6 (✆ **604/683-4421**).

The Consulate General for the **United States** in Vancouver is at 2100-1095 West Pender St., Vancouver, BC V6E 2M6 (✆ **604/685-4311**).

EMERGENCIES Dial ✆ **911** for fire, police, or ambulance. This is a toll-free call. In British Columbia, the Royal Canadian Mounted Police (RCMP) administer a Tourist Alert program by posting emergency notices at visitor information centers, at provincial park sites, and on BC ferries.

GASOLINE (PETROL) Gas prices are modestly higher than in the United States and significantly lower than in the United Kingdom. Taxes are already included in the printed price. One U.S. gallon equals 3.8 liters or .85 imperial gallons. Fill-up locations are known as gas or service stations. Canadian gas is sold by the liter and, by law, must be paid for in advance of purchase. In 2008, a controversial new "carbon tax" of C24¢/liter was introduced on all gas purchases in BC.

HOLIDAYS Banks; government offices; post offices; and many stores, restaurants, and museums are closed on the following legal national holidays: January 1 (New Year's Day), Good Friday, the third Monday in May (Victoria Day), July 1 (Canada Day), August 1 (British Columbia Day), the first Monday in September (Labor Day), the second Monday in October (Thanksgiving Day), November 11 (Remembrance Day), and December 25 (Christmas Day).

HOSPITALS & PHARMACIES Canada's health care system is similar to that in the U.S. except that its health insurance for Canadian citizens is managed nationally by the federal government. Hospitals, clinics, and pharmacies are as common as in the U.S. and western Europe.

Canadian hospitals have emergency rooms open 24 hours for emergency care. In addition, most cities and towns have walk-in clinics where nonemergency treatment is available.

Pharmacies are common, although in most small towns, they close at 7pm.

INSURANCE

Medical Insurance Although it's not required of travelers, health insurance is highly recommended. Most health insurance policies cover you if you get sick away from home—but check your coverage before you leave.

International visitors to Canada should note that, unlike many European countries, Canada does not usually offer free or low-cost medical care to its visitors. Visits by foreign tourists to doctors and hospitals can be expensive and, in most cases, will require advance payment. Good policies will cover the costs of an accident, repatriation, or death. Packages such as Europ Assistance's "Worldwide Healthcare Plan" are sold by European automobile clubs and travel agencies at attractive rates. CanmedNet (✆ **905/669-4333;** www.canmednet.com) is the agent for Europ Assistance in Canada. If you're ever hospitalized more than 150 miles from home, **MedjetAssist** (✆ **800/527-7478;** www.medjetassistance.com) will pick you up and fly you to the hospital of your choice in a medically equipped and staffed aircraft 24 hours day, 7 days a week. Annual memberships are US$225 individual, US$350 family; you can also purchase short-term memberships.

Canadians from other provinces should check with their provincial health plan offices or contact **Health Canada** (✆ **866/225-0709;** www.hc-sc.gc.ca) to find out the extent of their coverage, and they should always carry their provincial health cards.

Travelers from the U.K. should carry their European Health Insurance Card (EHIC), which replaced the E111 form as proof of entitlement to free/reduced cost medical treatment abroad (✆ **0845/606-2030;** www.ehic.org.uk). Note, however, that the EHIC only covers "necessary medical treatment," and for repatriation costs, lost money, baggage, or cancellation, travel insurance from a reputable company should always be sought (www.travelinsuranceweb.com).

Travel Insurance The cost of travel insurance varies widely, depending on the destination, the cost and length of your trip, your age and health, and the type of trip you're taking, but expect to pay between 5% and 8% of the vacation itself. You can get estimates from various providers through **InsureMyTrip.com** (www.insuremytrip.com). Enter your trip cost and dates, your age, and other information for prices from more than a dozen companies.

Most big travel agents offer their own insurance and will probably try to sell you their package when you book a holiday. Think before you sign. Britain's Consumers' Association recommends that you insist on seeing the policy and reading the fine print before buying travel insurance. **The Association of British Insurers** (✆ **020/7600-3333;** www.abi.org.uk) gives advice by phone and publishes *Holiday Insurance,* a free guide to policy provisions and prices. You might also shop around for better deals: Try **Columbus Direct** (✆ **0870/033-9988;** www.columbusdirect.net).

Trip Cancellation Insurance Trip-cancellation insurance will help retrieve your money if you have to back out of a trip or depart early, or if your travel supplier goes bankrupt. Trip cancellation traditionally covers such events as sickness, natural disasters, and State Department advisories. The latest news in trip-cancellation insurance is the availability of expanded hurricane coverage and the "any-reason" cancellation coverage—which costs more but covers cancellations made for any reason. You won't get back 100% of your prepaid trip cost, but you'll be refunded a substantial portion. **TravelSafe** (✆ **888/885-7233;** www.travelsafe.com) offers both types of coverage. Expedia also offers any-reason cancellation coverage for its air-hotel packages. For details, contact one of the following recommended insurers: **Access America** (✆ **866/807-3982;** www.accessamerica.com); **Travel Guard International** (✆ **800/826-4919;** www.travelguard.com); **Travel Insured International** (✆ **800/243-3174;** www.travelinsured.com); and **Travelex Insurance Services** (✆ **888/457-4602;** www.travelex-insurance.com).

LEGAL AID If you are "pulled over" for a minor infraction (such as speeding), never attempt to pay the fine directly to a police officer; this could be construed as attempted bribery, a much more serious crime. Pay fines by mail or directly into the hands of the clerk of the court. If accused of a more serious offense, say and do nothing before consulting a lawyer. Here, the burden is on the prosecution to prove a person's guilt beyond a reasonable doubt, and everyone has the right to remain silent, whether he or she is suspected of a crime or actually arrested. Once arrested, a person can make one telephone call to a party of his or her choice. International visitors should call your embassy or consulate.

LOST & FOUND Be sure to tell all of your credit card companies the minute you discover your wallet has been lost or stolen, and file a report at the nearest police precinct. Your credit card company or insurer may require a police report number or record of the loss. Most credit card companies have an emergency toll-free number to call if your card is lost or stolen; they may be able to wire you a cash advance immediately or deliver an emergency credit card in a day or two. **Visa's** North American emergency number is ✆ **800/847-2911** or 410/581-9994. **American Express** cardholders and traveler's check holders should call ✆ **800/221-7282. MasterCard** holders should call ✆ **800/307-7309** or 636/722-7111. For other credit cards, call the toll-free number directory at ✆ **800/555-1212.**

If you need emergency cash over the weekend when all banks and American Express offices are closed, you can have money wired to you via **Western Union** (✆ **800/325-6000;** www.westernunion.com). These numbers work both in Canada and the United States.

MAIL Canada Post is the national mail service provider across Canada. There are post offices in every small town from coast to coast.

If you aren't sure what your address will be in Canada, mail can be sent to you, in your name, c/o General Delivery at the main post office of the city or region where you expect to be. (Visit www.canadapost.ca for information on the nearest post office.) The addressee must pick up mail in person and must produce proof of identity (driver's license, passport, and so on). Most post offices will hold your mail for up to 1 month and are open Monday to Friday from 9am to 5pm. Always include postal codes when mailing items in Canada. If you don't know your zip code, visit www.canadapost.ca.

PASSPORTS The websites listed provide downloadable passport applications, as well as the current fees for processing applications. For an up-to-date, country-by-country listing of passport requirements around the world, go to the International Travel tab of the U.S. State Department at **http://travel.state.gov**. Allow plenty of time before your trip to apply for a passport. And keep in mind that if you need a passport in a hurry, you'll pay a HIGHER processing fee.

For Residents of Australia You can pick up an application from your local post office or any branch of Passports Australia, but you must schedule an interview at the passport office to present your application materials. Call the **Australian Passport Information Service** at ✆ **131-232** or visit the government website at www.passports.gov.au.

For Residents of Ireland You can apply for a 10-year passport at the **Passport Office,** Setanta Centre, Molesworth Street, Dublin 2 (✆ **01/671-1633;** www.irlgov.ie/iveagh). Those under age 18 and over 65 must apply for a 3-year passport. You can also apply at 1A South Mall, Cork (✆ **21/494-4700**) or at most main post offices.

For Residents of New Zealand You can pick up a passport application at any New Zealand Passports Office or download it from their website. Contact the **Passports Office** at ✆ **0800/225-050** in New Zealand or 04/474-8100, or head to www.passports.govt.nz.

For Residents of the United Kingdom To pick up an application for a standard 10-year passport (5-yr. passport for children under 16), visit your nearest passport office, major post office, or travel agency, or contact the **United Kingdom Passport Service** at ✆ **0870/521-0410** or search its website at www.ips.gov.uk.

SMOKING British Columbia by-laws prohibit smoking in public places, including restaurants, offices, shopping malls, and even transit shelters. There is also a 3m (9¾-ft.) smoke-free zone around most public and workplace doorways, open windows, and air takes. Although this is adhered to in the larger cities, individual pubs and bars in the province's interior sometimes turn a blind eye to the legislation. But ask before you light up publicly anywhere in the province.

TAXES British Columbia charges both a provincial sales tax (6%) and the federal goods and services tax (GST) of 5%, meaning you will be paying an additional 11% on most purchases.

TELEPHONES The telephone system in BC is similar to that across North America. Public telephones are sometimes available at trail heads.

In both Canada and the U.S., many convenience groceries and packaging services sell prepaid calling cards in denominations up to $50; for international visitors, these can be the least expensive way to call home. Many public pay phones now accept American Express, MasterCard, and Visa credit cards. Local calls made from pay phones in most locales cost either 25¢ or 35¢. Most long-distance and international calls can be dialed directly from any phone. For calls within Canada and to the United States, dial 1 followed by the area code and the 7-digit number. For other international calls, dial 011 followed by the country code, city code, and the number you are calling.

Calls to area codes 800, 888, 877, and 866 are toll-free. For reversed-charge or collect calls, and for person-to-person calls, dial the number 0, then the area code and number; an operator will come on the line, and you should specify whether you are calling collect, person-to-person, or both. If your operator-assisted call is international, ask for the overseas operator.

For local directory assistance ("information"), dial 411; for long-distance information, dial 1, then the appropriate area code and 555-1212.

TELEGRAPH, TELEX & FAX Telegraph and telex services are provided primarily by **Western Union** (✆ **800/325-6000;** www.westernunion.com). You can telegraph (wire) money, or have it telegraphed to you, very quickly over the Western Union system, but this service can cost as much as 15% to 20% of the amount sent.

Most hotels have fax machines available for guest use (be sure to ask about the charge to use it). Many hotel rooms are wired for guests' fax machines. A less expensive way to send and receive faxes may be at stores such as **The UPS Store.** They have 20 locations across British Columbia.

TIME Almost all of British Columbia is in the Pacific Time Zone, 3 hours behind the Eastern Standard Time and the same as in Seattle, San Francisco, and Los Angeles. Only the far eastern side of the province is in the Mountain Time Zone, the same as in the province of Alberta.

Daylight Saving Time is in effect from 1am on the second Sunday in March to 1am on the first Sunday in November. Daylight Saving Time moves the clock 1 hour ahead of standard time.

TIPPING Tips are a very important part of certain workers' income, and gratuities are the standard way of showing appreciation for services provided. (Tipping is certainly not compulsory if the service is poor!) Tipping etiquette is the same in Canada as in the U.S. In hotels, tip bellhops at least C$1 per bag (C$2–C$3 if you have a lot of luggage) and tip the chamber staff C$1 to C$2 per day (more if you've left a disaster area for him or her to clean up). Tip the doorman or concierge only if he or she has provided you with some specific service (for example, calling a cab for you or obtaining difficult-to-get theater tickets). Tip the valet-parking attendant C$1 every time you get your car.

In restaurants, bars, and nightclubs, tip service staff 15% to 20% of the check, tip bartenders 10% to 15%, tip checkroom attendants C$1 per garment, and tip valet-parking attendants C$1 per vehicle.

As for other service personnel, tip cab drivers 15% of the fare, tip skycaps at airports at least C$1 per bag (C$2–C$3 if you have a lot of luggage), and tip hairdressers and barbers 15% to 20%.

TOILETS You won't find public toilets or "restrooms" on the streets in British Columbia, but they can be found in hotel lobbies, bars, restaurants, museums, department stores, railway and bus stations, and service stations. Large hotels and fast-food restaurants are often the best bet for clean facilities. Restaurants and bars in resorts or heavily visited areas may reserve their restrooms for patrons.

VISAS For information about Canadian Visas go to **www.cic.gc.ca** and click on Visit. Or go to one of the following websites.

Australian citizens can obtain up-to-date visa information from the Canada High Commission in Australia, Level 5, 111 Harrington St., Sydney, NSW 2000 (✆ **02/9364-3050**).

British subjects can obtain up-to-date visa information by calling the High Commission of Canada to the United Kingdom, Canada House, Trafalgar Square, London SW1Y 5BJ (✆ **0207/258-6421**).

Irish citizens can obtain up-to-date visa information through the Embassy of Canada to Ireland, 7-8 Wilton Terrace, Dublin 2, Ireland (✆ **353/1-234-4000**).

Citizens of **New Zealand** can obtain up-to-date visa information by contacting the High Commission of Canada in New Zealand, Level III, 125 The Terrace, Wellington 6011 (✆ **644/473-9577**).

Other countries can find embassy listings at www.international.gc.ca.

U.S. citizens with a valid passport are allowed to stay for up to six months.

WATER Canada boasts some of the world's most pristine water. Population growth and industry are certainly threatening this quality, and water in British Columbia is a precious commodity.

TOLL-FREE NUMBERS & WEBSITES

MAJOR AIRLINES

Aeroméxico
✆ 800/237-6639 (in U.S.)
✆ 020/7801-6234 (in U.K., information only)
✆ 01/800/021-4000 (in Mexico)
www.aeromexico.com

Air Canada
✆ 888/247-2262 (in North America)
www.aircanada.com

Air France
✆ 800/237-2747 (in U.S.)
✆ 800/375-8723 (U.S. and Canada)
✆ 087/0142-4343 (in U.K.)
✆0820/012424 (in France)
www.airfrance.com

Air New Zealand
✆ 800/262-1234 (in U.S.)
✆ 800/663-5494 (in Canada)
✆ 0800/028-4149 (in U.K.)
✆ 0800/737000 (in New Zealand)
www.airnewzealand.com

Alaska Airlines/Horizon Air
✆ 800/252-7522
www.alaskaair.com

American Airlines
✆ 800/433-7300 (in U.S. and Canada)
✆ 020/7365-0777 (in U.K.)
www.aa.com

British Airways
✆ 800/247-9297 (in U.S. and Canada)
✆ 087/0850-9850 (in U.K.)
www.british-airways.com

Continental Airlines
✆ 800/523-3273 (in U.S. or Canada)
✆ 084/5607-6760 (in U.K.)
www.continental.com

Delta Air Lines
✆ 800/221-1212 (in U.S. or Canada)
✆ 084/5600-0950 (in U.K.)
www.delta.com

Frontier Airlines
✆ 800/432-1359
www.frontierairlines.com

Hawaiian Airlines
✆ 800/367-5320 (in U.S. and Canada)
www.hawaiianair.com

Japan Airlines
✆ 012/025-5931 (in Japan)
✆ 604/606-7770 (in Canada)
✆ 800/221-1081 (in U.S.)
www.jal.co.jp

JetBlue Airways
✆ 800/538-2583 (in U.S. or Canada)
✆ 080/1365-2525 (in U.K.)
www.jetblue.com

Lufthansa
✆ 800/399-5838 (in U.S.)
✆ 800/563-5954 (in Canada)
✆ 087/0837-7747 (in U.K.)
www.lufthansa.com

Northwest Airlines
✆ 800/225-2525 (in U.S.)
✆ 870/0507-4074 (in U.K.)
www.nwa.com

Quantas Airways
✆ 800/227-4500 (in U.S. or Canada)
✆ 084/5774-7767 (in U.K.)
✆ 13 13 13 (in Australia)
www.quantas.com

Southwest Airlines
✆ 800/435-9792 (in U.S., U.K., and Canada)
www.southwest.com

United Airlines
✆ 800/864-8331 (in U.S. and Canada)
✆ 084/5844-4777 (in U.K.)
www.united.com

US Airways
✆ 800/428-4322 (in U.S. and Canada)
✆ 084/5600-3300 (in U.K.)
www.usairways.com

Virgin America
✆ 877/359-8474
www.virginamerica.com

Virgin Atlantic Airways
✆ 800/821-5438 (in U.S. and Canada)
✆ 087/0574-7747 (in U.K.)
www.virgin-atlantic.com

WestJet
✆ 800/538-5696 (in U.S. and Canada)
www.westjet.com

CAR RENTAL AGENCIES

Advantage
✆ 800/777-5500 (in U.S.)
✆ 021/0344-4712 (outside of U.S.)
www.advantage.com

Alamo
✆ 800/GO-ALAMO (800/462-5266)
www.alamo.com

Avis
✆ 800/331-1212 (in U.S. and Canada)
✆ 084/4581-8181 (in U.K.)
www.avis.com

Budget
✆ 800/527-0700 (in U.S.)
✆ 087/0156-5656 (in U.K.)
✆ 800/268-8900 (in Canada)
www.budget.com

Dollar
✆ 800/800-4000 (in U.S.)
✆ 800/848-8268 (in Canada)
✆ 080/8234-7524 (in U.K.)
www.dollar.com

Enterprise
✆ 800/261-7331 (in U.S.)
✆ 514/355-4028 (in Canada)
✆ 012/9360-9090 (in U.K.)
www.enterprise.com

Hertz
✆ 800/645-3131 (in U.S. and Canada)
www.hertz.com

National
✆ 800/CAR-RENT (800/227-7368)
www.nationalcar.com

Rent-A-Wreck
✆ 800/535-1391
www.rentawreck.com

Thrifty
✆ 800/367-2277 (in the U.S. and Canada)
✆ 918/669-2168 (for all other countries)
www.thrifty.com

MAJOR HOTEL & MOTEL CHAINS

Best Western International
✆ 800/780-7234 (in U.S. and Canada)
✆ 0800/393-130 (in U.K.)
www.bestwestern.com

Comfort Inns
✆ 800/228-5150
✆ 0800/444-444 (in U.K.)
www.comfortinn.com

Courtyard by Marriott
✆ 888/236-2427 (in U.S.)
✆ 0800/221-222 (in U.K.)
www.marriott.com/courtyard

Crowne Plaza Hotels
✆ 888/303-1746
www.ichotelsgroup.com/crowneplaza

Days Inn
✆ 800/329-7466 (in U.S.)
✆ 0800/280-400 (in U.K.)
www.daysinn.com

Econo Lodges
✆ 800/55-ECONO (800/552-3666)
www.econolodge.com

Embassy Suites
✆ 800/EMBASSY (800/362-2779)
www.embassysuites1.hilton.com

Four Seasons
✆ 800/819-5053 (in U.S. and Canada)
✆ 0800/6488-6488 (in U.K.)
www.fourseasons.com

Hilton Hotels
✆ 800/HILTONS (800/445-8667) (in U.S. and Canada)
✆ 087/0590-9090 (in U.K.)
www.hilton.com

Holiday Inn
✆ 800/315-2621 (in U.S. and Canada)
✆ 0800/405-060 (in U.K.)
www.holidayinn.com

Howard Johnson
✆ 800/446-4656 (in U.S. and Canada)
www.hojo.com

Hyatt
✆ 888/591-1234 (in U.S. and Canada)
✆ 084/5888-1234 (in U.K.)
www.hyatt.com

InterContinental Hotels & Resorts
✆ 800/424-6835 (in U.S. and Canada)
✆ 0800/1800-1800 (in U.K.)
www.ichotelsgroup.com

Marriott
✆ 877/236-2427 (in U.S. and Canada)
✆ 0800/221-222 (in U.K.)
www.marriott.com

Motel 6
✆ 800/4MOTEL6 (800/466-8356)
www.motel6.com

Quality Inn
✆ 877/424-6423 (in U.S. and Canada)
✆ 0800/444-444 (in U.K.)
www.qualityinn. com

Radisson Hotels & Resorts
✆ 888/201-1718 (in U.S. and Canada)
✆ 0800/374-411 (in U.K.)
www.radisson.com

Ramada Worldwide
✆ 888/2-RAMADA (888/272-6232) (in U.S. and Canada)
✆ 080/8100-0783 (in U.K.)
www.ramada.com

Sheraton Hotels & Resorts
✆ 800/325-3535 (in U.S.)
✆ 800/543-4300 (in Canada)
✆ 0800/3253-5353 (in U.K.)
www.starwoodhotels.com/sheraton

Super 8 Motels
✆ 800/800-8000
www.super8.com

Travelodge
✆ 800/578-7878
www.travelodge.com

Westin Hotels & Resorts
✆ 800/937-8461 (in U.S. and Canada)
✆ 0800/3259-5959 (in U.K.)
www.starwoodhotels.com/westin

INDEX

See also Accommodations and Restaurant indexes, below.

General Index

Accommodations

Restaurants

New from Frommer's™!

Best Hiking Trips
All you need for every step of the trip!

Explore over 3,500 destinations.

Frommers.com makes it easy.

Find a destination. ✓ Book a trip. ✓ Get hot travel deals.
Buy a guidebook. ✓ Enter to win vacations. ✓ Listen to podcasts. ✓ Check
the latest travel news. ✓ Share trip photos and memories. ✓ And much mo

Frommers.co